A BREACH OF DUTY

Gefe de la punta de Langara.

José Cardero, *Jefe de la Punta de Lángara*, 1792 ("Chief" of the Point of Lángara, now Point Grey, the site of the main Musqueam Reserve, Vancouver). This portrait of the Musqueam leader was drawn by José Cardero, who accompanied Alcalá Galiano on his expedition in 1792. They were among the first Europeans to see the Musqueam (see p. 26), and the drawing is the earliest surviving image of an inhabitant of the area which is now the site of the city of Vancouver. (Courtesy Museo Naval, Madrid, Higueras 2946.)

A BREACH OF DUTY

Fiduciary Obligations

and

Aboriginal Peoples

James I. Reynolds

Purich Publishing Ltd.
Saskatoon, Saskatchewan
Canada

Purich Publishing Ltd.
Box 23032, Market Mall Post Office
Saskatoon, SK Canada S7J 5H3
Phone: (306) 373–5311   Fax: (306) 373–5315
Email: purich@sasktel.net
Website: www.purichpublishing.com

Library and Archives Canada Cataloguing in Publication
Reynolds, James I.
        A breach of duty : fiduciary obligations and Aboriginal
peoples / James I. Reynolds.

(Purich's aboriginal issues series)
Includes bibliographical references and index.
ISBN 1-895830-25-7

        1. Coast Salish Indians—British Columbia—Government relations. 2. Coast Salish Indians—Legal status, laws, etc.—British Columbia. 3. Indians of North America—
Canada—Government relations—1951– 4. Indians of North America—Canada—
Legal status, laws, etc. I. Title. II. Series.

KE7709.R49 2005   342.7108'72   C2005-901421-0
KF8205.R49 200

Series design by NEXT Communications Inc., Saskatoon, Saskatchewan.

Cover design by Duncan Campbell, Regina, Saskatchewan.

Copy-editing, design, and layout by Roberta Mitchell Coulter, Saskatoon, Saskatchewan.

Printed in Canada on acid-free paper.

The publisher acknowledges the financial assistance of the Government of Saskatchewan through the Cultural Industries Development Fund towards the publication of this book.

Readers will note that words like Aboriginal, Native, and Indigenous have been capitalized in this book except in some quoted material. In recent years, many Aboriginal people have argued that such words should be capitalized when referring to specific people, in the same manner that European and American are capitalized. We agree.
The Publishers

Contents

Illustrations

Foreword

Over twenty years ago, I appeared with Jim Reynolds, the author of this book, and other members of a Musqueam delegation before the House of Commons Special Committee on Indian Self-Government (the Penner Committee) to address issues of concern to the Band. Foremost among those concerns was the decision of the Federal Court of Appeal in the *Guerin* case that the doctrine of political trust meant that we were not able to hold the federal government legally responsible for leasing our lands to the Shaughnessy Heights Golf Club on terms to which we had not agreed and which would lock us into a very low rent for seventy-five years. The appearance before the committee took place just a few days before we were to apply for leave to the Supreme Court of Canada to appeal that decision. I remember how bitterly disappointed we were over the decision to deny us any legal remedy for the Crown's clear wrongdoing. It was a black moment in the long history of the Musqueam people. Fortunately, the Supreme Court of Canada did grant leave and, as explained in this book, we were successful in our appeal.

We are proud of our success in the *Guerin* case and in the subsequent *Sparrow* case that applied the fiduciary obligation of the Crown, as established in *Guerin*, to protect our Aboriginal right to fish. These cases have been important in protecting the rights of all Aboriginal Canadians. As shown in this book, the fiduciary doctrine, as restated in *Guerin*, has also been used to help other Canadians.

I am pleased that this book describes the background to the *Guerin* case, what was decided and its significance for Aboriginal rights and for fiduciary obligations generally. I hope that you will agree with Jim Reynolds that the story of how the Musqueam brought and succeeded in this case is a story worth telling.

Chief Ernest Campbell,
Musqueam Indian Band

Members of the legal team and the Musqueam Indian Band at the Supreme Court of Canada Building during the *Guerin* hearing, June 13 & 14, 1983: *(l to r)* Lewis Harvey, James Reynolds, Leona Sparrow, Andrew Charles, and Marvin Storrow. (Courtesy of the archives of the Musqueam Indian Band.)

Preface

This book tells the story of the determined search of the Musqueam people to find justice. In 1958, the Canadian government leased over one-third of their small reserve to an exclusive golf club at less than market value on terms to which they did not agree. They were repeatedly advised to drop the case but their tenacity led to the 1984 decision of the Supreme Court of Canada in *Guerin v. The Queen.*[1] That decision recognized, for the first time, that legally enforceable fiduciary obligations are owed to the Aboriginal peoples of Canada. In subsequent decisions, the Court applied the *Guerin* decision to give substance to the recent constitutional recognition of existing Aboriginal and treaty rights. The application and development of the fiduciary principle by the Supreme Court of Canada and other courts was a major factor in the dramatic changes in the laws affecting Aboriginal peoples over the last twenty years since *Guerin.* This book gives a detailed account of the law relating to fiduciary obligations and Aboriginal peoples. However, the impact of Guerin was not limited to Aboriginal peoples. It was instrumental in bringing about a general restatement of fiduciary law in Canada which has led to a vigorous and controversial development of that law. For this reason, I have also included a chapter which summarizes that development.

For five years, I had the good fortune to be part of the legal team that represented the Musqueam people in their groundbreaking legal struggle. In writing this record of the case, I have drawn upon the recollections of Delbert Guerin and other members of the Musqueam people and my own recollections and those of other members of the Musqueam legal team. I have also drawn upon the trial record, the reported decisions, and contemporary newspaper reports, as well as background research on the legal issues involved, the history of the Musqueam, and some of the key individuals involved in the case. The details of the Musqueam story give a compelling context for understanding the legal principles arising from the *Guerin* case and a great number of other legal decisions applying that case, principles that have transformed Aboriginal law in Canada over the last twenty years.

That transformation is not yet complete, and there are still a number of questions arising from the case. After setting out a comprehensive account of the legal developments in Canada following *Guerin* and a summary of developments in the United States, Australia, and New Zealand, I give my own views on how those questions should be answered. I hope that this book will be of practical assistance to lawyers advising clients in this area of law and have therefore included a chapter on the important practical issues of procedure, defences, and remedies which should be of assistance to them. Finally, I make some comments in the concluding chapter on the role played by *Guerin* in the development of the law.

The *Guerin* case has been ranked as the tenth most important decision of the Supreme Court of Canada in the twentieth century and among the top thirty significant legal events.[2] In *Wewaykum,* Binnie J. writing for the Supreme Court of Canada referred to *Guerin* as a watershed decision,[3] and in *Authorson v. Canada,* the Ontario Court of Appeal described it as a seminal case.[4] The leading authority on the law of trusts in Canada, Professor Donovan Waters, noted that "[f]or the first time, certainly so far as reserve lands are concerned, the Indians now have right of access to the courts in order to determine the propriety of the Crown's administration of their affairs and the Indians themselves regard this decision concerning their interests as perhaps the most important to have been handed down since Canada was formed."[5]

Other judges and scholars have also noted the significance of *Guerin* to Canadian law and the development of Aboriginal rights.[6] Judge David Arnot, the treaty commissioner for Saskatchewan, has written that "[t]he Supreme Court of Canada's unanimous rebuke of government privilege in *R. v. Guerin* is the milestone in restoring a system of law based on principles of fundamental justice over the exercise of individual discretion."[7] Professor Brian Slattery, one of Canada's leading authorities on Aboriginal law, noted in his influential article "Understanding Aboriginal Rights" that *Guerin* "provides the stimulus and much essential material for reflection on the fundamental nature and origins of aboriginal law." It had "a profound significance for aboriginal land claims" by ending the controversy over whether Aboriginal title existed as a legal right. Most important, "in *Guerin,* the Supreme Court shows a willingness to consider the topic of aboriginal rights afresh, and to initiate a dialogue concerning the broad principles that alone make sense of the subject."[8] Professor Tennant notes in his history of Aboriginal peoples and politics in British Columbia that the case "gave new life to land claims activity in British Columbia,"[9] and that "[i]t was evident almost immediately that the Guerin decision had major practical implications in British Columbia concerning the role of the courts and the means by which Indian groups could protect their interests in the land against the efforts of the Province."[10]

Guerin led to significant development of fiduciary law in Canada outside of the Aboriginal context. Professor Flanagan has commented that "[t]he development of modern Canadian law dealing with new fiduciary relationships can be traced to the Supreme Court of Canada's decision in *Guerin v. The Queen* in 1984," and that the case "opened the door to the extension of fiduciary obligations in relationships not traditionally recognized as fiduciary."[11] In *Authorson,* the Ontario Court of Appeal referred to *Guerin* as "the foundation of this line of general jurisprudence."[12] *Guerin* has been cited in over three hundred cases in Canada, involving both Aboriginal and non-Aboriginal people, and continues to influence the development of the law.

Although I was one of the counsel in *Guerin,* this book is intended to be more than a lawyer's "war story." In his account of *Mabo,* a landmark decision in the Aboriginal law of Australia, one of the counsel involved in that case commented that:

> [L]awyers' "war stories" about their favourite cases are generally of little interest to anyone, save the author. But the account which follows contains, I hope, some inherent justification and intrinsic interest.[13]

I hope that this is equally true of this book. Its aim is to provide a comprehensive, practical account of the fiduciary obligations owed to Aboriginal peoples in Canada.[14] It is intended primarily for legal practitioners and students, Aboriginal people, and those with a broader interest in the relationship of governments and the wider society with Aboriginal peoples. As a legal practitioner for over twenty-five years and a former law professor, I have tried to cover both the practical and the doctrinal aspects of the law. Of necessity, some of the discussion is technical in nature, but I have tried to explain the law in terms that "any intelligent person, taking the trouble to pay close attention, can understand."[15] I urge the reader to take that trouble. This is an important and exciting area of law.[16] It also has enormous political and economic consequences for Aboriginal peoples.[17]

The *Guerin* case shows that, with determination and confidence in the legal system, Aboriginal people can overcome some of the historical disadvantages under which they have struggled for too long and achieve some measure of justice. In the process of seeking justice for themselves, the Musqueam brought about fundamental improvements in the way the Canadian legal system deals with the rights of all Aboriginal people. In rejecting the argument that the Musqueam could not enforce the government's obligations to them in the courts, the Supreme Court of Canada strengthened the legal protection provided to all Canadians against the wrongdoings of governments. In that way, *Guerin* provided an example of how the Canadian legal system can "move us incrementally towards a just society."[18] I think that is a story worth telling.

Acknowledgements

Writing a book is essentially a solitary task with many hours spent alone re-searching in libraries, composing thoughts, typing and re-typing and reading and re-reading. However, in this task, I have had the assistance and support of many people whom I would like to acknowledge here.

My family, Pui-ah, Christopher, and Alistair, have been very understanding as I have juggled my time between them, my career as a practising lawyer, and my forays into writing. I thank them for that.

My colleagues at Ratcliff & Company in North Vancouver have been equally supportive. My partners readily made available the resources of what, by any standard, is one of Canada's leading law firms specializing in Aboriginal law. I have enjoyed discussing ideas with my colleagues at the firm although I cannot say that they have always been persuaded to my viewpoint. Special thanks are due to John Rich and Matt Kirchner, who kindly assisted on parts of the manuscript. The firm's librarian, Jennifer Galan, was never stumped by my constant requests for seemingly obscure and difficult to obtain material. It would soon appear on my desk with effortless ease. My secretary, Dolores Fossum, provided much appreciated assistance as this book took shape over the last couple of years. My lack of word-processing skills was overcome by the knowledge and expertise of Jennifer Jularbal and Audrey Randall, who prepared much of the first draft and were able to fix up my most egregious errors in subsequent revisions. As well, Lisa Glowacki used her Spanish language skills to assist me in obtaining a copy of the drawing that appears as the frontispiece from the Museo Naval in Madrid.

Special words of recognition are owed to the other members of the legal team who worked on the *Guerin* case that provided much of the material for this book. Marvin Storrow, the lead counsel, gave me encouragement in writing this book as he did over twenty years ago in writing the legal argument in the case itself. Other members of the team, Graham Allen, Bob Banno, Lew Harvey, Doug Sanders, and Steve Schachter, also deserve recognition for their contribution. Our success was due in large part to our ability to work together as a team.

I would also like to acknowledge the importance of legal scholars to the rapid development of Aboriginal law in Canada over recent decades. In *Citizens Plus: Aboriginal Peoples and the Canadian State*, Alan C. Cairns refers to "[t]he vanguard role of legal scholarship in providing roadmaps to a better future for Aboriginal peoples."[1] In common with judges and other legal practitioners, I have benefitted from the publications of scholars such as Richard Bartlett, John Borrows, Doug Harris, Michael Jackson, Patrick Maclem, Kent McNeil, Leonard Rotman, Doug Sanders, Brian Slattery, James (Sákéj) Youngblood Henderson, and Mark Walters. My debt to academic authors is recorded in the text and endnotes. I am especially indebted to Professors Harris and McNeil, who were generous enough with their time to read and give detailed comments on large portions of the manuscript. My debt extends beyond the Canadian border. Reid Peyton Chambers, a leading U.S. Indian Law practitioner and author of a 1975 article on the law which is still widely cited, was kind enough to provide me with U.S. materials, including copies of the *Navajo Nation* and *White Mountain Apache* decisions of the U.S. Supreme Court on the day they were released. David Bloch and Victoria Kingii provided comments on the chapter dealing with U.S. and New Zealand law.

When I first decided to write this book, I had no doubt who I wanted to publish it. I have long admired the books published by Don Purich and Karen Bolstad as part of Purich Publishing's Aboriginal Issues series. I was delighted when they agreed to include this book as part of that series and I greatly appreciate their comments and support as it developed. In his guide to aspiring authors, *The Joy of Writing,* Pierre Berton gives this eminently sensible advice: "*Suck up to your editor.* Treat her as you would a favourite teacher. Make it clear that you won't sulk if you get a touchy appraisal of your work. (And for God's sake, *don't sulk*)."[2] I had the good fortune to be assigned Roberta Coulter as my editor and so had little reason to sulk. I soon recognized that, whatever their potential harm to my ego, her comments were well-meant, well-founded, and would only improve the book. Her substantive review greatly improved its organization, and her editing skills exposed and corrected my rebellious and lazy inclination to avoid the stern discipline of the *Canadian Guide to Uniform Legal Citations*. If legal citations contain incorrect square brackets instead of correct parenthesis or errant commas, it is in spite of her tireless efforts.

Finally, I want to record my debt of gratitude to my Aboriginal clients over the last quarter of a century. I came to Canada from England almost thirty years ago as an English barrister and former law professor. I knew very little about the Aboriginal peoples of this country and of their cultures. Since my initial involvement in the *Guerin* case, I have acted for a number of Aboriginal

[1] (Vancouver: U.B.C. Press, 2000) at 211.

[2] (Random House, 2003) at 214.

groups in different areas of this vast country. Parts of this manuscript for this book were written in a hotel room in Yellowknife, in the kitchen of a bed and breakfast in Lax Kw'Alaams (Port Simpson) overlooking the Pacific Ocean in northwestern British Columbia, on an Indian reserve in central Alberta, in a Boeing 737 returning from clients in Sarnia, Ontario, on the Great Lakes, and in a small plane visiting the Quatsino First Nation of Vancouver Island. I have come to know many Aboriginal people as individuals and to have a better understanding of Aboriginal cultures and their contribution to the uniqueness of this wonderful country. As a group, Aboriginal people have suffered tremendous disadvantages, including the legal disadvantages described in this book. However, by and large, I have found little bitterness and a great deal of good humour (sometimes at my expense) and kindliness. It has been a privilege to be able to put at their service whatever knowledge and skills I have acquired.

This book tells a very small part of the long history of the Musqueam People. I am currently the General Counsel for the Musqueam Band. However, this book is purely a personal account and does not necessarily reflect the views of the Band or its members. The following members of the Band have reviewed chapter 2 dealing with that history: Andrew Charles; Delbert, Fran, and Victor Guerin; and Leona Sparrow. It has also been reviewed by Dr. Michael Kew, who has long been associated with the Band, both as a scholar and through marriage. I would like to thank them for their comments. I am grateful to Chief Ernest Campbell for providing the Foreword. To all the Musqueam People, I express my best wishes and thanks, "hay cᵛxʷ 'qa."

Table of Cases and Statutes

Cases

Statutes

Musqueam Reserve in 1958. See p. 44 for housing conditions on the reserve at the time of the lease to the Shaughnessy Heights Golf Club. (Courtesy *Vancouver Sun* and Vancouver Public Library, Special Collections, VPL 1994.)

Frank Leonard

is photograph shows the Shaughnessy Heights Golf Club clubhouse as it looked in 1958 (although e picture was taken on July 5, 1933) at the old location before the move to the Musqueam Reserve. The clubhouse was the scene of the "tea party" attended by Chief Ed Sparrow and Councillor Gertrude Guerin (see pp. 40–41). The Shaughnessy Heights Golf Club was founded in 1911 for the purposes of "social intercourse, mutual helpfulness, mental and moral improvement and rational recreation." (Courtesy Vancouver Public Library, Special Collections, VPL 12491.)

For Pui-ah, Christopher and Alistair

"You must be the change you wish to see in the world."
Mahatma Ghandi

Chapter 1

The Historical and
Legal Context

When the British first encountered Aboriginal people on the east coast of North America, they found groups such as the Mi'kmaq and the Iroquois, organized in societies and occupying the land as their ancestors had done for generations.[1] At the time, the British were mainly interested in trading for furs,[2] and they relied on the knowledge and capacity of the Aboriginal people to harvest the pelts. In the event of a conflict with their European competitors, particularly the French, the British wanted assistance from or at least the neutrality of the Aboriginal peoples. It only made sense for the British to enter into alliances to establish peaceful relations with the Aboriginal peoples and to encourage them to place themselves under the protection of the British Crown.[3] As the fur trade gave way to settlement of European populations, the Crown placed itself between the settlers and the Aboriginal peoples in order to protect them from exploitation.[4] No settler could take title to land directly from Aboriginals. Title had to be acquired from the Crown, but only if the Aboriginal group was first prepared to give up, or surrender, its Aboriginal title in the land to the Crown. Gradually, reserves were established. Legal title to reserve lands was held by the Crown for the benefit of Aboriginal peoples so there would be some protection from land-hungry settlers.[5]

The contemporary fiduciary relationship between the Crown and Aboriginal peoples has its roots in this early protection of Aboriginal interests. The obligation assumed by the British Crown to protect Aboriginal interests was frequently described as one of trust. However, until the *Guerin* case in 1984, there was uncertainty whether this was a legally enforceable obligation

1

or merely a political obligation assumed by the Crown that enjoyed no legal protection.

Historical Context

Courts have recognized that the basis of the fiduciary relationship between the Crown and Aboriginal peoples is rooted in their historical relationship. As Chief Justice Dickson (who gave the leading judgment in *Guerin*) explained in the subsequent decision of the Supreme Court of Canada in *Mitchell v. Peguis Indian Band*:[6]

> The recent case of *Guerin* took as its fundamental premise the "unique character both of the Indians' interest in land and *of the historical relationship with the Crown*." (at p. 343, emphasis added). That relationship began with pre-Confederation contact between the historic occupiers of North American lands (the aboriginal peoples) and the European colonizers (since 1763, "the Crown"), and it is this relationship between aboriginal peoples and the Crown that grounds the distinctive fiduciary obligation on the Crown.

In *R. v. Sparrow*,[7] which also involved the Musqueam band, Dickson C.J. and La Forest J., speaking for the Supreme Court of Canada, said:[8]

> The *sui generis* [unique] nature of Indian title, and the historic powers and responsibilities assumed by the Crown constituted the source of such a fiduciary obligation. In our opinion, *Guerin*, together with *R. v. Taylor and Williams* (1981), 34 O.R. (2d) 360, ground a general guiding principle for s. 35(1) [of the *Constitution Act, 1982*, which recognizes and affirms existing aboriginal and treaty rights]. That is, the Government has the responsibility to act in a fiduciary capacity with respect to aboriginal peoples. The relationship between the Government and aboriginals is trust-like, rather than adversarial, and the contemporary recognition and affirmation of aboriginal rights must be defined in light of this historic relationship.

This "historic relationship" was explained by Professor Brian Slattery in an article that has had a major impact on the development of the law.[9] He noted that most Aboriginal peoples were never conquered by the Crown. In a passage that has been quoted with approval by the Supreme Court of Canada[10] he said:[11]

> The Crown has a general fiduciary duty towards native people to protect them in the enjoyment of their aboriginal rights and in particular in the possession and use of their lands. This general fiduciary duty has its origins in the Crown's historical commitment to protect native peoples from the inroads of British settlers, in return for a native undertaking to renounce the use of force to defend themselves, and to accept instead the protection of the Crown as its subjects. In offering its protection, the Crown was animated less by philanthropy or moral sentiment than by the need to establish peaceful relations with peoples whose friendship was a source of military and economic advantage, and whose enmity was a threat to the security and prosperity of the colonies. The sources of the general fiduciary duty do not lie,

then, in a paternalistic concern to protect a "weaker" or "primitive" people, as has sometimes been suggested, but rather in the necessity of persuading native peoples, at a time when they still had considerable military capacities, that their rights would be better protected by reliance on the Crown than by self-help.

In the case of *Haida Nation v. British Columbia (Minister of Forests)*,[12] decided by the Supreme Court of Canada in 2004, Chief Justice McLachlin observed that the honour of the Crown gives rise to a fiduciary duty in situations in which the Crown has assumed discretionary control over specific Aboriginal interests.[13] Giving the judgment of the Court, she referred to "the historical roots of the principle of the honour of the Crown" in the assertion of British sovereignty.[14] In the companion case of *Taku River Tlingit First Nation v. British Columbia (Project Assessment Director)*[15], she stated that "[t]he duty of honour derives from the Crown's assertion of sovereignty in the face of prior Aboriginal occupation."[16]

The genesis of this fiduciary relationship can be traced back to earliest contacts between the British Crown and Aboriginal peoples on the east coast of North America.[17] In 1664, the British Crown and the Iroquois signed the *Treaty of Albany*. Under its terms, the British would receive the support of a powerful ally which had earlier supported the Dutch. In return, the Iroquois were assured of continued trading privileges and given recognition of their separate and independent existence and the protection of the British Crown. This treaty was preserved on a wampum belt presented by the Iroquois to the British as well as in a written treaty.

Until the constitutional recognition of Aboriginal and treaty rights in section 35 of the *Constitution Act, 1982*, the most important legal protection for Aboriginal peoples was found in the Royal Proclamation of 1763[18] issued by King George III. This document prohibited private purchases of Indian lands, prevented colonial governments from issuing patents for unceded Indian lands, and required settlers to remove themselves from such lands. It also stated that if the Indians were "inclined to dispose of [their] Lands, the same shall be Purchased only by Us . . . at some public Meeting or Assembly of the said Indians. To be held for that Purpose." In the *St. Catherine's Milling* case,[19] Mr. Justice Strong of the Supreme Court of Canada pointed out that the Royal Proclamation could not be ascribed to moral considerations or to "motives of humane considerations for the aborigines."[20] Rather, it was to ensure peace by avoiding further wars with the Indian tribes which, at the time, were a formidable threat to the North American colonies. He noted that it was successful in this objective as attested by the fact that "from the memorable year 1763, when Detroit was besieged and all the Indian tribes were in revolt, down to the date of confederation, Indian wars and massacres entirely ceased in the British possessions in North America, although powerful Indian Nations still continued for some time after the former date to inhabit these territories."[21] The truth of his comments is confirmed by the wording of the Royal Proclamation itself. It states:

> [I]t is just and reasonable and *essential to our Interest and the Security of our Colonies,* that the several Nations or Tribes of Indians, with whom We are connected, and *who live under Our Protection,* should not be disturbed in the Possession of such Parts of Our Dominions and Territories as, not having been ceded to, or purchased by Us, are reserved to them, or any of them, as their Hunting Grounds. [emphasis added]

Since the 1774 decision of the famous English judge Lord Mansfield in *Campbell v. Hall*,[22] it has been held that the Royal Proclamation had the force of statute and was binding on both the Imperial Crown and the colonial governments. In *Calder v. Attorney-General for British Columbia,* Mr. Justice Hall said that the Royal Proclamation was analogous to the status of the *Magna Carta* and thus had to be "regarded as a fundamental document upon which any just determination of original rights rests."[23]

There has been some debate as to the scope of the Royal Proclamation given its somewhat confusing description of the lands covered and the state of geographical knowledge at the time. It has even been held by the Ontario Court of Appeal,[24] somewhat surprisingly, that the surrender provision of the Royal Proclamation was repealed in Ontario by the *Quebec Act* of 1774,[25] a scant eleven years later, despite any plain and clear statement to that effect and the practice of colonial administrators, who were clearly under the impression that the Proclamation remained in force.

In *Guerin*, which involved lands in British Columbia, the Royal Proclamation was regarded as operable in that province.[26] The early colonial administration there initially pursued the same policy of making treaties with the Aboriginal peoples as was followed in most of the rest of the country.[27] Between 1850 and 1854, fourteen treaties were made with the tribes living around Victoria, Nanaimo, and Fort Rupert. Subsequent administrations refused to follow this policy, which has led to claims of unextinguished Aboriginal title to much of the province.[28] Even in the absence of treaties, the settlement of the province was largely peaceful.[29] Violent conflict such as the killing of settlers or the bombardment of Indian villages was the exception.[30] Colonial officials recognized the value of good relations with the Indians if peaceful settlement was to proceed. In 1856, Governor Douglas wrote to the colonial secretary: "[a]s the safety and prosperity of the colony depends . . . on our maintaining a good understanding with the native tribes, I have used every possible means to command their respect and conciliate their friendship by protecting their rights and giving them redress in all cases where they have suffered wrong, and with equal-handed justice severely punished their own delinquencies."[31] The first judge in the province, Matthew Begbie, regarded the Indian population as "very valuable inhabitants" because, without their skills as guides, packers, and trackers, the colony could not have been opened up to settlement.[32] He described them as "self-supported and self-supporting" and "a race of laborious independent workers."[33]

In short, the "historic relationship" between the Crown and Aboriginal peoples existed in British Columbia as much as in the rest of the country: the Indians allowed peaceful settlement and, in return, the Crown extended its protection to them.

Legal Context

Aboriginal Law

Aboriginal law has changed greatly over the last thirty years.[34] The case that started the rapid growth of Aboriginal law some thirty years ago was *Calder v. Attorney-General for British Columbia*,[35] in which the Nisga'a people claimed Aboriginal title to their traditional lands in the Nass River Valley. It was a split decision and, on balance, the Nisga'a were not successful in their claim. Three of the judges of the Supreme Court of Canada held that the Nisga'a had a legally recognized title that had not been extinguished by the British Crown or legislation. Three other judges seemed to accept that the Nisga'a had originally possessed some sort of Aboriginal rights to their traditional territory, but held that those rights had been extinguished by British Columbia legislation before Confederation. The seventh member of the Court expressed no opinion on these points and rejected the appeal on a procedural point.

Although the Nisga'a had to wait almost thirty years to achieve their objective through a treaty, the case was a significant indication that, contrary to the position of both the federal and provincial governments, there might be unextinguished Aboriginal rights. Largely as a result of the *Calder* case, the federal government announced a new policy indicating a willingness to negotiate on land claims.[36]

Calder also encouraged Aboriginal leaders to lobby for greater legal protection of their rights. This lobbying influenced the debate on the repatriation of the Canadian constitution in 1982 and led to the inclusion of section 35(1) of the *Constitution Act, 1982,* which recognizes and affirms the "existing aboriginal and treaty rights of the aboriginal peoples of Canada." In the *Sparrow* case, decided in 1990, Justices Dickson and La Forest of the Supreme Court of Canada paid tribute to their efforts by saying:[37]

S. 35(1) of the Constitution Act 1982 represents the culmination of a long and difficult struggle in both the political forum and the courts for the constitutional recognition of Aboriginal rights. The strong representations of native associations and other groups concerned with the welfare of Canada's Aboriginal peoples made the adoption of s. 35(1) possible and it is important to note that the provision applied to the Indians, the Inuit and the Metis. Section 35(1), at the least, provides a solid constitutional base upon which subsequent negotiations can take place. It also affords Aboriginal peoples constitutional protection against legislative power.

As we shall see in our discussion of the *Sparrow* case in Chapter 5, the Court used the somewhat vague wording of recognition and affirmation of existing Aboriginal and treaty rights in section 35 to incorporate the fiduciary relationship between the Crown and Aboriginal peoples (established in the *Guerin* decision) into the constitutional protection for such rights and so provide a mechanism to give them substance.

The Origins of Fiduciary Obligations

In his article "Demystifying the Fiduciary Mystique," Justice Gautreau wrote:[38]

> The origin of the fiduciary concept is to be found in equity. The original fiduciary was the trustee and trusts being creatures of the Court of Chancery came under its exclusive jurisdiction. Because of the dependence and vulnerability that was involved in trust situations, equity imposed special duties on the trustee which were known as fiduciary duties. These duties included such rules and obligations as: the trustee must act solely in the interests of the trust, he must avoid all conflict of interest and he is not to profit from the position entrusted. Not to do this would be to invite equitable fraud by way of abuse of power, position or opportunity that belongs to another.

Over the years, courts recognized that other relationships, such as partnerships and agency, involved similar elements of dependence and vulnerability as those found in express trusts. As a result, those relationships were also classified as fiduciary relationships and similar fiduciary duties were imposed on the partner and agent.

Fiduciary obligations form part of the law of equity and can only be understood if equitable principles are understood. To understand these principles, we must go a long way in both time and space from the present Aboriginal communities of Canada, back to medieval England.[39] English common law has its origins in the period from the Norman Conquest in 1066 to the reign of Henry III in the thirteenth century. But, although it continued to develop thereafter, it was not flexible enough to deal with new interests in land and novel claims such as breach of trust, and so claimants appealed directly to the king for a remedy. Some of these cases he referred to his chancellor, who eventually began to act on his own authority, thus leading to the Court of Chancery in the late fifteenth century. This court developed its own body of law to supplement the common law, a body of law which is referred to as equity. Since some of the early chancellors were clergymen, equity was more influenced by principles of conscience than the common law.

The nature of equitable principles is explained in the leading text on the law of equity, *Snell's Equity*:[40]

> Equity is thus a body of rules or principles which form an appendage to the general rules of law, or a gloss upon them. In origin at least, it represents the attempt of the English legal system to meet a problem which confronts all legal systems reaching a certain stage of development. In order to ensure the smooth running of society it is necessary to formulate general rules which work well enough in the majority of cases. Sooner or later, however, cases arise in which, in some unforeseen set of facts, the general rules produce substantial unfairness. When this occurs, justice requires either an amendment of the rule or, if (as in England some five or six centuries ago) the rule is not freely changeable, a further rule or body of rules to mitigate the severity of the rules of law. This new body of rules (or "equity") is therefore distinguishable from the general body of law, not because it seeks to achieve a different end (for both aim at justice), nor because it relates necessarily to a different subject-matter, but merely because it appears at a later stage of legal development.

It may also be noted that, in time, the rules of equity became as rigid and technical as those of the common law. By the Victorian era, the delays and corruption of the Court of Chancery led to the merciless indictment of the court by Charles Dickens in *Bleak House* (first published in 1852), which is based on the seemingly endless case of *Jarndyce v. Jarndyce*. The system of having separate courts of common law and equity was ended at this time in part to deal with this criticism. The English *Judicature Act* of 1873 enabled all courts to apply both the common law and equity and similar statutes were passed in other jurisdictions including the Canadian common law provinces.[41] However, this administrative fusion was not intended to fuse or merge the substantive law. The common law and equity remained distinct.

The application of equitable principles by the Court of Chancery led to the recognition of equitable interests in land and other property. The major example of an equitable interest was that of a beneficiary under a trust. A man might wish to avoid payment of feudal dues payable upon his death and so would transfer land to a friend to hold it for his benefit until his death and then for that of his children. The courts of common law refused to recognize any rights of the transferor or his children in the land and allowed the transferee to treat the land as his own. The beneficiaries began to petition the chancellor for relief and he ordered the transferee to hold the land for their benefit. Over time, the rights of these beneficiaries were upheld against other parties such as the transferee's heirs or a purchaser who took with knowledge of their interest. A purchaser who took the legal estate in the land without such knowledge was not subject to the interest of beneficiaries (the bona fide purchaser for value without notice doctrine). The interest of the beneficiaries in the land was thus recognized as a form of equitable interest since it was enforceable in equity but not at law. The legal interest remained in the transferee or trustee, which meant that he could deal with the land on behalf of the beneficiary. In practice, this made the beneficiary vulnerable to the actions of the trustee, who had the legal power to make a valid disposition of the land to a third party who was acting in good faith. Even if the disposition was contrary to the terms on which the trustee held the land, the interest of the beneficiary in the land would be defeated and he would be left with a claim for breach of trust against the trustee.

Given this vulnerability, courts imposed a heavy obligation of good faith and loyalty—a fiduciary duty—on the trustee. Although of ancient origin, trusts are still of great importance in our law and economy. They are still used extensively in wills and tax planning and in commercial transactions.

The term "fiduciary" is vague. At one time, the word "trust" was used to include a wide variety of relationships that are not technically trusts today. As the word "trust" came to be recognized as a formal term with a particular technical meaning, "fiduciary" was used to refer to relationships that are in some respects trust-like but that are not, strictly speaking, trusts.[42] The word "fiduciary" itself derives from the Latin word *fiducia*, meaning trust, and has been known to the English language since the late sixteenth century.

Fiduciary obligations are now well established in the Anglo-Canadian law and are best illustrated by the obligations owed by a trustee to act in a selfless manner for the benefit of the beneficiary of the trust. However, trustees are simply one example of a fiduciary; there are many other examples, such as agents, company directors, partners, parents, and solicitors. What they have in common is that the law holds them to a high degree of loyalty and good faith in order to protect the beneficiary, who is usually especially vulnerable and dependent on them.

Halsbury's Laws of England describes the importance of the principles of conscience to the early Courts of Chancery :[43]

> Early authorities refer to "conscience," "reason," and "good faith" as the principles which guided the Court of Chancery, and the term "equity" implies a system of law which is more consonant than the ordinary law with opinions current for the time being as to a just regulation of the mutual rights and duties of men living in a civilized society.

These principles influenced the development of the law of fiduciary obligations. La Forest J., writing for the majority of the Supreme Court of Canada in *Hodgkinson v. Simms*,[44] commented extensively on the rationale for the imposition of fiduciary obligations in certain relationships. He stated that the unique function of the fiduciary principle is that it "monitors the abuse of a loyalty reposed."[45] He also noted the important social function of the fiduciary principles:[46]

> The desire to protect and reinforce the integrity of social institutions and enterprises is prevalent throughout fiduciary law. The reason for this desire is that the law has recognized the importance of instilling in our social institutions and enterprises some recognition that not all relationships are characterized by a dynamic of mutual autonomy, and that the marketplace cannot always set the rules. By instilling this kind of flexibility into our regulation of social institutions and enterprises, the law therefore helps to strengthen them.

It was noted by Binnie J. in *R. v. Neil* that "[f]iduciary duties are often called into existence to protect relationships of importance to the public including, as here, solicitor and client. Disloyalty is destructive of that relationship."[47]

Fiduciary Obligations and Aboriginal Peoples: Canadian Law Prior to *Guerin*

In 1975, the year in which the *Guerin* action was commenced, an article was published that considered the tendency of some of those concerned with the rights of Aboriginal peoples "to claim that the rulers of these peoples stand in the position of trustees." Professor L.C. Green reviewed the American and Canadian case law on the trust obligation of the governments towards Indian peoples and then examined a trusteeship based upon treaties or international law. His conclusion was that:[48]

> . . . it is hardly possible to regard the relation between the Government and the Indians as one based on trusteeship, whether it be legal or political in character—unless, of course, the words ward and guardian and trust are to lack all meaning—legal, equitable or moral.

Although our review of the United States law later in this chapter will suggest that Professor Green was only partially correct in this conclusion, it cannot be said that he was incorrect in his statement that Canadian law did not recognize an enforceable trust obligation or indeed any other type of fiduciary obligation of the government towards Aboriginal peoples. Prior to *Guerin*, there was no clear judicial authority in support of such an obligation and the weight of authority denied its existence.

Legislation and other documents, however, indicated the existence of some type of duty. Indeed, the concept of the Crown holding land in "trust" for Indians has long been a feature of the relationship between the Crown and Aboriginal peoples. The critical legal issue was whether this "trust" was one that could be legally enforced or was simply political in nature. Early legislation affecting Indians often referred to the Crown being a form of trustee of their lands. For example, in 1849, legislation was passed for Crown lands in Upper Canada which applied to such lands "whether the same be held in trust or in the nature of a trust for the use of the Indians or of any parties whomsoever."[49] In 1850, *An Act for the Better Protection of the Lands and Property of the Indians in Lower Canada* provided:[50]

> That it shall be lawful for the Governor to appoint from time to time a Commissioner of Indian Lands for Lower Canada, in whom and in whose successors by the name aforesaid, all land or property in Lower Canada which are or shall be set apart or appropriated to or for the use of any Tribe or Body of Indians, shall be and are hereby vested, in trust for such Tribe or Body.

Clause 13 of the 1871 *British Columbia Terms of Union* stated that "[t]he charge of the Indians, and the trusteeship and management of the lands reserved for their use and benefit, shall be assumed by the Dominion Government."[51] The early *Indian Acts* contained similar provisions: section 4 of the 1876 Act provided that "[a]ll reserves for Indians or for any band of Indians, or held in trust for their benefit, shall be deemed to be reserved and held for the same purposes as before the passing of this Act, but subject to its provision."[52] Other examples of trust wording can be found in the *Ontario Boundary Act*[53] and its Quebec equivalent,[54] stating that " the trusteeship of the Indians in the said territory, and the management of any lands now or hereafter reserved for their use, shall remain in the Government of Canada subject to the control of Parliament."

However, the case law prior to *Guerin* was not clear as to the legal nature of this relationship and, in particular, whether the "trust" was one that could be legally enforced against the Crown or was merely a political or moral obligation without any effective remedies available from the court for its enforcement. The law prior to *Guerin* on the question of whether the Crown owed a fiduciary duty to Aboriginal peoples was sketchy and far from certain. There were only a few cases and they failed to provide any clear guidance, but they appeared to give a negative answer to this question.

Henry v. The King,[55] a 1905 decision of the Exchequer Court, was an early case that considered whether Aboriginal peoples could successfully sue the Crown for breach of trust. Unfortunately, jurisdictional problems obscured the discussion of the question. Band moneys of the Mississaugas of the Credit Indian Band, which had been promised to the band under the terms of a surrender of lands in 1820, had been incorrectly paid into the general accounts of the government. The band sought a declaration to have the moneys restored to band funds. The band claimed that the government was in breach of trust and relied upon provisions contained in pre- and post-Confederation statutes. The Crown denied any trust responsibility and defended on the basis of the "political trust" doctrine discussed below.

Burbidge J. of the Exchequer Court found that the moneys were held by the Crown in trust for the band:[56]

> [W]ith regard to the moneys arising from the sale of the lands surrendered by the Mississaugas of the Credit, it is clear, I think, that the Crown holds them in trust for that band of Indians. By the terms of the surrender of the 28th of February 1820, to which reference has been made, the lands were to be held upon the trust therein mentioned.

However, he went on to find that he lacked jurisdiction to hear the claim. Parliament alone had the authority to review the decisions and actions of the Crown.[57]

Attorney-General for Canada v. Giroux[58] was a 1916 decision of the Supreme Court of Canada that touched on the possibility of the Crown being a trustee for Aboriginal peoples. Duff J., speaking for himself and Anglin J., said of a surrender of lands:[59]

> The Indian interest being . . . ownership is by the terms of the surrender a surrender to Her Majesty in trust to be dealt with in a certain manner for the benefit of the Indians. The Dominion Parliament, having plenary authority to deal with the subject of the "Indian Lands" and having authorized such a transfer of the Indian title, it is difficult to see on what ground the transfer could be held not to take effect according to its terms *or on what ground the trusts, upon which the transfer was accepted can be treated as non-operative.*

It should be noted, however, that five years later, in *Attorney-General for Quebec v. Attorney-General for Canada* (the *Star Chrome* case),[60] the same judge speaking for the Privy Council denied that the legislation in question in both cases created "an equitable estate in lands set apart for an Indian tribe of which the Commissioner is made the recipient for the benefit of the Indians."[61]

In the 1935 case of *Dreaver v. The King*,[62] Angers J. of the Exchequer Court held that the Crown was liable for certain breaches of trust in the administration of funds generated from the sale of reserve lands surrendered by the Mistawisis Band of Indians to the Crown in trust. The surrender documents were signed after the band's adhesion to a treaty in 1876 and involved the surrender of some of the lands set aside under the treaty as reserve lands. The proceeds of disposition of the surrendered lands were to be held by the Crown for the band. The Crown made various charges against the moneys. For example, it charged for drugs and education, which the band considered should be provided under the treaty without charge. It also charged the salary of government officials. The Crown denied that any charges were improper.

It also defended on the grounds that the band had delayed too long in bring-ing the action, which was, therefore, outside the relevant limitations period. Angers J. rejected the Crown's defence of limitations, awarded the band part of its claim, and ordered the return of moneys wrongly charged to the band. He also restrained the Indian agent from farming part of the band's reserve without its approval. Although the case does not contain any explicit discus-sion of the Crown's fiduciary duty, it is notable for giving a legal remedy for wrongful administration of band assets.

The issue in *Re Kane*,[63] decided five years later, was whether Indians working off-reserve in Sydney, Nova Scotia, were required to pay a municipal poll tax and were liable for imprisonment for failure to do so. McArthur J. of the Nova Scotia County Court held that they did not have to pay the tax. He explained his decision on the following grounds:[64]

> For reasons which are quite apparent, the Indian has been placed under the guardian-ship of the Dominion Government. He is its ward, so long as he remains unenfran-chised, and the Minister of Interior, as Superintendent General of Indian Affairs, is given the control and management of all lands and property of Indians in Canada. They are looked upon and treated as requiring the friendly care and directing hand of the Government in the management of their affairs. They and their property are, so to speak, under the protecting wing of the Dominion Government, and I do not think in such circumstances, it was ever contemplated that the body of an Indian should be taken in execution under a civil process pure and simple.

Chisholm v. The King,[65] decided in 1948, was brought by the widow and executrix of a solicitor to obtain payment of her husband's account for legal services rendered to an Indian band. She sued the Crown in order to obtain payment out of funds held for the band. O'Connor J. held that the action could not succeed for various reasons, including a failure to obtain the writ-ten approval of the superintendent-general of Indian Affairs to the contract to provide the services as required by the *Indian Act*. However, he did state that "the Minister of Mines and Resources [who was then also the Minister of Indian Affairs] is and has been at all times material the trustee of the In-dians." It is not clear if he would have provided a legal remedy for breach of this trust responsibility.

The 1950 case of *Miller v. The King*[66] was an action brought by the chief councillor of the Six Nations of the Grand River, suing on behalf of himself and all other members of his tribe. It was alleged, *inter alia*, that the Six Na-tions had surrendered certain lands to the Crown in trust on terms that the Crown would sell the surrendered lands and hold the sale proceeds in trust for the benefit of the tribe. It was also alleged that the Crown breached this trust by investing $160,000 of the sale proceeds in the stock of a company which subsequently became insolvent. The case came before the Supreme

Court of Canada on the preliminary point of law of whether an action could be brought against the Crown for the relief sought. The Court held that the Crown could be an express trustee and that equitable relief would be available to enforce the trust obligation against the Crown and referred the matter back for trial.

The decision has a special significance since the Crown advanced the defence of "political trust" as is shown in the following passage from the judgment of Kellock, J.:[67]

> On behalf of the respondent it is first contended that the allegations of fact in the petition and particulars do not show any agreement by His Majesty or anything held by His Majesty in trust. It is said that reference to the Crown (presumably in documents or statutes) as trustee for the Indians and to the Indians as wards of His Majesty is not a technical use of such terms but such references are merely descriptive of the general political relationship between His Majesty and the Indians.

However, this contention was not considered at all by the Court.

Just a year before the Federal Court decision in *Guerin*, in *Pawis v. The Queen*,[68] Marceau J. of the same court considered and rejected a claim that the Lake Huron Treaty of 1850 created a trust. The subject matter of the trust was said to be the hunting and fishing rights confirmed by the treaty. He held that the rights could not be considered trust property. He also applied the political trust doctrine, which we will now consider.

The Political Trust Doctrine

In order to understand the decision in *Guerin* and how it changed the law, it is necessary to have an understanding of the political trust doctrine, which was a major issue in that case, especially in the Federal Court of Appeal.[69] The basis of the political trust concept is a line of cases holding that where the Crown is called a trustee, it may be a trustee in a political sense only, which means that its obligations are not enforceable in the courts but only in the political arena. Prior to the *Guerin* case, the status of the commonwealth law on the political trust doctrine was reflected in the following cases.[70]

The leading case was the 1881 decision of the English House of Lords in *Kinloch v. Secretary of State for India*[71] concerning claims to certain booty of war arising out of the Indian Mutiny. Lord Selborne L.C. said:

> Now the words "in trust for" are quite consistent with, and indeed are the proper manner of expressing, every species of trust—a trust not only as regards those matters which are the proper subjects for an equitable jurisdiction to administer, but as respects higher matters, such as might take place between the Crown and public officers discharging, under the directions of the Crown, duties or functions belonging to the prerogative and to the authority of the Crown. In the lower sense they are matters within the jurisdiction of, and to be administered by, the ordinary Courts

of Equity; in the higher sense they are not. What their sense is here, is the question to be determined, looking at the whole instrument and at its nature and effect.

In this strangely worded passage, he is saying that there are two classes of trusts: trusts "in the higher sense," which are trusts imposed on public officers and not legally enforceable, and trusts "in the lower sense," which are trusts that can be enforced by courts. Citizens who are told that they have no legal recourse for the misdeeds of a public officer may be forgiven for wondering in what sense the trust is "in a higher sense."

An example of the application of the political trust doctrine can be seen in another case from Victorian England, *Rustomjee v. The Queen*,[72] which arose out of the Treaty of Nanking in 1842 between Britain and China. The Emperor of China paid Queen Victoria to compensate British subjects for debts due to them by Chinese merchants. The petitioners sought to recover some of this money on the basis that it was received by the Crown on their behalf. The claim was rejected by the English Court of Appeal with some indignation:[73]

> The notion that the Queen of this country, in receiving a sum of money in order to do justice to some of her subjects, to whom injustice would otherwise be done, becomes the agent of those subjects, seems to me really too wild a notion to require a single word of observation beyond that of emphatically condemning it. In like manner, to say that the sovereign becomes the trustee for subjects on whose behalf money has been received by the Crown appears to be equally untenable.

A few years prior to the *Guerin* decision, the doctrine of political trust had been applied by Megarry V.C. in the English case of *Tito v. Waddell*,[74] where he held that South Sea Islanders were not entitled to claim as trust funds certain royalties payable to the local colonial official as the result of mining operations on their land. Placing particular reliance on the distinction recognized in *Kinloch*, he held that an agreement and certain ordinances did not create "a true trust" or impose any other fiduciary obligation on the Crown:[75]

> When it is alleged that the Crown is a trustee, an element which is of special importance consists of the governmental powers and obligations of the Crown; for these readily provide an explanation which is an alternative to a trust. If money or other property is vested in the Crown and is used for the benefit of others, one explanation can be that the Crown holds on a true trust for those others. Another explanation can be that, without holding the property on a true trust, the Crown is nevertheless administering that property in the exercise of the Crown's governmental functions. This latter possible explanation, which does not exist in the case of an ordinary individual, makes it necessary to scrutinise with greater care the words and circumstances which are alleged to impose a trust.

Another recent application in England was the 1978 decision of the

House of Lords in *Town Investments Ltd. v. Department of the Environment,*[76] where the issue was whether premises occupied under leases entered into by a minister of the Crown were occupied by the Crown or by the minister in trust for the Crown. Lord Simon noted that:[77]

> In public law even a phrase like "in trust for" may not betoken at all the relationship of trustee and cestui que trust [i.e., a beneficiary], but rather the imposition of a constitutional duty the sanction for which is political or administrative not legal (cf. Lord Selborne L.C. in *Kinloch v. Secretary of State for India,* 7 App. Cas. 619, 625, 626).[78]

Prior to *Guerin,* there were a few isolated cases going against the concept of a political trust and imposing a fiduciary obligation on municipal governments. *Roberts v. Hopwood*[79] was a decision of the English House of Lords. A municipality had paid a minimum wage to its employees which was above the market rate, and ratepayers challenged the payments. Upholding the challenge, the members of the House of Lords held that a municipality owes a fiduciary duty to the ratepayers. In the words of Lord Atkinson:[80]

> The indulgence of philanthropic enthusiasm at the expense of persons other than the philanthropists is an entirely different thing from the indulgence of it at the expense of the philanthropists themselves. The former wears quite a different aspect from the latter, and may bear a different legal as well as a moral character. A body charged with the administration for definite purposes of funds contributed in whole or in part by persons other than the members of that body owes, in my view, a duty to those latter persons to conduct that administration in a fairly businesslike manner, with reasonable care, skill, and caution, and with a due and alert regard to the interest of those contributors who are not members of the body. Towards these latter persons the body stands somewhat in the position of trustees or managers of the property of others. This duty is, I think, a legal duty as well as a moral one.

Several years later, the House of Lords reached a similar decision in *Bromley London Borough Council v. Greater London Council.*[81] This involved the question whether the Greater London Council could implement a reduction in bus fares under the relevant statutory provision that governed its powers. In the course of the judgment, Lord Wilberforce noted that the council "owes a duty of a fiduciary character to its ratepayers who have to provide the money."[82] Lord Scarman said the statutory provisions had to be considered "bearing in mind the existence of the fiduciary duty owed by the GLC to the ratepayers of London."[83]

Although the "political trust" concept developed from English colonial law, it was echoed in judgments of the Supreme Court of Canada. In *Hereford Railway Co. v. The Queen,*[84] the Supreme Court of Canada applied the *Kinloch* decision and held that money which the plaintiff railway company said the Crown had agreed to grant to it as a subsidy was not held by the Crown on its behalf in a trust that could be enforced in the courts.[85]

The Canadian law also provides some support for a fiduciary duty owed by a municipality to the ratepayers. In *MacIllreith v. Hart*,[86] a decision of the Supreme Court of Canada, a municipality refused to sue for the return of certain payments wrongfully paid to one of its officers. Mr. Justice MacLennan based his decision on the fiduciary position of the municipality:[87]

> The right of the inhabitants to compel the city corporation, that is the city council, as a body, to do its duty, rests on this:—That the corporation is a trustee for the inhabitants. —The city corporation is comprised of all the inhabitants and not merely of the ratepayers—whether inhabitants or not, all the ratepayers are also *cestui que trustent* of the city corporation.

However, in the subsequent case of *Norfolk v. Roberts*,[88] the Court affirmed the decision of the Ontario Court of Appeal that it was "erroneous to treat either the corporation or its council as trustees for the ratepayers."[89] This decision reflects the political trust doctrine: "[t]hey are, no doubt, in the sense in which the Sovereign is spoken of as a trustee for the people, trustees for the inhabitants of the municipality, but they are, in my opinion, in no other sense trustees."[90]

Two of the Court's judgments dealing with political trusts involved Aboriginal peoples. In *St. Catherine's Milling and Lumber Co. v. The Queen*,[91] Taschereau J. stated:[92]

> The Indians must in the future everyone concedes it, be treated with the same consideration for their just claims and demands that they have received in the past but, as in the past, it will not be because of any legal obligation to do so, but as a sacred political obligation, in the exercise of which the state must be free from judicial control.

It may be noted that, although the case concerned the legal position of Aboriginal peoples, they were not represented in the litigation.

In *St. Ann's Island Shooting and Fishing Club v. The King*,[93] one of the members of the Court used the expression "political trust," although it is not clear if he was intending to exclude legal liability. The Chippewa and Pottawatomie Indians of Walpole Island had surrendered reserve lands to the Crown. The lands were subsequently leased to the St. Ann's Island Shooting and Fishing Club by the Superintendent-General of Indian Affairs through a series of leases. Only the first lease had been authorized by an order in council as required by the *Indian Act*. The Supreme Court of Canada upheld the trial judge's ruling that the subsequent leases were void. In giving his judgment, Rand J. said:

> The language of the statute embodies the accepted view that these aborigines are, in effect, wards of the state, whose care and welfare are a political trust of the highest obligation. For this reason, every such dealing with their privileges must bear the

imprint of Governmental approval, and it would be beyond the power of the Governor in Council to transfer that responsibility to the Superintendent-General.[94]

Such was the law of Canada prior to the *Guerin* case.

United States Law[95]

In any consideration of Canadian Aboriginal law, it is relevant to review the law developed in the United States. Although the details of the law may differ, we share a common early history and a predominantly common law tradition. Both the successes and the failures of the United States law are relevant to the development of the Canadian law.

Canadian Aboriginal law is still very much in its youth. As one prominent practitioner, Thomas Berger, has noted, lawyers knew very little about the subject when he went to law school in the mid 1950s. It was not taught and the subject never came up.[96] In contrast, much of the foundation of United States Indian law can be traced to decisions of Chief Justice Marshall of the U.S. Supreme Court in the 1820s and 1830s.[97]

Canadian courts have long recognized the importance of cases from the United States in this area of the law. In *Guerin*, Dickson J. referred to the decisions of Chief Justice Marshall in his discussion of the Royal Proclamation of 1763.[98] As was pointed out by Mahoney J. of the Federal Court of Canada in the *Hamlet of Baker Lake* case:[99]

> The value of early American decisions to a determination of the common law of Canada as it pertains to Aboriginal rights is so well established in Canadian Courts, at all levels, as not now to require rationalization.

In *Van der Peet*,[100] Lamer C.J.C. agreed with Professor Slattery that the Marshall decisions are as relevant to Canada as they are to the United States, although he observed that their relevance arises from their articulation of general principles rather than their specific legal holdings.

United States cases on the fiduciary obligations owed towards Indian peoples are especially relevant because they are, ultimately, derived in part from the same colonial British document: the Royal Proclamation of 1763. The special protection given to Indians in that proclamation by the requirement of governmental involvement in the disposition of Indian lands was held by the Supreme Court of Canada in *Guerin* to form one source of the fiduciary relationship.[101] Chief Justice Marshall was also influenced by that protection in formulating his own early version of the fiduciary duty in the 1831 case of *Cherokee Nation v. Georgia*.[102] The Royal Proclamation had been restated by Congress in the *Trade and Intercourse Act* of 1790. This statute has been held to establish a legally enforceable trust obligation on the part of the United States government towards Indian peoples.[103]

The trust responsibility of the United States has been recognized as a central concept in American Indian law. It has been described by writers as "one of the primary cornerstones of Indian Law"[104] and "one of the most important principles in Indian Law."[105] In 1970 President Nixon recognized that"[t]he United States Government acts as a legal trustee for the land and water rights of American Indians" and has "a legal obligation to advance the interests of the beneficiaries of the trust without reservation and with the highest degree of diligence and skill."[106]

The law relating to the fiduciary duty of the United States government to Indian people has a long history in United States law. As observed by Reid Peyton Chambers, a leading United States practitioner and scholar in this area,[107] the fiduciary concept stems from the comments of Chief Justice Marshall of the United States Supreme Court in the 1831 decision in *Cherokee Nation v. Georgia,*[108] where he said:

> [The Indians] are in a state of pupilage; their relation to the United States resembles that of a ward to his guardian. They look to the government for protection; rely upon its kindness and its power.

Chambers has described the importance of the *Cherokee* case and the price paid by the Indians for the protection given by the government:[109]

> An overriding legal consequence of Marshall's guardianship concept was to integrate Indian occupancy and ownership of land into the system of American land tenure. A treaty was in essence a land transaction whereby the tribe ceded some lands in return for federal protection and sovereign recognition of Indian occupancy of the retained lands. By concluding treaties with and submitting to the protection of the United States, the tribe acknowledged that it was a sort of federal vassal or loyal subject. A guardian-ward relationship can thus be seen as a natural incident of such land tenure, since Indians were not citizens, the guardianship concept provided a way in which their ownership of real property could be acknowledged and protected.

In effect, therefore, as noted by Professor Green,[110] the Indians acknowledged that they were subject to the jurisdiction of the United States in return for the protection of that government.

Some of the subsequent decisions of the Supreme Court emphasized the legislative jurisdiction of Congress over Indians resulting from the duty of protection recognized in the *Cherokee* case. As the Court commented in *United States v. Kagama,* "these Indian tribes are the wards of the nation. They are communities dependent on the United States. . . . From their very weakness and helplessness . . . there arises the duty of protection and *with it the power.*"[111] The Court accordingly upheld a statute giving the courts of the United States the jurisdiction to try and punish an Indian who had killed another on an Indian reservation. Another leading decision was *Lone Wolf v. Hitchcock*[112] in which the plenary power of Congress to manage Indian property was held to entitle it to abrogate treaties.

On the other hand, there is another line of cases which hold that the trust relationship creates legally enforceable fiduciary duties for federal officials in their dealings with Indians. These cases indicate that an action may be maintained against officials of the executive branch of government for equitable or declaratory relief for breach of trust. [113] For example, in 1937, the United States Supreme Court decided *Shoshone Tribe v. United States*.[114] The government had allowed the Arapahoe to occupy part of the Shoshone reservation despite the objections of the Shoshone and in breach of a treaty. The court found in favour of the Shoshone. In giving the judgment of the court, Cardozo J. summarized the relevant legal principles as follows:[115]

> Power to control and manage the property and affairs of Indians in good faith for their betterment and welfare may be exerted in many ways and at times even in derogation of the provisions of a treaty. . . . The power does not extend so far as to enable the government "to give the tribal lands to others, or to appropriate them to its own purposes, without rendering, or assuming an obligation to render, just compensation; . . . for that would not be an exercise of guardianship, but an act of confiscation." . . . The right of the Indians to the occupancy of the lands pledged to them may be one of occupancy only, but it is "as sacred as that of the United States to the fee." . . . Spoliation is not management.

Perhaps the most significant of this line of cases was the decision in *Seminole Nation v. United States*,[116] decided in 1942, which involved claims based on various treaties, agreements, and acts of Congress. The claims related to payments made to Seminole tribal officials who were allegedly corrupt and misappropriated the funds. The following quotation shows the high fiduciary standard expected of the government:[117]

> Furthermore, this Court has recognized the distinctive obligation of trust incumbent upon the Government in its dealings with these dependent and sometimes exploited people. . . . In carrying out its treaty obligations with the Indian tribes the Government is something more than a mere contracting party. Under a humane and self-imposed policy which has found expression in many acts of Congress and numerous decisions of this Court, it has charged itself with moral obligations of the highest responsibility and trust. Its conduct, as disclosed in the acts of those who represent it in dealings with the Indians, should therefore be judged by the most exacting fiduciary standards. Payment of funds at the request of a tribal council which, to the knowledge of the Government officers charged with the administration of Indian affairs and the disbursement of funds to satisfy treaty obligations, was composed of representatives faithless to their own people and without integrity would be a clear breach of the Government's fiduciary obligation.

The lead given by the United States Supreme Court was followed in lower court decisions.[118] In 1944, the Court of Claims summarized the state of the law by noting that the special jurisdictional statute providing that "the Court shall apply as respects the United States the same principles of law as would be applied to an ordinary fiduciary—add[s] little to the settled doctrine that the United States, as regards its dealings with the property of the Indians, is a trustee."[119] The District Court for the District of Columbia held in *Pyramid Lake Paiute Tribe of Indians v. Morton*[120] that the trust responsibility extended to protection of the water right of the tribe and noted that "[t]he Secretary [of the Interior]'s trust obligations to the Tribe are paramount."[121] In *United States v. The Oneida Nation of New York*, the Court of Claims stated:[122]

> There can be no doubt that a fiduciary relationship does exist between the Indians and the United States Government. This was first established by the *Trade and Intercourse Act of 1790* which required governmental consent prior to any sale or conveyance of Indian lands.

Again in *Manchester Band of Pomo Indians Inc. v. United States*[123] the District Court observed, "[i]t is unquestioned that the United States has a solemn trust obligation to the Indian people" and held the government liable for depositing trust funds in treasury accounts either bearing no interest or interest at a lower rate than was available in other authorized depositories.

In *Joint Tribal Council of the Passamaquoddy Tribe v. Morton*,[124] decided in 1975, the United States Court of Appeals, First Circuit answered the question of whether there was a trust relationship between the tribe and the United States government as follows:[125]

> The district court found that the *Nonintercourse Act* establishes a trust relationship between the United States and the Indian Tribes, including the Passamaquoddy Tribe. It relied on a series of decisions by the Court of Claims . . ., while also finding support in an extensive body of cases holding that when the Federal Government enters into a treaty with an Indian Tribe or enacts a statute on its behalf, the Government commits itself to a guardian-ward relationship with that tribe. . . .
>
> We agree with the district court's conclusions and in large part with its reasoning and analysis of legal authority. That the *Nonintercourse Act* imposes upon the Federal Government a fiduciary's role with respect to protection of the lands of a tribe covered by the Act seems to us beyond question, both from the history, wording and structure of the Act and from the cases cited above and in the district court's opinion. [Citations omitted.]

In 1980, the United States Supreme Court decided *United States v. Mitchell (Mitchell I)*[126] which, together with its sequel, *Mitchell II*[127] in 1983, was described by Justice Ginsburg, giving the opinion of the Court in the 2003 decision in *Navajo Nation*, as "the pathmaking precedents on the question whether a statute or regulation (or combination thereof) can fairly be interpreted as mandating compensation by the Federal Government."[128] The key issue in the two cases was whether the relevant legislation and regulations mandated the award of monetary damages for breach of a fiduciary duty. It is axiomatic in United States constitutional law that the government cannot be sued without its consent.[129] The *Indian Tucker Act*[130] provided such consent. However, it is still necessary to find a substantive right to recover money damages in some other source of law such as the Constitution, Act of Congress, regulation, or executive order

In *Mitchell I*,[131] the Court of Claims held that the *General Allotment Act*[132] imposed a trust obligation on the government to manage certain timber lands. The *Act* provided that "the United States does and will hold the land thus allotted . . . in trust for the sole use and benefit of the Indian." On appeal,[133] the Supreme Court decided that the statute created only a limited trust relationship between the United States and the allottee and did not impose any fiduciary duty on the government for the management of the timber resources.[134] In particular, the statute indicated that the Indian allottee and not a representative of the government was to be responsible for managing the lands.[135] The *Act* did not authorize, much less require, the government to manage timber resources for the benefit of Indian allottees and so established no right to recover monetary damages for the mismanagement of such resources.[136] Since the Court of Claims had not considered the argument that other statutes rendered the government liable for mismanagement, the court remanded the case for re-consideration.[137] Upon remand,[138] the Court of Claims decided that these other statutes "broadened the special trust imposed by the *Allotment Act* to create a general fiduciary obligation on the Government in the management of the forest lands with which Interior was entrusted."[139] The decision was affirmed by the United States Supreme Court when the case came before them again on appeal in *Mitchell II*.[140] Giving the opinion of the majority, Justice Marshall distinguished the earlier decision as follows:[141]

> In contrast to the bare trust created by the *General Allotment Act*, the statutes and regulations now before us clearly give the Federal Government full responsibility to manage Indian resources and land for the benefit of the Indians. They thereby established a fiduciary relationship and define the contours of the United States' fiduciary responsibilities.

After reviewing the relevant statutes and regulations, he concluded that they mandated compensation by the federal government for the damages sustained and referred to general trust principles in support of this conclusion:[142]

> Our construction of these statutes and regulations is reinforced by the undisputed existence of a general trust relationship between the United States and the Indian people. This Court has previously emphasized "the distinctive obligation of trust incumbent upon the Government in its dealings with these dependent and

sometimes exploited people." *Seminole Nation v. United States*, 316 U.S. 286, 296 (1942). This principle has long dominated the Government's dealings with Indians. [citations omitted].

Because the statutes and regulations at issue in this case clearly establish fiduciary obligations of the Government in the management and operation of Indian lands and resources, they can fairly be interpreted as mandating compensation by the Federal Government for damages sustained. Given the existence of a trust relationship, it naturally follows that the Government should be liable in damages for the breach of its fiduciary duties. It is well established that a trustee is accountable in damages for breaches of trust. See *Restatement (Second) of Trusts* 205–212 (1959); G. Bogert, *Law of Trusts and Trustees* 862 (2d ed. 1965); 3 A. Scott, *Law of Trusts* 205 (3d ed. 1967). This Court and several other federal courts have consistently recognized that the existence of a trust relationship between the United States and an Indian or Indian tribe includes as a fundamental incident the right of an injured beneficiary to sue the trustee for damages resulting from a breach of the trust.

The majority of the court also held that:[143]

... a fiduciary relationship necessarily arises when the Government assumes such elaborate control over forests and property belonging to Indians. All of the necessary elements of a common law trust are present: a trustee (the United States), a beneficiary (the Indian allottees) and a trust corpus (Indian timber, land and funds).

The court went on to award monetary compensation for mismanagement of Indian timber lands, citing in support standard texts on the law of trusts. It rejected the government's argument that the court should only award remedies to prevent future breaches of its fiduciary obligations such as an injunction. The court stated that, in the circumstances of this case, these remedies were "totally inadequate." An award of damages for past breaches was necessary to ensure that the government's duties were performed. The Indian allottees were in no position to monitor federal management of their lands on a consistent basis. In addition, by the time government mismanagement became apparent, the damage to Indian resources might be so severe that a prospective remedy might be next to worthless.

Conclusion

The situation in 1979, when the trial of the *Guerin* case commenced in the Federal Court of Canada, was that there were no Canadian precedents in favour of a ruling imposing legally enforceable obligations on the Crown with respect to its relationship with Aboriginal peoples. The United States law provided support for such a ruling, but United States law is not binding on Canadian courts. Such Canadian decisions as existed were not conclusive but tended to the opposite conclusion, including the decision earlier in that year in *Pawis,*[144] in which Marceau J. of the same court applied the political trust doctrine to reject a claim of an enforceable trust.[145] In the opinion of Professor Douglas Sanders, "[i]t was clear that Musqueam had to lose the case. The First Nation had to lose if the prior judicial decisions were respected."[146] Another leading Aboriginal law scholar, Professor Richard Bartlett, observed that "[a]t the commencement of the 1980s, it remained unclear under what circumstances and to what extent the Crown was accountable at law to the aboriginal peoples. . . . The matter required further consideration by the Supreme Court of Canada."[147] The *Guerin* case was to provide the opportunity for such further consideration.

"Sordid Living Conditions on Musqueam Indian Reserve Scored by Alderman
Back-door steps of this home on the reserve consist of plank ramp. Other houses do not even have this for steps. Indians would like council to find work for men. Only 10 of 250 people on reserve have regular employment. . . . 'There's no point in Ald. Rathie throwing dirt at the department of Indian Affairs, either. They do a good job and assist us whenever possible,' said [Chief] Mrs. [Gertrude] Guerin. 'We don't want sympathy, just an opportunity to give our men work,' she said." (Courtesy *Vancouver Sun,* Wednesday, Feb. 21, 1962, p. 29. Caption quotes text from both the original caption and news article.)

Chapter 2

Roots of the *Guerin* Case

The Musqueam

The Musqueam form part of the Central Coast Salish people and are the descendants of the original inhabitants of the Vancouver area of British Columbia. [1] As evidenced by middens found in various parts of the city, their presence in the area goes back thousands of years. Such archaeological evidence shows that the present Musqueam village has been occupied for over three thousand years.

Their main reserve, Musqueam Indian Reserve No. 2, is the site of their main winter village and was the reserve involved in the *Guerin* case. It is strategically located on the Pacific coast at the entrance to the North Arm of the Fraser River. Their territory extended over much of what is now the Greater Vancouver region.

The Coast Salish depended on the land as well as the sea and the rivers for their survival. The sea and rivers were the source of fish, sea mammals, and shellfish. The land supported game and provided roots, leaves, shoots, bulbs, and berry crops, as well as bark and reeds used for clothing. It provided the wood used for large plank houses that made up the winter villages and canoes made of dug-out and steam-shaped logs.

Spring and summer were periods of great activity as successive migrations of salmon were fished, game was hunted, and various root and berry crops were gathered. At this time, there was intensive use of the economic hinterland beyond the winter villages located on the coast. During the winter months, many families would live together in the plank houses within the winter village. Many important ceremonies or "dances" were held at this time of the year. The size of the Musqueam population before contact with Europeans is not known, but it was substantial. [2] The diary of the explorer Simon Fraser in 1808 describes houses that could easily have accommodated a thousand people. [3] As will be seen, that population was to fall dramatically post-contact.

The history of contact between the Indians of the northwest coast and Europeans can be summarized in the following progression: first the Europeans came to trade, then they came in search of gold, and finally, they came to settle.[4] The Musqueam and other Coast Salish had some direct contact with Europeans from the time of the Spanish and British expeditions from 1791 onwards.[5] Simon Fraser's diary records a hostile reception from Musqueam "howling like so many wolves, and brandishing their war clubs,"[6] but other explorers appear to have been welcomed. The journal of a Spanish expedition in 1792 states: "[w]hen they came alongside, they at once gave us a salmon without showing that they looked for any return or taking any interest in the beads we gave them."[7] In the same year, Captain Vancouver had a similar welcome in Burrard Inlet: "[h]ere we were met by about fifty Indians, in their canoes, who conducted themselves with the greatest decorum and civility, presenting us with several fish. . . . These good people finding as we were inclined to make some return for their hospitality, shewed much understanding in preferring iron to copper."[8]

After these early expeditions, because of the relative scarcity of the sea otter, which was the basis of the fur trade, the Coast Salish were left very much to themselves until the middle decades of the 1800s.[9] In 1848, the Hudson's Bay Company moved its headquarters from Fort Vancouver on the Columbia River to Victoria. The colonial era began in 1849 with the establishment of the colony of Vancouver Island. In 1858, the colony of British Columbia was declared on the mainland, and in 1866, the two colonies were united.

Increasing contact with Europeans brought great changes to the way of life that had existed for thousands of years. Diseases for which the Indians had no immunity decimated their numbers.[10]

Government action undermined the traditional Aboriginal society but did nothing to replace it with a new viable way of life. Central to this action were measures to dispossess the traditional owners by allocation of most of the land to settlers through the process of pre-emption. Pre-emption enabled settlers to claim land, settle on it, and then purchase it at a low rate after having cleared and improved it. This led to the confinement of Aboriginal groups to the winter villages, which became reserves.[11] As we saw earlier, such villages only satisfied the needs of the population during the colder months when economic activity was at a low and people survived on what had been accumulated during the preceding spring and summer. To sustain their economy and culture, they needed access to the rest of their traditional territory, their economic hinterland, to obtain food and supplies to be preserved and stored for the winter months. The winter villages alone were never a viable economic base.

In 1874, the Indians of the Fraser River complained in vain to government officials of their treatment by the settlers and the British Columbia colonial and provincial governments that represented the interests of the settlers:[12]

> We have been at a loss to understand the views of the Local Government of British Columbia in curtailing our land as much as to leave, in many instances, but few acres of land per family.
>
> Our hearts have been wounded by the arbitrary way the Local Government of British Columbia have dealt with us in locating and dividing our Reserves. . . .
>
> For many years we have been complaining of the land left us being too small. We have laid our complaints before Government officials nearest to us; they sent us to some others; so we had no redress up to the present and we have felt like men trampled on, and are commencing to believe that the aim of the white man is to exterminate us as soon as they can, although we have always been quiet, obedient, kind and friendly to the whites.
>
> Discouragement and depression have come upon our peoples. . . .
>
> We consider that 80 acres per family is absolutely necessary for our support, and for the future welfare of our children. We declare that 20 or 30 acres of land per family will not give satisfaction, but will create ill feelings, irritation amongst our people, and we cannot say what will be the consequences.

In the case of the Musqueam, the pressure from neighbouring settlers was felt soon after land was surveyed by the Royal Engineers and pre-emption in the area began in 1859.[13] The land south of the main winter village along the Fraser River was pre-empted and sold during the next decade. The land to the north and east was leased as timberlands to the Hastings Saw Mill Company. Fitzgerald McCleery, who came from County Down in Ireland and settled in 1862 near the village, recorded in his diary that the settlers could go to the winter dances being held there.[14] Once the settlers acquired land by pre-emption, they took steps to have the Indians removed. For example, one William Smith wrote in 1875 to the Indian superintendent to complain about Indians, presumably Musqueam, trespassing on his lands at the mouth of the Fraser:[15]

> There is some Indians settled on my Preemption and I can not get them off also their dogs are a bothering my Stock and Stealing every thing they can get hold of and the Indians are tramping down my dykes and when I say any thing to them they call me all the mean names they can think of so I think it is time they was moved off with stick [sic] orders not to come back on the place any more.

The Musqueam were now considered trespassers on land that they had occupied for thousands of years, land that they had never given up and for which they had received no compensation. The customary law of the Coast Salish relating to ownership of land[16] had to give way to imported English common law concepts. The law of the settlers was now used to support them in their conflict with Aboriginal peoples over the land. Professor Harris notes that "suddenly there were survey lines and fences on the land. There were owners who could identify trespassers, tell them to get off, and know their commands would be backed, if need be, by the full apparatus of the state. Native people suddenly found that they could not go where they had; there were too many watchmen (property owners) backed by too much power."[17] Although the early colonial administration under Governor Douglas recognized Aboriginal title and entered into a few treaties to acquire the land by agreement on Vancouver Island, later administrations simply denied its existence.[18]

No treaties were made with the Musqueam, but they were increasingly confined to the area of their main winter village at the mouth of the Fraser by the pressure of European settlement. The current Reserve No. 2 was informally established by the colonial government before the colony entered the Confederation of Canada in 1871. It was first laid out in 1864 on the orders of Magistrate Brew acting under instructions of Governor Douglas and was to consist of "all the land N. of a line drawn from the Black Stump to the River," but it was not surveyed.[19]

The earlier, more liberal policies of Governor Douglas were soon replaced by a harsher policy leading to reduction in the size of reserves. On August 28, 1867, Colonial Commissioner of Lands Joseph Trutch criticized the policy of Douglas and the size of reserves and expressed his opinion that "these reserves should, in almost every case, be very materially reduced."[20] In 1870, the Musqueam reserve was surveyed and reduced in size by another magistrate, and a settler named Bates took over the cut-off lands, making it difficult to restore those lands when the reserve was later formally established in 1879.[21]

After Confederation in 1867,[22] the federal government had jurisdiction over "Indians, and the Lands reserved for the Indians." When British Columbia joined Canada in 1871, the federal government expressly assumed "[t]he charge of the Indians and the trusteeship and management of the lands reserved for their use and benefit."[23] To discharge this fiduciary responsibility, the federal government attempted to obtain land from the province to be set aside for reserves. For its part, the province took every opportunity to frustrate the process (which was not completed until 1938) and to perpetuate the small size of British Columbia reserves, which were considerably smaller than those in the rest of the country.

During the early discussions between the federal and provincial governments, the federal government suggested that reserves should be allocated on the basis of eighty acres per family, but the province countered with an offer of only ten.[24] Dr. Powell, the Indian superintendent appointed by the federal government, managed to get a short-lived agreement on twenty acres.[25] In

1874, Dr. Powell completed a survey of the Musqueam Reserve and wrote as follows to the chief commissioner of Lands and Works for the province:[26]

> Indian Office, Victoria, July 31 st, 1874
>
> SIR, — I have the honour to inform you that the survey of the Musqueam Indian Reserve, lately undertaken by my office, is now finished, and the quantity of land is insufficient to give each head of a family an allotment of 20 acres. The actual number of families in the tribe is 70, consequently 1,400 acres of land will be required to make up the full quantity. Of this the present reserve contains 314 acres, 114 of which is quite useless.
>
> I now make application for 1,197 acres, and request that the surveyor may be allowed to choose the land in the immediate vicinity, or as near the present reserve as may be found practicable. . . .
>
> I have, & (Signed) I.W. Powell.

On the basis of twenty acres for each family and a population of seventy families, the Musqueam should have received fourteen hundred acres for their reserve. In reply to his request for this amount of land, Dr. Powell received a letter from the provincial Commissioner of Lands and Works raising a number of petty questions clearly designed to obstruct the survey.[27] The provincial government then changed its position and restricted the grant of twenty acres for each family to new reserves only. In the light of this reversal of the provincial position, another letter was sent by Dr. Powell:[28]

> Department of Indian Affairs, Victoria, August 15th., 1874.
>
> SIR, — Pursuant to the arrangement of granting 20 acres of land to every head of an Indian family in British Columbia, I had the honour of applying to the Honourable Chief Commissioner of Lands and Works for land to make up deficiency in the present reserves of Musqueam and Tsowassen.
>
> . . . As many of the present reserves do not contain *five* acres of land to each head of a family, the injustice with which the Indians having such reserves would be treated in case they were not extended, and the serious complications which would at once be consequent upon such treatment are so great, that I sincerely trust the interpretation seemingly conveyed in the Honourable Commissioner's letter, of confining the grant to new reserves, is not that intended by the Government in lieu of *all* reserves containing 20 acres to every head of a native family. . . .
>
> I have &., (Signed) I.W. Powell

Despite Dr. Powell's efforts and the clear wording of the order in council making the allotment, the provincial government insisted that its agreement to allocate twenty acres for each family did not apply to existing reserves such as those for the Musqueam and Tsawwassen.[29]

The reaction of the federal government to the position taken by the provincial government was to use critical words but to take no effective action. The Minister of the Interior saw the position as "little short of a mockery" of the claims of the Indians.[30] He said the policies of the former colonial and the provincial governments "fall far short of the estimate entertained by the Dominion Government of the reasonable claims of the Indians" and expressed concern that the discontent among them might possibly lead "in the near future [to] an Indian War with all its horrors."[31] However, in the face of the determined opposition of the provincial government, the federal government effectively abdicated its recently assumed fiduciary obligations to protect the interests of the Aboriginal peoples of the province and took no action.

The federal government did little to support Dr. Powell in his efforts to get more land for existing reserves. In 1875, it agreed with a provincial proposal (made at the suggestion of the missionary William Duncan) to abandon any specific acreage per family.[32] As one writer noted:[33]

> To all appearance the Province had now taken a position that could only lead to a complete deadlock with the Dominion. Most surprisingly, however, the Dominion Government for reasons that seem incomprehensible expressed its readiness to adopt the proposals of the Province. It seems difficult to understand how the Dominion Government so readily yielded this point. It is indeed anomalous that at the very moment when the Canadian Government was in a strong position, when the Imperial Government was roused to action and determined to give every support to the Dominion Government, that the latter should have surrendered almost every point for which it had long contended.

Under the *Terms of Union*, the federal government could have referred the dispute to the Secretary of State for the Colonies, who had indicated support for its position, but it did not do so. It took no effective action at all to protect the land base of the Aboriginal peoples of the province. Within five years of expressly assuming a fiduciary obligation for "the charge of the Indians and the trusteeship and management of the lands reserved for their use and benefit" under the *Terms of Union*, the federal government had shown that it did not have the will to oppose the hunger of the local non-Indian population for Indian land. Its fiduciary obligation to the Aboriginal peoples meant little in practice.

A joint reserve commission consisting of three members was set up to look at each situation individually.[34] The commission began its work at Musqueam, and in 1879, a reserve of just under four hundred acres was formally allocated to the band.[35] This was just under six acres per family, less than one-third of what Dr. Powell had requested. It was also less than what the band had understood it was to receive. In 1913, a Musqueam chief complained to another joint commission, the McKenna-McBride Commission, which finally settled the boundaries of reserves in the province, that "[s]ince these posts were put down by Sir James Douglas for the Indians, the land has been lessened twice. The Indians were not notified or consulted . . . and after that three persons came here to Musqueam and told some of the Indians that the posts . . . meant nothing at all."[36]

From the beginning, the reserve provided an insufficient land base. Some effort was made by band members to become farmers, and in 1877, twenty-two acres were under cultivation.[37] But such cultivation had never been part of the Coast Salish way of life, and band members were not equipped to support themselves by agriculture. In any event, the size and quality of land that the band was permitted to retain as reserve was simply inadequate for farming. In 1913, the McKenna-McBride Commission determined that it consisted of 416.82 acres or 4.11 acres per capita.[38] The average for the New Westminister Agency, of which it formed a part, was 16.30 acres per capita.[39] In fact, the Musqueam Reserve had the lowest per capita acreage in the agency and almost the entire province and, almost certainly, among the lowest in the country since British Columbia reserves were considerably smaller than those in the rest of the country.[40]

The quality of much of the land was also poor. The McKenna-McBride Report effectively confirmed Dr. Powell's assessment that 114 acres was "quite useless,"[41] noting that "approximately one-third" was "low and marshy—good if drained."[42] Eighty years later, the Musqueam were to suffer the loss of use of over one-third of even this meagre amount of land with the lease of much of the higher, better land to the Shaughnessy Golf and Country Club for seventy-five years because of the further breach of the fiduciary duty of the federal government to protect what remained of the traditional territory of the Musqueam.

Other traditional Musqueam villages, located in what is now much of Greater Vancouver, were not given reserve status and so received no protection at all from the demands of settlers. They soon ceased to exist.[43]

Aboriginal people were also being denied the opportunity to acquire interests in land under the newly introduced legal system based on European legal concepts.[44] Governor James Douglas had seen the pre-emption of land by Indians as the means by which they could integrate into settler society. However, this changed when Joseph Trutch was appointed Chief Commissioner of Lands and Works for British Columbia in 1864.[45] He thought that Indians were not capable of using land in a productive way and should only be given minimal amounts of land. Under his administration, much of the land set aside by Douglas for reserve lands was taken away. It was his opinion that to allow Indians to pre-empt land would create an "embarrassing precedent."[46] In 1866, a land ordinance prevented Indians from pre-empting land without the written permission of the governor.[47]

By 1875, there was only one case of an Indian pre-empting land under this provision.[48] In that year, the attorney-general, George Walkem, noted that the provision "is now in force, but the practice of giving these permissions has been discontinued, lest it should interfere with the Dominion policy of concentrating the Indians upon Reserves."[49] Meanwhile, Trutch was implementing measures that would increase the amount of land that a settler could acquire. A 1865 land ordinance allowed each settler to purchase up to 480 acres in addition to a pre-emption of 160 acres.[50] At the same time, he expected an Indian family to subsist on 20 acres of reserve land, and even less in the case of bands such as the Musqueam.

Writing in 1955, just three years before the lease over the main Musqueam reserve was signed by the Department of Indian Affairs with the Shaughnessy Heights Golf Club, Professor Barnett gave this gloomy summary of the state of the Coast Salish:[51]

> At present the old culture is practically dead. There has been very little displacement of the Indian population, and reserves for the most part comprise the traditional village locations; but the material basis, the technology, and the spirit of the aboriginal economy are gone. The plentiful sources of salmon, once so easy to exploit, have gradually receded to the north under the onslaught of cannery operations, and most of the young men go in summer to Rivers Inlet north of the Salish territory for the commercial fishing season. Others, with their families make annual excursions to the hop fields of Washington. Dugout canoes are still made, but "gas boats" and row boats have taken the field. Houses are built in the modern manner. The ancient handicrafts are modified or have ceased altogether to be practiced. Wood and fiber working, formerly foundation crafts, have given way to wage labor and ready-made products. I have seen (during six summer months) three men making canoes, one woman making baskets, and three others carding wool for sweaters. Utensils and furnishings are of white manufacture and pattern, and today it is not easy to find even wooden spoons of a simple type.

It is of little surprise that many of the Musqueam's traditional forms of economic activity and social organization broke down under the pressures created by the city growing next to them. As Dr. Kew points out, "within the span of a single lifetime the timbered peninsula of Point Grey gave way to modern city suburb."[52] They could no longer go into their traditional economic hinterland to hunt, obtain wood and other materials, or gather berries and other crops. Their access to fish was severely limited both by the declining salmon stocks noted by Barnett and by legislation in existence since 1888 which permitted Indian people to catch fish for their own consumption but prohibited them from selling or trading fish without a commercial fishing licence.[53] They obtained some seasonal part-time jobs at the bottom end of the new economy as unskilled or semi-skilled workers in fishing and the canneries and saw mills.[54]

As a result, Kew comments, ". . . the Musqueam population of 1960 contained within its ranks virtually no persons with work experience or skills in such fields as commerce, accounting or business management. It was not prepared by experience for developments to come."[55]

Most of the people at Musqueam were converted to the Catholic religion, but, perhaps because of the relatively small population, the Musqueam village never attracted sufficient attention from the missionaries to have a permanent mission or school such as those established by the missionary William Duncan in Port Simpson for the Tsimpsean. [56] There were no schools on the reserve and few children attended schools off the reserve because of lack of space, resistance from parents to sending children away from the family to attend residential schools and the non-acceptance of Indian children by local public schools. Provincial and Vancouver city schools were not generally open to Indians until 1958 and, by 1955, only two or three Musqueam youths had graduated from high school and only one had attained a little university experience.[57] Part of the difficulty was that the public schools required payment for Indian children, which the Department of Indian Affairs refused to provide for off-reserve schooling.

Those who attended public schools faced discrimination. Writing in 1965, Wilson Duff referred to "the social barrier which still discourages many of these people from entering fully into the social life of the communities which surround them. . . . Any impartial observer can see that some degree of prejudice still operates to segregate the Indians socially."[58] An editorial in the Vancouver *Province* of June 5, 1941 gives some indication of the prevailing attitude towards Indian settlements such as the Musqueam village as obstacles to progress to be relocated to some unstated destination:[59]

> The City's case [ie., the *Chow Chee*[60] case, which ruled that the city of Vancouver could tax non-Indian lessees of Musqueam reserve lands] touches but barely touches the Indian Reserve problem which has become a vexed one in Greater Vancouver. The reserves, by the very fact of their existence, stand in the way of orderly community development. Town-planning cannot be made completely effective while these areas lie athwart the path of development.
>
> It is not good for the Indians to be domiciled on undeveloped tracts in the centre or on the outskirts of a big city and it is certainly not good for the City to have them there.

This overt racism may have been toned down somewhat by the time of the Shaughnessy lease in January 1958. However, the marriage of a Musqueam woman with a non-Indian was considered newsworthy enough for the May 6, 1958 issue of *The Sun* to have a headline declaring "Indian Marries White Man." The wife's parents complained of her difficulty in finding employment and the extent of the prejudice that existed against Indians.

Although limiting their advancement in the wider society, this prejudice, together with the strength and resolve of the community, may have helped to keep alive some aspects of Musqueam culture such as spirit dancing and pot-laching (gift-exchange ceremonies) which continue to be part of Coast Salish and Musqueam life.[61] As Kew comments, "in the face of segregation and social restriction encountered in the larger community they provided Musqueams of all ages with rewarding and compensating roles and statuses. They have been essential means of providing positive self-images for Musqueams."[62] He points out the contrast that still exists in the lives of many Musqueam and other Coast Salish people:[63]

> Musqueams may pass though the automatically opened doors of a bustling, air conditioned supermarket and within five minutes step into a dirt floored, fire-lit structure where painted Indians are singing and dancing under the instructions of guardian spirit powers.

The spirit dancing existed as an unbroken link to a culture that still survives despite or, perhaps, in part, because of the pressures of the larger community to which the Musqueam also belong.

The Department of Indian Affairs

The traditional system of governance broke down in the face of pressures from the wider society and was replaced by government imposed by the colonial and federal authorities. Under the terms of Canadian Confederation, "Indians, and Lands reserved for the Indians" are within the federal and not the provincial jurisdiction.[64] At the time of Confederation in 1867, Indian Affairs was the responsibility of the Secretary of State;[65] in 1873, it became a branch of the Department of Interior; in 1880, it was made a separate Department of Indian Affairs; in 1936, it became a branch of the Department of Mines and Resources; and in 1950, it formed part of the Department of Citizenship and Immigration. A commissioner of Indian Affairs was the senior officer for Indian Affairs in the province of British Columbia; at the time of the negotiations for the lease with the Shaughnessy Heights Golf Club in 1957–58, Mr. William Arneil filled this position.[66] Reporting to him were the Indian superintendents (or Indian agents) in charge of the twenty agencies existing at the time. The Musqueam came under the Vancouver Agency; Mr. Frank (Earl) Anfield was Indian superintendent for that agency for most of the negotiations, although he was promoted to assistant Indian commissioner towards the end of these negotiations and replaced by Mr. Jack Letcher. Department officials in Ottawa also had some involvement in the negotiations.

The power of the Indian superintendent or Indian agent over the lives and property of band members was extensive, and their independence was correspondingly diminished. That power came formally from the *Indian Act*, which is a federal statute. "In matters of schooling, management of band monies, reserve lands, wills and estates, local by-laws, community improvements, matters of health and welfare, the Department and especially the Superintendent, were the guiding and controlling powers."[67] Underlying this bureaucratic structure and regulation was the belief that Indians were incapable of managing their own affairs. They therefore had to be subjected to what was essentially a colonial system of government, and reserves became, in Dr. Kew's words, "a series of internal colonies."[68] However, having set up the system, the federal government failed to adequately fund or staff it. Witnesses from the department complained at the *Guerin* trial of insufficient funds to discharge their responsibilities.

The Indian agent also had a role in the community which went beyond his formal powers. Kew states:[69]

> Musqueam people, as did all registered Indians in some degree, came to depend upon the Superintendent for [services under the *Indian Act*] and this dependence extended beyond the sphere of normal business matters and into the inter-personal and even domestic affairs. Complaints about misbehaviour of neighbours' children, visitors who had outstayed their welcome, family discord and so on, were at times taken to the Superintendent. He in turn sometimes took action—issuing orders for non-members to leave the reserve, delivering horticultural lectures or whatever the case and circumstances required. The Indian Superintendent was, within the social system of the village, a figure of authority, a step above that of chief and council.

It is little wonder that some Indian agents let this power go to their heads.

The Indian agent whose power was to have a great impact on the destiny of the members of the Musqueam band was Mr. F. Earl Anfield, the agent at the time of negotiations over the Shaughnessy lease in 1957. At the *Guerin* trial, his assistant, Mr. William Grant, recalled that Anfield would often say that, from the womb to the tomb, the Indians were his responsibility, and he described Anfield as very paternalistic. The combination of power, paternalism, and an inability to discharge his heavy responsibilities to the band members was to have dramatic and still continuing consequences for them.

Earl Anfield appears to have been concerned for the interests of Aboriginal people under his care. He was the former principal of a residential school for Indian children in Alert Bay and an Anglican minister. In his history of residential schools, Professor Miller singles him out as an exceptional example of a principal who respected the Indian community, understood their language, and treated children under his care considerately.[70] He left the ministry and became an Indian agent in Bella Coola. Judged by the standards of the day, he seems to have been relatively enlightened and progressive. In their history of the laws against spirit dancing and the potlach, Douglas Cole and Ira Chaikin refer to an incident where he chanced upon an illegal dance at a cannery.[71] Based on his own account, he seems to have handled the matter in good humour and, instead of prosecuting the offenders, made them take up a collection for the Red Cross. He then "chased them all off to their boats" and admonished them to get a permit for dances off the reserve next time. Compared with some of the agents described by Cole and Chaikin, he was relatively moderate in his approach to enforcing the laws.

When he was transferred to the Vancouver Agency and became responsible for the Musqueam, he demonstrated some vision and regard for the wishes of the band members. Before he became involved in the negotiations for the Shaughnessy lease, he recognized the department's lack of expertise and the value of the lands to the members of the band:[72]

> It seems to me that the real requirement here is the services of an expert estate planner with courage and vision and whose interest and concern would be as much the future of the Musqueam Indians as the revenue use of the lands unrequired [sic] by these Indians. It is essential that any new village be a model community. The present or any Agency staff set up could not possibly manage a project like this, and some very realistic and immediate plans must be formulated to bring about the stated wish of these Musqueam people, the fullest possible use and development for their benefit, of what is undoubtedly the most potentially valuable 400 acres in metropolitan Vancouver today.

For reasons which were never sufficiently explained at the trial, he lost sight of this broader vision and became focussed on only one object: having a lease signed with the golf club on any terms. The band never did receive the benefit of the "expert estate planner with courage and vision" concerned with their future. Anfield himself clearly lacked that expertise. But it was not merely a case of a man out of his depth. He actively worked to further the interests of the club when he must have realized that they were adverse to those of the band members.

Because he was not alive at the time of the trial to explain his actions, one can only speculate on why Anfield lost his concern for the interests of the band members and the objectivity that he had shown earlier. As found by the trial judge, these actions included failing to disclose all the terms of the proposed lease to the appraiser, leading to an opinion that the appraiser testified at the trial he would not have given had he known all the facts,[73] and then "over-stating" the opinion to the band.[74] He gave information on the appraised value to the representatives of the club during the negotiations which he did not disclose to the band.[75] He ignored expressions of interest from other potential lessees of the land which would have generated a higher return for the band.[76] He told William Guerin,[77] a member of the band council at the time, that if the band was "unreasonable" in its demands, the department could lease the land without a surrender (something that would have violated a requirement of law going back to the Royal Proclamation of 1763[78]) and for any sum it wished. Once he obtained the surrender of the lands from the band members, he did not return to them to explain that the terms of the lease as signed were not the terms approved by the band.[79] Indeed, the department refused to give them a copy of the lease for another twelve years.[80]

The trial judge ruled out fraud in the sense of deceit, dishonesty, or moral turpitude.[81] One is therefore left wondering if this was a case of a middle-level civil servant being blinded to his duty by the rare opportunity to dine and rub shoulders with the wealthy and powerful representatives of an exclusive club[82] who were able to use this short-term relationship to their advantage. Another possibility is that he was acutely aware that an officer of the club had contacted a deputy minister to lobby on the club's behalf. The deputy minister then told his subordinates to report on the progress of the negotiations.[83] Anfield would have realized that his actions would likely be closely and critically scrutinized if the club were to complain to his superiors about his conduct towards them.

There is much that is puzzling about the Rev. Earl Anfield. How did an English-born clergyman end up in the remote Indian community of Alert Bay in British Columbia in the 1930s as the principal of the St. Michael's Residential School? What did he know of the abuse that we now know took place in such institutions? Why did he leave the school to become a bureaucrat in the Department of Indian Affairs? Why did he behave as he did during the Shaughnessy lease negotiations? He was clearly not a stupid man and saw the need for an "expert estate planner with courage and vision" who would keep in mind the future of the Musqueam. He must have realized that a lease with rents at below market value could never be in their best interests. How could he have lost his expressed concern for those under his care and actively assisted in obtaining a lease for the golf club that was clearly so unfavourable to them? Did he ever think back to his earlier proposal for "what is undoubtedly the most potentially valuable 400 acres in metropolitan Vancouver today" and ask himself how he could have gone so far wrong?

Was it again the conflict between theory and practice? The theory was easy: the federal government had to act in the best interests of the Indians. The practice was very different. As we have seen, in the face of the determined opposition of the settler society represented by the provincial government, the federal government failed to take any effective steps to discharge its fiduciary duty to act in the best interests of the Musqueam Band by obtaining a reserve of adequate size for its needs. The result was that the Musqueam reserve was less than a third of the twenty acres per family sought by the federal government in 1874, which was already much less than the eighty acres per family it had originally sought, which was the standard in other provinces. In the same way, Anfield's recommendation for vision and courage in the planning of the Musqueam lands gave way in the face of the determination of the golf club to have a lease on its terms. When push came to shove, the federal government again breached its fiduciary duty and gave in to the pressure from the club to lease over a third of the reserve at less than market rent. The limited land base of the Musqueam became even smaller. They will live with the consequences of that breach until the lease ends in 2033.

The other side of the coin to the extensive powers of the department was the powerlessness and dependency of the band. The superintendent directed affairs of the band council.[84] He called and chaired meetings and drew up the agenda. He arranged for the minutes to be typed. It was not until 1963 when Willard Sparrow became chief at Musqueam that council meetings were held without the presence of the superintendent.[85] The band did not have a band office at the time of the Shaughnessy lease negotiations.[86] They lacked private telephones and typewriters. As noted above, they also lacked formal education and relevant experience. Legally, their powers were limited by the *Indian Act* and the need to obtain department approval to do any number of things and, in particular, for any use of reserve lands. They had no say in the passage of this legislation. Except in very specific cases such as war veterans, Indians were denied a vote in federal elections until 1960. The first federal election in which they were eligible to vote was that of 1962. They had no political power and were unavoidably dependent on the department.

In their report written in 1958, the same year as the Shaughnessy lease was signed, Professors Hawthorn, Belshaw, and Jamieson described this paternalistic system:[87]

> We have been astonished to find . . . that all business of a financial kind is transacted through the superintendent's office, and that officials of the band council seldom come face to face with representatives of the groups with whom they have business. This is one of the most revealing lacks in the administration of Indian Affairs, since it documents with clarity our contention that the focus of administrative action is not the education of the Indian, except in a narrow formal sense, but the manipulation of his property.

The result of this bureaucratic control of band assets was that band members had little or no opportunity to manage their own affairs, including use of their reserve. Reflecting this lack of power, when the Shaughnessy lease—162 acres of the best land out of a total of 416 acres, one-third of the whole reserve, for seventy-five years—was made on January 22, 1958 between Her Majesty The Queen in right of Canada and the Shaughnessy Heights Golf Club, the band was not even a party to the agreement. During negotiations with the golf club, the band was represented by bureaucrats from the Department of

Indian Affairs and primarily by an ex-residential school principal without any business experience. No legal advice was made available to either the bureaucrats or the band.

The Golf Club

On the other side of the table, representing the Shaughnessy Heights Golf Club (now the Shaughnessy Golf and Country Club) were vice-presidents of the leading corporations of the province who had contacts at the highest level in the federal government. They also had available to them the services of a leading law firm, who prepared the lease which was ultimately signed without any significant amendments.

The Shaughnessy Heights Golf Club was, and is, an exclusive golf club with sizeable admission and green fees. As of 2004, the club charged approximately $50,000 for full memberships for men. Membership is subject to a ballot and a strict dress code is enforced. The club has always been *the* club for Vancouver's business elite, where discreet deal-making is every bit as important as hitting golf balls around the manicured fairways, which are always kept green and lush.

In 1956, the club was located in the Shaughnessy area of Vancouver, which is an area of larger homes and generally upper-income people. Shaughnessy Heights was part of a large amount of land acquired by the Canadian Pacific Railway (CPR) in return for bringing the railway to Vancouver and so providing a link to the rest of the country, which was the condition of British Columbia's agreement to join Canada. The Shaughnessy area was designed as Vancouver's Nob Hill, and the golf club was part of that design to provide recreation for the wealthy residents.[88] However, by the 1950s, the surrounding area had become too developed for the golf club to remain and the CPR wanted to develop the golf course lands. Witnesses at the trial spoke of golf balls having to be retrieved from neighbouring Oak Street, which had become a busy road. The club was told by the CPR that its lease would not be renewed. It started to look for an alternative location, and the Musqueam Reserve became the object of its interest.

The history of the club is given as follows on its website:

> The Shaughnessy Heights Golf Course, today the Shaughnessy Golf and Country Club, had its beginning at 4 pm on the afternoon of April 26, 1911 in the office of CPR executive Richard Marpole. Nine businessmen, all residents of the prestigious and quickly developing enclave of Shaughnessy, agreed to turn 67 acres of land leased from the CPR into the Shaughnessy Heights Golf Course. And by November 2 of the following year, they had. The first nine holes opened on that date, the second nine the next year. In the decades to follow, many of the names that played a prominent role in Vancouver's growth and prosperity also appeared

on Shaughnessy's membership roster.

... In 1956, it became evident that the CPR wanted the valuable land on which the Shaughnessy Heights Golf Club stood for real estate development. After a search, a long-term lease was signed with the Musqueam Indian Band for the present beautiful 162-acre site of the new Shaughnessy Golf and Country Club. The last crack of a ball being shot struck on the original fairways echoed down Granville Street in early November 1960. The Club was then moved to the new site—without any interruption of play.

Although the play of Vancouver's business elite may have continued uninterrupted on the fairways of the Musqueam Reserve, the club's move to the Musqueam Reserve would cause an interruption of seventy-five years in the band's ability to enjoy a fair return on its lands. The fairways of the club were anything but fair to the band members.

It was clear from the witnesses for the club at the trial[89] that they were very concerned at the prospect of having to relocate to the suburbs. They did not want members to have to drive from their homes on the west side of Vancouver to the suburbs in order to get their recreation.[90] Another major concern was the restriction on having alcohol on the reserve, and they successfully lobbied senior officials to get a waiver. It was also clear from that evidence that they were concerned that the membership fees should not rise and so the rent had to be kept low.[91] For this reason, they successfully negotiated a restriction on any increase in rent of 15 percent for the second rent period of fifteen years, and a restriction for all rent periods that the lands were to be valued on the fiction that they were uncleared and unimproved and with limited use. They insisted on a provision that would give the club a unilateral right to terminate the seventy-five year lease on six months notice and another provision that permitted them to remove the improvements at the end of the lease.

From the viewpoint of the club, it was undoubtedly an excellent lease which reflected the superior negotiating skills and legal advice available to them.

A Clash of Cultures and Power

The band members had little involvement in the lease negotiations, which were primarily conducted between the department and the club. There is, however, one poignant account of the clash of cultures in the evidence of Ed Sparrow, who was chief at the time of the lease negotiations. He describes a social meeting attended by Councillor Gertrude Guerin and himself at the old clubhouse, a "tea party" in his words.[92] A witness from the golf club said that it was a chance "to discuss and be on social terms with our very delightful friends from the Reserve."[93] It was clearly an awkward meeting with representatives of the impoverished, powerless band sitting down on the other side of the table to the representatives of the affluent, powerful business elite at their exclusive club. The imposing clubhouse, where the meeting took place, stood as a silent monument to that affluence and power—a world away from the poverty of the nearby reserve. They ate their cookies and drank their tea with little conversation until, starting with Anfield, the Indian agent who sat on the same side of the table as the representatives of the club, the others got up one by one without comment and went to a lounge, leaving their guests alone at the table. One club official stood silently by the exit. Finally, Gertrude Guerin looked at Chief Sparrow and said it seemed as if they were no longer welcome and should go.

This is how Chief Sparrow described the meeting at the trial:[94]

> We had . . . we were just talking across the table, chatting away, nothing in particular. Then we had our tea and cookies, whatever we had there, and we got finished. Anfield gathered up his papers and left the room. He left the room first before . . . the Golf Club people did, and left us sitting there. They finally all went in to a lounge room and left us sitting there.
>
> . . . [T]hey left Gertie Guerin and I sitting right at the table, and there was one man waiting at the door. And then Gertie says, "Well, I guess that's all. I guess we're not wanted," and we walked off. They didn't even bid us good-bye or anything. . . . They went to see [Anfield] in the room.

Gertrude Guerin's son, Delbert, recalls how she arrived home furious at the treatment received from their prospective tenants. She never forgot the insult. She felt humiliated both as an individual and as a representative of her people, a people who have always placed great value on personal dignity. She was deeply offended by the lack of manners of the golf club representatives.

Whatever might be the usual balance of power in the landlord/tenant relationship, this was not the case here. The club had all the power and it is still enjoying the benefits of the favourable lease that resulted from the exercise of that power. The consequences of the unequal bargaining positions will continue until the end of the lease in 2033.

Delbert Guerin[95]

Delbert Guerin was nineteen at the time of the fateful meeting on October 6, 1957 when Anfield held the pencils of adult band members as they voted on the surrender of a large part of the reserve for lease to the golf club.[96] He was too young to be allowed to vote. Also, as his wife of over forty years, Fran, testified at the trial, those under twenty-one were expelled from the meeting by Anfield when they started to object to his use of a proposed Christmas distribution of monies as a reason to vote in favour.[97] This happened even though some of them, like her, had been specifically asked to attend by the elders who did not understand English too well and wanted them to explain what was involved in the surrender. Delbert stood outside of the band hall in which the meeting was held and was joined by them when they were told to leave. With them, he looked in through the window as their future and that of the next couple of generations of band members was decided.

Delbert Guerin was born in 1938 and is now in his mid-sixties. He is impressive in appearance with a physique reflecting a lifetime spent as a long-shoreman on the Vancouver docks. A serious accident in 1975 left him with a permanent limp, but he has rarely missed a day's work. He usually worked the evening or graveyard shift to have time to spend on band business. He has also continued to fish over the years.

The work ethic was drilled into him as a child. From the age of ten, he delivered newspapers on the Squamish Reserve, where he was raised by his parents because of the housing shortage at Musqueam until the family moved back to Musqueam in 1953. It was delivering papers that gave him his intro-duction to some of the issues confronting Aboriginal people.

On his newspaper route lived Andrew Paull, a member of the Squamish Nation and an outstanding Indian leader. In 1916, he had been a founder of the Allied Tribes of British Columbia which was one of the earliest intertribal Indian organizations in the country and which he led with Rev. Peter Kelly, a member of the Haida Nation.[98] The Musqueam and other Coast Salish nations were members of the Allied Tribes. The organization kept alive the issue of the unextinguished Aboriginal title in the province, especially in opposition to the recommendations in the McKenna-McBride report to "finally" settle the question of reserves in British Columbia.

In 1927, Andrew Paull and Peter Kelly had appeared before a hearing of a Special Committee of the Senate and the House of Commons to present a petition for judicial determination of the validity of their claim.[99] Wilson Duff has described this as "a major climax in the history of the Indian title question."[100] Unfortunately, the hearing turned out to be little more than a farce as committee members blatantly displayed their prejudice and constantly insulted the counsel for the Allied Tribes, Arthur O'Meara. The committee's report rejected the request for a judicial determination and the committee took it upon itself to deny the existence of Aboriginal title in the province of British Columbia.[101] Contrary to all the evidence so carefully and patiently put before the committee, it stated that the province had been acquired by conquest and the claim of Aboriginal title was first presented as a legal claim only fifteen years earlier. It denied that there were "any tribal records" of such title and claimed that the Indians had concurred in "the whole policy of the government both as to reserves and other benefits which they accepted without demur." In an obvious reference to O'Meara, the report referred to "designing white men" who, as "a source of livelihood," had deceived the Indians and led them "to expect benefits from claims more or less fictitious." Legal restrictions on pursuing land claims were introduced the same year to prevent any judicial determination of the validity of the claim of Aboriginal title.[102]

Andrew Paull took a liking to the young newspaper boy and they had many conversations together about Paull's experiences before the Special Committee and in advancing the interests of his people.[103] He would talk of some of the things he had done and what he thought should be done to help Indian people. In this way, Delbert Guerin was introduced to some of the issues that would be so important to him for the rest of his life.

Delbert Guerin had direct experience of the power and influence of the Indian agent during the 1940s and 1950s. He recalls climbing up, at the age of eight or so, into the attic of the Squamish meeting hall with other children in order to witness a meeting attended by the Indian agent, Mr. Ball, the predecessor of Mr. Anfield. The chief and council were dressed up in their best suits and greeted him with such formality that Delbert thought Ball was the king.

As a student at the St. Paul's Indian Residential School from grade one to grade eight, he also had first-hand experience of a system of education which has had such a devastating effect on generations of Indian people.[104] After the family moved back to the Musqueam Reserve in 1953, Delbert enrolled in a public school off-reserve; he was one of the first Indian children to be accepted in the provincial system. He has mixed feelings about the move from the Indian residential school to the public school system. He, and other Musqueam students, now faced racist taunts, and he became involved in fights with some of the non-Indian children as a result. Some of the Musqueam children could not take the abuse and dropped out of school, but he "fought it right through" and graduated from high school. He had some hopes of going on to further education, but financial pressures meant he had to find employment.

One of his earliest jobs as a twenty year old in 1958 was helping on the development of the reserve for the Shaughnessy golf course. He worked on the drainage system as a manual labourer and driving a backhoe, where his abilities won praise from his supervisors. However, they became upset and could not understand when he gave notice in order to help his uncle to fish during the season at River's Inlet. They did not understand that Delbert and his people had fished in this way for centuries and, however incompatible with the wage economy, he could not let his uncle down. Again, there was a clash of cultures.

Delbert Guerin is not critical of the members who voted in favour of the surrender for lease. He explains the pressure placed on them by the Indian agent, who had misrepresented the appraisal report to them and failed to disclose the true terms of the proposed lease. He also notes the financial pressure that they were under. They were living in third-world conditions on the doorstep of Canada's third largest city, lacking facilities that the residents of Vancouver took for granted. Sometimes this had tragic consequences. On Christmas Eve, 1957, just a few weeks before the Shaughnessy lease was signed, six children died in a fire caused by an overheated wood heater at a house on the reserve. One of the chief factors in the loss of life was the failure of the Department of Indian Affairs to provide long-requested fire hydrants. The coroner noted that the cause of death could be ascribed to a form of neglect.[105] There were no public buildings except a church and the band hall (which was actually a house converted into a band hall when the owner died without heirs and the property came into the hands of the band). The reserve had no running water,[106] no electricity, and no municipal services. The road to the reserve was a rough dirt road full of potholes. An article in *The Vancouver Sun* on February 21, 1962 reported on the squalid living conditions:

> Women wash their clothes in buckets after carrying water from outside taps near their homes. The wooden houses are badly in need of repair. . . . There's no drainage system, few families have bathroom facilities and the only toilets are ramshackle shacks behind the houses. . . . Many are elevated basementless homes and you have to literally climb, or walk along narrow strips of plank to reach the front door. . . . Jack Campbell, a 53-year old carpenter who lives in a 10-year old home at the west end of the reserve overlooking the Fraser River, said: "It floods here every year to a depth of about three feet and there's a swamp under the house but we can't do anything about it. There's no plumbing inside, the place needs fixing up, there's no drainage and the toilet is over there."

Overcrowding was also a problem, with about thirty tumbledown houses for the 250 or so band members.

There was no economic activity on the reserve, no sources of employment. Only a handful of men had regular employment and, as a result, the band members had very limited income: an average annual income of about $2,000 for each wage earner.[107] The only band income was the low rent received from Chinese market gardeners who had informal or "buckshee" leases. Social assistance was only a few dollars a month. Members received some income from the seasonal fishing and did a variety of things to make ends meet. As a child, Delbert Guerin would go beachcombing to find things that he could sell. He recalls Musqueam women going down to Washington State to pick berries and, when the season was over, returning to go to Sardis and Sumas to pick hops. Many were involved in weaving baskets.[108] Some members would go to the neighbouring University Endowment Lands to strip bark off the barberry bushes, dry it, and then chop it into chips, which were sold to traditional Chinese herbal shops in Chinatown.[109] Guerin recalls even his blind grandfather picking berries and hanging fishing nets.

Because of the poverty of the people on the reserve, it was an overwhelming temptation when the Indian agent, Earl Anfield, urged and bullied them into leasing the lands to the wealthy Shaughnessy Heights Golf Club, especially when he told them that, after the low rent during the first rent period of fifteen years, during which the club would increase the value of the lands with expensive improvements such as a clubhouse, they could "hit" the club for a large increase.[110]

What the band members were not told about were the restrictions in the lease on the rent increases and that the club had the right to remove the improvements at the end of the lease. Delbert Guerin remembers the shock of his mother and that of the other members of the band council during the time of the negotiations, Ed Sparrow and Bill Guerin, when he finally obtained the lease and told them what it contained. They were totally aghast and said that they had no idea that the lease contained such terms. It was the discovery of the lease by Delbert Guerin in 1970 that led to the commencement of the *Guerin* case in 1975.[111]

Delbert Guerin was first elected to band council in 1964. One of his first responsibilities was to represent the band in negotiations with the City of Vancouver over tax sharing and the provision of municipal services to the reserve. As noted in the above quotation from the *Province* of June 5, 1941,[112] the British Columbia Court of Appeal held in the *Chow Chee* case that the city could tax the non-Indian lessees of reserve lands. The band had objected to such taxation as an infringement on its own taxation jurisdiction (such jurisdiction was not expressly recognized until amendments made to the *Indian Act* in 1987) and said, in its submission to the city, that "if there is any tax to be paid by the said Chinese it should come to the Musqueam Reserve for the benefit of the Reserve."

Despite the band's objection, the city continued to be the exclusive beneficiary of the reserve tax base for some time, so that, in the case of the Shaughnessy Golf Club, the city was collecting property taxes in 1967 of $33,000 while the rent paid to the band was only $29,000. The city was deriving a greater benefit from these reserve lands than the band![113]

Starting in 1966, the band commenced a campaign to get a share of the taxes received from the reserve. It lobbied the provincial government and presented a submission to the city, in which it said:

Hence, here you have Musqueam, the tiny but elder neighbour, with a history back to around 400 B.C., coming to Vancouver, the modern giant, requesting harmonious and prompt rectification of a situation that was unfair yesterday, unfair today and will become even more unfair tomorrow.

The Musqueams say—"Let us have a fair deal. We are legally, morally and economically entitled to one."

The band's claim was rejected by the mayor with the comment "[t]hey're trying to scalp me."[114] Delbert and other members of the band's negotiating committee met with Harry Rankin, an opposition member of city council who supported their claim. He suggested that the band consider a protest demonstration outside city hall. Delbert and the others decided to adopt this suggestion. He recalls the protest as an exciting example of the protest politics of the sixties. He was especially encouraged by the support received from passing motorists.

Under this pressure, the city changed its position and the band was successful in obtaining an agreement in 1970 with the city under which the band would finally receive some basic municipal services in return for a payment of about a quarter of what the city initially demanded.[115] The neophyte politician had learnt the lesson of determination and persistence. It was to serve him, the Musqueam, and other Aboriginal people well as he turned his attention from the negotiations with the city to the upcoming negotiations with Shaughnessy Golf Club on the amount of rent to be paid for the second fifteen-year rent period of the Shaughnessy lease.

Chapter 3

The Trial and
Federal Court of Appeal

Getting to Trial[1]

The Department of Indian Affairs was aware at least as early as 1968 that the terms of the Shaughnessy lease did not reflect a fair market rent. A confidential report prepared for the department (the Fields-Stanbury Report, dated September 1968) contained a severe criticism by D.P. Squarey and Associates, a firm of valuers, of the rents to be received under the lease. The report was especially critical of the restriction on rent increases. It was never given to the band and only became public when it was leaked to the press in 1972 by Mr. Frank Howard, M.P.[2] In 1970, Delbert Guerin and other members of the band council did not even know of the terms of the lease substantially drafted by the solicitor for the golf club and signed by the government in 1958. They were anticipating a large rent increase on the first rent review date in 1973 in order to obtain a market rent. At a meeting in March, 1970, with Graham Allen, who was then a lands officer with the department, Chief Guerin mentioned that he expected to be able to negotiate a significant increase in the rent at the rent review. Allen checked the lease and wrote him a letter to say that there was a 15 percent restriction on the permitted increase for the period from 1973 to 1988.[3] This came as a great shock to Chief Guerin and the other members of the band who had no idea of this restriction and the other unfavourable provisions in the lease. He remembers being "totally vehement, wild over it."

Chief Guerin insisted on getting a copy of the lease and, after some initial resistance, he was permitted by department officials to go down to the "cage" in the basement of the department's building to look for the lease and related documents. He recalls the look of horror from Mr. Anfield's former secretary as she heard him demand a copy of the lease. She was about five feet tall but he describes her as "bouncing off the ceiling." He feels she knew that, at long last, the band would find out the truth. The "cage" was a cramped, wired enclosure about ten feet by ten feet wide, full of boxes including some marked "Musqueam" which he eagerly opened. His head swam as he tried to make sense of them. He describes his feelings of surprise, then growing anger and amazement as he read document after document dealing with Musqueam lands. He spent hours looking at the documents and trying to copy them on an old-fashioned copying machine which was "tormentingly slow." By the time the other department officials had left for the day leaving Graham Allen behind, he had only copied a few of the documents. Finally, Allen said that he would have to leave and would be back in a few minutes to lock up the "cage" and Chief Guerin would have to do what he had to do before he came back. Delbert Guerin took this as a hint that he should take away the relevant documents. He seized the opportunity, scooped up a pile of documents, and left the department's office with an armful of documents. He had offered a lift home to Allen, who lived on the route back to the reserve. On the half-hour journey, they never discussed the lease and Allen never once mentioned the pile of papers occupying the back seat, which was as inconspicuous as an elephant. True to his English background, he turned a blind eye in the best tradition of Admiral Nelson.

Delbert Guerin read the documents over the next few days with increasing despondency. He and the other members of the band gradually realized just how badly band members had been misled on the terms of the lease. It did not contain the terms that the members had voted on but terms that were much less favourable. The first rent increase was limited to 15 percent; rent periods after the first were fifteen years, not ten years as understood by the band; the subsequent rent increases were based not on the market rent or even a developed golf course but on the fiction that the lands were uncleared and unimproved and limited as to their use; the club had a unilateral right to terminate the lease on six months notice and could take the improvements. The band had clearly been taken advantage of. The practical and immediate result was that, instead of the sizeable rent increase they had expected to receive starting in 1973 (the big "hit" Anfield had promised to band members before they voted),[4] they were going to receive only an increase of just over $4,000, so that the annual rent for the second term of the lease from 1973 to 1988 would be $33,500. This was about the same amount as the city of Vancouver was receiving in property taxes.

The question for Chief Guerin and other members of the council was what could they do about it? Their energies were initially focussed on the rent review in 1973. For a couple of years, the band council put pressure on the Department of Indian Affairs in an unsuccessful attempt to get them to negotiate a change in the terms of the lease. They then tried to negotiate directly with the golf club to get them to agree to waive the 15 percent restriction. The club refused. In a letter dated April 9, 1973, the club's solicitor said the lease was not the subject of negotiations. Articles in the *Province* of May 8 and 9, 1973 reported that the band had written directly to club members appealing for the rent to be increased and pointing out that, based on recent appraisals, a market rent would be $800,000 yearly. The plea fell on deaf ears. A club member was quoted as saying that he believed the membership was not inclined to be sympathetic with the band's point of view because of high membership costs. (At that point, the club had an annual income of about $419,000, so at an annual rent of $29,000, it was paying only approximately 7 percent of its income on rent to the band.) Despite this low expense for its most important asset, the band complained that the club had defaulted five or six times in the previous fifteen years. In another letter dated May 11, 1973, the club's solicitor threatened legal action after a band member hinted that the band might organize a demonstration at the entrance to the club. The government lawyer wrote back on May 30, 1973 to say that the band had no authority to negotiate the renewal of the rent on behalf of the Crown. The club then refused to deal with the band. The 15 percent restriction was applied.

Having failed to negotiate an increase outside of the lease terms, the band council sought legal advice on whether it could obtain a remedy for the failure of the government to ensure that the lease contained the terms understood by the members of the band before they voted on the surrender of the lands for the purpose of the lease.

The solicitors for the band were not optimistic over the prospects for a successful action. Given the status of the law at the time, there seemed little chance of success. The band might only be wasting its money if it pursued a claim. They recommended against doing so.

At the time, Delbert Guerin was attending meetings in different parts of the country to represent Aboriginal interests and he came to know several lawyers advising Aboriginal groups. He took every opportunity to buttonhole them on the potential case against the government or the golf club. Over time, he became something of a nuisance. At the end of the meetings he would seek out lawyers in bars or coffee shops and ask for their advice. One by one, they would excuse themselves to go to the washroom but they never came back. Many lawyers just turned him away. Others were clearly reluctant to get involved. They had no desire to take on the federal government or the powerful members of the golf club. Those who were willing to consider the claim at all were worried about how they would be paid. If they looked at the matter in any detail, they saw insurmountable legal problems. He was repeatedly advised that the band would not be successful.

The major problem was the delay in bringing any action. There were statutes of limitation which required actions to be brought within six years.[5] It was over twelve years since the lease was signed. The events leading up to the case took place in 1957–1958 with the surrender of the lands on October 6, 1957 and the signing of the lease on January 22, 1958. However, the band was not aware of the Crown's breach of fiduciary duty—by entering into the lease on terms much less favourable to the band than those authorized by the members—until it was finally able to obtain a copy of the lease in 1970.

One lawyer consulted by the band expressed his views as follows: "I have agonized over the Statute of Limitations problem in this case and reluctantly have come to the conclusion that there is no legal answer to the defence that [you] have not brought this case in time. In my opinion success in the lawsuit is barred by the Statute of Limitation. . . . I cannot advise that you proceed with this case." Even if the statute of limitations could be overcome, courts still had a discretion to refuse a remedy on the grounds that the band had delayed for too long in bringing the claim.[6]

The passage of time also meant that it would be difficult to prove the claim. The band's claim rested on the recollection of members involved in the surrender. Some of them had died or were elderly and in ill health. Nobody knew at the time that government documents and witnesses from the Crown would support the band's claims when the case was finally heard.

As discussed in chapter 1, no band had ever obtained judgment against the Crown for breach of trust or other breach of fiduciary obligation. The matter had never been squarely dealt with by the courts in Canada, but actions against the British Crown had been rejected on the basis that any obligation of the government was political and not legal. Courts would not enforce such obligations. There were cases from the United States that supported the claim, but they were not binding on Canadian courts, and the constitutional law of that country was quite different.[7] All in all, the consensus of those with whom he spoke about the claim was that Chief Guerin was being quite unrealistic and unreasonable in thinking he could succeed in any action.

Eventually, after being repeatedly advised to drop the case by several lawyers including many experienced in Aboriginal law, Chief Guerin obtained the opinion of Doug Sanders. Sanders was then a young lawyer, but he had gained some experience in the practice of Aboriginal law and had taught the subject. He was the editor and person primarily responsible for the first edition of *Native Rights in Canada*, a pioneering study of Aboriginal law, published by the Indian–Eskimo Association of Canada in June, 1970. The band had retained him to assist them in preparing their land claim. He was a sole prac-titioner and did not have the resources to take the matter to trial. He also had serious concerns about the defence of limitations. He made it very clear that his involvement would be limited. However, in order to reduce the chance of a successful limitations defence, he agreed to file the statement of claim and so commence the action within the period of six years from the band's knowledge of the terms of the lease. This period would expire early in 1976.

The claim was filed and served just before Christmas on December 22, 1975. Guerin drove Sanders to the Federal Court Registry in Vancouver and then to the offices of the Department of Justice where government lawyers could accept service for the government. He had to spend some time track-ing down someone who would accept service until he persuaded a somewhat disgruntled Department of Justice lawyer to interrupt his Christmas party to do so.

The full name of the *Guerin* case is "Delbert Guerin, Joseph Becker, Eddie Campbell, Mary Charles, Gertrude Guerin and Gail Sparrow, suing on their own behalf and on behalf of all the other members of the Musqueam Indian Band versus Her Majesty The Queen." The action was, therefore, brought in the name of all the members of the band and not just in the name of Delbert Guerin. The reason why the names of all the then council members were listed in the Statement of Claim commencing the action is that the legal status of a band was, and still is, uncertain. Therefore, the action was commenced in the names of the council as representatives of all the band members. Delbert Guerin was then the chief, so his name came first, and the case is consequently referred to by his name, as is common practice. Having said that, it is also appropriate that his pivotal role in bringing the case should be acknowledged. It was his persistence that led to the true terms of the lease being known to the band and to the action being commenced.

Since Sanders was not in a position to pursue the matter to trial, Chief Guerin still had to find a lawyer able and willing to do so. Robert Banno, a solicitor at Davis & Company, had been advising the band on other mat-ters. Chief Guerin was involved in a motor accident and called him to get a referral to a litigation lawyer who could act for him. The lawyer he chose was unable to make the appointment and he decided to refer Chief Guerin to a new lawyer at the firm, Marvin Storrow.[8] Storrow had recently joined the firm after being with the Department of Justice handling tax litigation in Ottawa and was free to take on new work. He had been both a prosecutor and defence lawyer and had extensive trial experience. He agreed to meet Chief Guerin to discuss the motor vehicle case. When they met, Chief Guerin was a bit nervous and, to put him at ease, Storrow asked what else was happening with him. Delbert Guerin explained his frustration at not being able to find a lawyer willing and able to take the claim against the government to trial. As Guerin explained the facts, Storrow became more and more fascinated and agreed to take the case.

Subsequently, other lawyers at Davis & Company joined the legal team, including me (I was also counsel at all levels of the case), Lewis Harvey (who was counsel at the Supreme Court of Canada), and Steve Schachter (who appeared at the trial and the Federal Court of Appeal). Robert Banno remained an active member of the team. Our knowledge, experience, and skills complemented each other and we functioned well together as a team.

The Crown was represented at the trial by Gunnar Eggertson,[9] Alan Louie, and Carol Pepper of the local office of the Department of Justice. At the time of the hearing dealing with interest on the award before Mr. Justice Collier in August 1981, the Crown was represented by Ian Binnie and Cindy Roth. Binnie was a prominent Ontario lawyer who had lectured on Aboriginal rights at Osgoode Hall Law School and who was to be counsel for the Crown before the Federal Court of Appeal and the Supreme Court of Canada. During the *Guerin* appeals, from 1982 to 1986, he was associate deputy minister of Justice for Canada.[10] As counsel for the Crown in the *Guerin* case before the Supreme Court of Canada, he was accompanied by Mitch Taylor and M. Freeman.

The pre-trial proceedings were complex and involved a lot of legal wrangling. The government served a list of documents numbering about 1,700. It took a great deal of time for the band's legal team to review each document and try to relate them to each other and to the information provided by the band members. In the view of the legal team, many of the documents were of only marginal relevance, and, in fact, there were only 186 exhibits entered at the trial.

Possible witnesses had to be tracked down and interviewed. Some had since died, such as the former chief, Willard Sparrow. Some had moved away from the reserve. Others were elderly and in poor health, such as the chief at the time of the lease, Ed Sparrow, who was born in 1898. Delbert Guerin's wife, Fran, was very helpful in assisting the legal team to locate and interview witnesses.

The band's lawyers were impressed by the account provided by the witnesses, which was consistent on its main points with the documentary evidence obtained from the department and with the other oral evidence. It seemed that proving the facts would not be a major problem. The challenge would lie in persuading a court to adopt the band's legal argument that those facts gave rise to a legal remedy.

The Trial

The trial commenced on September 18, 1979, before Mr. Justice Frank Collier of the Federal Court of Canada, Trial Division.[11] In his opening for the band, Marvin Storrow said that, to his knowledge, it was the first case of its kind to be brought before the courts of Canada.[12] He itemized the misrepresentations made by government officials as to the terms of the lease which led the band members to agree to surrender the land for lease. He also described other breaches of the government's duty, including failure to advertise or tell the band members of other parties who had indicated an interest in leasing the lands for residential development which would have led to a higher rent. According to expert witnesses acting for the band, the loss suffered by the band was in excess of forty million dollars. The band was seeking this amount plus exemplary damages given the high-handed and wilful nature of the government's breaches of duty.

In his opening, the lead counsel for the Crown, Gunnar Eggertson, said the evidence demonstrated that "the Crown was to negotiate and have the freedom to negotiate the lease that was actually signed."[13] He submitted:[14]

> The Crown will show that the Plaintiffs' position is so improbable that they must have deceived themselves, given the long passage of time and all the benefits of hindsight into believing that a state of facts existed which do not exist.

He also said that, if there were any damages, they were less than a million and a half dollars.

The first witness for the band was Dr. Michael Kew,[15] an anthropologist. His report gave some of the band's history, culture, and socio-economic background. Another witness, Bud Kelly, a real estate developer, gave evidence of the interest expressed by him to the Department of Indian Affairs in developing the land for residential purposes. This would have generated far more than the initial rent of $29,000 each year produced by the lease to the golf club.[16] He expressed his anger at the way he was treated by the officials of the Department of Indian Affairs. Eventually, adjacent lands on the reserve were successfully developed on the basis that he had proposed.

A number of band members were called as witnesses. Andrew Charles[17] had been secretary for the band at the time of the surrender in 1957. He described the circumstances of the band in the 1950s and explained that they lacked any band office and that his bedroom was used for that purpose. There was no typewriter and no private telephone, so much to his embarrassment band business had to be discussed over a public telephone located in a store. The Indian agent had great powers over their affairs. He called and chaired meetings of the band council and typed the minutes. Charles described what took place at the various meetings relating to the Shaughnessy lease and the terms of the lease as understood by the band members present. Their understanding differed significantly from the lease as signed. He also described the repeated requests made by them to obtain a copy of the lease and the reply of the department officials that "we were not allowed to have a copy of the lease."[18] Band members were not told of the interest expressed by other potential lessees. Nor were they informed of the communications between the department and the appraiser and the golf club. They were told that they were "not allowed to engage professional people outside of the Department of Indian Affairs."[19] He explained how, during the vote on the surrender, Anfield marked the ballots as each voter held the eraser-end of the pencil. His evidence took about two days, and at the end of it, it was clear that the essential facts had been proven both through his testimony and the documents introduced through him.

Ed Sparrow, the chief at the time of the surrender, also gave evidence.[20] He was eighty-two years old at the time of the trial and in ill health. He needed assistance to hold the book of documents to which he was referred, and giving evidence was clearly a strain on him. But he was mentally very alert, and his humour was evident on occasion despite the gruelling cross-examination. His voice had a distinctive "clip" to it, which revealed that his first language was Hunquminim rather than English. He gave his recollections regarding the surrender and the lease, which were consistent with those of Andrew Charles. He also gave an insight into the relationship between the band, the golf club, and the Department of Indian Affairs. During his examination, he described the already-mentioned meeting with officials from the golf club at the old clubhouse and the embarrassment and humiliation that he felt at being summarily dismissed from the meeting without a word.[21] Later in his evidence, he confirmed that a major concern of the club was to get the removal of a restriction on selling liquor on the reserve.

Other band members who gave evidence were William Guerin, Fran Guerin, and Delbert Guerin. William Guerin[22] was a member of the band council from 1957 to 1958, and his evidence was consistent with that given by Andrew Charles and Chief Ed Sparrow. He testified that, at a meeting on September 17, 1957, Mr. Anfield told him that, if the band was "unreasonable" in its demands, the department could lease the land without a surrender and for any sum it wished.[23] Fran Guerin was too young to vote at the surrender meeting, but she objected at the meeting to the references made by Anfield to a possible distribution of lease monies before Christmas, which she saw as a blatant attempt to bribe members to vote in favour of the golf club lease.[24] Anfield ruled that she was out of order and told her to leave the meeting.

Delbert Guerin was already outside of the meeting hall and observed some of what was going on by looking through the window, not realizing the influence that those events would have upon him and the other members of the band. He described his excitement at finding the lease in the basement of the Department of Indian Affairs building, his efforts to obtain legal advice, and the filing of the statement of claim.[25]

Chief Guerin's evidence was supported by Graham Allen, the former Department of Indian Affairs officer who had provided the lease to him. Allen also expressed his concern at its contents.[26] For example, in his opinion, which was based on years of involvement in leases and his qualification as a professional appraiser, the provision saying the rent had to be based on the lands in their unimproved condition created "something of a travesty in trying to look at land separated from its improved condition."[27] The 15 percent ceiling on the first rent increase "was a reckless provision . . . an extremely unfortunate thing to include in the lease and [he] hadn't seen it in any of the other leases."[28] The tenant's unilateral right of termination was "a rather remarkable concession."[29] He was familiar with over eight hundred department leases and had not seen another lease that gave the tenant the right to remove improvements.[30] Another witness was the current Director of Lands for the department, Peter Clark, who contrasted the department's standard practices with those in the case of the Shaughnessy lease.[31] He had not seen restrictions on rent renewal similar to those in that lease.[32]

The band produced expert witnesses to quantify the loss suffered which was estimated at over forty million dollars. George Oikawa was the band's appraiser.[33] In his opinion, a realistic market rent as at the last rent review date of January 22, 1983 would have been $1,884,563 instead of the $33,500 that was received. According to Oikawa, if the land were developed in 1958 at its highest and best use, the band would have been the owner, at the end of a ninety-nine year lease, of a subdivision of 438 first-class houses together with the associated subdivision services.

After the band closed its case, the Crown produced their witnesses, starting with Dr. Michael Goldberg, a professor in the Faculty of Commerce at the University of British Columbia.[34] He had been asked by the Crown to produce a report on the micro-economic environment surrounding the lease negotiations. In his view, given that environment and the trends in real estate during that time period, "the lease entered into by Anfield appears reasonable."[35] Under cross-examination, he admitted that he had been out of the country for most of the time since the report was commissioned and that an assistant had worked on it under his direction. His attention was directed to a very important report, the Turner Report, written in 1956 on the potential development of the adjacent University Endowment Lands. Despite the reference to it in the report submitted under his name, he admitted that he had not read it in detail and had not had a chance to critique it.[36]

The Crown also called George McIntosh, the solicitor for the golf club.[37] McIntosh had drafted the lease, including the rent restriction provision. Under cross-examination, he described the backgrounds of those negotiating for the club. One was vice-president of B.C. Telephone Company, another the vice-president of a leading forestry company, and another owned a printing business. He confirmed that there were no members of the band present when he met with officials from the Department of Indian Affairs. He had assumed that department officials were reporting back to them, which was not, in fact, the case. There were no other lawyers present at those meetings. He also confirmed that the club had contacted a minister of the federal government to make sure that things moved quickly.

Some of the officials of the golf club also provided evidence. They recalled a meeting at the reserve where they were asked to wait outside while the band council discussed the lease with Anfield. Their recollection of the meeting at the clubhouse with Chief Ed Sparrow and Councillor Gertrude Guerin was vague, but one witness recalled Mrs. Guerin as "a most charming and delightful person to talk with."[38] The meeting "was a chance to discuss and be on social terms with our delightful friends from the Reserve, from the Band."[39] Their concern was the ability of the club to pay the agreed rent and avoid moving out to the suburbs as they could no longer stay at the current location in the Shaughnessy area of Vancouver where most of their members lived. "We had truly our own selfish point of view, what we felt we could pay, taking a long gamble."[40] The department officials had not tried to increase the rent by telling them of the other offers for the land. They had met for a "lunch or two" with Anfield at the golf club but he felt that "he should not accept club lunches where he had no opportunity of signing a chit, indefinitely" and refused a lunch invitation to the Yacht Club.[41] One former director of the club described his visits to Ottawa, where he lobbied a senior Department of Indian Affairs official.[42]

The Crown called Alfred Howell, who had prepared the appraisal report for the department in 1957.[43] His evidence turned out to be very favourable to the band. His original report gave a value for the lands and then used a capitalization rate of 6 percent, which gave a rent of $53,450 each year. Anfield gave that value to the golf club officials but not to the band. The club countered with $25,000, which was less than half the annual rent in Howell's original report. Instead of terminating the negotiations because of the failure of the club to come anywhere close to the appraised rent, Anfield wrote to

Howell to ask him if a rent of $25,000 for the first fifteen years of the lease would be "just and equitable." Howell was not given any other details of the proposed lease and, in particular, the clauses limiting the future rents and giving the golf club the right to remove the improvements. He changed his opinion to reduce the capitalization rate from 6 percent to 3 percent each year on the assumption that the improvements would revert to the band and, as he stated in his letter giving the revised opinion, "he had assumed that the Department will be in a much stronger position to negotiate an increase in rental in fifteen years time after the Club had made a considerable capital investment." Under cross-examination, he said that if he had known the improvements would not revert to the band, he would have recommended a rate of return of 4 to 6 percent. He had assumed, in giving his opinion, the renegotiation of the rent would be based on the improved condition of the land and on the highest and best use principle, and he was not aware of the provision in the lease that rent was to be determined on the basis that the land was to be regarded as if it were unimproved and uncleared and limited in use. He expressed shock at the ultimate terms of the lease limiting the initial rent increase to 15 percent.[44]

The next witness for the Crown, William Grant, also greatly assisted the band's case.[45] He was Anfield's assistant and had accompanied him to the surrender meeting. His account of the meeting and the understanding of the band members supported that given by the witnesses for the band. In particular, he said that the band members did not approve the rent restriction provisions that appeared without the knowledge of the band in the lease as signed. In fact, Anfield had told the band members that, in ten years, the band could "hit" the club for "quite an increase," "a good increase."[46] He also misstated the appraisal report from Howell. Grant was clear that the position of the band members was that no lease was to be signed except on the terms as understood by them—"the Band didn't give him [Anfield] authority to change things around after."[47] He agreed that there was "very little resemblance" between the lease terms approved by the band members and the lease as signed.[48]

Anfield had died in 1961, but witnesses for the Crown, including Grant, gave an insight into his background and personality. He was born in England in 1900 and was the principal of an Anglican residential school for Indian children in Alert Bay for a number of years. He was then known as the Reverend Anfield. He subsequently joined the Department of Indian Affairs and served as Indian agent at Prince Rupert and Bella Coola before joining the department in Vancouver. According to Grant, after twenty-five to thirty years in the residential school system and at the Department of Indian Affairs, Anfield had become very paternalistic, although he meant well. He was fond of saying that "the Indians are my responsibility from the womb to the tomb."[49] He liked "to have things done his own way, whether it was with [Grant] or the Band or anyone else."[50] As confirmed by other witnesses, this paternalistic attitude was apparent in the voting procedure at the surrender meeting, when Anfield made the mark for the voter who held the other end of the pencil. In answer to the question whether he found this procedure to be incredible, Grant said:[51]

> It . . . yes, I imagine incredible would be a word that would describe it, it's a—but knowing Mr. Anfield, a different . . . it was part of his makeup that rather than use the ballot box and these people were familiar with the ballot box . . . [he] reverted back to the father/child attitude, this paternalism, and you know, it was decided it was better to do it that way.

The Crown called witnesses from Ottawa to explain the handling of Indian monies, the different roles within the Department of Indian Affairs, and the policy of the government on the retention of records. As explained by witnesses, it was not the practice of the Department of Indian Affairs to provide copies of documents to bands.[52] The Musqueam Band only obtained a copy of the lease as the result of the efforts of Delbert Guerin, who was the chief in the early seventies.[53] Another witness was Jack Letcher, who had succeeded Anfield.[54] He had finished up some of the administrative work that had to be completed with respect to the lease with the golf club. He was asked if anyone had asked for a copy of the lease. In his reply, he referred to a request in 1964 from Professor White of the University of British Columbia, who was acting for the band in connection with another lease.[55] Professor White had been provided with a copy of the lease with the golf club together with other information. This was a very significant and potentially damaging piece of evidence as it could have supported a successful defence that the band had not acted reasonably in trying to obtain the lease and had accordingly delayed too long in bringing its claim. Letters between Letcher and Professor White regarding the transmittal of documents, including the lease with the golf club, were produced from a government file.

During a short mid-morning break in the proceedings, we obtained the file from the government's lawyers and reviewed these letters. We also found another which, through oversight, had not been listed by the Crown in its List of Documents. This letter from Professor White, dated April 15, 1964, was very critical of the department's lack of cooperation in providing a copy of the lease being proposed to another tenant and its insistence that the tenant had to consent to a copy being given to him. He had tried several times to obtain the terms of that proposed lease but had been put off by officials. He referred to the department's "absurd and irregular proceedings" and said:[56]

> I fail entirely to understand these procrastinations and excuses. . . . As I understand the position, the land in question belongs to the Band, and I regard it as nothing short of monstrous that the person asked by the Band to advise them as to the disposition of their property is denied access to the terms of the disposition by those who have acted on their behalf.

He said he would hold the department responsible for its lack of cooperation. Gunnar Eggertson, counsel for the Crown, had said that the relevance of the letter entered by him into evidence was that the Court could draw the inference that, since Letcher had made the Shaughnessy lease available to Professor White on request, it would have done the same if the band members had made such a request. The letter dated April 15, 1964, buried deep in the government's file and not listed on their List of Documents, showed that, in fact, Professor White's request for a copy of the lease that he was interested in had been rebuffed on several occasions and it took a strongly worded and somewhat threatening letter from a well-qualified person to obtain essential information as to the lease terms. Far from supporting the Crown's position, the evidence regarding Professor White supported the band's claim that requests from band members for a copy of the Shaughnessy lease had been denied.

After the Crown had put in evidence through its experts on the value of the lands and the maximum loss suffered by the band, the trial closed on November 8, 1979 with legal argument. The Crown urged the defence of political trust, namely that any obligation that the Crown had was not enforceable by a court. In reply, Marvin Storrow said:[57]

> By defending this action on the basis of "political trust" the Department is essentially saying to Indian peoples across this country that we as a Government can control your lives through the Indian Act, that we can control your lands, that we can do things to affect your lives that we cannot do to any other group in Canada and when we do these things you have absolutely no recourse to the courts of this Country.
>
> It is submitted that this position is one which cannot be condoned by the courts of this Country.

It was also submitted that the Crown had failed to plead the defence of political trust. Mr. Justice Collier agreed that the defence should have been pleaded by the Crown. He gave leave to do so but on condition that either the Minister of Indian Affairs or the Minister of Justice be made available for examination for discovery on that point.[58] This was a significant ruling and would have enabled us to cross-examine a senior minister on government policy, which might have been very revealing. However, perhaps to avoid this possibility, the Crown withdraw the defence.[59]

Three months after the trial had closed, the Crown was successful in a motion to re-open it so the evidence of John Ellis, a real estate developer, could be given.[60] He claimed that, during his negotiations in 1963 with the band on a subsequent lease of adjacent lands, someone on the band council had asked for a 15 percent limit on rent increases "because this was the limit that they had on the Shaughnessy lease."[61] He thought the statement about the limit in the Shaughnessy lease had been made by the late Willard Sparrow. Witnesses were called on behalf of the band to rebut this new evidence as to the band's knowledge of the terms of the Shaughnessy lease. They each denied knowing of the lease and having any reason to think that the late Willard Sparrow knew of the lease terms. In his Reasons for Judgment, Mr. Justice Collier accepted the evidence of the band members over that of Ellis, which he found to be, understandably, vague and imprecise.[62] He pointed out that it was not in the interests of the band for the band council to propose a 15 percent limit on rent increases as Ellis had testified.

The Judgment

After about thirty days of evidence and argument, the trial finally came to an end on March 25, 1980. Mr. Justice Collier reserved judgment, which was not delivered until July 3, 1981. The judgment takes up fifty-nine pages in the official law report. Except for the amount of compensation, it was a great success for the band. Mr. Justice Collier rejected the Crown's contention that the band's claim was based on hindsight and that they had convinced themselves of things that did not happen. He found the witnesses from the band "to be honest, truthful witnesses. They did not, in my assessment, conjure up the key evidentiary matters disputed by the defendant. Nor, in my view, was their evidence based on hindsight and reconstruction. On some matters . . . the Band members' testimony is, on analysis, supported by other evidence."[63]

After a careful and detailed review of the evidence given at the trial both orally and in documentary form, he concluded that:

(a) the band was not told of any interest in or proposals for development of the land other than that of the golf club;[64]

(b) during the negotiations on the rent, Anfield gave information on the appraised value of the land to the golf club but not to the band;[65]

(c) not all the terms of the club's proposals were given to the band council by Anfield;[66]

(d) Anfield did not give all the details of the club's proposal to Howell when he asked him for his opinion on the rent being proposed;[67]

(e) Howell would not have expressed his opinion the way he had if he had all the facts before him;[68]

(f)   Anfield's advice to Chief Sparrow that Howell considered a 3 percent return to be "a very satisfactory return" was "an overstatement";[69]

(g)   before the band members voted to surrender the lands for leasing, they understood that[70]

(i)   apart form the first rent period, the lease would have rent periods of ten years;

(ii)   there would be no 15 percent limitation on rental increases;

(h)   members also had no knowledge that the club had the right to remove improvements at the end of the lease, that the future rents were to be based on the uncleared and unimproved condition of the lands with restrictions as to its use rather than its market value, and that the club had a unilateral right to terminate the lease;[71]

(i)   after the surrender meeting, the department failed to consult the band on the provisions increasing subsequent rent periods to fifteen years, restricting the increase for the second period to 15 percent, restricting future increases to the uncleared and unimproved condition, allowing the club to take the improvements, and giving the club the unilateral right of termination;[72]

(j)   the terms of the lease that was ultimately entered into "bore little resemblance to what was discussed at the surrender meeting";[73]

(k)   the balance of probabilities was that the majority of those who voted at the surrender meeting "would not have assented to a surrender of the 162 acres if they had known all the terms of the lease of January 22, 1958";[74]

(l)   despite requests for copies of the lease, the band was unsuccessful in obtaining a copy until March 1970;[75]

(m)   the band had no reason to think that a lease with terms different from what they had been led to believe would be the case had been entered into.[76]

In short, the band's account of what took place, including the misrepresentations and the concealment by Department of Indian Affairs officials, was held to be correct.

Having reached the above findings of facts, the next issue was to determine the legal effect of those findings. Mr. Justice Collier reviewed the cases on whether the Crown could be a trustee. He concluded that there was, in the case before him, a legal trust created between the Crown and the band.[77] The Crown had become a trustee effective the date of the surrender of the 162 acres and the band was the beneficiary.[78] He referred to the defence of political trust and said that, since the Crown had not amended the pleadings to add this defence, he would not deal with it.[79]

He then considered the terms of the trust upon which the lands were to be leased, which he found to be those understood by the band members at the time of the surrender vote:[80]

(a) a total term of seventy-five years;

(b) the rental revenue for the first fifteen years to be $29,000;

(c) the remaining sixty years of the lease to be divided into six ten-year terms;

(d) future rental increases to be negotiated for each new term and no provisions regarding arbitration or the manner in which the land would be valued;

(e) no 15 percent limitation on rental increases;

(f) all improvements on the land, on the expiration of the lease, to revert to the Crown.

Since the lease contained terms which were substantially different from those authorized by the band and the Crown had failed to get authorizations for those changes, there had been a breach of trust.[81]

Mr. Justice Collier then considered the defences of the Crown based on the alleged unreasonable delay of the band in bringing the claim.[82] The lease was entered into on January 22, 1958 and the claim was commenced almost eighteen years later in December 1975. The Crown said that it was prejudiced in being able to make a defence since key witnesses such as Anfield and Arneil, the Commissioner of Indian Affairs for British Columbia at the time of the lease negotiations, had died before the trial. It tried to demonstrate through the evidence of Mr. Ellis and Professor White's report in 1964 that the band either knew of the terms of the lease or, acting reasonably, could have known and so should have brought the action much earlier. It submitted that the action was barred either by the six-year limitations period in the *Statute of Limitations* or the equitable doctrine of laches that defeats a plaintiff who "sleeps on his rights."

Mr. Justice Collier rejected those defences on the basis of his finding that the band did not know of the terms of the lease until March 1970. They had been unsuccessful in obtaining a copy of the lease until then despite their requests. The department officials had failed to return to the band after the surrender meeting to advise the true terms of the lease or to get another authorization for the changes. This conduct was "unconscionable" and "a concealment amounting to equitable fraud" which prevented the defences being used against the band.[83] He found, however, that there was no fraud in the sense of deceit, dishonesty or moral turpitude.[84]

He also considered and rejected the Crown's request that it be granted relief under a provision in the *Trustee Act* that enables a court to relieve a trustee from personal liability if the trustee has acted honestly and reasonably.[85] In his view, this provision only applied to the Supreme Court of British Columbia not the Federal Court. But, even if he had jurisdiction, he would not grant relief in the circumstances. The Indian Affairs officials had acted honestly but not reasonably in signing the lease without first going back to the band. It would not be fair to excuse the Crown.

Finally, Mr. Justice Collier considered the "extremely difficult question of damages."[86] As he pointed out, a great deal of evidence at the lengthy trial was on that subject and given by experts in various fields. Having found that the band would not have accepted the terms that appeared in the Shaughnessy lease, he turned his attention to how to put the band in the position it would have been in if the lease had not been signed. One of the most difficult questions was what would have happened to the land if the lease had not been signed. He reviewed a number of possibilities, including a development based on a ninety-nine year prepaid lease for residential use as proposed by the band's appraiser, George Oikawa. The three appraisers called by the Crown did not agree that this was a possibility at the time. After considering the proposed development at around the same time of the adjacent University Endowment Lands in the Turner Report and the interest expressed by potential developers in leasing the lands, he accepted the opinion of Oikawa over the appraisers for the Crown. However, he was not persuaded that the area would have been developed as quickly as Oikawa had opined. The land may have remained undeveloped for a few years after 1958. "Development might have been, at first, slow, limited, and somewhat experimental. In my view, the area would probably have been well on the road to full development, on a leasehold basis, by approximately 1968 to 1971."[87]

He then turned to the amount of the damages to be awarded. The band had put forward four suggested approaches which estimated losses at between forty-five million dollars and seventy-one million dollars. In his view, "none of those suggested approaches are completely unrealistic. The calculations, based on acceptance of all the plaintiff's evidence as to damages, are, to my mind, relatively conservative."[88] However, he could not accept these calculations because of two factors. None of the approaches took into account "a very realistic contingency in 1988, or at a later rent review period, the golf club may decide, because of the obviously high rents in sight, to terminate the lease."[89] Also, they were based on Oikawa's opinion on the possibility of a development in 1958 as opposed to the later date found by him. Having rejected full acceptance of the band's calculations, he considered the Crown's submissions on the loss suffered and also rejected them. He summarized his views: "[M]y views are, in effect, somewhere between those of the plaintiff and those of the defendant. But I have no doubt the plaintiffs, by the breach of the trust by the defendant, have suffered a very substantial loss."[90]

He referred to cases which said that a court has to assess damages as best as it can even if it involves guesswork, and he then assessed the damages at ten million dollars.[91] He said he had experimented with various approaches to set out some, perhaps even vague, mathematical basis for coming to this sum. "But I found myself unable to set out a precise rationale or approach, mathematical or otherwise. The dollar award is obviously a global figure. It is a considered reaction based on the evidence, the opinions, the arguments and, in the end, my conclusions of fact."[92] He then set out some of the factors and contingencies which he had in mind, including the contingency that the area might not have been satisfactorily developed; the astonishing increase in land values; inflation and interest rates since 1958; the possibility that the lease will remain in effect until its expiry in 2033; "the very real contingency" that it may be terminated at some future rental review period; the monies already received and to be received by the band under the lease, and finally, the value of the improvements.[93] He rejected the band's claim for exemplary damages. The actions of the department officials could not be seen as "oppressive or arbitrary conduct, warranting punishment by way of exemplary damages."[94]

The award of only ten million dollars rather than the minimum amount claimed of forty-five million dollars came as a big disappointment to the band and its legal team. With respect to Mr. Justice Collier, his rejection of the band's "relatively conservative" calculations on the basis of the contingency that the golf club might move in 1988 or later was untenable. As we have seen, he referred to the "obviously high rents in sight" as a reason why the club might do so.[95] Yet, unknown to the band members at the time they approved the surrender of the land for the lease to the club, the lease ties the rent throughout its duration to the fiction that the lands are to be considered as if "in an uncleared and unimproved condition . . . considering the restricted use" rather than the market rent as understood by the band and the government's appraiser, Mr. Howell. It seems that Collier J. overlooked the effect of this restriction on the rent and the other terms of the lease which were favourable to the club in his consideration of the contingency that the club might move before 2033, the termination date for the lease. Many of the witnesses at the trial, including the director of lands for the Department of Indian Affairs and a former lands officer for the department, gave evidence to demonstrate just how unusually pro-tenant the lease is.[96] It is difficult to see why the club would want to move or where they could hope to find a more favourable lease. The lease has achieved for them exactly what they set out to achieve, namely artificially low rents; a long-term security of tenure which they alone can terminate on six months notice; and the ability to continue the club on the west side of Vancouver without having to suffer the inconvenience of driving out to the suburbs, which was the fate of other clubs similarly situated.[97] The club has not, of course, moved and there is no reasonable basis to think that they will do so until they are forced to in 2033 when the lease expires.

In August of 1981, the band sought interest on the award from January 22, 1958 (the date of the lease) to July 12, 1981, which was the date that the award was formally made, and post-judgment interest at a higher rate than the statutory rate of 5 percent per annum to reflect the higher then-current interest rates. Giving judgment from the bench, Mr. Justice Collier rejected these applications.[98] He found that section 35 of the *Federal Court Act* prohibited the award of interest against the Crown unless a contract or statute authorized the award. In his view, there was no contract or statute which provided such authorization. He also held that he had no power to vary the rate of post-judgment interest.[99] This ruling added to the disappointment of the band and its legal team over the monetary aspect of the decision. However, the band had still won a great victory in obtaining a ruling that it had a legal remedy for the Crown's failure to live up to its obligations.

The Federal Court of Appeal

After the decision of Mr. Justice Collier, the band tried to negotiate a settlement with the federal government to avoid the risk and costs associated with an appeal. Their efforts were unsuccessful. Mr. John Munro, Minister of Indian Affairs, refused to discuss the case, and the Crown appealed the judgment of Mr. Justice Collier to the Federal Court of Appeal. The band cross-appealed, seeking an increase in the amount of damages, a reversal of his refusal to award pre-judgment interest, an increase in the post-judgment rate of interest, and costs at a higher rate.

Many legal arguments were advanced on behalf of the government to persuade the Federal Court of Appeal that the trial judge was wrong.[100] Despite its withdrawal by the Minister of Justice at the trial, the political trust doctrine was strongly pursued[101] and reliance was placed on cases such as *Kinloch*,[102] *Tito*,[103] and *St. Ann's Island Shooting and Fishing Club*[104] (discussed in chapter 1). Reference was made to the practical consequences flowing from the imposition of a legally enforceable trust obligation on the government.

On behalf of the band, we opposed the political trust defence both on procedural grounds and on the merits.[105] We maintained that if the Crown disagreed with the trial judge's ruling disallowing the defence except on terms, the Crown should have appealed that ruling. It was not free simply to ignore it and so it could not now raise the defence. We argued that the cases relied upon by the Crown to support the defence were not applicable, and reliance was placed instead upon *Miller*,[106] *Dreaver*[107] and a recent decision of the Federal Court, *Kruger v. The Queen*,[108] in which Mahoney, J. held that the Crown had title to a reserve under "a true trust" and not "a political trust." We pointed out that when the alleged breaches of trust took place, Indian people (save for limited exceptions) were forbidden to vote in federal elections:[109] "[T]he doors of Parliament were then closed to our Native people, the Appellant now seeks to close the doors of the Courts of Justice."[110] Further, we said that a defence of political trust would deny Indian people equal protection of the law contrary to the *Canadian Bill of Rights*[111] and the spirit of the *Canadian Charter of Rights and Freedoms*.[112]

Another argument of the Crown was to dispute the judge's statement that the reserve lands were the lands, the potential investment, and the future of the Musqueam Band. In the government's submission, the federal government could terminate the interest of the band in the reserve lands at its pleasure. Therefore, there could be no legally enforceable trust because the band owned no interest in the reserve lands which could form the subject matter of a trust.[113]

In reply for the band, we argued that Indian peoples *do* have a proprietary interest in their lands.[114] We also argued that in any event, the cases cited by the Crown to deny such an interest did not relate to reserve laws but Aboriginal title lands and so could be distinguished by the Court.[115] Section 18 of the *Indian Act*, which provides that reserves are held by the Crown "for the use and benefit" of the band, recognizes the band's beneficial interest in the reserve and rendered the Crown a trustee. Even if those cases were relevant, the nature of Indian title is not to be found by an analysis using common law concepts but by way of an inquiry into the actual form of enjoyment of land by the Aboriginal people in question.[116] In the case of the Musqueam Band, there was expert evidence that the occupants of their villages took a general proprietary interest in the lands and waters in the vicinity of the villages.

Cases from the United States indicated that Indians had sufficient interest in lands set aside for their exclusive occupation to make a taking of these lands compensable under the Fifth Amendment.[117]

There were other arguments. In particular, the government said all terms of the proposed lease had to be set out in the document that had been prepared by it for the band to give up its interest in the golf course lands (the surrender document) if they were to be binding on the government.[118] In reply, we argued that the rule of law relied upon by the government (the parol evidence rule) did not prevent the band from relying upon the oral terms of the trust under which the surrender document was delivered to the government.[119] We referred to cases where courts had permitted evidence to be given that a document which was unconditional on its face had, in fact, been delivered subject to a condition that had to be satisfied before it became effective.[120] Further, we said that to ignore the oral terms would, in effect, reduce the surrender meeting to a mere sham and constitute a gross fraud on the band members.

The Judgment

The appeal was heard in June of 1982 and, on December 10, 1982, the Federal Court of Appeal handed down its unanimous judgment.[121] It allowed the government's appeal, rejected the band's cross-appeal for greater compensation, and awarded costs to the government. The judgment can be summarized in three statements:

1. The interest of the band in reserve lands is in the nature of a property right and so could be the subject of a trust;

2. The terms of the trust were contained only in the surrender document and there could be no oral terms to the trust;

3. Neither the provisions of the *Indian Act* nor the surrender created a legally enforceable trust but only a governmental obligation or "political trust."

On the issue of whether the Indian title or interest in reserve lands was a property right, Le Dain J., giving the judgment of the court, reviewed prior judicial commentary, especially in the *St. Catherine's Milling*,[122] *Star Chrome*,[123] and *Calder*[124] cases. He also referred to United States cases holding the interest of Indians in certain reservations to be property within the Fifth Amendment,[125] to the Privy Council decision in *Amodu Tijani*,[126] which dealt generally with the concept of Native title, to cases dealing specifically with the *Indian Act* provisions relating to reserve lands,[127] and finally to an article[128] in which Professor K. Lysyk expressed the view that the Indian title amounts to a beneficial interest in the land. Based on this detailed analysis of Indian title, he concluded:[129]

> For the reasons suggested by Viscount Haldane in *Amodu Tijani*, to which Professor Lysyk also makes reference, if the Indian title cannot be strictly characterized as a beneficial interest in the land it amounts to the same thing. It displaces the beneficial interest of the Crown. As such, it is a qualification of the title of the Crown of such content and substance as to partake, in my opinion, of the nature of a right of property. I am, therefore, of the opinion that it could be the subject of a trust.

So far as Aboriginal title is concerned, the decision of the Federal Court of Appeal in *Guerin* can be seen as a significant recognition of that title as being in the nature of a property right.

The finding that the terms of the alleged trust were to be found only in the surrender document was based upon an analysis of the provision of the *Indian Act* dealing with the surrender of reserve lands[130] and, in particular, the requirement that the surrender be accepted by the Governor in Council.[131] The oral terms of the surrender found by the trial judge were not accepted by the Governor in Council, nor was there any evidence that any official of the Department of Indian Affairs had accepted the oral conditions, even assuming that such conditions could be validly accepted by a departmental official. No reference was made to our argument on this issue save for a reference to the decision of the Ontario Court of Appeal in *R. v. Taylor and Williams*[132] which allowed oral terms as part of a treaty.

The third and, for present purposes, most important issue dealt with by the Federal Court of Appeal in the *Guerin* case was whether either the *Indian Act* or the surrender document created a legally enforceable equitable obligation. Before considering this issue, Le Dain J. noted:[133]

> The appeal raises squarely and unavoidably the question whether the legal relationship of the Crown, or the Government to the land in a reserve and to reserve land which is surrendered "in trust" for the purpose of lease, is that of a trustee in the private law sense, that is, whether it is an equitable obligation enforceable in the Courts.

He pointed out that there is nothing in principle to prevent the Crown from acting as a trustee,[134] and then proceeded to note the distinction between "a true trust" and a trust "in the higher sense" or "a government obligation" in cases such as *Kinloch*,[135] *Hereford Railway Co. v. The Queen*,[136] *Tito*,[137] and *Town Investments Ltd. v. Department of the Environment*[138] (these cases were considered in chapter 1).

Our argument that the Crown was not free to plead governmental obligation or "political trust" was rejected, as was our contention that *Miller v. The King*[139] supported a finding of a true trust. With respect to our argument that the *Kinloch*,[140] *The Hereford Railway*,[141] and *Tito*[142] cases could be distinguished and so were not binding on the Court, he said:[143]

> The respondents insisted that the facts in *Kinloch, The Hereford Railway* and *Tito v. Waddell* are quite different and distinguishable from the facts in the present case. There can be no doubt of that, but the distinction that is affirmed in those cases and the policy considerations which underlie it are relevant to the issues in the present case.

Section 18 of the *Indian Act* was considered.[144] Subject to the terms of any treaty or surrender, this section confers upon the Governor in Council a discretion to determine whether any purpose for which lands in a reserve are used or are to be used is for the use and benefit of the band. Le Dain J. concluded that the discretionary authority conferred by section 18 indicated that:[145]

> [I]t is for the Government and not the courts to determine what is for the use and benefit of the Band. That provision is incompatible, in my opinion, with an intention to impose an equitable obligation, enforceable in the courts, to deal with the land in a reserve in a certain manner, and particularly, an obligation to develop or exploit the reserve so as to realize its potential as a source of revenue for the Band, which is in essence the obligation that is involved in the present case.

Other provisions of the *Indian Act* supported him in that view. He concluded:[146]

> All of this, it seems to me, clearly excludes an intention to make the Crown a trustee in a private law sense of the land in a reserve. How the government chooses to discharge its political responsibility for the welfare of the Indians is, of course, another thing. The extent to which the government assumes an administrative or management responsibility for the reserve of some positive scope is a matter of governmental discretion, not legal or equitable obligation.

An analysis of the surrender document led to the same conclusion. That document conferred a discretion upon the government to lease the lands to such person or persons and upon such terms as the government deemed most conducive to the welfare of the band. The surrender was construed so as to confer an authority to lease but not a duty to do so. Reference was also made to the use of the words "in trust," which had appeared in surrenders for well over one hundred years and also in the *Terms of Union*[147] upon which British Columbia was admitted into Canada and the provincial order in council that conveyed the reserve from the province to the dominion. Concluding this analysis, Le Dain J. said:[148]

> Within the context of statute and inter-governmental agreement it is my opinion that the words "in trust" in the Surrender Document were intended to do no more than indicate that the surrender was for the benefit of the Indians and conferred an authority to deal with the land in a certain manner for their benefit. They were

not intended to impose an equitable obligation or duty to deal with the land in a certain manner.

The decision of the Federal Court of Appeal was a great shock and disappointment to the members of the band and their legal team. The Court of Appeal had not reversed any finding of fact made by Mr. Justice Collier. In fact, the statement of the facts set out by Mr. Justice Le Dain closely followed his account but is more detailed in parts. The critical finding by Mr. Justice Collier remained: the band had voted on certain terms and the lease as signed bore little resemblance to those terms. The government officials had acted in a manner that would have been a clear breach of trust for any private trustee. How could the Crown escape liability on those facts? It was so patently unjust and unfair by any reasonable standards. How could the legal system allow the government to lease the lands on terms that were so unfavourable to the band and so favourable to the club? I and other members of the band's legal team had real trouble reconciling this rejection of the band's claim by the court with basic concepts of the rule of law in a democratic society as a restraint on the arbitrary exercise of governmental powers and of the equal protection of the law. What other group of citizens would be effectively barred from seeking justice on the plea of political trust, which seemed to have more to do with seventeenth-century theories of the absolute right of kings[149] than with a twentieth-century democratic society?

The decision raised serious questions about the ability of the Aboriginal peoples of Canada to resolve their legitimate grievances through the legal system. In April 1982, just months before the Federal Court of Appeal decision and after much effort by Aboriginal peoples, Parliament had added a provision to the Canadian Constitution recognizing and affirming "existing aboriginal and treaty rights."[150] What value would that hard-won constitutional provision have? The recognition and affirmation of non-enforceable "rights" would be a cynical mockery of the Constitution. We had very real difficulty answering the questions of band members and trying to explain the decision to them.

We prepared an opinion on the chances of a successful appeal to the Supreme Court of Canada and recommended an appeal. The opinion analyzed in detail the relevant legal principles, but the basis of our recommendation was simply that the decision of the Federal Court of Appeal and the position of the Government of Canada on the political trust issue was so unjust and the stakes were so high that the issue had to go to the highest court in Canada for resolution. At a well-attended meeting held just a few days before Christmas 1982, the members of the band unanimously voted to approve that recommendation, and the focus now moved to the Supreme Court of Canada.

Chapter 4

The Supreme Court of Canada

On January 26, 1983, we filed notice of application for leave to appeal the decision of the Federal Court of Canada in the registry of the Supreme Court of Canada on behalf of the Musqueam. The application stated that the essential question of law for the Court to determine was whether the *Indian Act* and the surrender of the land for leasing imposed "an equitable obligation upon the Crown enforceable in the courts."[1] In order to demonstrate the importance of the question, an affidavit was filed in support of the application setting out the concerns of Aboriginal leaders and of Dr. Donovan Waters, Canada's leading expert in the law of trusts, confirming that the matter was one of fundamental importance to the law of trusts.[2] On February 21, 1983, a panel consisting of Chief Justice Bora Laskin and Justices Estey and Wilson granted leave to appeal.[3] A critical hurdle had been overcome, but the real work on the appeal now began.

The amount of material relevant to the appeal is indicated by the fact that the Case on Appeal containing the pleadings, the transcript of the trial, the exhibits, and the judgments below took 3,651 pages bound in 18 volumes. Twenty copies of each set of volumes had to be filed with the Court. The factum or written argument that we prepared for the band was 122 single-spaced pages, and twenty-one copies had to be filed with the Court. Over 120 cases were cited. Copies of these authorities were collected in Books of Authorities, which were also filed with the Court. The Crown's factum in reply was about the same length and cited additional cases. There was also a factum from the lawyers for the National Indian Brotherhood.

In our factum for the band, we submitted that the Federal Court of Appeal was incorrect to allow the government to argue political trust as a defence in view of its failure to specifically plead this defence as required by the ruling trial judge.[4] The doctrine of political trust was also attacked on its merits as being inappropriate for a government to use against its own citizens[5] and objectionable on several policy grounds as granting immunity to the government for its misconduct.[6] The Federal Court of Appeal's analysis of the case law and especially the *Miller* case was criticized,[7] as was the analysis of the statutory provisions and especially section 18 of the *Indian Act*.[8] The existence of a wide discretionary power did not exclude the existence of an enforceable equitable obligation.[9] It was submitted that technical rules ought not to be applied strictly against Indian people and reference was also made to the fiduciary obligation of the United States government towards American Indians.[10] We sought an order that the band's appeal should be allowed, that the government pay pre-judgment interest, punitive damages, and post-judgment interest at a rate higher than 5 percent, and that the damages awarded by the trial judge be increased.

The band's appeal was supported by the National Indian Brotherhood, representing status Indians in Canada, which had been allowed to intervene.[11] In their factum, they stressed the special importance of reserve lands as Aboriginal people depend upon them for the planning and development of their future.[12] They argued that the desperate economic conditions that Indian people suffer is a source of anguish for most Canadians. Those bands in Canada that have shown the ability to overcome their depressed economic condition, by and large, have been those that have enjoyed the full development of reserve resources. A declaration of breach of trust and for damages against the Crown was the only significant legal recourse available to ensure fair administration of surrendered lands.

In its factum, the Crown responded to the various points made on behalf of the band. It was contended that the trust alleged by the band would be void as being in conflict with various binding statutory enactments.[13] The trust found by the trial judge was void for uncertainty,[14] and in any event, the band's interest in unsurrendered reserve lands was not in law property capable of being the subject matter of a trust.[15] In order for the Crown to be bound by an express trust, the terms had to be clearly communicated to the executive and acceptance "manifested by Order in Council or other authentic testimony."[16] The American law was not relevant because the United States had developed a different conceptual framework in relation to Indians.[17]

The Hearing

The hearing took place before the nine judges of the Supreme Court of Canada on June 13 and 14, 1983. It was a hot, humid day in Ottawa and we sweated as we carried heavy bags full of law books up the many steps of the Supreme Court of Canada building. Unfortunately, the elderly Ed Sparrow, a former chief of the Band, also had trouble climbing those steps and stumbled but, with characteristic good humour, he got up and continued on his way. The journey to the Court had been long and difficult with more than one stumble along the way, but finally the band would have a hearing before Canada's highest court despite the determined effort of the Crown to deny them a legal remedy for the wrong done to them. Chief Ernest Campbell and three former chiefs—Ed Sparrow, Gertrude Guerin, and Delbert Guerin—and other members of the Band including Fran Guerin, Leona Sparrow, George Guerin, and Andrew Charles accompanied the legal team to the Court. They were joined by the leaders of the neighbouring Squamish Nation, another Coast Salish group, and by other Aboriginal leaders, including the current chief of the B.C. First Nations Summit, Ed John. The presence of so many Aboriginal people in the courtroom could not but help to impress upon the members of the Court the importance of the case to Aboriginal people generally.

The complexity of the case was evidenced by the tall stack of eighteen appeal books, factums, and books of legal authorities piled high before each judge. Chief Justice Laskin kept thing moving along as the lawyers for the parties went over their written arguments and answered questions from the judges. He tried to hurry Marvin Storrow along in his account of the facts by saying the judges were familiar with them. Storrow stressed that the facts were very important. When he went into them, the judges showed great interest. It became obvious that the judges had read the legal arguments and were well prepared.[18] The only resistance to the band's argument came when Storrow alleged that the Crown's action constituted fraud. The chief justice said that was a pretty harsh designation to level against the Crown and told Ian Binnie, the lawyer for the government, that he did not have to reply to the allegation or to the claim for punitive damages. One moment of humour came as Chief Justice Laskin leaned over to Mr. Justice Dickson at one point and said, without realizing that his microphone was on, "Gerrry [Mr. Justice Le Dain] got it wrong." At the end of the hearing, we felt that it had gone well and assessed our chances of a win at 75 percent.

The Decision

The Supreme Court of Canada rendered judgment on November 1, 1984.[19] Chief Justice Laskin had died before judgment was given. The eight remaining judges were unanimous in their decision that the appeal should be allowed, the decision of the Federal Court of Appeal should be set aside, and the judgment of the trial judge reinstated without variation, with costs to the band in all courts. They differed, however, in their reasons for reaching this decision.

Three separate judgments were delivered: Mr. Justice Dickson delivered judgment for himself and for Beetz, Chouinard, and Lamer J.J.; Madam Justice Wilson delivered judgment for herself and for Ritchie and McIntyre J.J.; Estey J. delivered his own judgment.

Decision of Dickson J.

Justice Dickson summarized the facts as found by the trial judge and his decision as well as that of the Federal Court of Appeal. He expressed some doubt as to the cogency of the terminology of "higher" and "lower" trust as used by Le Dain J. following the *Kinloch*[20] case, but he agreed that the existence of an equitable obligation was the *sine qua non* for liability.[21] However, such an obligation is not limited to relationships which can be strictly defined as trusts. Indeed, in his view, the Crown's obligation vis-à-vis the Indians could not be defined as a trust, but this did not mean that the Crown owed no enforceable duty to the Indians in the way in which it deals with their land. He summarized his conclusion as follows:[22]

> In my view, the nature of Indian title and the framework of the statutory scheme established for disposing of Indian land places upon the Crown an equitable obligation, enforceable by the courts, to deal with the land for the benefit of the Indians. This obligation does not amount to a trust in the private law sense. It is rather a fiduciary duty. If, however, the Crown breaches this fiduciary duty it will be liable to the Indians in the same way and to the same extent as if such a trust were in effect.
>
> The fiduciary relationship between the Crown and the Indians has its roots in the concept of aboriginal, native or Indian title. The fact that Indian bands have a certain interest in lands does not, however, in itself give rise to a fiduciary relationship between the Indians and the Crown. The conclusion that the Crown is a fiduciary depends upon the further proposition that the Indian interest in the land is inalienable except upon surrender to the Crown.

Dickson J. noted that an Indian band is prohibited from directly transferring its interest to a third party. Any sale or lease can only be carried out after a surrender has taken place, with the Crown then acting on the band's behalf. The Crown first took this responsibility upon itself in the Royal Proclamation of 1763[23] and it was still recognized in the surrender provisions of the *Indian Act*. In his view, "the surrender requirement, and the responsibility it entails, are the source of a distinct fiduciary obligation owed by the Crown to the Indians."[24] In order to explore the character of this obligation, he first considered the basis of Aboriginal or Indian title and the nature of the interest in land which it represents.

The existence of Indian title was traced through the decisions in *Calder*,[25] *St. Catherine's Milling*,[26] *Johnson v. McIntosh*,[27] *Worcester v. Georgia*,[28] *Amodu*

Tijani,[29] and *Star Chrome.*[30] These were decisions that we had urged upon the Federal Court of Appeal to support our argument that the band's interest in the lands could form the subject matter of a trust. Le Dain J. had also relied upon them to reach his decision that the Indians had a beneficial interest in the land, although he went on to find that it was one which was not protected by a legally enforceable equitable obligation on the part of the Crown. Dickson J. commented that Indian title is an independent legal right which, although recognized by the Royal Proclamation of 1763, nonetheless predates it.[31] For this reason, *Kinloch, Tito,* and other "political trust" decisions were inapplicable to the present case. Those cases concerned essentially the distribution of public funds or other property held by the government. The situation of the Indians was entirely different as their interest in their lands is a pre-existing legal right not created by the Royal Proclamation, the *Indian Act,* or any other executive order or legislative provision.[32] It did not matter that the present case was concerned with reserve lands rather than "unrecognized aboriginal title" in traditional tribal lands. The Indian interest in the land is the same in both cases.[33]

The nature of Indian title was next examined. The *St. Catherine's Milling,*[34] *Johnson v. McIntosh,*[35] *Amodu Tijani,*[36] and *Star Chrome*[37] cases were cited as authorities for the proposition that Indian title was "a personal and usufructuary right."[38] On the other hand, this characterization had sometimes been questioned, as in the *Calder,*[39] *Giroux,*[40] and *Cardinal*[41] decisions of the Supreme Court of Canada and the *Sarcee Developments*[42] decision of the Alberta Court of Appeal. Those cases supported the view of Le Dain J. that the Indian title in reserve lands was a beneficial interest. In *Miller v. The King,*[43] Kellock J. seemed implicitly to adopt a similar position. Dickson J. reconciled this apparent conflict between these cases[44] by pointing out that in describing what constitutes a unique interest in land the courts have almost invariably found themselves applying a somewhat inappropriate terminology drawn from general property law. There was a core of truth in the way that each of the two lines of authority had described Native title, but in neither case was the categorization quite accurate.

Dickson J. expressed his own view of the nature of Indian title as follows:[45]

> The nature of the Indians' interest is therefore best characterized by its general inalienability coupled with the fact that the Crown is under an obligation to deal with the land on the Indians' behalf when the interest is surrendered. Any description of Indian title which goes beyond these two features is both unnecessary and potentially misleading.

He then proceeded to describe the nature of the Crown's fiduciary obligation to Indian people. The concept of fiduciary obligation originated long ago in the jurisdiction of the courts of Chancery.[46] In the present case, its relevance was based on the requirement of a "surrender" to the Crown before Indian land can be alienated.[47] This requirement had been continuously maintained since the Royal Proclamation of 1763 and was now found in sections 37–41 of the *Indian Act*. The purpose of this requirement was clearly to interpose the Crown between the Indians and the prospective purchasers or lessees of their land so as to prevent the Indians from being exploited.[48]

Section 18(1) of the *Indian Act* conferred upon the Crown a discretion to decide for itself where the Indians' best interests really lie. The Federal Court of Appeal had found that this discretion ousted the jurisdiction of the courts to regulate the relationship between the Crown and the Indians. Dickson J. thought it had quite the opposite effect and transformed the Crown's obligation into a fiduciary duty.[49] He quoted from an article by Professor Ernest Weinrib[50] and said that he agreed:[51]

> That where by statute, agreement or perhaps by unilateral undertaking, one party has an obligation to act for the benefit of another, and that obligation carried with it a discretionary power, the party thus empowered becomes a fiduciary. Equity will then supervise the relationship by holding him to the fiduciary's strict standard of conduct.

These words may be regarded as the *ratio decidendi* or governing principle of his judgment and would have an important impact outside the area of Aboriginal law (as will be seen in chapter 6). He went on to say that "the categories of fiduciary, like those of negligence, should not be considered closed."[52] The performance of public law duties does not typically give rise to a fiduciary relationship, but the Crown's obligation to the Indians with respect to their interest in land was not a public law duty. While it is not a private law duty in the strict sense either, it is nonetheless in the nature of a private law duty. Therefore, in this unique or *sui generis* relationship, it was not improper to regard the Crown as a fiduciary.[53]

The broad discretion of the Crown in dealing with surrendered land which was conferred by section 18 of the *Indian Act* and the surrender document was subject to control by virtue of the fiduciary obligation:[54]

> When, as here, an Indian band surrenders its interest to the Crown, a fiduciary obligation takes hold to regulate the manner in which the Crown exercises its discretion in dealing with the land on the Indians' behalf.

He went on to distinguish the fiduciary obligation from a trust obligation.[55] The law of trusts is a highly developed, specialized branch of the law. An express trust requires a settlor (somebody to create the trust), a beneficiary (someone to benefit from the trust), a trust corpus (trust property), words of settlement, certainty of object, and certainty of obligation (wording which shows sufficient intention by the settlor to create a trust in favour of beneficiaries who can be clearly identified). Not all of these elements were present. There was not even a trust corpus:[56]

> As the *Smith* decision, *supra*, makes clear, upon unconditional surrender the Indians' right in the land disappears. No property interest is transferred which could constitute the trust *res*, so that even if the other *indicia* of an express or implied trust could be made out, the basic requirement of a settlement of property has not been met.

Dickson J. went on to say that the surrender did not give rise to a constructive trust, which depends upon the principle of unjust enrichment.[57] The Crown was not enriched by the surrender transaction, whether unjustly or otherwise. The Crown's obligation to the Indians was not a trust, but this did not prevent the obligation being trust-like in character:[58]

> As would be the case with a trust, the Crown must hold surrendered land for the use and benefit of the surrendering band. The obligation is thus subject to principles very similar to those which govern the law of trusts concerning, for example, the measure of damages for breach.

The fiduciary relationship between the Crown and the Indians also bears a certain resemblance to agency, since the obligation can be characterized as a duty to act on behalf of the Indian bands who have surrendered lands when negotiating for the sale of the lease of the land to third parties. However, he continued:[59]

> But just as the Crown is not a trustee for the Indians, neither is it their agent; not only does the Crown's authority to act on the band's behalf lack a basis in contract but the band is not a party to the ultimate sale or lease, as it would be if it were the Crown's principal. I repeat, the fiduciary obligation which is owed to the Indians by the Crown is *sui generis*. Given the unique character both of the Indian's interest in land and of their historical relationship with the Crown, the fact that this is so should occasion no surprise.

Having considered the nature of the fiduciary obligation, Dickson J. went on to consider the breach of that obligation.[60] The trial judge had found that the Crown's agents promised the band to lease the land in question on certain specified terms and then, after surrender, obtained a lease on different terms. The lease obtained was much less valuable. The oral terms that the band understood would be embodied in the lease were not incorporated as conditions into the surrender, but the Crown could not ignore those terms:[61]

> Nonetheless, the Crown, in my view, was not empowered by the surrender document to ignore the oral terms which the band understood would be embodied in

the lease. The oral representations form the backdrop against which the Crown's conduct in discharging its fiduciary obligation must be measured. They inform and confine the field of discretion within which the Crown was free to act. After the Crown's agents had induced the band to surrender its land on the understanding that the land would be leased on certain terms, it would be unconscionable to permit the Crown simply to ignore those terms. When the promised lease proved impossible to obtain, the Crown instead of proceeding to lease the land on different unfavourable terms, should have returned to the band to explain what had occurred and seek the band's counsel on how to proceed. The existence of such unconscionability is the key to a conclusion that the Crown breached its fiduciary duty. Equity will not countenance unconscionable behaviour in a fiduciary, whose duty is that of utmost loyalty to his principal.

The Crown could not promise the band that it would obtain a lease of its land on certain stated terms, thereby inducing the band to alter its legal position by surrendering the land, and then simply ignore that promise to the band's detriment. He concluded:[62]

> In obtaining without consultation a much less valuable lease than that promised, the Crown breached the fiduciary obligation it owed the band. It must make good the loss suffered in consequence.

Dickson J. then turned to a consideration of the Crown's contention that the claim was barred by the *Statute of Limitations* and by the doctrine of laches.[63] (Laches is the doctrine that a plaintiff, who delays too long in bringing an equitable claim, may be denied her day in court.) The argument based on the *Statute of Limitations* was rejected because of the concealment of the lease from the band. He agreed with Collier J. that this amounted to equitable fraud and was unconscionable although not dishonest. The limitation period did not therefore start to run until the discovery of the lease in March 1970. The defence of laches was also swiftly disposed of.[64] Since the conduct of the Indian Affairs branch personnel amounted to equitable fraud, since the band did not have actual or constructive knowledge of the actual terms of the lease until March 1970, and since the Crown suffered no disadvantage in making its defence by reason of the delay between March 1970 until suit was filed in December 1975, there was no ground for application of the equitable doctrine of laches.

Finally, Dickson J. considered the question of amount of damages, which in his opinion was to be determined by analogy with the principles of trust law.[65] He saw no error in principle in the judgment of the trial judge and was content to adopt the quantum of damages awarded at trial.

Decision of Wilson J.
Madam Justice Wilson gave judgment for herself and for Ritchie and McIntyre

J.J. She noted that in any breach of trust action, the facts are extremely important[66] and set out the facts as found by the trial judge.[67] She then considered
the contention made on behalf of the band that section 18 of the *Indian Act*
imposed on the Crown a fiduciary obligation enforceable in the courts.[68] In
her view, section 18 did not *per se* create a fiduciary obligation which has its
roots in the Aboriginal title of Canada's Indians as discussed in the *Calder*[69]
case. Section 18 acknowledged a historic reality, namely that Indian bands
have a beneficial interest in their reserves and that the Crown has a responsibility to protect that interest and make sure that any purpose to which reserve
land is put will not interfere with it. This is not to say that the Crown either
historically or by section 18 holds the land in trust for the bands. The bands
do not have the fee (ie. the absolute ownership) in the lands; their interest is
a limited one, but it is an interest that cannot be derogated from or interfered
with by the Crown's utilization of the land for purposes incompatible with the
Indian title unless, of course, the Indians agree. She continued:[70]

> I believe that in this sense the Crown has a fiduciary obligation to the Indian Bands
> with respect to the uses to which reserve land may be put and that s. 18 is a statutory
> acknowledgment of that obligation. It is my view, therefore, that while the Crown
> does not hold reserve land under s. 18 of the Act in trust for the Bands because
> the Bands' interests are limited by the nature of Indian title, it does hold the lands
> subject to a fiduciary obligation to protect and preserve the Bands' interests from
> invasion or destruction.

She next considered the Crown's submission that any obligation imposed
on the Crown by section 18 is political only and unenforceable in courts of
equity as held by the Federal Court of Appeal.[71] In her opinion, the discretion
conferred on the Governor in Council by the section was not unfettered. This
discretion had to be exercised on proper principles and not in an arbitrary
fashion. The "political trust" cases were inapplicable because the band had
a beneficial interest in its reserve and those cases concerned funds which
were the property of, or in the possession of, the Crown.[72] Continuing her
analysis of section 18, she noted that the Governor in Council's discretion
was "subject to the terms of any treaty or surrender" so that a band could
pre-empt that discretion.

She also considered the Crown's submission that it could rely upon the
terms of the surrender document, which gave the Crown complete discretion
both as to the lessee and the terms of the lease.[73] This submission was also
rejected. The Crown was well aware that the terms of the lease were important to the band. It ill became the Crown to obtain a surrender of the band's
interest for lease on terms voted on and approved by the band members at a
meeting specially called for the purpose and then assert an overriding discre-

tion to ignore those terms at will:[74]

> It makes a mockery of the Band's participation. The Crown well knew that the lease it made with the golf club was not the lease the Band surrendered its interest to get. Equity will not permit the Crown in such circumstances to hide behind the language of its own document.

She then returned to section 18 and considered the effect of the surrender of the land in trust for a lease on specific terms upon the Crown's fiduciary duty under the section:[75]

> It seems to me that s. 18 presents no barrier to a finding that the Crown became a full-blown trustee by virtue of the surrender. The surrender prevails over the s. 18 duty, but in this case there is no incompatibility between them. Rather, the fiduciary duty which existed at large under the section to hold the land in the reserve for the use and benefit of the band crystallized upon the surrender into an express trust of specific land for a specific purpose.

In the circumstances of this case, the Crown was compelled in equity upon the surrender to hold the surrendered land in trust for the purpose of the lease that the band members had approved as being for their benefit. The Crown was no longer free to decide that a lease on some other terms would do. Its hands were tied. When the golf club refused to enter into a lease on the approved terms, the Crown should have returned to the band and told them:[76]

> I think the learned trial judge was right in finding that the Crown acted in breach of trust when it barrelled ahead with a lease on terms which, according to the learned judge, were wholly unacceptable to its *cestui que trust* [the beneficiary].

Wilson J. then considered the band's claim in deceit[77] and noted that the trial judge had rejected this claim because there was no dishonesty or moral turpitude on the part of the government officials. The trial judge's findings were sufficient to dispose of this ground of appeal. Nevertheless, there was concealment amounting to equitable fraud which prevented the Crown from applying for relief from liability for breach of trust under section 98 of the *British Columbia Trustee Act*.[78]

Finally, Wilson J. considered in some detail the measure of damages, interest, and costs.[79] This was one of the most difficult issues. She concluded that the trial judge had not committed any error in principle in approaching the damages issue on the basis of a lost opportunity for residential development. She did not think it was the function of the Court to interfere with the quantum of damages awarded by the trial judge if no error in principle in determining the measure of damages had been demonstrated. The trial judge was entitled to treat the termination of the lease by the club as a contingency tending towards diminution of the band's damages and it was not for the Supreme Court of Canada to substitute the value it would have put upon that contingency for his. His refusal to award punitive damages and pre-judgment interest and his award for post-judgment interest at 5 percent were also upheld.

Decision of Estey J.

In his judgment, Estey J. expressed his view that the action "should be disposed of on the very simple basis of the law of agency."[80] He distinguished between "surrenders" in which the Indian band severed entirely its connection with the land, which he thought would be better described as a release, and "surrenders" in which the band did not release its interest but appointed the Crown as its agent to develop and exploit their interest in their lands by a lease or licence. In this case, the band had given detailed instructions to the representatives of the Government of Canada on the terms of the lease. These representatives did not carry out these instructions, nor keep the band apprised of the negotiations.[81] Most seriously of all, the Crown did not give the instructing Indians a copy of the lease or a written description of its contents for many years after the lease was executed. He concluded:[82]

> The fact that the agent is prescribed by statute in no way detracts in law from the legal capacity of the agent to act as such. The further consideration that the principal (the Indian band as holder of the personal interest in the land) is constrained by statute to act through the agency of the Crown, in no way reduces the rights of the instructing principal to call upon the agent to account for the performance of the mandate. . . . For these reasons, I would, with great respect to all who hold a contrary view, hesitate to resort to the more technical and far-reaching doctrines of the law of trusts and the concomitant law attaching to the fiduciary. The result is the same but, in my respectful view, the future application of the Act and the common law to native rights is much simpler under the doctrines of the law of agency.

It may be true that using doctrines of the law of agency simplifies the application of the *Indian Act* and the common law to Aboriginal rights. However, as Professor Bartlett has pointed out, this analysis of the relationship between the Crown and Aboriginal peoples as based on agency law is startling and unusual.[83] It is inconsistent with basic principles of agency law. Agents do not have title to the property of the principal, but the Crown has title to reserve lands under section 18 of the *Indian Act*. Agency is based on an agreement, but there is no agreement between the Crown and Aboriginal peoples. The major role of an agent is to create contractual relationships between her principal and a third party, but the Crown does not enter into agreements on behalf of Aboriginal peoples. The judgment of Estey J. has not been followed in other cases.

Although not directly mentioned in the judgment of any member of the Court, the momentous developments in our Constitution that took place between the *Guerin* trial in 1979 and the decision of the Supreme Court of Canada in 1984[84] may well have encouraged it to take a bolder approach than it otherwise would have done. This is suggested by the statement made by Justices Dickson and La Forest in the *Sparrow* decision that followed a few years later in 1990 that "it is essential to remember that the *Guerin* case was decided after the commencement of the *Constitution Act 1982.*"[85]

Almost ten years after having commenced legal action and twenty-seven years after the surrender of its land, the Musqueam Band was successful in its claim that the Crown was in breach of its fiduciary duty. The band had also obtained a ruling from the Supreme Court of Canada that the Crown's obligation was one that could be enforced by the courts and was not merely political in nature. This was a ruling that, in addition to achieving some measure of justice for the Musqueam, would have great implication for the rights of Aboriginal peoples generally (as shown in the next chapter and chapter 10). In giving its judgment, the Court had restated the requirements to demonstrate the existence of a fiduciary relationship in a manner that (as shown in chapter 6) was also to have significant impacts on the general law relating to fiduciary obligations.

Chapter 5

Aboriginal Law in Canada since *Guerin*

The Fiduciary Relationship

In the 2002 decision of *Wewaykum*, Binnie J., speaking for the Supreme Court of Canada, said that "[s]ince *Guerin*, Canadian courts have experienced a flood of 'fiduciary duty' claims by Indian bands across a whole spectrum of possible complaints."[1] This "flood," however, took some years to build up following the giving of the decision in 1984. It took a few years for lawyers acting for Aboriginal clients to fully realize the implications of the decision and then a few more years before the litigation, which was commenced in the light of that realization, reached the courts.[2] A review of the cases shows a slow build-up during the rest of the 1980s and no leading cases.

It was another Supreme Court of Canada decision involving the Musqueam, the *Sparrow*[3] decision in 1990, which led to an increasing number of cases in the first part of the 1990s. In 1995, the Supreme Court of Canada decided the *Blueberry River*[4] case and the pace picked up in the latter part of the decade and into the new century. The great majority of cases reported to date on the fiduciary obligations owed to Aboriginal peoples were decided during that period. This seemed to lead to a reaction by some judges and an attempt to reverse the trend by denying that the relationship between the Crown and Aboriginal peoples is fiduciary *per se* and limiting fiduciary obligations to specific fact situations.[5] However, with the decisions of the Supreme Court of Canada in *Osoyoos*,[6] *Ross River Dena*,[7] and *Wewaykum*,[8] this attempt appears to have failed, and the role of the fiduciary relationship as a cornerstone of Canadian Aboriginal law seems assured.[9]

Because "not all obligations existing between the parties to a fiduciary relationship are themselves fiduciary in nature,"[10] there still exists doubt as to the circumstances in which a fiduciary duty will arise in the course of the relationship between the Crown and Aboriginal people. There is little doubt, however, as a result of *Guerin* and subsequent cases, that the relationship itself is fiduciary in nature.[11]

Decisions of the Supreme Court of Canada have made this clear. In *Sparrow*, Dickson C.J. and La Forest J. said:[12]

> [T]he Government has the responsibility to act in a fiduciary capacity with respect to aboriginal people. The relationship between the government and aboriginals is trust-like, rather than adversarial, and contemporary recognition and affirmation of aboriginal rights must be defined in light of this historic relationship.

Speaking for the Court in *Quebec (Attorney-General) v. Canada (National Energy Board)*, Iacobucci J. said, "[i]t is now well settled that there is a fiduciary relationship between the federal Crown and the aboriginal peoples of Canada: *Guerin v. The Queen* [1984] 2 S.C.R. 335."[13] More recently, in *Ross River Dene*, Le Bel J. said on behalf of the Court, "[i]t must be kept in mind that the process of reserve creation, *like other aspects of its relationship with First Nations*, requires that the Crown remain mindful of its fiduciary duties and of their impact on this procedure."[14] Other courts have generally followed the lead of the Supreme Court of Canada. Gerein J. of the Saskatchewan Queen's Bench said in *Lac La Ronge Indian Band v. Canada*, "[t]here is a fiduciary relationship between Canada and Indian peoples. This is beyond doubt and does not warrant a lengthy discussion."[15] The existence of a fiduciary relationship was also recognized by the Royal Commission on Aboriginal Peoples in its 1996 report:[16]

> [T]he government cannot treat Aboriginal peoples as if they were adversaries. On the contrary, it must be mindful of the trust-like relationship with them and recognize and protect their Aboriginal rights as a trustee would protect them.

Fiduciary Obligations Applicable to Reserve Lands

Like *Guerin* itself, many of the cases following *Guerin* have considered the fiduciary obligations arising out of dealings with reserve lands. Binnie J. noted in *Wewaykum*, land "has generally played a central role in aboriginal economies and cultures."[17] There seems little doubt that fiduciary obligations apply to all aspects of the Crown's dealings with such lands. This was confirmed as early as 1988 when, in *Canadian Pacific Ltd v. Paul*, the Supreme Court of Canada commented that "in *Guerin* this court recognized that the Crown has a fiduciary obligation with respect to the land it holds for them."[18] Le Bel J., speaking for the Court, said in *Ross River Dena*, "it must not be forgotten that the actions of the Crown with respect to the lands occupied by the Band will be governed by the fiduciary relationship which exists between the Crown and the Band."[19]

Kruger v. R.[20] was one of the first cases after *Guerin* to consider the Crown's fiduciary relationship with Aboriginal peoples. The Crown expropriated land from the Penticton Indian Band for use as an airport. The band claimed that the compensation given was inadequate. The trial judge found that the claim was barred by the applicable limitation period, and the Federal Court of Appeal dismissed the appeal. All the judges in the Federal Court of Appeal agreed that the claim was statute barred. However, Heald J. dissented from his colleagues on whether the Crown was in breach of its fiduciary duty. Speaking for himself and Stone J., Urie J. said the Crown was under such a duty even though there was no surrender. An expropriation of the land created the same kind of fiduciary obligation, and the Crown was under an obligation to ensure that the Indians were properly compensated. However, on the facts, there had been no breach of that duty.

The issue before the Ontario Court of Appeal in *Skerryvore Ratepayers Assoc. v. Shawanaga Indian Band*[21] was whether a road passing through a reserve had become a public highway. The land in question had never been surrendered by the band under the *Indian Act*. However, the province argued that the conduct of officials of the Department of Indian Affairs resulted in the dedication of the road to public use. The court rejected this argument:[22]

> In sum, the Crown owed a fiduciary obligation to the Shawanaga Band in respect of their land and was incapable of disposing of that land without consulting with them; and a disposition could not be inferred in the absence of clear statutory language. Accordingly, the conduct of government officials was incapable of resulting in a dedication of Shawanaga Road to public use. Moreover, this argument proceeds on the assumption that unsurrendered land on a reserve is capable of dedication, be it by the band or by government officials. We are of the view that it is not.

The road was declared to be a private road. This case demonstrates that the Crown owes fiduciary obligations with respect to reserve lands even prior to a surrender of the interest of the band in the lands. Like *Guerin*, it also illustrates that consultation with the Aboriginal group is one of the fiduciary obligations owed by the Crown.

Lower Kootenay Band v. Canada[23] was a 1992 decision of the Trial Division of the Federal Court of Canada. In 1934 the Lower Kootenay Band surrendered some of its reserve lands to the Crown for leasing to a land reclamation company for a fifty-year term. Throughout the years, the band considered that the terms of the lease were unfavourable to it as they did not provide for any increase in rent over time. They applied pressure on the Department of Indian Affairs to have the lease terminated. The Crown discovered in 1948 that there was no order in council accepting the surrender as required by section 51 of the *Indian Act, 1927*. This information was not conveyed to the band for twenty-five years.

Dube J. of the Federal Court reviewed the facts in detail and set out his findings on the issues in the case in a series of questions and answers:[24]

1) *Was the Crown in breach of its fiduciary duty, and or negligent or both, vis-à-vis the band at the time of the surrender and the lease in 1934?*

[The Crown was] . . . under the obligation to be reasonably prudent and provident, and more so, where it had decided not to award the pro rata contribution recommended by the Royal Commission. Knowing well that the Indians were very reluctant to be locked into a long-term lease, the Crown should at least have secured a more realistic "escalator" clause or a "review" clause and ought not to have bound the band for fifty years to "Depression-era prices." . . .

4) *Was the Crown in breach of its fiduciary duty, and or negligent, or both, from 1948 until the date of termination of the lease in 1982, as the Crown knew, or ought to have known, that the lease was null and void ab initio* [from the beginning] *and took no steps to inform the band or to terminate the said lease?*

In my view, the Crown was both negligent and in breach of its fiduciary duty. It was also clearly negligent in failing to obtain the order in council in 1934. It seems obvious to me that it was part of the Crown's fiduciary obligations to follow the prescriptions of the *Indian Act* which, after all, is the basic legislation that governs the activities of the Department of Indian Affairs. Having decided to proceed under s. 51, the Crown was duty bound to proceed according to that section. . . .

Since the surrender, and therefore the lease, were void ab initio, had the Indians been so informed earlier, they might have been successful in obtaining more satisfactory rentals from [the land reclamation company], or they might have decided to treat the lease as being void and chosen to seek other, more suitable, arrangements with other parties. In any event, the Crown failed in its duty in not informing the plaintiffs, as it was duty bound to do, as soon as it discovered that there was no order in council.

5) *Was the Crown in breach of its fiduciary duty, and or negligent or both, in not taking steps to terminate the lease when it was contacted repeatedly by the band, from 1974 onwards, with requests to take steps to terminate the lease when it was apparent that there were valid legal grounds for such termination?*

Again, the answer is in the affirmative. By 1974, all those who were interested knew, or ought to have known, that the lease rentals were inadequate and that the Indians wanted to terminate the lease. There were obvious grounds for such termination, apart from the fact that the lease was null and void ab initio.

In the *Blueberry River*[25] case, decided in 1995, the Supreme Court of Canada applied *Guerin* in finding the government liable for breach of its fiduciary duty in the management of reserve lands. The facts were somewhat complex but, in essence, an Indian band in 1940 surrendered to the Crown mineral rights on its reserve "to lease" for its benefit and, subsequently in 1945, surrendered the reserve to the Crown. In 1948, the Department of Indian Affairs transferred the lands to the Director of the Veterans Land Act. There was no reservation of mineral rights. The land was then sold to veterans. Oil and gas were discovered on the lands and the revenues went to the veterans and not the band. The successor bands sued in respect of several breaches of fiduciary duty. The Court rejected most of the claims but held that the transfer of the mineral rights constituted a breach of fiduciary duty. Unfortunately, the decision fails to provide very much useful clarification of the fiduciary obligations owed by the Crown to Aboriginal people. It is largely dominated by the difference of approach taken by the judges on how to interpret the surrenders and the 1927 *Indian Act.*

Consistent with the approach taken by Dickson J. in *Guerin,* Gonthier J. found that by accepting the 1945 surrender, the Department of Indian Affairs took "on the obligations of a trustee in relation to" the surrendered reserve, such that it "was under a fiduciary duty to deal with the lands in the best interests of the members of the Beaver Band. This duty extended to both the surface rights and the mineral rights."[26] The department's discretion to sell or lease the reserve on terms virtually of its own choosing stemmed from the 1945 surrender agreement itself. This discretion and the department's "longstanding policy" to retain mineral rights for the benefit of Aboriginal peoples when surrendered lands were sold off, together with the absence of any "clear mandate from the Band to sell the mineral rights," justified the conclusion that the Department of Indian Affairs was under a fiduciary duty to retain the mineral rights for the benefit of the band when it sold the surface rights to the Director of the Veterans Land Act.[27] Gonthier J. attributed the Department of Indian Affairs' failure to do so to "inadvertence."

He concluded that the department's failure to continue leasing the band's mineral rights and its sale of these rights to the Director of the Veterans Land Act constituted a breach of its fiduciary duty. Like McLachlin J., he also found the department was under a continuing fiduciary duty to safeguard the band's mineral rights, so long as it had the power to do so.[28] Since s. 64 of the 1927 *Indian Act* gave the department the power to reacquire the lands in order to lease the mineral rights, and the department became aware early on of facts which ought to have made it act to recover the mineral rights for the band, the department was under an additional fiduciary obligation: to correct the previous error it had committed through inadvertence.[29] Specifically, the Department of Indian Affairs as fiduciary was required to act "with reasonable diligence," and its failure to correct the error and reacquire the mineral rights for the band was "a clear breach of the [Department of Indian Affairs'] fiduciary duty to deal with I.R. 172 according to the best interests of the Band."[30]

In her separate judgment, McLachlin J. made these comments on the pre-surrender obligation of the Crown:[31]

It follows that under the *Indian Act*, the Band had the right to decide whether to surrender the reserve, and its decision was to be respected. At the same time, if the Band's decision was foolish or improvident—a decision that constituted exploitation—the Crown could refuse to consent. In short, the Crown's obligation was limited to preventing exploitative bargains.

And on the post-surrender obligation of the Crown, she said:[32]

> The matter comes down to this. The duty on the Crown as fiduciary was "that of a man of ordinary prudence in managing his own affairs": *Fales v. Canada Permanent Trust Co.*, [1977] 2 S.C.R. 302, at p. 315. A reasonable person does not inadvertently give away a potentially valuable asset which has already demonstrated earning potential. Nor does a reasonable person give away for no consideration what it will cost him nothing to keep and which may one day possess value, however remote the possibility. The Crown managing its own affairs reserved out its minerals. It should have done the same for the Band.

McLachlin J. then considered whether the particular factual circumstances of the case before her superimposed a fiduciary relationship on the Crown quite apart from the *Indian Act*'s regime for the alienation of Indian lands. She concluded it did not since there was no evidence that the band had completely entrusted its power of decision over surrender of the reserve to the Crown.[33] Thus, she found the evidence did not support the existence of a fiduciary duty on the Crown prior to the 1945 surrender of the reserve.

She also considered what she referred to as "Post-surrender Duties and Breaches Regarding Surface Rights." She did so in the context of the Crown's concession that the 1945 surrender imposed a fiduciary duty on it with respect to the subsequent sale or lease of the lands. Considering what was reasonable at the time and the fact the band's interests and wishes were given utmost consideration, she declined to find that the Crown had breached its fiduciary duty by deciding to sell the reserve land to the Director of the Veterans Land Act. She also disagreed with the trial judge that the Crown was in breach of its fiduciary obligation to sell the land at a fair value, finding the band had failed to adduce evidence showing the sale price to be unreasonably low.[34]

Lastly, she considered whether the Crown breached its fiduciary obligations under the heading, "Post-surrender Duties and Breaches Regarding Mineral Rights." Unlike Gonthier J., she attributed importance to the 1940 surrender of the mineral rights, concluding that since the mineral rights were conveyed to the Crown in trust to lease for the welfare of the band, it followed that the Crown thereafter owed a fiduciary duty with respect to the mineral rights.[35]

McLachlin J. found that there were two grounds on which to argue that the transfer of the minerals to the Director of the Veterans Land Act in 1948 constituted a breach of fiduciary duty by the Crown. First, the transfer violated the terms of the 1940 surrender, which restricted the Department of Indian Affairs to leasing the mineral rights. In this connection, she noted: "A fiduciary is at very least bound to adhere to the terms of the instrument which bestows his powers and creates the trust."[36] Alternatively, if the 1945 surrender revoked the 1940 surrender (as the majority held), the 1945 surrender itself imposed an obligation on the Crown to lease or sell "*in the best interests of the Band*" (emphasis in the original). Ultimately, she found that a breach was made out on the first ground.[37] The majority found a breach had been made out on the second ground.

While McLachlin J. stated that the fiduciary duty associated with the administration of Indian lands "may have" terminated with the sale of the reserve lands in 1948, she too found an ongoing fiduciary duty existed both before and after 1948 "to act to correct error in the best interests of the Indians," which duty had been breached. This duty stemmed both from s. 64 of the *Indian Act*, which empowered the Department of Indian Affairs to revoke erroneous grants of land "even as against bona fide purchasers," and from the jurisprudence on fiduciary obligations. She explained:[38]

> Where a party is granted power over another's interests, and where the other party is correspondingly deprived of power over them, or is "vulnerable," then the party possessing the power is under a fiduciary obligation to exercise it in the best interests of the other: *Frame v. Smith, supra,* per Wilson J.; and *Hodgkinson v. Simms, supra.* Section 64 gave to [Department of Indian Affairs] power to correct the error that had wrongly conveyed the Band's minerals to the [Director of the Veterans Land Act]. The Band itself had no such power; it was vulnerable. In these circumstances, a fiduciary duty to correct the error lies.
>
> The [Department of Indian Affairs'] duty was the usual duty of a fiduciary to act with reasonable diligence with respect to the Indians' interest. Reasonable diligence required that the [Department of Indian Affairs] move to correct the erroneous transfer when it came into possession of facts suggesting error and the potential value of the minerals that it had erroneously transferred.

Semiahmoo Indian Band v. Canada[39] was a decision of the Federal Court of Appeal. The Crown negotiated an absolute surrender of reserve lands to improve customs facilities adjacent to the reserve. However, most of the land was not used for that or any other purpose. The band brought an action alleging the Crown breached its fiduciary duty to the band with respect to the surrender in failing to obtain an adequate price and in failing to protect the best interests of the band when it consented to an absolute surrender of the land. The Federal Court of Appeal found a breach and a constructive trust of the land in favour of the band.

In their analysis of the Crown's fiduciary duty, the Court applied *Guerin* and the above quotation from McLachlin J.'s judgment in *Blueberry River* regarding the Crown's pre-surrender duty to avoid an exploitative bargain in the surrender.[40] The Crown breached this duty because it was not known what, if any, use would be made of the land. The Crown should have refused to consent to the surrender or should have ensured that the surrender was qualified. The Court held that the claims of breaches of fiduciary obligation that took place prior to the surrender of the lands were barred by the passage of time and the defence based on the statute of limitations. However, it went on to find that there was a post-surrender fiduciary duty to correct any earlier breach since the Crown retained control of the land. The band's claim in respect of the Crown's post-surrender breach was not statute-barred. Chief Justice Isaac, writing for the Court, noted that the nature and scope of the fiduciary duty depends upon the specific facts:[41]

> The authorities on fiduciary duties establish that courts must assess the specific relationship between the parties in order to determine whether or not it gives rise to a fiduciary duty and, if yes, to determine the nature and scope of that duty. (See e.g. *Apsassin* [*i.e.* the *Blueberry River* case] (S.C.C.), *supra*; *Frame v. Smith* [1987] 2 S.C.R. 99, 42 D.L.R. (4th) 81; and *Lac Minerals Ltd. v. International Corona Resources Ltd.*, [1989] 2 S.C.R. 574, 61 D.L.R. (4th) 14.). This approach applies equally in the context of the fiduciary duty owed to Indian Bands when they surrender reserve land. In my view, while the statutory surrender requirement triggers the Crown's fiduciary obligation, the Court must examine the specific relationship between the Crown and the Indian Band in question in order to define the nature and scope of that obligation.

In this case, the band was particularly vulnerable to the influence of the Crown because the Crown had previously expropriated reserve lands and they knew that this could happen again.

The 1999 case of *Fairford First Nation v. Canada (Attorney General)*[42] was an action for breach of fiduciary duty brought by the Fairford First Nation against the Government of Canada. They claimed that the construction of a dam on a river next to their reserve caused flooding for which they had been inadequately compensated. Rothstein J. of the Federal Court, Trial Division rejected the action except for a finding of breach of fiduciary duty with respect to the delay and failure to consult by the federal government in the course of negotiations with the province.

Tsartlip Indian Band v. Canada (Minister of Indian Affairs)[43] was a decision of the Federal Court of Appeal which dealt with a decision by the Minister of Indian Affairs to lease part of an Indian reserve on behalf of a "locatee" (a member of the band who held a right to possession of part of the reserve in his individual capacity) under s. 58(3) of the *Indian Act*. The chief and council of the band claimed that the decision was unreasonable and in breach of the Crown's fiduciary obligations to the band. The Court held that the minister's decision was unreasonable but it rejected the claim of breach of fiduciary duty. It quoted with approval the earlier decision of the Court in *Boyer v. R.*[44] to the effect that the minister owed no fiduciary duty to the band when a lease was granted under s. 58(3) since "no interest of the Band can be affected by such a lease."[45]

The facts of *Mathias v. Canada*[46] involved claims by three bands (the Squamish, Musqueam, and Burrard bands) to an interest in what, prior to its surrender in 1946, constituted an eighty-six acre reserve known as the False Creek Reserve in Vancouver. The plaintiff bands alleged, among other things, that the federal government breached its fiduciary obligations to them by improperly allocating the reserve, mismanaging it, improperly taking its surrender, and selling it when it should have been leased over the long term. Simpson J. of the Federal Trial Court considered in some detail (and very restrictively) cases dealing with the existence of a pre-surrender fiduciary duty on the part of the Crown and concluded there was no fiduciary duty in the circumstances of the case. She summarized her views as follows:

> [527] There is no general all-encompassing Private Law Fiduciary Duty or general *sui generis* fiduciary duty which automatically arises under or is automatically superimposed on the Indian Act.
>
> There is the possibility that a *sui generis* fiduciary duty could be superimposed on the actions of the Crown during reserve administration, but only in special circumstances.
>
> There is no possibility that a Private Law Fiduciary Duty could arise in connection with the administration of reserves, even in special circumstances. In my opinion, any fiduciary duty found to be owing by the Crown would always be *sui generis*.

In *Lac La Ronge Indian Band v. Canada*,[47] the plaintiff band claimed entitlement to land and monies pursuant to Treaty No. 6 and to lands once set aside as a reserve. Gerein J. of the Saskatchewan Court of Queen's Bench partially upheld their claims and, in doing so, considered the Crown's fiduciary obligations:[48]

> The plaintiffs submit that Canada failed in its fiduciary obligation in respect to the Band Council Resolution of May 8, 1964 [which purported to accept certain lands in settlement of a treaty claim], and in withdrawing its claim to the lands at Candle Lake. As to the first, I hold the view that Canada had an obligation in 1964 to ensure that the Lac La Ronge Indian Band did not wrongly or imprudently extinguish its Treaty land entitlement and in carrying out that obligation it had a duty to fully inform the Band about the various possible approaches.

However, he went on to hold that, although there had been a breach of the Crown's fiduciary obligation, it was not necessary to grant a remedy as the court had already held the band council resolution to be invalid because of a lack of informed consent.

The question before the Supreme Court of Canada in *Osoyoos Indian Band v. Oliver (Town)*,[49] decided in 2001, was whether a strip of land located on a reserve remained part of the reserve after a federal order in council consented to the taking of the land by the province. A majority decided that it maintained its reserve status and reversed the decision of the British Columbia Court of Appeal. Iacobucci J. gave the opinion for the majority. In the course of his judgment, he made the following comments on the fiduciary obligations of the Crown:

> [47] Land may be removed from a reserve with the participation of the Crown, which owes a fiduciary duty to the band, as discussed below. Fiduciaries are held to a high standard of diligence. For this reason, as well as by reason of the foregoing principles, it follows that a clear and plain intention must be present in order to conclude that land has been removed from a reserve. . . .

> [52] In my view, the fiduciary duty of the Crown is not restricted to instances of surrender. Section 35 [of the *Indian Act*] clearly permits the Governor in Council to allow the use of reserve land for public purposes. However, once it has been determined that an expropriation of Indian lands is in the public interest, a fiduciary duty arises on the part of the Crown to expropriate or grant only the minimum interest required in order to fulfill that public purpose, thus ensuring a minimal impairment of the use and enjoyment of Indian lands by the band. This is consistent with the provisions of s. 35 which give the Governor in Council the absolute discretion to prescribe the terms to which the expropriation or transfer is to be subject. In this way, instead of having the public interest trump the Indian interests, the approach I advocate attempts to reconcile the two interests involved.

> [53] This two-step process minimizes any inconsistency between the Crown's public duty to expropriate lands and its fiduciary duty to Indians whose lands are affected by the expropriation. In the first stage, the Crown acts in the public interest in determining that an expropriation involving Indian lands is required in order to fulfill some public purpose. At this stage, no fiduciary duty exists. However, once the general decision to expropriate has been made, the fiduciary obligations of the Crown arise, requiring the Crown to expropriate an interest that will fulfill the public purpose while preserving the Indian interest in the land to the greatest extent practicable. . . .

> [55] . . . [T]he duty includes the general obligation, wherever appropriate, to protect a sufficient Indian interest in expropriated land in order to preserve the taxation jurisdiction of the band over the land, thus ensuring a continued ability to earn income from the land.

Gonthier J. gave judgment for the minority which expressly agreed with the comments above from the judgment of Iacobucci J. regarding the contents of the Crown's fiduciary duty. However, they could not agree that the Crown's fiduciary obligation regarding its adoption of the order in council included a duty to protect an Indian interest in expropriated land sufficient to preserve the band's taxation jurisdiction. The band had no taxation jurisdiction to preserve in 1957, when the order in council was adopted.

In *Ross River Dena Council Band v. Canada*,[50] the Supreme Court of Canada set out the requirements for the legal creation of a reserve. It upheld the decision of the majority of the Yukon Territory Court of Appeal that, on the facts of this case, no reserve had been established. Finch J.A. had dissented on the grounds that the appropriate government official had set apart certain land intending it to be reserved for the use and benefit of the band. To hold otherwise would be inconsistent with the Crown's fiduciary obligations. However, Lebel J., giving the judgment of the majority of the Supreme Court of Canada, observed:

> [68] It should be noted that the parties did not raise, in the course of this appeal, the impact of the fiduciary obligations of the Crown. It must be kept in mind that the process of reserve creation, like other aspects of its relationship with First Nations, requires that the Crown remain mindful of its fiduciary duties and of their impact on this procedure, and taking into consideration the *sui generis* nature of native land rights: see the comments of Lamer C.J. in *St. Mary's Indian Band v. Cranbrook (City)*, [1997] 2 S.C.R. 657, at paras. 14–16.

He had earlier noted that, although not at stake in the present appeal, the exercise of the power to create reserves "remains subject to the fiduciary obligations of the Crown" as well as to the constitutional rights and obligations which arise under s. 35 of the *Constitution Act, 1982*.[51]

In *Wewaykum Indian Band v. Canada*,[52] decided in 2002, the Supreme Court of Canada applied *Guerin* to the process of reserve creation in British Columbia. The case involved actions by two Indian bands (the Wewaykum or Cape Mudge Band and the Wewaikai or Campbell River Band) against the federal Crown for alleged breach of fiduciary duty arising out of the creation of two reserves.

The essential facts were that certain reserves were set aside in 1888 for the Laich-Kwil-tach Nation. Each of the appellant bands was part of this nation. Schedules of reserves prepared by the Department of Indian Affairs showed both of the reserves in question (reserves numbers 11 and 12) as being set aside for one of the bands (the Wewaykum Band). This was done by writing the name of that band against Reserve 11 and then showing ditto marks against Reserve 12. A dispute arose between the two bands as to fishing rights which led to a dispute over possession of Reserve 11. The dispute led to a resolution passed by the Wewaykum Band in 1907 ceding any claim over Reserve 11 to the Wewaikai Band. The effect of the resolution was recorded in a change to the departmental schedule. The name of the Wewaikai Band was entered opposite Reserve 11 but, in what became known as the "ditto-mark error," the ditto marks against Reserve 12, directly beneath it, remained unchanged. The result was that it looked as if the Wewaikai Band had an interest in both reserves. The schedule was subsequently appended to orders in council.

In 1985, the Wewaikai brought action against both the Crown and the Wewaykum on the grounds that it had a "legislated entitlement" to Reserve 12. The Wewaykum counter-claimed for exclusive entitlement to both reserves and added a claim against the Crown. After eighty days of evidence and submissions, the Federal Court, Trial Division, dismissed the claims of both bands. The Federal Court of Appeal upheld that decision. The further appeals by the bands to the Supreme Court of Canada were also dismissed by a unanimous Court. Binnie J. wrote the judgment of the Court. He referred to the finding of the trial judge that the Crown had acted fairly and honourably. The wishes of the Indians themselves had been sought out and respected. Each of the bands had formally abandoned the claim to the other's reserve by the time that the reserve-creation process had been completed in 1938. Over the intervening sixty or so years, band members had relied on the status quo to make improvements to the reserves on which they reside. In the circumstances, he concluded that no fiduciary duty had been breached and no equitable relief was available either by injunction or equitable compensation. In any event, all such claims would have been barred by the expiry of the applicable limitation periods.

After reviewing the facts and the reserve creation process in British Columbia, he expressed his opinion that "the solution to these appeals . . . does not lie in the law of rectification but in the law governing the fiduciary duty alleged and the equitable remedies sought by the appellant bands."[53] His analysis of the fiduciary duty owed by the Crown to the bands commenced with the court's "watershed decision in *Guerin*."[54]

Turning to the facts before him, he explained why the submissions of the bands with respect to the existence and breach of a fiduciary duty could not succeed under the following headings:[55]

1   The content of the Crown's fiduciary duty towards aboriginal peoples varies with the nature and importance of the interest sought to be protected. It does not provide a general indemnity.

2   Prior to reserve creation, the Crown exercises a public law function under the *Indian Act* which is subject to supervision by the courts exercising public law remedies. At that stage a fiduciary relationship may also arise but, in that respect, the Crown's duty is limited to the basic obligations of loyalty, good faith in the discharge of its mandate, providing full disclosure appropriate to the subject matter, and acting with ordinary prudence with a view to the best interest of the aboriginal beneficiaries.

3 Once a reserve is created the content of the Crown's fiduciary duty expands to include the protection and preservation of the band's quasi-proprietary interest in the reserve from exploitation.

4 In this case, as the appellant bands have rightly been held to lack any beneficial interest in the other band's reserve, equitable remedies are not available either to dispossess an incumbent band that is entitled to the beneficial interest, or to require the Crown to pay "equitable" compensation for its refusal to bring about such a dispossession.

5 Enforcement of equitable duties by equitable remedies is subject to the usual equitable defences, including laches and acquiescence.

Each of the propositions was then discussed. During the period of reserve creation, there was a fiduciary duty in existence:[56]

> It cannot reasonably be considered that the Crown owed no fiduciary duty during this period to bands which had not only gone into occupation of provisional reserves, but were also entirely dependant on the Crown to see the reserve-creation process through to completion.

The issue was to define the content of that duty. This was not the same situation as in *Guerin,* which involved the disposition of an existing Indian interest but "the creation of an altogether new interest in lands to which the Indians made no prior claim by way of treaty or aboriginal rights."[57]

During the period prior to reserve creation, the Crown exercised a public law function under the *Indian Act* which was subject to supervision by the courts exercising public law remedies. The imposition of a fiduciary duty attached the additional obligations of "loyalty, good faith, full disclosure appropriate to the matter in hand and acting in what it reasonably and with diligence regards as in the best interests of the beneficiary."[58] After the reserve is created, the content of the fiduciary duty expands to include the protection and preservation of the band's interest from exploitation. He referred to the statement by Wilson J. in *Guerin* that, prior to any disposition, the Crown has "a fiduciary obligation to protect and preserve the Bands' interest from invasion or destruction."[59] In his view:[60]

> Wilson J.'s comments should be taken to mean that ordinary diligence must be used by the Crown to avoid invasion or destruction of the band's quasi-property interest by an exploitative bargain with third parties or, indeed, exploitation by the Crown itself. (Of course, there will also be cases dealing with the ordinary accountability by the Crown, as fiduciary, for its administrative control over the reserve and band assets.)

He rejected the claim by the Wewaykum or Cape Mudge Band that the *1907 Resolution* ceding Reserve 11 was exploitive:[61]

> [T]his argument rests on a misconception of the Crown's fiduciary duty. The Cape

Mudge forbears, whose conduct is now complained of, were autonomous actors, apparently fully informed, who intended in good faith to resolve a "difference of opinion" with a sister band. They were not dealing with non-Indian third parties (*Guerin*, at p. 382). It is patronizing to suggest, on the basis of the evidentiary record, that they did not know what they were doing, or to reject their evaluation of a fair outcome. Taken in context, and looking at the substance rather than the form of what was intended, the *1907 Resolution* was not in the least exploitative.

The "bold attempt of the appellant bands to extend their claim to fiduciary relief on the present facts [was] overly ambitious."[62] On the other hand, the trial judge and the Federal Court of Appeal had adopted too restrictive a view of the content of the fiduciary duty owed by the Crown to the bands with respect to their existing quasi-proprietary interest in their respective reserves. The Crown did not discharge its fiduciary duty by balancing the interests of the two bands:[63]

With respect, the role of honest referee does not exhaust the Crown's fiduciary obligation here. The Crown could not, merely by invoking competing interests, shirk its fiduciary duty. The Crown was obliged to preserve and protect each band's legal interest in the reserve which, on a true interpretation of events, had been allocated to it. In my view it did so.

He concluded by rejecting the availability of any equitable remedies pointing out that "a mandatory injunction is not available to dispossess the rightful incumbent. Nor is there any requirement on the Crown to pay equitable compensation to a claimant band to substitute for an equitable or beneficial interest that does not belong to it."[64] Further, the defences of laches and acquiescence would have applied and, in any event, the claims of the appellant bands were statute barred.[65]

The Protection of Aboriginal Rights and Title

The fiduciary relationship between the Crown and Aboriginal peoples has played a key role in the interpretation and application of section 35(1) of the *Constitution Act, 1982,* which states that "the existing aboriginal and treaty rights of the aboriginal peoples of Canada are hereby recognized and affirmed." The scope of this vaguely worded provision was the subject of considerable debate.[66] It was often referred to as "an empty box." Section 35 was not contained in the *Canadian Charter of Rights and Freedoms*. Section 1 expressly guaranteed the rights and freedoms set out in the *Charter* subject only to such reasonable limits prescribed by law as can be demonstrably justified in a free and democratic society. Since they were outside the *Charter*, there was no such guarantee for existing Aboriginal and treaty rights recognized and affirmed by section 35 and nor was there any other mechanism to provide substantive protection for such rights. This raised the concern that these rights were not guaranteed by, or entrenched in, the Constitution and could be extinguished or arbitrarily infringed by government. Arguably, the section merely recognized and affirmed those rights that had been legally acknowledged at the time of the passage of the *Act* and, at most, created a rule of statutory interpretation that there was a presumption against future extinguishment or infringement. There was obviously the potential for it to receive a conservative, restrictive interpretation which would have severely limited the protection provided. One leading academic specializing in Aboriginal law went so far as to say that "it may properly be asserted that the [s. 35 of the *Constitution Act, 1982*], far from protecting or guaranteeing the rights of the aboriginal peoples of Canada, provides for the diminution and abrogation of such rights without their consent."[67] Fortunately for Aboriginal peoples, the Supreme Court of Canada has held that section 35 should be interpreted in the light of the fiduciary principle and should receive a liberal and generous interpretation. This judicial incorporation of the fiduciary principle into the Constitution has provided the substantive protection for Aboriginal and treaty rights that the politicians failed to provide.

The first decision of the Supreme Court of Canada to consider section 35 was *R. v. Sparrow*,[68] which, like *Guerin*, was another landmark case on the development of Aboriginal rights in Canada involving the Musqueam Band. The Court first noted that:[69]

> Section 35(1) at the least provides a solid constitutional base upon which subsequent negotiations can take place. It also affords aboriginal peoples constitutional protection against provincial legislative power. We are, of course, aware that this would, in any event, flow from the *Guerin* case, *supra*, but for a proper understanding of the situation, it is essential to remember that the *Guerin* case was decided after the commencement of the *Constitution Act 1982*.

The Court later observed:[70]

> In our opinion, *Guerin*, together with *R. v. Taylor and Williams* (1981), 62 C.C.C. (2d) 227, 34 O.R. (2d) 360 ground a general guiding principle for s.35(1). That is, the government has the responsibility to act in a fiduciary capacity with respect to aboriginal peoples. The relationship between the government and aboriginals is trust-like, rather than adversarial, and contemporary recognition and affirmation of aboriginal rights must be defined in light of this historic relationship.

The fiduciary relationship was relied upon as the basis for importing into section 35 some restraint on the exercise of the sovereign power to restrict Aboriginal rights:[71]

> There is no explicit language in the provision that authorizes this Court or any court to assess the legitimacy of any governmental legislation that restricts aborigi-

nal rights. Yet, we find that the words "recognition and affirmation" incorporate the fiduciary relationship referred to earlier and so import some restraint on the exercise of sovereign power. . . .

[F]ederal power must be reconciled with federal duty and the best way to achieve that reconciliation is to demand the justification of any government regulation that infringes upon or denies aboriginal rights. Such scrutiny is in keeping with the liberal interpretive principle enunciated in *Nowegijick, supra,* and the concept of holding the Crown to a high standard of honourable dealing with respect to the Aboriginal peoples of Canada as suggested in *Guerin v. The Queen, supra.*

The Court later explained how the fiduciary relationship could be applied as the basis for a test of justification to determine the validity of governmental restrictions on an Aboriginal right. This test is considered below.[72]

A few years later, in *Van Der Peet,*[73] the Court again ruled that the fiduciary relationship mandated a generous and liberal interpretation of section 35(1) as well as treaties and other statutory and constitutional provisions protecting the interests of Aboriginal peoples:

[24] . . . The Crown has a fiduciary obligation to aboriginal peoples with the result that in dealings between the government and aboriginals the honour of the Crown is at stake. Because of this fiduciary relationship, and its implication of the honour of the Crown, treaties, s. 35(1), and other statutory and constitutional provisions protecting the interests of aboriginal peoples, must be given a generous and liberal interpretation: *R. v. George* [1966] S.C.R. 267, at p.279. This general principle must inform the Court's analysis of the purposes underlying s.35(1) and of that provision's definition and scope.

[25] The fiduciary relationship of the Crown and aboriginal peoples also means that where there is any doubt or ambiguity with regards to what falls within the scope and definition of s. 35(1), such doubt or ambiguity must be resolved in favour of aboriginal peoples.

Prior to the enactment of section 35(1) in 1982, the federal government was able to unilaterally extinguish Aboriginal rights. In *Sparrow,* the Supreme Court of Canada held that, for a pre-1982 provision to have this effect, it was necessary to demonstrate a clear and plain intention to do so.[74] In his dissenting judgment in *R. v. Gladstone,* La Forest J. found that the right in question had been extinguished. However, he commented that "the fiduciary nature of the relationship between the Crown and aboriginal peoples must be taken into account in assessing whether or not a clear and plain intention to extinguish an aboriginal right exists in a given scheme."[75]

After the enactment of section 35(1), governments may not extinguish Aboriginal rights but they may still infringe upon such rights if they can satisfy the test of justification set out in *Sparrow.* In that case, the Court explained the basis of this burden on the Crown as arising from interpreting the section in the light of the fiduciary relationship:[76]

> Section 35(1) suggests that while regulation affecting aboriginal rights is not pre-
> cluded, such regulation must be enacted according to a valid objective. . . . By giving
> aboriginal rights constitutional status and priority, Parliament and the provinces
> have sanctioned challenges to social and economic policy objectives embodied in
> legislation to the extent that aboriginal rights are affected. Implicit in this consti-
> tutional scheme is the obligation of the legislature to satisfy the test of justification.
> The way in which a legislative objective is to be attained must uphold the honour
> of the Crown and must be in keeping with the unique contemporary relationship,
> grounded in history and policy, between the Crown and Canada's aboriginal peoples.
> The extent of legislative or regulatory impact on an existing aboriginal right may
> be scrutinized so as to ensure recognition and affirmation. . . . The government
> is required to bear the burden of justifying any legislation that has some negative
> effect on any aboriginal right protected under s.35(1).

The Court then proceeded to set out the test of justification, which was summarized as follows by the British Columbia Court of Appeal in *R. v. Jack*:[77]

> *The Sparrow Principles*
>   In *Sparrow*, the Supreme Court of Canada stated that a generous liberal inter-
> pretation of the words in the constitutional provisions of s.35(1) was demanded
> (*Sparrow*, 1106).
>   The court set out the test to determine whether the regulation or conservation
> measure for a fishery has the effect of interfering with an existing Aboriginal right to
> fish. There are two stages to the test. The first stage requires establishing a *prima facie*
> infringement [i.e., an infringement that has been established at first sight rather than
> on the usual test of a balance of probabilities] and if that is established, the second
> stage asks whether there is any justification for the *prima facie* infringement.
>   In the first stage of the test, the following questions need to be answered to
> determine whether there is a *prima facie* infringement of s. 35(1) of the *Constitu-
> tion Act* :
>
> 1. Is the limitation unreasonable?
>
> 2. Does the regulation impose undue hardship?
>
> 3. Does the regulation deny to the holder of the Aboriginal right their preferred
>   means of exercising that right?
>
>   The individual or group who challenges the regulation bears the onus of proving
> a *prima facie* infringement. (*Sparrow*, 1112).
>   If a *prima facie* infringement is found, the analysis proceed to the second stage
> of the test, whether there was justification for the infringement. Under the second
> stage the following enquiries are made:
>
> 1. Is there a valid legislative objective to the interference?
>   When considering this question the court emphasized that the honour of the
> Crown is at stake in dealings with Aboriginal peoples. The special trust relationship
> and the responsibilities of the government *vis-a-vis* Aboriginal [sic] must be the first

consideration in determining whether the legislation or action can be justified.

2. Has the allocation of priorities after valid conservation measures have been taken given top priority to the Indian right to fish for food and social and ceremonial purposes? (*Sparrow*, 1101). Any regulation that does not do so is in violation of s.35(1). (*Sparrow*, 1116).

Has the brunt of the conservation measures been borne by the sports and commercial fisheries and not by the Indian food and social and ceremonial fishing? (*Sparrow*, 1116).

3. Has there been as little infringement as possible to effect the desired conservation result? (*Sparrow*, 1119).

4. Has the Aboriginal group been consulted with respect to the conservation measures being implemented? (*Sparrow*, 1118–1119).

The justificatory standard to be met may place a heavy burden on the Crown. (*Sparrow*, 1119).

A number of cases have considered whether the requirements of the *Sparrow* justification test have been met on the evidence before the court. In many cases, an Aboriginal defendant has been acquitted because the Crown was unable to discharge the burden of the test. This is illustrated by three decisions of the British Columbia Court of Appeal delivered in 1995: *Jack*,[78] *Little*,[79] and *Sampson*.[80] In each case, the Court decided that the appeal should be allowed and the convictions set aside. The government had failed to give priority to Aboriginal fishers over other fishers as required by *Sparrow*. There was also evidence of inadequate consultation. Likewise, in *Adams*,[81] the Supreme Court of Canada quashed the conviction of an Indian who had been found guilty of illegal fishing. The Court said that:[82]

> [I]n light of the Crown's unique fiduciary obligations towards aboriginal peoples, Parliament may not simply adopt an unstructured discretionary administrative regime which risks infringing aboriginal rights in a substantial number of applications in the absence of some explicit guidance. . . . In the absence of such specific guidance, the statute will fail to provide representatives of the Crown with sufficient directives to fulfil their fiduciary duties, and the statute will be found to represent an infringement of aboriginal rights under the *Sparrow* test.

In *Gladstone*,[83] the Court remanded the case for further consideration on the question whether a regulation placing restrictions on the Aboriginal right to fish could be justified as consistent with the Crown's fiduciary obligations. *Powley*[84] was a decision of the Court involving the Aboriginal rights to hunt of Métis people in Ontario. The Court held that the legislation in question failed to satisfy the justification test because it failed to give *any* recognition to such rights.

The duty of government to justify any infringement of an Aboriginal right is not limited to criminal proceedings. In *Union of Nova Scotia Indians v. Canada (Attorney General),*[85] Mackay J. of the Trial Division of the Federal Court held that the governmental approval for dredging the sea bottom should be set aside because the dredging would infringe an Aboriginal right to fish and the government had failed to show the effect on that right was warranted. Richard A.C.J. of the same court held in *Nunavik Inuit v. Canada*[86] that the federal government had a duty to consult with the Inuit before it established a national park in their territory which might have infringed their Aboriginal rights.

Lack of consultation as part of the *Sparrow* test led to a similar result by the British Columbia Court of Appeal in *Taku River Tlingit First Nation v. British Columbia (Project Assessment Director).*[87] A mining company wanted to develop a mine in the traditional territory of the First Nation and, without addressing their concerns, the provincial government had issued an approval for the project. It took the position, accepted in some other cases,[88] that the Aboriginal right first had to be determined by legal proceedings before the duty of consultation arose. The British Columbia Court of Appeal rejected this argument on the grounds that it ignored "the responsibility of government to protect the rights of Indians arising from the special trust relationship created by history, treaties and legislation" and "would largely negate the purpose of the constitutional protection provided by s. 35(1) of the *Constitution Act, 1982.*"[89] Although upholding the existence of the duty prior to determination of the Aboriginal right, the Supreme Court of Canada held that, on the facts, there had been adequate consultation and allowed the appeal of the province.[90]

The *Delgamuukw* decision of the Supreme Court of Canada in 1997 applied the *Sparrow* test to Aboriginal title.[91] Chief Justice Lamer said that, in the case of Aboriginal title, the role of the fiduciary duty as part of the test of justification for infringement may be articulated in a manner different from other Aboriginal rights. For example, the idea of priority may not apply. However, the government would still have to demonstrate that, in allocating a resource, it took into account the interests of the holders of Aboriginal title in the land. This might entail participation of Aboriginal people in the development of the resource and require that the conferral of fee simple titles, leases and licences reflect their prior occupation of the land. Economic barriers to Aboriginal uses of the land (e.g., licensing fees) might be somewhat reduced. This list was illustrative but not exhaustive. He noted that the "fiduciary relationship between the Crown and aboriginal peoples may be satisfied by the involvement of aboriginal peoples in decisions taken with respect to their lands. There is always a duty of consultation." Further, Aboriginal title had an inescapable economic aspect which suggested that compensation is relevant to the question of justification as well. "Compensation for breaches of fiduciary duty [is] a well-established part of the landscape of aboriginal rights: *Guerin*. In keeping with the duty of honour and good faith on the Crown, fair compensation will ordinarily be required when aboriginal title is infringed." The amount of compensation would vary with the nature of the particular Aboriginal title affected and with the nature and severity of the infringement and the extent to which Aboriginal interests were accommodated.

The Protection of Treaty Rights

As indicated above, section 35(1) of the *Constitution Act* in 1982 recognizes and affirms existing treaty rights as well as existing Aboriginal rights. Prior to the enactment of that section, there was little protection for treaty rights which could be extinguished or infringed by legislation.[92] After its enactment, the courts extended to treaties the protection of the fiduciary principle which requires governments to justify any infringement of an Aboriginal right using the *Sparrow* test discussed above.[93]

An early application of the *Sparrow* test to treaty rights was *R. v. Noel*.[94] Halifax J. of the Northwest Territories Territorial Court acquitted an Aboriginal hunter who was charged with discharging a firearm contrary to certain regulations. The defendant argued that he had a treaty right to hunt. Halifax J. applied the test to hold that the regulations did not validly restrict the treaty right because there had been inadequate consultations.

The application of the *Sparrow* test to treaty rights was expressly upheld by the Supreme Court of Canada in *R. v. Badger*.[95] Cory J. noted that , "[i]n *Sparrow,* certain criteria were set out pertaining to justification. . . . While that case dealt with infringement of aboriginal rights, I am of the view that those criteria should, in most cases, apply equally to the infringement of treaty rights."[96]

In *Halfway River First Nation v. British Columbia*,[97] a majority of the British Columbia Court of Appeal held that a cutting permit issued by the Ministry of Forests should be set aside as it would infringe the hunting rights of the First Nation protected under a treaty. The provincial Crown had failed to honour its fiduciary duty to have meaningful consultations with the First Nation.

A similar decision was reached by Hansen J. of the Trial Division of the Federal Court in *Mikisew Cree First Nation v. Canada (Minister of Canadian Heritage)*.[98] The decision of Parks Canada to approve a winter road though the traditional territory of the First Nation without meaningful consultation was held to be an unjustified infringement of their treaty rights and was set aside. On appeal, a majority of the Federal Court of Appeal held that the approval was a "taking up" within the treaty. As such, the First Nation had no continued right to hunt on the land taken up for the road and there was no violation of section 35 of the *Constitution Act, 1982*. There was, therefore, no need to apply the *Sparrow* analysis. Although, as a matter of good practice, the Minister might have consulted more extensively with the First Nation before approving the road, she was not constitutionally obliged to do so.

The fiduciary relationship may also be relevant to the negotiation and implementation of treaties. In *Gitanyow First Nation v. Canada*,[99] Williamson J. of the British Columbia Supreme Court granted a declaration that the federal and provincial governments were obliged to negotiate a treaty in good faith. He did so on the basis of the fiduciary obligation owed to the band. A similar ruling had been made by Richard A.C.J. of the Federal Court, Trial Division in *Nunavik Inuit v. Canada*.[100]

On the other hand, the Federal Court of Appeal said in *Eastmain Band v. Canada* that "when the Crown negotiates land agreements today with the Aboriginals, it need not and cannot have only their interests in mind. It must seek a compromise between that interest and the interest of the whole society, which it represents and of which the Aboriginals are part, in the land in question."[101] In *Lac La Ronge Indian Band v. Canada*,[102] the Saskatchewan Court of Appeal agreed with the observation of the trial judge that not every breach of a treaty would constitute a breach of a fiduciary obligation.

Litigation

As is evident from the number of cases discussed in this chapter, there has been considerable litigation since *Guerin* between the Crown and Aboriginal peoples. The existence of the fiduciary relationship has been relevant to the conduct of some of this litigation.

Some Aboriginal groups have maintained that the Crown is under a fiduciary obligation to fund litigation which the group wants to bring to protect its interests. An early case was *Ominayak v. Minister of Indian Affairs*[103] in which Strayer J. of the Federal Court, Trial Division refused to strike out a claim that the Crown was under an obligation to fund litigation brought by the Lubicon Lake Band to obtain a reserve although he expressed serious doubts about the claim.

In *British Columbia (Minister of Forests) v. Jules*, the British Columbia Court of Appeal rejected an argument that there was a specific fiduciary duty to provide funding to enable a band to go to trial to prove its Aboriginal title and the Supreme Court of Canada upheld its decision.[104] Giving the judgment of the Court, Madam Justice Newbury agreed with the Chambers Judge that there was "nothing in the specific circumstances of this case that would give rise to a 'fiduciary expectation' of funding."[105] However, the Court went on to exercise its discretion to award costs in favour of the Band and, in doing so, it took into account the "Crown's broad fiduciary duty" and the honour of the Crown in its dealings with Aboriginal people."[106] In the words of Madam Justice Newbury, "it is simply unrealistic for the Crown in this case to fold its hands and say that the Band will have to manage without counsel."[107]

The existence of the fiduciary relationship is also relevant to procedural matters arising during the Crown's conduct of litigation with Aboriginal peoples. In *Guerin*, the Crown's conduct in raising the defence of political trust in the Federal Court of Appeal after failing to plead the defence and appearing to abandon it at trial was criticized by Madam Justice Wilson in the Supreme Court of Canada.[108] Jerome A.C.J. of the Federal Court, Trial Division referred to this criticism in *Dick v. The Queen*[109] in the context of his consideration of a band's application for an order that the Crown give further answers to interrogatories which it had previously been ordered to answer. He commented that "[n]or can the nature of the relationship between the parties involved in this action be overlooked" and referred to the Crown's "fiduciary obligation towards native persons."[110] He ordered the Crown to answer the questions. In *Montana Band v. Canada*,[111] Huggerson J. of the same court said:

> Even within the adversarial relationship created by litigation between them, the Crown continues to owe an historic fiduciary duty to deal fairly and openly with first nations. This is not to say that there are special rules for Aboriginal claims, but simply that the nature of any claim is part of the context in which any objection to interrogatories is to be decided and that where a claim is in respect of alleged historical injustice by the Crown, that context may be determining.

The conflict between the right to discovery of documents and the right to withhold privileged documents was considered by the Federal Court of Appeal in *Samson Indian Nation and Band v. Canada*.[112] The Court held that the Band was entitled to receive documents if it could establish a prima facie trust relationship and if the documents had been obtained or prepared by the Crown in the course of carrying out duties as a trustee. It ordered disclosure of some of the documents which the Crown claimed were privileged but rejected the Nation's claim to obtain *all* relevant documents relating to a trust of which the Nation was a beneficiary. Desjardin J.A. said that he agreed with the following statement by the case management judge:[113]

> The plaintiffs urge that the general fiduciary relationship of the Crown to the Indians, in light of its treaty, statutory and contractual responsibilities has trust-like responsibilities that warrant close examination of any claim to privilege of relevant documents. I am not persuaded at this stage that the general relationship of the parties, aside from relations arising out of the specific variation of a trust in Indian land created by the surrenders of natural resources, and derivative responsibilities

arising from the surrenders, warrants an order to produce documents on a wider scale than that now outlined.

In *Begetikong Anishnabe v. Canada*,[114] Dube J. of the Trial Division of the Federal Court applied the *Samson* case to deny the Band's request for a copy of the legal opinion prepared by the Department of Justice regarding the Band's claim under the Comprehensive Land Claim Policy. He concluded "[t]he special fiduciary relationship between the Crown and the Indians does not favour disclosure in this instance."[115]

Funding

As we have just seen, there is authority for taking into account the fiduciary relationship in considering the question of funding the costs of Aboriginal peoples in litigation. The question of funding has also come up in other contexts. In *Desjarlais v. Canada*,[116] Strayer J. said that the Crown might have a fiduciary duty with regard to additional funds to cover the demand for housing created by the amendments to the *Indian Act* made in 1985 by Bill C-31 which added additional members to bands lists.

In *Cree School Board v. Canada*,[117] Croteau S.C.J. of the Quebec Superior Court considered an application for a declaratory judgment challenging the validity of certain administrative arrangements between Quebec and Canada concerning budgetary approval for funding the Cree School Board. In the course of his judgment, he said that the funding arrangement was subject to the fiduciary obligations of Quebec and Canada and that "the ultimate aim of Canada and Quebec's fiduciary duty towards the Crees must be to ensure that the Cree School Board's mission and constitutional rights are respected."[118]

On the other hand, in *Southeast Child & Family Services v. Canada*,[119] MacInnes J. of the Manitoba Court of Queen's Bench rejected a claim that Canada was in breach of its fiduciary obligation to Aboriginal peoples by terminating funding to First Nation agencies which provided services to children and families resident on reserves in Manitoba.

Disclosure of Band Information

Attempts by bands to prevent the disclosure by the Crown of band information to third parties under access to information legislation on the basis that such disclosure would be a breach of the Crown's fiduciary duty have failed to win acceptance by the courts. This argument was rejected by the Federal Court in *Montana Band of Indians v. Canada*,[120] *Timiskaming Indian Band v. Canada*[121] and *Chippewas of Nawash First Nation v. Canada*.[122] In the latter case, the Federal Court of Appeal commented that "[t]his case is about whether certain information submitted to the government by the appellants should be disclosed under the *Access To Information Act.* The government is acting pursuant to a public law duty. Fiduciary obligations do not arise in these circumstances."[123] On the other hand, in *Buffalo v. Canada*[124] that Court upheld a ruling of MacKay J. of the Trial Division of the Federal Court who rejected the attempt by the Crown to obtain details of how the plaintiff bands had invested funds under their control. The Crown had been sued for its handling of Band monies under its control and sought these details in order to defend the claim and on the issue of damages. MacKay J. held that how the plaintiff bands managed funds under their control was irrelevant.

Duty to Consult and Accommodate[125]

Part of the *Sparrow* test of justification is whether the Aboriginal people have been consulted on the proposed measure that would infringe their Aboriginal or treaty right. However, the duty to consult is also an independent example of a fiduciary obligation. As we have also seen, it had its origins in *Guerin* where the Supreme Court of Canada said the Crown should have consulted with the Musqueam when it was realized that it would not be possible to obtain the lease terms authorized by the Band members.[126] In *Haida Nation v. British Columbia (Minister of Forests)*,[127] Lambert J.A. of the British Columbia Court of Appeal said "[a]ll the principles which must inform the tests for justification of a *prima facie* infringement, such as consultation, accommodation, and minimal impairment, represent examples of the Crown's fiduciary duty to the Indian peoples." He noted in the original reasons for the judgment of the Court:[128]

> The discharge of the obligation to consult, as expressed in *Sparrow, Gladstone,* and *Delgamuukw,* has been framed as an element among the circumstances which would justify a *prima facie* infringement of the aboriginal title or aboriginal rights. As I have said, the consultation must take place before the infringement. But, where there are fiduciary duties of the Crown to Indian peoples it is my opinion that the obligation to consult is a free standing enforceable legal and equitable duty. It is not enough to say that the contemplated infringement is justified by economic forces and will be certain to be justified even if there is no consultation. The duty to consult and seek an accommodation does not arise simply from a *Sparrow* analysis of s. 35. It stands on the broader fiduciary footing of the Crown's relationship with the Indian peoples who are under its protection.

When the case came before the Supreme Court of Canada, Chief Justice McLachlin, speaking for the Court, said that, in view of the facts, the duty to consult and accommodate arose from the principle of the honour of the Crown rather than as a fiduciary duty.[129] This was because Aboriginal rights and title had been asserted but not yet defined or proven. The Aboriginal interest in question was insufficiently specific for the honour of the Crown to mandate that the Crown act in the Aboriginal group's best interest, as a fiduciary, in exercising discretionary control over the subject of the right or title.[130] However, if the Aboriginal right or title has been proven, the above statement by Lambert J.A. would appear to be applicable. Lamer C.J.C. pointed out in *Delgamuukw* that in the case of a proposed infringement of an Aboriginal or treaty right, "there is always a duty of consultation."[131] In *Marshall*, Binnie J. of the Supreme Court of Canada noted the "the special trust relationship includes the right of treaty beneficiaries to be consulted about restrictions on their rights."[132]

The question of who owes fiduciary obligations to Aboriginal peoples is discussed in detail below.[133] Here, it may be noted that the duty to consult and accommodate is owed by both the federal and the provincial Crowns. The federal Crown's duty to consult and accommodate is well established by several cases including the decision of the Supreme Court of Canada in *Delgamuukw*.[134] This duty also extends to the provincial Crown as held by the British Columbia Court of Appeal in *Halfway River*[135] and the Supreme Court of Canada in the *Haida Nation* case.[136] It cannot be delegated to a third party.[137]

A majority of the British Columbia Court of Appeal held in *Haida Nation* that the duty to consult with Aboriginal peoples falls not only on the federal and provincial Crowns but also on third parties who receive a benefit from the Crown in circumstances in which they knew, or should have known, that there was a *prima facie* breach by the Crown of its fiduciary duty including the duty to consult.[138] As discussed below, this part of the judgment was reversed on appeal by the Supreme Court of Canada, which held that third parties are under no duty to consult or accommodate Aboriginal concerns.[139]

It should be noted that Aboriginal people themselves have a duty to participate in the consultation process. In the *Haida Nation* case, Chief Justice McLachlin said:[140]

> At all stages, good faith on both sides is required. . . . As for Aboriginal claimants, they must not frustrate the Crown's reasonable good faith attempts, nor should they take unreasonable positions to thwart government from making decisions or acting in cases where, despite meaningful consultation, agreement is not reached. . . . Mere hard bargaining, however, will not offend an Aboriginal people's right to be consulted.

The complex nature of Aboriginal right and title and of the organizational structure of Aboriginal peoples means that there may be difficult issues in terms of the proper party or parties to be consulted. There may be overlapping claims between different Aboriginal groups as yet unresolved. In *Delgamuukw*,[141] Chief Justice Lamer observed that more than one Aboriginal group may have rights in a particular area. The facts of *Mikisew Cree*[142] provide an example.

In such cases, it will be necessary to consult with all those groups. A related question is who within the Aboriginal group should be consulted. In some First Nations, there is a question whether the chief and council elected under the *Indian Act* have power to negotiate issues affecting traditional territory or whether hereditary leaders of clans or families with claims to the land are the proper persons to do so.

It is not necessary for the Aboriginal group to have obtained a judicial determination of the existence of the Aboriginal or treaty right in order for the duty to consult and accommodate to arise, although in such cases, the duty will not be a fiduciary duty but arises out of the honour of the Crown. As already noted, the Supreme Court of Canada held in the *Haida Nation* case that, prior to such determination, the Aboriginal interest in question is insufficiently specific for a fiduciary duty to arise.[143] This "pre-determination" duty to consult arises "when the Crown has knowledge, real or constructive, of the potential existence of the Aboriginal right or title and contemplates conduct that might adversely affect it."[144]

In order to satisfy the requirement that the consultation be meaningful, it must occur "early in the planning stages of the project" and not after a decision has "essentially been made."[145] In *Mikisew Cree First Nation v. Canada (Minister of Canadian Heritage)*, Hansen J. observed that "[a]t the meetings that were finally held between Parks Canada and Mikisew, a decision had essentially been made, therefore, the meeting could not have been conducted with the genuine intention of allowing Mikisew's concerns to be integrated with the proposal."[146] Consultation must take place before an infringement of an Aboriginal right or title occurs if it is to form part of the justification for the infringement.[147]

In *Mikisew Cree*, Hansen J. found that the existence of a standard public consultation process did not meet the test for Aboriginal consultation, and the failure of the Mikisew Cree to participate in that process did not preclude them from a successful complaint:[148]

> This communication [ie. public notice] was of the same form and substance as the communication being distributed to all interested stakeholders. In my view, taken alone, it does not constitute First Nations consultation as required by s.35(1) of the *Constitution Act, 1982*.
>
> The applicant has asserted interference with a constitutionally protected right. At the very least, Mikisew is entitled to a distinct process if not a more extensive one. This finding would justify Mikisew's failure to adhere to the Minister's timelines for public participation. Mikisew, in my opinion, has not frustrated a "First Nations consultation" process at all. Instead, they have refused to accede to the Minister's expectation that a public consultation process is sufficient to discharge her constitutional duty towards them.

There is a duty on the party owing the duty to consult and accommodate to ensure that the Aboriginal party is fully informed of the measures that may infringe upon their rights. In *R. v. Jack*, the British Columbia Court of Appeal said:[149]

> [T]here was a duty on the DFO to ensure that the Indian Band was provided with full information on the conservation measures and their effect on the Indians and other user groups. The DFO had a duty to fully inform itself of the fishing practices of the aboriginal group and their views of the conservation measures.

In most cases, the cost of consultation to the Aboriginal peoples will itself be an early topic of consultation. In *Halfway River*,[150] the court held that the Aboriginal group cannot impose unreasonable conditions as a precondition to consultation so any request for funding from them must be reasonable. Although there appears to be no case finding a specific legal duty to provide funding, as a practical matter, given the positive duty to fully inform the Aboriginal group of the project, funding might be a reasonable requirement in many cases. Also, if the proponent wishes to proceed in a reasonably expeditious manner, providing funding for the process may be advisable from a business perspective.

The question of the required content of consultation and accommodation has been considered in some of the cases but courts have declined to set down rigid rules. The British Columbia Court of Appeal said in *R. v. Sampson*:[151]

> [N]o useful purpose would be served by attempting to define for general application the meaning of the word consulted as expressed in *Sparrow*. In our view, the determination of whether aboriginal people were consulted will depend on the facts and circumstances of each particular case.

In *Delgamuukw*,[152] Chief Justice Lamer said "the nature and scope of the duty of consultation will vary with the circumstances." Speaking for the Supreme Court of Canada in *Haida Nation*, Chief Justice McLachlin noted that "[i]n general terms . . . it may be asserted that the scope of the duty is proportionate to a preliminary assessment of the strength of the case supporting the existence of the right or title, and to the seriousness of the potentially adverse effect upon the right or title claimed."[153] At one end of the spectrum, the duty to consult and accommodate is a mere duty to "give notice, disclose information, and discuss any issue raised in response to the notice."[154] At the other end of the spectrum, the duty is one of "deep consultation" that "may entail the opportunity to make submissions for consideration, formal participation in the decision-making process, and provision of written reasons to show that Aboriginal concerns were considered and to reveal the impact they had on the decision."[155] The Court suggested that the government may wish to adopt dispute resolution procedures like mediation or adminstrative regimes with impartial decision-makers in complex or difficult cases.[156] Between these two extremes will lie other situations which will have to be approached individually and with flexibility. The Court set out the general principles as follows:[157]

> The controlling question in all situations is what is required to maintain the honour of the Crown and to effect reconciliation between the Crown and the Aboriginal peoples with respect to the interests at stake. Pending settlement, the Crown is bound by its honour to balance societal and Aboriginal interests in making decisions that may affect Aboriginal claims. The Crown may be required to make decisions in the face of disagreement as to the adequacy of its response to Aboriginal concerns. Balance and compromise will then be necessary.

Meaningful consultation may oblige the Crown to make changes to its proposed action based on information obtained through consultation. When the consultation process suggests amendment of Crown policy, this constitutes accommodation.[158]

There is not yet sufficient guidance from the case law as to the required content of appropriate consultation and accommodation. It will require many more decisions before the detailed rules emerge. The Supreme Court noted in *Haida Nation* that its task was "the modest one of establishing a general framework for the duty to consult and accommodate, where indicated, before Aboriginal title or rights claims have been decided. As this framework is applied, courts, in the age-old tradition of the common law, will be called upon to fill in the details of the duty to consult and accommodate."[159] The existing cases turn mostly upon whether consultation and accommodation is required rather than what it must cover. However, we can draw some tentative principles from the case law.

Consultation must "substantially address the First Nations concerns."[160] It must be "meaningful" and "appropriate to the circumstances."[161] The duty to consult requires the government to "allocate the resources in a manner respectful" of the interests of Aboriginal peoples.[162] The duty to consult may include a duty to accommodate as noted above.

The burden of proving meaningful consultations is on the Crown. In *Mikisew Cree*, Hansen J. pointed out that "[t]he Mikisew do not bear the burden of proving that the Crown did not adequately consult with them."[163]

It is important to understand that the duty to consult and accommodate is more than a procedural step. It must address the concerns of the Aboriginal group and respect their interests. These interests may be both cultural and economic. Speaking for the British Columbia Court of Appeal in *Haida I*, Mr. Justice Lambert held that the obligation to consult and accommodate "extended to both the cultural and the economic interests of the Haida people."[164] Accommodation of economic interests may require that compensation be paid to the Aboriginal group. As noted by Chief Justice Lamer in *Delgamuukw*, "[c]ompensation is relevant to the question of justification . . . compensation for breach of fiduciary duty [is] a well-established part of the landscape of aboriginal rights: *Guerin*."[165] It should, therefore, be included as a part of the consultation and accommodation whenever appropriate as recognized by Mr. Justice Lambert in *Haida II*, "[c]ompensation for damage to Haida title or rights should become a subject of negotiations."[166] On the other hand, in some cases, compensation may not be an appropriate or sufficient form of accommodation and the only appropriate remedy to prevent an unjustified form of infringement of Aboriginal right or title may be the termination of the infringement as in *Mikisew Cree* involving the construction of a road which would infringe the right of an Aboriginal group to trap and hunt.[167]

The duty to accommodate may require that the allocation of resources by the government reflect the priority of Aboriginal people to a resource. The Supreme Court of Canada first articulated the doctrine of priority in *Sparrow*[168] and elaborated on it in *Gladstone* by saying that it required:[169]

> . . . that the government demonstrate that, in allocating the resource, it has taken account of the existence of aboriginal right and allocated the resource in a manner respectful of the fact that those rights have priority over the exploitation of the fishery by other users. This right is at once both procedural and substantive; at the stage of justification the government must demonstrate both the process by which it allocated the resource and the actual allocation of the resource which results from that process reflect the prior interest of aboriginal rights holders in the fishery.

The Court held in *Gladstone* that, where the Aboriginal right is one without an internal limitation, the government does not need to give exclusivity to the right, but must take into account the existence and importance of such rights. Further, the Court noted the requirements of consultation and compensation referred to in *Sparrow*, and then expanded upon the list of factors to be considered in the justification analysis. Prime among these included whether the government's objectives in enacting a particular regulatory scheme reflect the need to take into account the priority of Aboriginal rights holders.

In *Delgamuukw*, Chief Justice Lamer gave some of the factors which are relevant to determining whether there has been sufficient accommodation:[170]

- whether the government has accommodated the exercise of the Aboriginal right to participate in the industry through, for example, reduced fees;

- whether the government's objective in enacting a particular regulatory scheme reflects the need to take into account the priority of Aboriginal rights holders;

- the extent of the participation in the industry of Aboriginal rights holders relative to their percentage of the population;

- how the government has accommodated different Aboriginal rights in a particular industry (for example, in the case of fishing, food fishing versus commercial fishing);

- how important the industry is to the economic and material well-being of the Aboriginal group in question;

- the criteria taken into account by the government in, for example, allocating commercial licences amongst different users.

Duty to Negotiate

There has been a conflict in the cases on whether the fiduciary relationship imposes a duty on governments to negotiate with Aboriginal peoples on matters that may infringe their Aboriginal or treaty rights. In *Ardoch Algonquin First Nation v. Ontario*,[171] an Aboriginal person was charged with a hunting offence. The trial judge had ordered the provincial government to negotiate with the Aboriginal people of the Province on new enforcement measures. The Ontario Court of Appeal allowed the Crown's appeal holding "there is no positive duty on the government to negotiate with aboriginal communities for the purpose of reaching agreement upon a set of game and fish enforcement measures."[172]

On the other hand, Richard A.C.J. of the Trial Division of the Federal Court held in *Nunavik Inuit v. Canada*[173] that the federal government was obligated to negotiate with the Nunavik Inuit regarding the establishment of a national park in their traditional territory. He also stated "[a]ny negotiations should also include other Aboriginal nations which have a stake in the territory claimed. The Crown is under a moral, if not a legal, duty to enter into and conduct those negotiations in good faith."[174] In the case of *Gitanyow First Nation v. Canada*,[175] the First Nation successfully applied for a declaration that both the federal and British Columbia governments were obliged to negotiate a treaty in good faith. Williamson J. of the British Columbia Supreme Court said he agreed with the importation by Richard A.C.J. in the *Nunavik Inuit* case of "the honour of the Crown and its fiduciary obligation to act in good faith into the treaty negotiation process."[176] Entering into the treaty process did not displace the fiduciary relationship between the Crown and Aboriginal peoples.

The decision of the Supreme Court of Canada in the *Haida Nation* case appears to have settled the issue in favour of a duty to negotiate. The Court held that, where treaties remain to be concluded, the honour of the Crown requires negotiations leading to a just settlement of Aboriginal claims, and that Aboriginal rights be determined, recognized, and respected. It continued, "[t]his, in turn, requires the Crown, acting honourably, to participate in processes of negotiation."[177]

The Exercise of Governmental Powers Generally

In an early decision, Mr. Justice Strayer of the Trial Division of the Federal Court suggested, *obiter*, that there might be a duty to exercise governmental powers where it would be reasonable and lawful for the government to do so in order to carry out a specific fiduciary obligation to a band. In *Bruno v. Canada*, in which a band claimed that the Crown was under a duty to pass regulations under the *Indian Oil and Gas Regulations* which would have increased royalty revenue to the band, Strayer J. commented:[178]

> One can deduce from the protective stance taken by the Crown ever since the *Royal Proclamation 1763* that the Crown kept to itself the exclusive right to acquire and dispose of Indian title because it had taken the unique power and responsibility to act as an appropriate protector of the interests of the people who inhabited this land before the arrival of the Europeans. It is wholly consistent with this view that the Crown should exercise these governmental powers which only it has, where this may be reasonably and lawfully done to perform adequately the specific fiduciary obligation it owes to a given band whose Indian title has been surrendered to the Crown.

However, since breach of fiduciary duty was not put to the Court in the stated case before him, it was not open to determination.

Binnie J. of the Supreme Court of Canada indicated, in the *Wewaykum* decision,[179] that there are limits to the extent to which a fiduciary duty will be imposed on the Crown in exercising governmental powers. Giving the judgment of the Court, he referred to the positive aspects of the fiduciary relationship and continued:

> [81] But there are limits. The appellants seemed at times to invoke the "fiduciary duty" as a source of plenary Crown liability covering all aspects of the Crown-Indian band relationship. This overshoots the mark. The fiduciary duty imposed on the Crown does not exist at large but in relation to specific Indian interests. In this case we are dealing with land, which has generally played a central role in aboriginal economies and cultures. Land was also the subject matter of *Ross River* ("the lands occupied by the Band"), *Blueberry River* and *Guerin* (disposition of existing reserves). Fiduciary protection accorded to Crown dealings with aboriginal interests

in land (including reserve creation) has not to date been recognized by this Court in relation to Indian interests other than land outside the framework of s.35 (1) of the *Constitution Act, 1982.*

[82] Since *Guerin*, Canadian courts have experienced a flood of "fiduciary duty" claims by Indian bands across a whole spectrum of possible complaints, for example:

(i) to structure elections (*Batchewana Indian Band (Non-resident members) v. Batchewana Indian Band*, [1997] 1 F.C. 689 (C.A.) at para. 60; subsequently dealt with in this Court on other grounds);

(ii) to require the provision of social services (*Southeast Child & Family Services v. Canada (Attorney General)*, [1997] 9 W.W.R. 236 (Man. Q.B.);

(iii) to rewrite negotiated provisions (*B.C. Native Women's Society v. Canada*, [2000] 1 F.C. 304 (T.D.));

(iv) to cover moving expenses (*Paul v. Kingsclear Indian Band* (1997), 137 F.T.R. 275); *Mentuck v. Canada*, [1986] 3 F.C. 249 (T.D.); *Deer v. Mohawk Council of Kahnawake*, [1991] 2 F.C. 18 (T.D.));

(v) to suppress public access to information about band affairs (*Chippeywas of the Nawash First Nation v. Canada (Minister of Indian and Northern Affairs)* (1996), 116 F.T.R. 37 aff'd (1999), 251 N.R. 220; *Montana Band of Indians v. Canada (Minister of Indian and Northern Affairs)*, [1989] 1 F.C. 143 (T.D.); *Timiskaming Indian Band v. Canada (Minister of Indian and Northern Affairs)*, (1997), 132 F.T.R. 106);

(vi) to require legal aid funding (*Ominayak v. Canada (Minister of Indian Affairs and Northern Development)*, [1987] 3 F.C. 174 (T.D.));

(vii) to compel registration of individuals under the *Indian Act* (rejected in *Tuplin v. Canada (Indian and Northern Affairs)*, (2001), 207 Nfld. & P.E.I. R. 292 (P.E.I.T.D.));

(viii) to invalidate a consent signed by an Indian mother to the adoption of her child (rejected in *G. (A.P.) v. A. (K.H.)*, (1994), 120 D.L.R. (4th) 511 (Alta. Q.B.)).

[83] I offer no comment about the correctness of the disposition of these particular cases on the facts, none of which are before us for decision, but I think it desirable for the Court to affirm the principle, already mentioned, that not all obligations existing between the parties to a fiduciary relationship are themselves fiduciary in nature (*Lac Minerals, supra*, at p.597), and that this principle applies to the relationship between the Crown and aboriginal peoples. It is necessary, then, to focus on the particular obligation or interest that is the subject matter of the particular dispute and whether or not the Crown has assumed discretionary control in relation thereto sufficient to ground a fiduciary obligation.

He later said that the creation of a fiduciary relationship depends "on identification of a cognizable Indian interest, and the Crown's undertaking of discretionary control in relation thereto in a way that invokes responsibility 'in the nature of a private law duty'."[180] He did not specify the "cognizable Indian interests" although, as we have seen,[181] he had earlier indicated that, to date, the Supreme Court of Canada has only recognized such interests in the case of land and those interests recognized and affirmed in section 35(1) of the *Constitution Act, 1982*, that is to say, existing Aboriginal and treaty rights.

The practical effect of the decision in *Wewaykum* appears to be the recognition of fiduciary obligations with respect to land and other interests to which Aboriginal peoples have Aboriginal or treaty rights but to exclude them from governmental programs for Aboriginal peoples not based on such rights. These exclusions may cover elections, social services, legal aid funding, child welfare, and registration under the *Indian Act*. It will be necessary to determine on a case by case basis if an Aboriginal or treaty right to the particular government program existed in the circumstances.

Who Has a Fiduciary Relationship with Aboriginal Peoples?

The question of who has a fiduciary relationship with Aboriginal peoples has been considered by the courts in a number of cases. The decision of the Supreme Court of Canada in *Guerin* clearly established that the federal Crown has such a relationship.[182] It now seems equally clear that the provincial Crown has such a relationship.[183] In the *Haida Nation* case, the Supreme Court of Canada rejected the argument of the Province of British Columbia that any duty to consult or accommodate rests solely with the federal government, and there seems little reason to attempt to distinguish that duty from other fiduciary duties.[184]

Some doubt regarding the scope of the fiduciary duties owed by provincial governments to Aboriginal peoples was expressed by Laskin J.A. speaking for the Ontario Court of Appeal in the *Bear Island* case:[185]

> [34] The appellants claim an interest in the disputed lands as a remedy for Ontario's breach of fiduciary duty. I am doubtful whether the provincial Crown owes fiduciary duties to Aboriginal people that, on breach, would allow for the transfer of land. The fiduciary duty of the Crown to Aboriginal people is fundamentally a duty of the federal Crown. It is the federal government that has legislative responsibility for Indians and lands reserved for Indians under s.91(24) of the *Constitution Act 1867*. As the Supreme Court said in *Mitchell v. Peguis Indian Band*: "The provincial Crown bears no responsibility to provide for the welfare and protection of native peoples."

> [35] In *Perry v. Ontario*, this court recognized that the province may have a fiduciary duty to Aboriginal peoples who have an Aboriginal or treaty right to hunt and fish and whose exercise of that right is affected by a provincial regulation. In such a case, the province's duty is "a restraint against regulations improperly af-

fecting aboriginal [or treaty] rights." Breach of the duty may render the provincial regulation unenforceable against Aboriginal people exercising these rights. But the fiduciary duty owed by the provincial Crown is a "shield and not a sword". Ordinarily, the affirmative obligation to provide for the welfare of Aboriginal peoples and to implement the terms of treaties belongs to the federal Crown. Nonetheless, for the purposes of this appeal, I will assume, without deciding, that Ontario has a fiduciary obligation to the appellants and that a breach of that obligation may be remedied by the grant of an interest in land.

However, it must be noted that, when the case had earlier came before the Supreme Court of Canada, the Court observed in a brief judgment that "[i]t is conceded that the Crown [an apparent reference to the provincial Crown in the context of the case] has failed to comply with some of its obligations under this agreement, and thereby breached its fiduciary obligations to the Indians. These matters currently form the subject of negotiations between the parties."[186] The comments of Laskin J.A. overlook this statement.

The fiduciary nature of the relationship between provincial governments and Aboriginal peoples is now established. In *Badger*,[187] the Supreme Court of Canada applied the *Sparrow*[188] requirement to justify an infringement of an Aboriginal right (which is based on the existence of the Crown's fiduciary relationship) to the infringement of treaty rights by the Alberta government. The British Columbia Court of Appeal upheld the decision of the chambers judge in *Halfway River First Nation v. British Columbia*[189] to quash a cutting permit on the basis that the infringement of a treaty right to hunt had not been justified because the provincial Ministry of Forests had breached its fiduciary obligation to engage in adequate consultation with the First Nation. A similar decision was reached by a majority of that court in *Taku River Tlingit First Nation v. British Columbia (Project Assessment Director)* involving an approval given under the provincial *Environmental Assessment Act*, although this decision was reversed by the Supreme Court of Canada on the facts.[190]

In *Gitanyow First Nation v. Canada*,[191] Williamson J. of the British Columbia Supreme Court expressly rejected the argument of the province of British Columbia that only the federal Crown owed a fiduciary obligation to Aboriginal people:[192]

> In 1867, the powers, duties and responsibilities of the Crown pre-Confederation were enumerated and assigned to either the Crown in Right of Canada and or the Crown in Right of the Provinces. But, as can be seen above, the fiduciary obligation of the Crown which characterized its relationship with Aboriginal peoples has continued after 1867 as before. As a result, in its dealings with native peoples within its jurisdictional powers, the Crown in Right of British Columbia must act in light of that duty even as its predecessor, the Crown of colonial times, should have done. . . .
>
> I conclude that the duty to negotiate in good faith, founded upon the fiduciary

relationship between Aboriginal people and the Crown, apples equally to the Crown in Right of Canada and the Crown in Right of British Columbia.

The rationale for recognizing the fiduciary nature of the relationship between the provincial Crown and Aboriginal peoples is to be found in the judgment of Chief Justice Dickson in *Mitchell v. Peguis Indian Band* in which he said:[193]

> On its facts, *Guerin* only dealt with the obligation of the *federal* Crown arising upon the surrender land by Indians and it is true that, since 1867, the Crown's role has been played, as a matter of the federal division of powers, by Her Majesty in right of Canada, with the *Indian Act* representing a confirmation of the Crown's historic responsibility for the welfare and interests of these peoples. However, the Indians' relationship with the Crown or Sovereign has never depended on the particular representatives of the Crown involved. From the aboriginal perspective, any federal-provincial divisions that the Crown has imposed upon itself are internal to itself and do not alter the basic structure of Sovereign-Indian relations. This is not to suggest that aboriginal peoples are outside of the Crown, nor does it call into question the divisions of jurisdiction in relation to aboriginal peoples in federal Canada.

In my view, the following statements by Mr. Justice Lambert in the *Haida I*[194] case accurately reflect the current state of the law:

> [23] [T]he authorities do establish, as a matter of law, that the federal Crown stands in a fiduciary relationship with all Aboriginal peoples of Canada, *and the provincial Crown stands in a similar relationship to the Aboriginal peoples of British Columbia.*

> [34] The trust-like relationship is now usually expressed as fiduciary duty *owed by both the federal and Provincial Crown* to the aboriginal people. . . .

It is not entirely clear, however, if all government departments have a fiduciary relationship with Aboriginal people. In *Blueberry River*,[195] the plaintiff bands had argued that the fiduciary obligation owed by the Crown followed the transfer of land from the Department of Indian Affairs ("DIA") to the Director of Veterans Land Act ("DVLA"). Madam Justice McLachlin rejected this argument on the facts. She found that the fiduciary obligation did not continue because it would have been "problematic from a practical point of view."[196] Further, the two departments operated at arm's length and the Director of Veterans Land Act had no knowledge of obligations owed by the Department of Indian Affairs:

> [110] . . . the Bands argue that the 1948 transfer to the DVLA was not a transfer at all, but merely an administrative allocation within the bosom of the unified Crown. Thus the Crown's fiduciary duty continued, although it was transferred for administrative purposes to the DVLA after 1948. Consequently, the cause of action did not arise until the land was alienated from the DVLA to the veterans.

> [111] I cannot accept this argument. Although the transfer was from one Crown

entity to another, it remained a transfer and an alienation of title. First, the transfer converted the Band's interest from a property interest into a sum of money, suggesting alienation. Second, the continuing fiduciary duty proposed for the DVLA is problematic from a practical point of view. Any duty would have applied, at least in theory, both to the mineral rights and the surface rights. Each sale to a veteran would have required the DVLA to consider not only those matters he was entitled to consider under his Act, but sometimes conflicting matters under the *Indian Act*. This would have made the sale in 1948 pointless from the DVLA's point of view and have rendered it impossible to administer. Moreover, it is not clear that the DVLA had any knowledge of the fiduciary obligations which bound the DIA. In fact, the DVLA and the DIA acted at arm's length throughout, as was appropriate given the different interests they represented and the different mandates of their statutes.

Giving the majority opinion of the Court, Gonthier J. did not consider this issue.

In my view, McLachlin J.'s analysis in *Blueberry River* of the fiduciary obligations of the DVLA to the bands in question is not convincing. The fiduciary relationship, based as it is on the historical relationship between the Crown and Aboriginal peoples,[197] is between the unified Crown and the Aboriginal peoples and not merely the department that has primary responsibility for Indian affairs at any given time. As noted in the statement by Chief Justice Dickson in *Mitchell v. Peguis Indian Band* quoted above,[198] the Indians' relationship with the Crown has never depended on the particular representative of the Crown involved and, from an Aboriginal perspective, any internal divisions that the Crown has imposed upon itself do not alter the basic structure of Crown–Indian relations. Also, the ignorance of the DVLA of its fiduciary obligations is surely no basis for a finding that no such obligations exist. If this was so, the Crown would have succeeded in *Guerin* on the basis of its denial of the existence of such an obligation.

Other cases have held that the fiduciary obligation is not restricted to the Department of Indian Affairs and may be owed by other government departments. In *Kruger*, Heald J. of the Federal Court of Appeal said that it was no defence for the Crown to say that the Department of Transport had competing interests with those of the Department of Indian Affairs: "[T]he federal Crown cannot default on its fiduciary obligations to the Indians through a plea of competing considerations by different departments of government."[199] Likewise, in *Union of Nova Scotia Indians v. Canada*,[200] MacKay J. of the Trial Division of the Federal Court of Canada found a breach of fiduciary duty by reason of the failure by the Departments of Fisheries and Oceans and of the Environment to consider the impact on Aboriginal fishing rights of a proposal to dredge the sea bottom. He noted:

[20] The Crown's fiduciary duty to the applicants as representing Aboriginal people

continued throughout the assessment process and thereafter. It may be that within the public service, at least on this occasion, the perception was that the sole responsibility for discharge of that duty was that of [the Department of Indian Affairs]. . . . There simply was no reference by the responsible authorities here involved, acting on behalf of the Ministries of Fisheries and Oceans and of Environment, to the fiduciary duty owed by Her Majesty's government to the Mi'kmaq Aboriginal people. . . .

[21] I am persuaded that by their failure to consider the fiduciary duty here owed to the applicants, when the decision was made on behalf of the Ministers, those acting on behalf of the Ministers did breach that duty.

Judicial and quasi-judicial bodies, however, do not owe a fiduciary obligation to Aboriginal peoples. This was made clear by the Supreme Court of Canada in *Quebec (Attorney-General) v. Canada (National Energy Board)*[201] in which the Grand Council of the Crees of Quebec brought an appeal against the decision of the National Energy Board to grant Hydro Quebec a licence for the export of electrical power. One of the arguments made was that the Board owed them a fiduciary duty in considering applications for such licences since the Board was an agent of government established by Parliament. In rejecting this argument on behalf of the Court, Iacobucci J. said:[202]

The courts must be careful not to compromise the independence of *quasi*-judicial tribunals and decision-making agencies by imposing upon them fiduciary obligations which require that their decisions be made in accordance with a fiduciary duty. . . . Therefore, I conclude that the fiduciary relationship between the Crown and the appellants does not impose a duty on the Board to make its decisions in the best interests of the appellants, or to change its hearing process so as to impose superadded requirements of disclosure. When the duty is defined in this manner, such tribunals no more owe this sort of fiduciary duty than do the courts. Consequently, no such duty existed in relation to the decision-making function of the Board.

Whether Crown agencies other than quasi-judicial bodies may owe a fiduciary obligation to Aboriginal peoples has yet to be decided. In *Gitanmaax Indian Band v. British Columbia Hydro and Power Authority*,[203] Millward J. of the British Columbia Supreme Court rejected an argument that the Hydro Authority owed such an obligation on the basis that "although the defendant is an emanation of the Crown, it is not the Crown but a separate entity."[204]

A potentially far-reaching decision of the British Columbia Court of Appeal in 2002 held that non-Crown parties may have a fiduciary duty towards Aboriginal peoples if they knowingly receive the benefit of a breach by the Crown of its fiduciary duty or wish to justify an infringement of Aboriginal rights or title. In *Haida Nation v. British Columbia (Minister of Forests) and Weyerhaeuser*,[205] the provincial government had granted a tree farm licence to a forest company which was subsequently transferred to Weyerhaeuser

Company Ltd and renewed. The Haida claimed Aboriginal title to the area covered by the licence and the chambers judge found that they had a good *prima facie* case of title but he held there was no legal duty to consult on the part of the Province. On appeal, the British Columbia Court of Appeal held, in a unanimous decision, that the Province had breached its fiduciary obligation to consult with the Haida and accommodate their interests. The Court made a declaration that both the Province and Weyerhaeuser were under a duty to consult and accommodate those interests.[206] Unfortunately, the original reasons did not explain the basis on which the declaration was made against Weyerhaeuser. The company sought clarification and also opposed the declaration against them on procedural grounds.

After a further hearing, one judge in the Court of Appeal (Low J.A.) reversed his concurrence in the original reasons on procedural grounds. He stated that he thought the Court had "erred in extending that duty [to consult and accommodate] to Weyerhaeuser. *I do not say that the duty on Weyerhaeuser does not exist.* I simply say that the issue is not properly before the court."[207] Chief Justice Finch confirmed the declaration against Weyerhaeuser with a minor modification as to the period covered. In his view, it was necessary to extend the duty to consult and accommodate to Weyerhaeuser in order to grant an effective remedy to the Haida Nation. Without such an extension, Weyerhaeuser would have continued to hold, unimpaired, the exclusive right to harvest timber from the area specified in the licence which covers one-quarter of the Haida territory of Haida Gwaii. He concluded:[208]

> [118] A declaration of the Crown's duty to consult, without more, would therefore have been a completely hollow or illusory remedy. Weyerhaeuser might choose to co-operate in the consultation or not. If it refused to co-operate, the Crown would be unable to make any effective accommodation. The Crown's duty of consultation and accommodation would be frustrated.

> [123] In my view, Weyerhaeuser's duty to consult arose from the particular circumstances of this case. Those circumstances in essence are the issuance by the Minister of Forests of a tree farm licence in breach of the Crown's duty to consult, and receipt by Weyerhaeuser of a licence which therefore suffered a legal defect, which cannot be remedied without its participation. In other words, Weyerhaeuser's duty to consult existed at least when it received replacement TFL 39 in 2000, and when this Court declared that the licence was issued by the Minister of Forests in breach of the Crown's duty to consult. Upon that finding, Weyerhaeuser became possessed of a licence with a fundamental legal defect. It is a defect that absent a declaration of invalidity, can only be remedied by the participation of Weyerhaeuser and the Crown in consultation with the Haida.

Mr. Justice Lambert gave the most detailed reasons to explain his decision to extend the fiduciary duty to consult and accommodate to Weyerhaeuser.

He said that Weyerhaeuser's duty of consultation and accommodation came from three sources:[209]

1.   the provisions of the *Forest Act* and the tree farm licence in question imposed such a duty;

2.   Weyerhaeuser's "knowing receipt" of the licence in circumstances where the Crown and Weyerhaeuser "both knew, or, on reasonable and necessary inquiry, could, and should have known, that the Crown was in breach of its fiduciary duty to the Haida people in granting, renewing and transferring T.F.L. 39 in 1999 and 2000 without consulting the Haida people"[210]; and

3.   Weyerhaeuser's opportunity to put up a defence of justification to any claim against it for violation of Aboriginal title or Aboriginal rights.

The first source was dependent on the particular wording of the legislation and licence in question and will not be further discussed but the other two sources are of more general relevance.

The "knowing receipt" source of the duty was based on the principle that "the title, if any, that is passed to the third party in breach of the fiduciary duty, is clogged by the fiduciary's breach of duty, so that the third party is itself a constructive trustee and, in that capacity, owes a trust or fiduciary duty to the original beneficiary of the original fiduciary obligation."[211] Applying that principle to the facts before him, Mr. Justice Lambert concluded:

> [71] In my opinion, MacMillan Bloedel [the predecessor licence holder] and Weyerhaeuser must have been aware of the provincial Crown's fiduciary duty to the Haida people, including a duty to consult the Haida people before renewing or transferring T.F.L. 39, and must have been aware of the strong *prima facie* case of the Haida people to aboriginal title and aboriginal rights in at least a significant part of the land area of T.F.L. 39, and must have been aware, or at least, could have become aware on reasonable and necessary inquiry, of the Crown's breach of its fiduciary duty to the Haida people, particularly in the Crown's failure to consult the Haida people and to seek reasonable accommodations with them in the renewal and transfer of T.F.L. 39.

> [72] In those circumstances, the principles of "knowing receipt" apply and Weyerhaeuser, in taking title to T.F.L. 39 must be regarded as a constructive trustee, owing a third party fiduciary duty to the Haida people, a duty which was breached immediately, as it was acquired, at the time of the renewal and transfer of T.F.L. 39, and a fiduciary duty which continues throughout the period that Weyerhaeuser is a licensee of T.F.L. 39 and which applies to Weyerhaeuser's management, administration, and operation of T.F.L. 39.

> [73] . . . The principles of "knowing receipt" giving rise to a constructive trust

with fiduciary obligations on the third party that are similar to the obligations of the fiduciary who transfers the title, including the obligations of consultation and accommodation in dealing with T.F.L. 39, meet this case exactly.

The third source of the duty was based on the *Sparrow* justification test for an infringement of Aboriginal rights or title.[212] Mr. Justice Lambert expressed some doubt whether either the Province or a third party could invoke the defence of justification for such an infringement.[213] In the case of a third party, he said:

> [80] There is a further question of whether the law in relation to justification for an infringement can be invoked by a party other than the provincial Crown. No doubt such a third party would wish the law of justification for an infringement to be available to safeguard the activities of that third party since, if that law were not available, the third party would be guilty of violating the aboriginal title or rights in question and would be liable for compensatory damages and perhaps aggravated and punitive damages as well.

He proceeded to deal with the question of justification for an infringement on the assumption that a third party like Weyerhaeuser would be entitled to justify an infringement. To do so, it would have to ensure that the infringements in which it was participating with the Crown could be justified. It would also have to ensure that any infringements for which it alone was responsible could be justified.

Weyerhaeuser appealed the finding that it owed a duty of consultation and accommodation to the Supreme Court of Canada and was successful.[214] As we have seen, that Court found that the Crown's duty to consult and possibly accommodate was based on the honour of the Crown rather than a fiduciary obligation in cases where the Aboriginal interest or title had yet to be determined.[215] Therefore, strictly speaking, the decision does not cover situations in which a third party takes an interest from the Crown in breach of the Crown's fiduciary duty to Aboriginal peoples. However, the language used by the Court strongly suggests that third parties will not be held liable even in such situations.

Chief Justice McLachlin gave the decision for the Court.[216] First, she rejected the suggestion of Lambert J.A. that a third party's obligation to consult Aboriginal peoples may arise from the ability of the third party to rely on justification as a defence for infringement of the Aboriginal right or title.[217] Since the Court had found that the duty to consult and accommodate arose from the honour of the Crown, this theory provided no support for an obligation on third parties to consult or accommodate. The Crown alone remains legally responsible for the consequences of its actions and interactions with third parties that affect Aboriginal interests. She commented:[218]

> The Crown may delegate procedural aspects of consultation to industry proponents seeking a particular development. . . . However, the ultimate legal responsibility for consultation and accommodation rests with the Crown. The honour of the Crown cannot be delegated.

She then turned to the alternative suggestion by Lambert J.A. that third parties might have a duty to consult and accommodate on the basis of the trust law doctrine of "knowing receipt."[219] In answer to this suggestion, she referred to her earlier ruling that the duty to consult in this case was not based on a fiduciary duty because there was no particular cognizable Aboriginal interest.[220] Furthermore, in *Guerin*, the Court had made it clear that the "trust-like" relationship between the Crown and Aboriginal peoples is not a true "trust."[221] She then asserted, "[t]here is no reason to graft the doctrine of knowing receipt onto the special relationship between the Crown and Aboriginal peoples."[222] She also thought it was questionable whether businesses acting on licence from the Crown could be analogized to persons who knowingly turn trust funds to their own ends. Finally, she rejected the suggestion of Chief Justice Finch that it was necessary to hold third parties to a duty to consult and accommodate in order to provide an effective remedy. In her view, the government had sufficient powers to achieve meaningful consultation and accommodation.

It is now well established that the chief and members of the council of a band are fiduciaries for the band members.[223] In the words of Skipp J. of the British Columbia Supreme Court in *Gilbert v. Abby*,[224] "[t]here can be no question that a duly-elected chief as well as the members of a band council are fiduciaries as far as all other members of the band are concerned. The chief [and a member of a band council] upon being elected, undertakes to act in the interests of the members of the band." Therefore, they must not allow their interests to conflict with their duties to the band members. Accordingly, they should disclose any conflict and not participate in the decision making process in such situations.[225] A failure to do so will render the decision invalid and require the turning over of any benefit gained to the band.[226]

In *Gilbert v. Abby*, a chief had obtained payment from the band for her student loan, private school fees for her sons, and for her housing costs in breach of her fiduciary obligations to the band. The Court ordered her to repay the money. Likewise, in *Silver v. Ned and Kelly*,[227] a former chief and a member of council were found liable to the band for breach of fiduciary duty when they obtained in their own names a permit to sell tobacco on the reserve in circumstances in which they should have allowed the band to benefit from the opportunity. They were ordered to pay damages to the band equivalent to the net profits which they had earned.

On the other hand, in *Assu v. Chickite*,[228] Romilly J. of the British Columbia Supreme Court held that there was no breach of fiduciary duty when the common-law spouse of a member of council was appointed as band manager. The councillor did not vote on the motion appointing the band manager or fixing her salary. In reaching his decision, the judge noted that, given the small size of the band and the close relationships among band members, it would be unrealistic to apply too rigorous a test of conflict.

Chamberlist J. of the same Court held in *Klahoose First Nation v. Cortes Ecoforestry Society*[229] that a council had a fiduciary duty to consult with band members on proposed amendments to a woodlot management licence. The consultative approach was so integral to the woodlot operation that any significant change to its development required consultation with members.

In the case of distributions of band funds to members, the council is likely to be held to be trustees of the funds for the members. Accordingly, they must deal fairly and equally with all members. In *Barry v. Garden River Band of Ojibways*,[230] the Ontario Court of Appeal held that a band council could not discriminate against women who had regained their band membership under changes made to the *Indian Act* in 1985 by reducing their distribution payments by the amounts that they had received when they left the band. Other members did not have their distribution payments reduced by the amounts which they owed to the band. The Court also held that the band council had fixed the distribution payment date in a manner that unlawfully discriminated against the children of these women. The band council was under a duty to make reasonable efforts to ensure that the children received payment. *Moon (Guardian Ad Litem For) v. Campbell River Indian Band*[231] was a somewhat similar case in which the band council was also held to be a trustee of funds being held for distribution to members and could not discriminate against the adopted children of a band member with respect to the distribution. In order to determine the applicable limitation period, it became necessary to decide if "a trust relationship or merely a fiduciary duty" existed.[232] Reed J. of the Trial Division of the Federal Court held, in a decision affirmed by the Federal Court of Appeal, that the funds were specific, identifiable trust property and the band council was a trustee and so applied the limitation period for breach of trust which is ten years in British Columbia rather than the period for breach of fiduciary duty which is six years.

To Whom Is the Duty Owed?

Most of the cases on the fiduciary duty to Aboriginal peoples have involved Indian bands or first nations recognized under the *Indian Act*. Clearly, these groups have a fiduciary relationship with the Crown. *Guerin*[233] was such a case. However, the term "aboriginal peoples of Canada" as defined in section 35(2) of the *Constitution Act, 1982* "includes the Indian, Inuit, and Metis peoples of Canada" and case law has applied the fiduciary relationship to both the Inuit and the Métis. In *Nunavik Inuit v. Canada*,[234] Richard A.C.J. of the Trial Division of the Federal Court of Canada granted declaratory relief to the Nunavik Inuit to require the federal Crown to negotiate with them regarding the establishment of a national park. *R. v. McPherson*[235] and *R. v. Powley*[236] were examples of the recognition of a fiduciary relationship between Métis people and the Crown. In the latter case, the Ontario Court of Appeal referred to "the Crown's trust-like relationship with the Metis people"[237] and applied the *Sparrow* test of justification[238] to an infringement of Métis hunting rights. This decision was upheld by the Supreme Court of Canada.[239]

A number of cases have considered the possible application of the fiduciary relationship to individual Indian people but the question of whether an individual can successfully bring such an action has not been decided. In *Mintuck v. The Queen*,[240] a claim by a band member against the Crown for allegedly failing to honour an arrangement to assist him to move off a reserve and compensate him for lost improvements was rejected on the facts. In other cases, courts have rejected applications by defendants to strike out claims brought by individuals without allowing them to go to trial on the grounds that they disclose no valid legal claim.[241] These rejections do not indicate that the claims that the claims will be successful at trial but only that the plaintiff is entitled to have his or her day in court. However in one such case, *Derrickson v. Canada*,[242] Teitelbaum J. commented:

[44] . . . [T]he question as to whether the Crown's fiduciary duty applies only to aboriginal collectivities or to native individuals is yet to be determined. As stated by John Hurley ((1985) McGill Law Journal p. 595), in principle, no reasons appear why native individuals should not be able to invoke the Crown's fiduciary duty.

Where the property of an individual Indian is held by the Minister of Indian Affairs on his or her behalf as in the case of a mentally incompetent Indian or an infant Indian under sections 51 and 52 of the *Indian Act*,[243] there would seem to be no valid objection to an action for breach of fiduciary obligation on behalf of that individual. If, however, the alleged breach of fiduciary duty relates to dealings with reserve lands which were or are held for the collective benefit of all band members, the proper plaintiff is the band not individual band members.[244] Further, a band cannot validly assign its Aboriginal rights to a corporation, even one which it controls, and the Crown owes no fiduciary obligation to the corporation to justify an alleged infringement of those rights.[245]

"Personal inspection of Musqueam Indian Reserve by city council is urged by Alderman Bill Ruthie in effort to improve degrading conditions there. Mrs. Esther Sparrow lives in four ground floor rooms of a two-storey house with her husband, an unemployed fisherman, and seven children." (Courtesy *Vancouver Sun,* Wednesday, Feb. 21, 1962, p. 29. Caption quotes text from both the original caption and news article.)

Chapter 6

Fiduciary Law in Canada Since *Guerin*

In *Guerin*,[1] fiduciary obligations owed by the Crown to Aboriginal peoples were discussed in the context of the general law applying to fiduciaries.[2] Subsequent cases have continued to do so while noting that the relationship between the Crown and Aboriginal peoples is unique, or *sui generis*. Therefore, in order to understand the law relating to fiduciary obligations owed to Aboriginal peoples, it is necessary to have an understanding of general fiduciary law. The converse is also true. Dickson J. restated the law in *Guerin* on what gives rise to a fiduciary relationship in a manner that has significantly influenced not only the law as it relates to Aboriginal peoples but the development of fiduciary law outside of the Aboriginal context. Professor Flannigan, for example, has stated that *Guerin* "has had a profound and problematic significance in the Canadian jurisprudence."[3] This restatement set the Canadian law on fiduciary obligations on a course that is significantly different from that of other Commonwealth jurisdictions and has been controversial. In my view, this development is to be commended and offers the promise of achieving greater justice for all Canadians, although it must be said that the law is still in its infancy and requires further development.

The Development of the Fiduciary Principle in Canada

Guerin has been key to the recent and rapid development of fiduciary law in Canada. Prior to the *Guerin* case, fiduciary law in Canada closely followed the English law. It was quite restrictive and largely confined fiduciary obligations to traditional categories such as trustee, director, partner, and agent. Professor Flannigan has observed that, "[i]n the three decades preceding the *Guerin* decision, most of the decisions of the Supreme Court of Canada employed a restrictive approach to imposing liability."[4] The decision introduced a far more expansive concept of the "fiduciary principle" and took the law into new, uncharted, and uniquely Canadian waters. Ten years after it was decided, its influence was recognised by La Forest J. of the Supreme Court of Canada in his decision in *Hodgkinson v. Simms*:[5]

> [O]ver the past ten years or so this Court has had occasion to consider and enforce fiduciary obligations in a wide variety of contexts, and this has led to the development of a "fiduciary principle" which can be defined and applied with some measure of precision. One may begin with the following words of Dickson J. (as he then was) in *Guerin v. The Queen*, [1984] 2 S.C.R. 335, at p. 384:
>
> > [W]here by statute, agreement, or perhaps by unilateral undertaking, one party has an obligation to act for the benefit of another, and that obligation carries with it a discretionary power, the party thus empowered becomes a fiduciary. . . .
> >
> > It is sometimes said that the nature of fiduciary relationships is both established and exhausted by the standard categories of agent, trustee, partner, director and the like. I do not agree. It is the nature of the relationship, not the specific category of actor involved that gives rise to fiduciary duty. The categories of fiduciary, like those of negligence, should not be considered closed.

In *Authorson v. Canada*, the Ontario Court of Appeal said that, over the years since *Guerin*, the Supreme Court of Canada has significantly developed this area of the law. That development began with the "seminal case of *Guerin,*" which is treated as "the foundation of this line of general jurisprudence."[6]

The Supreme Court of Canada has considered the fiduciary principle in several cases following *Guerin,* and they illustrate the wide application of that principle.[7] *Frame v. Smith*[8] was decided three years after *Guerin*. Wilson J. wrote a dissenting judgment supporting the contention of a parent that his former spouse was in breach of a fiduciary obligation owed to him when she interfered with his access to his children. She noted that there had been reluctance throughout the common law world to affirm the existence of, and give context to, a general fiduciary principle that can be applied in appropriate circumstances. She suggested the three-part "rough and ready guide" noted below[9] and held that the relationship between custodial and non-custodial parent fitted within the fiduciary principle:[10]

> Accordingly, it would be my view that the cause of action for breach of fiduciary duty should be extended to this narrow but extremely important area of family law where the non-custodial parent is completely at the mercy of the custodial parent by virtue of that parent's position of power and authority over the children.

She would have awarded compensation to the plaintiff but the majority of the Court rejected the claim, whether based on tort or fiduciary duty. They did so primarily on the grounds that the matter was now governed by statute.

International Corona Resources Ltd. v. Lac Minerals Ltd.,[11] decided in 1989, discusses the possible application of the fiduciary principle in a commercial setting. Two mining companies were in negotiations to enter into a joint venture. One of the companies used information acquired from the other in confidence for its own benefit. The Supreme Court of Canada found liability for breach of confidence but a majority held that the facts were not sufficient to create a fiduciary relationship. The defendant company did not have the required discretionary power over the plaintiff company and the plaintiff company lacked the degree of vulnerability necessary for the relationship. A minority of the court would have found a fiduciary duty arising out of the specific circumstances. This case illustrates that fiduciary relationships are not likely to be found in commercial situations where the parties are dealing at arm's length.

The 1991 case of *Canson Enterprises Ltd. v. Boughton & Co.*[12] was an example of the fiduciary duty owed by a solicitor to a client. The Supreme Court of Canada was divided on the issue of what principles should apply to determine the compensation to be paid for breach of the duty, but the existence of the duty was plain. In that case, a solicitor acted for a purchaser of land, who then proceeded to develop the land by erecting a warehouse on it. The warehouse sank because of the failure of the underpinning. After this happened, the purchaser discovered for the first time that the solicitor had also acted for the vendor, who had made a substantial profit by "flipping" the property, which was overpriced. The solicitor had not shared in the secret profit but was held liable to pay this amount to the purchaser because he would not have purchased the land if he had known of the secret profit. However, the solicitor was not held liable to pay compensation for the loss arising from the sinking of the warehouse because this loss was not reasonably foreseeable.

In 1992, the Supreme Court of Canada decided two cases involving the fiduciary duties owed by a physician to a patient. In *McInerney v. MacDonald*,[13] the Court recognized a patient's right to gain access to his or her medical records and confirmed the fiduciary nature of the doctor-patient relationship. Speaking for the Court, La Forest J. said that a doctor has a duty to act with utmost good faith and loyalty and to hold information received from the patient in confidence. *Norberg v. Wynrib*[14] was a shocking example of a breach of the fiduciary relationship. A doctor supplied drugs to an addict in return for sexual favours. McLachlin J., supported by L'Heureux-Dube J., said that characterizing the doctor's duty as fiduciary effectively negated the patient's consent and provided a remedy not available under contract or tort. She was critical of the reluctance of the other judges to apply fiduciary principles and commented:[15]

> The principles alluded to by Wilson J. in *Frame v. Smith* and applied by this Court in its earlier decision in *Guerin v. The Queen*, [1984] 2 S.C.R. 335, are principles of general application, translatable to different situations and the protection of dif-

ferent interests than those hitherto recognized. They are capable of protecting not only narrow legal and economic interests, but can also serve to defend fundamental human and personal interests, as recognized by Wilson J. in *Frame v. Smith*.

The relationship of parent and child formed the subject matter of the fiduciary relationship in *M.(K.) v. M.(H.)* also decided in 1992.[16] The Court agreed that incest constituted a breach of the fiduciary obligation owed by a father to his daughter. Giving the majority judgment, La Forest J. wrote:[17]

> It is intuitively apparent that the relationship between parent and child is fiduciary in nature, and that the sexual assault of one's child is a grievous breach of the obligations arising from that relationship. Indeed, I can think of few cases that are clearer than this. For obvious reasons society has imposed upon parents the obligation to care for, protect and rear their children. The act of incest is a heinous violation of that obligation. Equity has imposed fiduciary obligations on parents in contexts other than incest, and I see no barrier to the extension of a father's fiduciary obligation to include a duty to refrain from incestuous assaults on his daughter.

In the course of his judgment, he reviewed the development of the "fiduciary principle" over the preceding years since *Guerin*.

Hodgkinson v. Simms,[18] decided in 1994, was similar in some ways to the *Canson* case, although it involved an investment counsellor rather than a lawyer. The counsellor did not disclose that he had received a commission from the developer in whose project the client invested. The trial judge found the counsellor liable for all the losses suffered on the basis that the client would not have made the investment if there had been full disclosure. The British Columbia Court of Appeal set aside the finding of a breach of fiduciary duty, but it was restored by a majority of the Supreme Court of Canada. The majority of the Court found the necessary degree of reliance and vulnerability. However, the minority concluded that the facts were not capable of demonstrating the unilateral exercise of power by the counsellor and the correlative total reliance by the investor required to establish a fiduciary obligation.

In 2002, the Court again considered the fiduciary obligations of a solicitor to a client in *R. v. Neil.*[19] The lawyer's firm gave information to the police about the client's involvement in a forgery and acted for a fellow accused. The Court found the lawyer to be in a conflict of interest. Giving the opinion of the Court, Binnie J. set out a "bright line" to prevent such conflicts of interest: a lawyer may not represent a client whose interests are directly adverse to the immediate interests of another current client—even if the two mandates are unrelated—unless both clients consent after receiving full disclosure (and preferably independent legal advice) and the lawyer reasonably believes that he or she is able to represent each client without adversely affecting the other.

The potential liability of a provincial government as a fiduciary for children in its care has been the subject of some recent decisions of the Supreme Court of Canada. The existence of a fiduciary relationship has not been in doubt,[20] but the scope of the fiduciary obligation assumed by the government has been in issue. In the leading case of *K.L.B. v. British Columbia*,[21] the Court considered the content of the duty that this relationship imposes on the government when it undertakes the responsibilities of a parent. Those representing children who had been abused while in care urged the Court to find a duty to act in the best interests of the children. The government, on the other hand, argued for a more narrowly defined duty: a duty to avoid harmful actions that constitute a betrayal of trust. The Court concluded that the government's view must prevail. Giving the opinion of the Court, Chief Justice McLachlin noted:

> [40] First a procedural point. Fiduciary duties arise in a number of different contexts, including express trusts, relationships marked by discretionary power and trust, and the special responsibilities of the Crown in dealing with aboriginal interests. Although the parties' view seemed to be that the Superintendent's fiduciary duty was a private law duty arising from the relationship between the Superintendent and the children, they also suggested at times that it arose from the public law responsibilities imposed on the Superintendent by the *Protection of Children Act*. On the latter view, the Superintendent's fiduciary obligations would be closer to the fiduciary obligations of the Crown toward aboriginal peoples, which have been held to include a requirement to use due diligence in advancing particular interests of aboriginal peoples: *Wewaykum Indian Band v. Canada*, 2002 SCC 79; *Blueberry River Indian Band v. Canada (Department of Indian Affairs and Northern Development)*, [1995] 4 S.C.R. 344; *Guerin v. The Queen*, [1984] 2 S.C.R. 335. In my opinion, this latter view of the Superintendent's fiduciary obligation cannot succeed. A fiduciary obligation to promote the best interests of foster children while in foster care cannot be implied from the statute.

She then reviewed the content of the fiduciary duty arising as a private law duty from the relationship of discretionary power and trust between the superintendent and the children:

> [48] . . . The traditional focus of breach of fiduciary duty is breach of trust, with the attendant emphasis on disloyalty and promotion of one's own or others' interests at the expense of the beneficiary's interests. Parents stand in a relationship of trust and owe fiduciary duties to their children. But the unique focus of the parental fiduciary duty, as distinguished from other duties imposed on them by the law, is breach of trust. Different legal and equitable duties may arise from the same relationship and circumstances. Equity does not duplicate the common law causes of action, but supplements them. Where the conduct evinces breach of trust, it may extend liability, but only on that basis.

In the case of the parental fiduciary relationship, the duty imposed is to act loyally and not put one's own or others' interests ahead of the child's in a manner that abuses the child's trust. Negligence, even aggravated negligence, will not ground parental fiduciary liability unless it is associated with breach of trust in this sense. In this case, the superintendent's fault was not disloyalty but failure to take sufficient care. Therefore, the government did not breach its fiduciary duty to the children.[22]

Authorson v. Canada[23] was a significant decision of the Ontario Court of Appeal extending *Guerin* to apply to the relationship between disabled veterans and the Crown. The plaintiff was a disabled war veteran whose pension was administered for him by the Department of Veterans Affairs. During the years of its administration, the department neither invested the funds nor accrued interest on them. The motions judge found that the Crown was a fiduciary to the veterans and had breached its fiduciary duty. The Ontario Court of Appeal upheld this decision.

It rejected the Crown's argument based on the *Kinloch*[24] and *Tito*[25] cases that, if there was any trust, it was at most a political trust. Those cases were distinguishable on the grounds that the funds in question were owned by the veterans rather than public funds, which was the situation in those cases. Further, it was not necessary that the relevant legislation expressly state that the Crown hold the funds as a trustee or fiduciary, although the purpose of the statute was important:

> [61] Nor can these cases be said to require that the express terms of "trust" or "fiduciary" appear in the relevant legislation before such an obligation will be found to bind the Crown. The seminal case of *Guerin, supra*, demonstrates as much. In his famous judgment in that case, Dickson J. (as he then was) found that a fiduciary obligation rested on the Crown although the statutory framework which was in part the source of that obligation, namely the *Indian Act*, did not explicitly say so.

> [62] The "political trust" cases do however sound a proper note of caution that should be exercised before a court places a fiduciary obligation on the Crown. This is so because the Crown has many tasks to perform in the discharge of its legislative, executive, and public administration responsibilities which are governmental functions to be enforced in the political arena rather than encumbered with court-imposed remedies. Thus, the debate is about the nature of a task given to the Crown by a particular statute.

The Court also rejected the argument that *Guerin* was distinguishable because it was based on the special nature of Indian title. It stated that there is no suggestion in the case that the Crown can be a fiduciary only in the context of Native people. Dickson J.'s "most famous passage" in the judgment regarding the creation of a fiduciary duty (i.e., when one party has an obligation to act for the benefit of another and that obligation carries with it a discretionary power[26]) described the law of fiduciary duty as being of general application "reaching the Crown no less than any other party."[27] The subsequent development of the law by the Supreme Court of Canada "has proceeded with no suggestion that *Guerin* is to be confined to its facts or to the Crown or to situations of aboriginal title. Rather, *Guerin* is treated as the foundation of this line of general jurisprudence."[28]

The Court concluded:[29]

> [72] In our view, therefore, *Guerin* does not have the limited scope contended for by the appellant. It sets out principles that are relevant to this case. Brockenshire J. did not err in relying on it.

> [73] Thus, in our view, the attacks mounted by the appellant on the finding that the Crown is subject to a fiduciary duty all fall short. Rather, we agree with Brockenshire J. that when the Crown through the DVA is directed to administer for the benefit of a veteran his funds, which he is incapable of managing himself, the Crown shoulders a fiduciary obligation to that veteran. The legislation that results in this administration, its nature and effect and its context make this clear.

It was unnecessary to determine if the Crown can properly be described as a trustee. As a fiduciary, the Crown had a duty to invest the funds given the circumstances, and it breached that duty. The Court went on to find that a statutory provision which would have barred the claim was inoperative because it was in breach of the provisions of the *Canadian Bill of Rights* protecting rights to property. The Supreme Court of Canada reversed the decision of the Ontario Court of Appeal on this latter point but there was no appeal on the finding of a breach of a fiduciary obligation.[30]

What Gives Rise to a Fiduciary Relationship?

Despite the centuries-old recognition of fiduciary relationships,[31] until recently, the law relating to them had received little attention in legal texts and the courts still largely fail to set out or apply the underlying principles in a consistent fashion. In something of an understatement, Justice McLachlin has observed, "It should be noted that it is still not entirely clear, even in Canada, what gives rise to a fiduciary obligation."[32]

A general definition of fiduciary relationships has proven impossible.[33] Rather, the obligation has been considered on a case-by-case basis. A number of positions, such as agent, trustee, partner, and director, have been recognized as giving rise to a fiduciary obligation; these are the so-called *per se* fiduciary relationships. In such cases, there is a strong presumption that the obligations owed by the fiduciary are themselves fiduciary in nature and the onus is on the fiduciary to rebut this presumption.[34] Courts have pointed out that even in this first class of fiduciary relationship, "not all obligations between the parties to a fiduciary relationship are themselves fiduciary in nature."[35] There is also a second class of fiduciary relationship, which are relationships not ordinarily considered to be fiduciary but in which, on the particular facts, one party owes a fiduciary obligation to the other. This is the so-called *ad hoc* class of fiduciary relationships. In such cases, the onus is on the plaintiff to demonstrate that the defendant owes a fiduciary obligation to him.[36] In the decision of the English Court of Appeal in *Lloyd's Bank v. Bundy*, Sir Eric Sachs said:[37]

> As was pointed out in *Tufton v. Sperni* [1952] 2 T.L.R. 516, the relationships which result in such a duty must not be circumscribed by reference to defined limits; it is necessary to "refute the suggestion that, to create the relationship of confidence, the person owing the duty must be found clothed in the recognizable garb of guardian, trustee, solicitor, priest, doctor, manager, or the like." (Sir Raymond Evershed M.R., at p. 522.)
>
> Everything depends on the particular facts, and such a relationship has been held to exist in unusual circumstances as between purchaser and vendor, as between great uncle and adult nephew, and in other widely differing sets of circumstances. Moreover, it is neither feasible nor desirable to attempt closely to define the relationship, or its characteristics, or the demarcation line showing the exact transition point where a relationship that does not entail that duty passes into one that does (*cf.* Ungoed-Thomas J. in *In re Craig, decd.* [1971] Ch. 95, 104).

It was noted by earlier Canadian courts[38] and repeated by Dickson J. in *Guerin* that "the categories of fiduciary, like those of negligence, should not be considered closed."[39]

One important element in determining whether a person is a fiduciary is the existence of a discretion that is to be exercised for the benefit of another.[40] The critical importance of such discretion was established by Dickson J. in *Guerin*:[41]

> Where by statute, agreement or perhaps by unilateral undertaking, one party has an obligation to act for the benefit of another, and that obligation carries with it a discretionary power, the party thus empowered becomes a fiduciary. Equity will then supervise the relationship by holding him to the fiduciary's strict standard of conduct.

As one writer has said in words which were quoted by Dickson J. in that case:[42]

> [Where there is a fiduciary obligation] there is a relation in which the principal's interests can be affected by, and are therefore dependent on, the manner in which the fiduciary uses the discretion which has been delegated to him. The fiduciary obligation is the law's blunt tool for the control of this discretion.

In the words of another writer:[43]

> A person becomes a fiduciary through his independence in the position he occupies. If he serves a beneficiary who has not the general right to say how he wishes to be served then Equity steps in to ensure that the fiduciary does serve that beneficiary's

interests. Though his position gives him autonomy Equity circumscribes that autonomy, it channels the direction of his activities.

In *Guerin*, Le Dain J. of the Federal Court of Appeal had concluded that the government's discretion ousted the court's jurisdiction to regulate the relationship between the Crown and the Indians.[44] However, Dickson J. reached the opposite conclusion. He thought the discretion had the effect of transforming the Crown's obligation into a fiduciary one subject to the supervision of the court.[45] This recognition by the Supreme Court of Canada of the critical importance of a discretion to act for another as a key indicia of a fiduciary relationship served to restate the legal requirement for a fiduciary relationship and, thereby, re-invigorate the fiduciary principle in Canadian law.

Three years later, in her dissenting opinion in *Frame v. Smith*,[46] Wilson J. expanded on the comments made by Dickson J. in *Guerin*. She outlined "common features" of relationships in which fiduciary obligations have been found to exist:[47]

> Relationships in which a fiduciary obligation have been imposed seem to possess three general characteristics:
>
> 1. The fiduciary has scope for the exercise of some discretion or power.
> 2. The fiduciary can unilaterally exercise that power or discretion so as to affect the beneficiary's legal or practical interests.
> 3. The beneficiary is peculiarly vulnerable to or at the mercy of the fiduciary holding the discretion or power.

Sopinka J., writing for the majority of the Supreme Court of Canada in *Lac Minerals*,[48] approved of Wilson J.'s approach as "a rough and ready guide." He also noted the *Frame* criteria were not conclusive:[49]

> It is possible for a fiduciary relationship to be found although not all of these characteristics are present, nor will the presence of these ingredients invariably identify the existence of a fiduciary relationship.

In *Norberg v. Wynrib*,[50] McLachlin J. summarized the requirements for a fiduciary duty as including an undertaking by the fiduciary to look after the interests of the beneficiary:[51]

> The criteria for the imposition of a fiduciary duty already enunciated by this Court in cases such as *Frame*, *LAC Minerals* and *Guerin* provide a good starting point for the task of defining the general principles which determine whether such a relationship exists. As we have seen, an imbalance of power is not enough to establish a fiduciary relationship. It is a necessary but not sufficient condition. There must also be the potential for interference with a legal interest or a non-legal interest of "vital and substantial 'practical' interest." And I would add this. Inherent in the notion of fiduciary duty, inherent in the judgments of this Court in *Guerin* and

Canson, is the requirement that the fiduciary have assumed or undertaken to "look after" the interest of the beneficiary.

However, in *M.(K.) v. M.(H.)*,[52] La Forest J. suggested that "fiduciary obligations are imposed in some situations even in the absence of any unilateral undertaking by the fiduciary."

A couple of years later, in *Hodgkinson v. Simms*, La Forest J. included the expectations of the parties as being relevant to the existence of a fiduciary relationship:[53]

> The existence of a fiduciary duty in a given case will depend upon the reasonable expectations of the parties, and these in turn depend on factors such as trust, confidence, complexity of subject matter and community or industry standards.

He noted that the expectation that another person will act as a fiduciary must be reasonable and justified by the kind of factors mentioned by him.

In the subsequent case of *Blueberry River*, McLachlin J. gave a further description of the typical characteristics of a fiduciary relationship which stressed the vulnerability of the beneficiary:[54]

> Generally speaking, a fiduciary obligation arises where one person possesses unilateral power or discretion on a matter affecting a second "peculiarly vulnerable" person: see *Frame v. Smith* (1987), 42 D.L.R. (4th) 81, [1987] 2 S.C.R. 99, 42 C.C.L.T. 1; *Norberg v. Wynrib* (1992), 92 D.L.R. (4th) 449, [1992] 2 S.C.R. 225, 12 C.C.L.T. (2d) 1; and *Hodgkinson v. Simms* (1994), 117 D.L.R. (4th) 161, 57 C.P.R. (3d) 1, [1994] 3 S.C.R. 377. The vulnerable party is in the power of the party possessing the power or discretion, who is in turn obligated to exercise that power or discretion solely for the benefit of the vulnerable party. A person cedes (or more often finds himself in the situation where someone else has ceded for him) his power over a matter to another person. The person who has ceded power trusts the person to whom power is ceded to exercise the power with loyalty and care. This is the notion at the heart of the fiduciary obligation.

And later:[55]

> Where a party is granted power over another's interest, and where the other party is correspondingly deprived of power over them, or is "vulnerable," then the party possessing the power is under a fiduciary obligation to exercise it in the best interests of the other. . . .

Binnie J. noted in the 2002 case of *R. v. Neil*[56] that loyalty is often cited as one of the defining characteristics of a fiduciary and referred to the following definition by Professor Donovan Waters:[57]

> In putting together words to describe a "fiduciary" there is of course no immediate obstacle. Everyone would say that it is a person in whom trust and confidence is placed by another on whose behalf the fiduciary is to act. The other (the beneficiary) is entitled to expect that the fiduciary will be concerned solely for the beneficiary's

interests, never the fiduciary's own. The "relationship" must be the dependence or reliance of the beneficiary upon the fiduciary.

The Duties of a Fiduciary

Once a fiduciary relationship is found to exist, the discussion turns to the nature of the obligations owed by the fiduciary. In *Guerin*, Dickson J. referred to "the fiduciary's strict standard of conduct"[58] and said that the Crown's fiduciary obligation was "trust-like in character."[59] The obligation was therefore subject to principles very similar to those that govern the law of trusts. The general obligation of a fiduciary is "that of utmost loyalty to his principal."[60] Laskin J. said in *Canadian Aero Service Ltd. v. O'Malley* that a fiduciary relationship "in generality betokens loyalty, good faith and avoidance of a conflict of duty and self-interest."[61]

In *Lac Minerals*, La Forest J. also described the fiduciary's duty of loyalty:[62]

> The obligation imposed may vary in its specific substance depending on the relationship, though compendiously it can be described as the fiduciary duty of loyalty and will most often include the avoidance of a conflict of duty and interest and a duty not to profit at the expense of the beneficiary.

He noted in *Hodgkinson* that it is the existence of loyalty, trust, and confidence in a fiduciary relationship that distinguishes the fiduciary duty from the duty of care in negligence:[63]

> [T]he fiduciary duty is different in important respects from the ordinary duty of care. In *Canson Enterprises Ltd. v. Boughton & Co.*, [1991] 3 S.C.R. 534 at 571–73 I traced the history of the common law claim of negligent misrepresentation from its origin in the equitable doctrine of fiduciary responsibility; see also *Nocton v. Lord Ashburton*, [1914] A.C. 932 at pp. 968–71, per Lord Shaw of Dunfermline. However, while both negligent misrepresentation and breach of fiduciary duty arise in reliance-based relationships, the presence of loyalty, trust, and confidence distinguishes the fiduciary relationship from a relationship that simply gives rise to tortious liability. Thus, while a fiduciary obligation carries with it a duty of skill and competence, the special elements of trust, loyalty and confidentiality that obtain in a fiduciary relationship give rise to a corresponding duty of loyalty.

In that case, Justices Sopinka and McLachlin said that:[64]

> At the heart of the fiduciary relationship lie the dual concepts of trust and loyalty. This is first and best illustrated by the fact that the fiduciary duties find their origin in the classic trust where one person, the fiduciary, holds property on behalf of another, the beneficiary. In order to protect the interest of the beneficiary, the express trustee is held to a stringent standard; the trustee is under a duty to act in a completely selfless manner for the sole benefit of the trust and its beneficiaries (*Keech v. Sandford* (1726), 25 E.R. 223) to whom he owes "the utmost duty of loyalty." (Waters *Law of Trust in Canada* 2nd ed. (Toronto: Carswell, 1984) at p.

31). And while the fiduciary relationship is no longer confined to the classic trustee-beneficiary relationship, the underlying requirements of complete trust and utmost loyalty have never varied.

Often, the duty of the fiduciary is expressed to be that of acting in the best interests of the beneficiary. In his judgment in *Guerin*, Dickson J. said that the fiduciary obligation which arises from the fiduciary relationship of the Crown and an Indian band is "to deal with the land for the benefit of the Indians."[65] Similarly, Gonthier J. stated in *Blueberry River* that:[66]

> . . . By the terms of the surrender instrument, the DIA was required to act in the best interests of the Band in dealing with the mineral rights. In fact, the DIA was under a fiduciary duty to put the Band's interests first.
> . . . By taking on the obligations of a trustee in relation to I.R. 172, the DIA was under a fiduciary duty to deal with the land in the best interests of the members of the Beaver Band.

However, in recent cases dealing with the parental fiduciary obligation, the Supreme Court of Canada has rejected the argument that the obligation is always to act in the best interests of the child. Instead, it is "to act loyally and not to put one's own or others' interests ahead of the child in a manner that abuses the child's trust."[67]

In the case of *R. v. Sparrow,* the Supreme Court of Canada referred to the high standard of conduct to be met by the Crown as a fiduciary. It said that the Crown would be held to "a high standard of honourable dealing with respect to the aboriginal peoples of Canada."[68] Writing in *The Law of Restitution*, Maddaugh and McCamus cite with approval the statement of Chief Justice Cardozo of the New York Court of Appeal, describing the high standards of conduct set by courts for fiduciaries:[69]

> Many forms of conduct permissible in a workaday world for those acting at arm's length, are forbidden to those bound by fiduciary ties. A trustee is held to something stricter than the morals of the market place. Not honesty alone, but the punctilio of an honor the most sensitive, is then the standard of behavior. As to this there has developed a tradition that is unbending and inveterate. Uncompromising rigidity has been the attitude of courts of equity when petitioned to undermine the rule of undivided loyalty by the "disintegrating erosion" of particular exceptions. . . . Only thus has the level of conduct for fiduciaries been kept at a level higher than that trodden by the crowd.

The high standard expected of a fiduciary was underlined by Reid J. in *Re Collins and Pension Commissioner of Ontario*: "My conclusion is that the duty owed . . . was equivalent to that of a trustee. I have no hesitation in calling it a fiduciary duty, the law knows none higher."[70]

A number of specific fiduciary duties have been identified, including the following:[71]

1. not to delegate discretions, so that the fiduciary must exercise any discretion herself and not allow another to do so on her behalf;

2. not to act under another's dictation, so that a fiduciary must act independently;

3. not to place "fetters" on discretions, so that a fiduciary must not do anything that would prevent the free exercise of a discretion in the future;

4. to consider whether a discretion should be exercised, so that a fiduciary must not act according to rigid rules;

5. not to act for her own benefit or for the benefit of any third person, but only for that of the beneficiary;

6. to treat principals equally where they have similar rights, so that, if there is more that one principal or beneficiary with similar rights, they must be treated equally;

7. to treat principals fairly where they have dissimilar rights, so that, even if the principals or beneficiaries do not have equal rights, they must still be treated fairly;

8. not to act capriciously or totally unreasonably, so that the fiduciary must always act prudently;

9. not to exercise undue influence, so that the fiduciary never puts pressure on the beneficiary or takes advantage of him;

10. not to misuse property held in a fiduciary capacity, so that property held in a fiduciary capacity must always be used for the benefit of the beneficiary;

11. not to misuse information derived in confidence, so that any confidential information must always be used for the purpose for which it was given;

12. not to purchase property if to do so would conflict with her fiduciary obligation;

13. not to allow any personal interest to conflict with her fiduciary obligation, so that the fiduciary must always act in the interests of the beneficiary and not her own interests;

14. not to allow her duty to another to conflict with her fiduciary

obligation, so that the fiduciary must avoid situations where her fiduciary obligation would be in conflict with the duty owed to a third party.

It must be noted that not every fiduciary is subject to each of these duties.[72] A fiduciary for one rule is not necessarily a fiduciary for all or indeed for any other rule. It is pointless to describe a person as a fiduciary unless at the same time it is said for which rule that description is being used: "These rules are everything. The description 'fiduciary' means nothing. It has gone much the same way as did the general descriptive term 'trust' one hundred and fifty years ago."[73] As emphasized by Laskin J. in *Canadian Aero Service Ltd. v. O'Malley*,[74] the obligations of a particular fiduciary will depend upon the circumstances. In *Guerin*, Dickson J. commented that "the fiduciary obligation which is owed to the Indians by the Crown is *sui generis*,"[75] and, in *Osoyoos*,[76] Gonthier J. noted that "the Crown's fiduciary obligation . . . will vary with the facts."[77]

Just because a relationship is fiduciary in nature does not mean that all of the obligations arising in that relationship are necessarily fiduciary ones. As Sopinka J. pointed out in *Lac Minerals*, "not all obligations existing between the parties to a well-recognized fiduciary relationship will be fiduciary in nature."[78] There may be statutory, contractual, tort, or public law obligations that exist independent of any fiduciary obligation(s) whose breach does not give rise to any remedy under fiduciary law. Thus, it is important not to assume that a breach of an obligation by a fiduciary automatically gives rise to liability for breach of fiduciary duty. For example, incorrect advice by a solicitor may constitute negligence or a breach of a contractual obligation to take care but not breach of a fiduciary obligation.[79]

This point has been made in cases involving claims by Aboriginal peoples. The Federal Court of Appeal in *Wewaykum*[80] noted that while the fiduciary nature of the relationship between the Crown and Aboriginal peoples is generally well-established in Canadian law, a fiduciary duty "does not arise in every facet of Crown–Native relations nor is the content of the fiduciary responsibilities of the Crown identical in every transaction."[81] Likewise, in *Quebec (Attorney General) v. Canada (National Energy Board)*,[82] Iacobucci J. noted:[83]

> It is now well settled that there is a fiduciary relationship between the federal Crown and the aboriginal peoples of Canada: *Guerin.* . . . Nonetheless, it must be remembered that not every aspect of the relationship between fiduciary and beneficiary takes the form of a fiduciary obligation: *Lac Minerals.* . . . The nature of the relationship between the parties defines the scope, and the limits, of the duties that will be imposed.

Fiduciary Obligations and Other Causes of Action

Ryan J.A., in separate concurring reasons in *A(C) v. Critchley*,[84] agreed that the Crown's appeal from the trial judge's finding of breach of fiduciary duty against the provincial government for abuse suffered by children in its care should be allowed. She stressed the need to maintain a distinction between negligence and breach of fiduciary duty, noting the Crown's incompetence was not disloyalty, but rather negligent behaviour.[85] A breach of fiduciary duty occurs only when the risk inherent in the relationship materializes, meaning the fiduciary exercises the power entrusted to it to the detriment of the beneficiary, or for the benefit of someone other than the beneficiary.[86] She also stressed that a fiduciary does not breach its duty by simply failing to obtain the best result for the beneficiary.[87]

This distinction between breach of fiduciary duty and negligence is significant for cases involving the fiduciary obligations owed to Aboriginal peoples since there are cases where lower courts have declined to hold that the Crown breached fiduciary obligations to a plaintiff band because the Crown's conduct was held to be only negligent. In *Wewaykum*,[88] for example, the trial judge stressed that the Crown's "technical failure" to interpret correctly the surrender requirements of the *Indian Act*, or to advise the plaintiff bands of their legal claims to the disputed reserves, did not necessarily amount to a breach of fiduciary duty.[89] He relied on *Blueberry River*,[90] where the Federal Court of Appeal found that non-compliance with the certification provisions of the *Indian Act* relating to a surrender did not constitute a breach of fiduciary duty. The trial judge in *Wewaykum* also stated that if he was wrong and a surrender had been necessary to give effect to the allocation of the reserves in dispute, the Crown's failure to discharge its duty to use reasonable care in interpreting the provisions of the *Indian Act* and advising the plaintiffs on these issues could not be construed as a breach of fiduciary duty. In support of this conclusion, he relied on Sopinka J.'s statement in *Lac Minerals*[91] that not all obligations existing between the parties in a fiduciary relationship are fiduciary in nature. Neither the Federal Court of Appeal[92] nor the Supreme Court of Canada[93] specifically addressed this aspect of the trial judge's decision.

On the other hand, La Forest J. observed in *Hodgkinson* that "a fiduciary obligation carries with it a duty of skill and competence,"[94] and, in *Blueberry River*, the Supreme Court of Canada attributed the breach of fiduciary duty to inadvertence on the part of the Crown. The Court noted that "the duty on the Crown was 'that of a man of ordinary prudence' in managing his affairs. . . . The [Department of Indian Affairs'] duty was the usual duty of a fiduciary to act with reasonable diligence with respect to the Indians' interest."[95] Likewise, in *Wewaykum*, the Court said that an obligation of "acting with ordinary prudence with a view to the best interests of the aboriginal beneficiaries" exists even prior to reserve creation.[96] Thus, it would appear that acts and omissions that are "negligent" in character can still, when they occur within the context of a fiduciary relationship, constitute a breach of a fiduciary obligation of prudence.[97]

Breach of fiduciary obligation has its origin in the law of equity. Like all equitable actions, it is more flexible than common law actions. As discussed in detail in chapter 9, a claim of breach of fiduciary obligation has the following advantages for the plaintiff over a claim in common law such as for breach of contract or negligence:[98]

- a fiduciary is held to the highest duty of loyalty and honesty, and it may be easier to prove a breach of a fiduciary obligation than a breach of contract or negligence;[99]

- a reverse onus of proof may be applied, and the fiduciary will have to disprove a breach of the obligation once the plaintiff has shown sufficient facts to show a possible breach;

- statutory limitation periods are more favourable in some jurisdictions to a plaintiff in a breach of fiduciary obligation action;

- a broader range of remedies may be available than at common law;

- equitable compensation is calculated at the date of trial, not the date of breach of fiduciary obligation, as with common law damages, and the plaintiff obtains the benefit of any increase in market value since the date of breach;

- presumptions may operate in favour of the plaintiff when determining compensation, such as the presumation that a plaintiff would have made the most advantageous use of an asset if not wrongly deprived of it;

- technical principles of foreseeability, remoteness, and mitigation may be applied more flexibly, leading to greater recovery by the plaintiff; and

- the principles of causation either do not apply or are applied more flexibly, and a fiduciary may be found liable even if there is some doubt if his breach caused the harm suffered by the plaintiff.

However, common law remedies are available as of right but equitable remedies are in the discretion of the court. Therefore, a plaintiff may establish a breach of fiduciary obligation only to have the court decide in the exercise of its discretion not to give a remedy for the breach or not to give the remedy sought by the plaintiff.

One question to which no clear answer has yet been provided is the relationship between ancient equitable principles reflected in the law of fiduciary obligations and the relatively new branch of law known as restitution or unjust enrichment.[100] According to Chief Justice McLachlin, the decisions of the Supreme Court of Canada on breach of fiduciary obligations, including *Guerin*[101] and *Blueberry River*[102] involving Aboriginal peoples, are examples of the principle of unjust enrichment.[103] A leading authority on the law of restitution has noted "fiduciary obligation surfaces as a chapter in the restitution books as one of a large number of common law and equitable doctrines creating causes of action which are now seen to rest upon or find their justification in the unjust enrichment principle."[104] As yet, there is no clear answer to the question raised by Chief Justice McLachlin of "how does unjust enrichment mesh with other equitable doctrines such as breach of fiduciary duty?"[105]

Governments As Fiduciaries

As demonstrated by the concept of the political trust discussed in chapter 1, the traditional view has been that governments do not owe a fiduciary duty to citizens. Despite his rejection of that concept in *Guerin*, Dickson J. observed in that case:[106]

> It should be noted that fiduciary duties generally arise only with regard to obligations originating in a private law context. Public law duties, the performance of which requires the exercise of discretion, do not typically give rise to a fiduciary relationship.

However, this immunity is gradually being eroded mainly as the result of *Guerin* itself, as evidenced by the recent decision of the Ontario Court of Appeal in *Authorson* discussed above.[107] Mark Ellis notes in *Fiduciary Duties in Canada*:[108]

> In recent years, courts are allowing a wide variety of actions against governments of all levels to at least go to trial, often on the basis of the more famous dictum in *Guerin* that the categories of fiduciary should not be considered closed, but rather depend on the facts of the particular relationship. In any event, certain governmental authorities will be found to owe a fiduciary duty to those for whom it has a mandate to protect or serve.

The following governmental bodies or individuals have been held to owe a fiduciary duty:[109] the Ontario Pension Commission,[110] elected officials,[111] the Workers' Compensation Board of Alberta,[112] superintendents of mental health institutions,[113] provincial child care agencies,[114] and the British Columbia Oil and Gas Commission.[115]

It was noted by Binnie J. in *Wewaykum* that finding a fiduciary obligation adds "an array of equitable remedies" to those available at public law against government. It also "attaches to the Crown's intervention the additional obligations of loyalty, good faith, full disclosure appropriate to the matter at hand and acting in what it reasonably and with diligence regards as the best interests of the beneficiary."[116]

Conclusion

As discussed in chapter 10,[117] the above developments in fiduciary law have been controversial and some critics have recommended a return to the relative simplicity of the pre-Guerin law or that the general law of fiduciaries be "formally disconnected" from that applying to Aboriginal peoples.[118] My view is that, although the law certainly needs to be simplified and clarified, the general thrust has been positive in requiring a higher standard on the part of governments and other fiduciaries and providing a greater range of remedies than other areas of law such as contract, tort, or public law would require. Any attempt to turn back the clock to the pre-Guerin law is both too late and unjustified.[119]

Chapter 7

American, Australian, and New Zealand Law

The United States, Australia, and New Zealand also have a common law tradition and significant Aboriginal populations, and their consideration of fiduciary obligations and Aboriginal peoples is of interest and may be instructive for us in Canada. However, there are significant historical, social, and constitutional differences in those jurisdictions which should be kept in mind. As Justice Kirby of the High Court of Australia said in *Fejo v. Northern Territories*[1] with respect to the question of Aboriginal title:

> 101. [C]are must be exercised in the use of judicial authorities of other former colonies and territories of the Crown because of the peculiarities which exist in each of them arising out of historical and constitutional developments, the organization of the indigenous peoples concerned and applicable geographical or social considerations. . . .

> 103. The ways in which each of the former colonies and territories of the Crown addressed the reconciliation between native title and the legal doctrine of tenure sustaining estates in land varied so markedly from one former territory to the other and were affected so profoundly by local considerations (legal and otherwise) that it is virtually impossible to derive applicable common themes of legal principle.

United States Law, 1983–2004

As discussed in chapter 1, the trust responsibility of the United States towards Aboriginal peoples has long been recognized as a central concept in American Indian law.[2] However, after *Mitchell II*,[3] which was decided in 1983 at the time of the hearing of *Guerin* in the Supreme Court of Canada, and until the 2003 decisions in *Navajo Nation*[4] and *White Mountain Apache*,[5] the U.S. Supreme Court did not consider that responsibility in any detail, although it has touched upon it in a couple of cases. In the 1987 decision of *United States v. Cherokee Nation of Oklahoma*, the Court noted: "[I]t is, of course, well established that the Government in its dealings with Indian tribal property

145

acts in a fiduciary capacity."[6] However, the Court found no breach on the facts of the case. Likewise, in *Lincoln v. Virgil*,[7] the Court held that the fiduciary relationship did not limit the government's ability to reallocate Indian health services from a subgroup of beneficiaries to a broader class of beneficiaries.

Other courts, including the United States Court of Appeals, decided a number of cases on the fiduciary relationship in the period after *Mitchell II*.[8] The 1995 case of *Short v. United States*[9] involved a claim by Indians who lived on a reservation but who had been denied their rightful share of timber proceeds. The United States Court of Appeals for the Federal Circuit reviewed the statutes in question and held that they gave the plaintiffs a right to damages including interest. The court relied upon *Mitchell II*[10] for the establishment of the fiduciary relationship and held that interest may be appropriately included in a damage award against the United States for breach of its fiduciary obligation to a tribe.

Brown v. United States[11] involved claims for lost rent and profits allegedly due to breaches of trust by the Secretary of the Interior in managing commercial leases. The United States Court of Appeals for the Federal Circuit found that the relevant legislation gave sufficient control over the leases to impose a fiduciary relationship. It was not necessary that the secretary also supervise or manage the leases. *Mitchell II* only required control *or* supervision. Also, the Supreme Court had not qualified "control" or "supervision" with modifiers such as "significant" or "comprehensive." However, it was still necessary for the plaintiffs to show a breach of statute or regulation to establish liability for damages: "[w]here no specific statutory requirement or regulation is alleged to have been breached by the Secretary, the money claim against the government must fail."[12] The court expressed some doubt whether such a breach could be shown but remanded the case for review by the court of federal claims.

Loudner v. United States[13] was a 1997 decision of the United States Court of Appeals for the Eighth Circuit. The plaintiffs based their claims on being descendants of a tribe which had been dispersed during the Civil War by the military and had lost their lands. The government had set aside a fund to distribute among such descendants but, in the view of the court, made only minimal efforts to notify the beneficiaries of the existence of the funds. The court said there was a presumption that, absent explicit language to the contrary, all funds held by the United States for Indian tribes are held in trust. This trust relationship extended not only to the tribes but to tribal members living collectively or individually on or off the reservation. The government had not pointed to any statutory language relieving it of its obligations. Accordingly, it had the obligation to act as a trustee in its management of the fund, and its conduct had to be judged by the most exacting fiduciary standards. The court then considered the duty of a common law trustee to provide beneficiaries with adequate notice of their entitlement and found that the Secretary of the Interior had breached this duty. This breach prevented the application of the statute of limitations to defeat the claims.

The case of *Cobell v. Norton*[14] reveals widespread breaches by the Departments of the Interior and Treasury of their fiduciary duty to manage individual Indian accounts. Those accounts originated with the policy adopted in the 1887 *General Allotment Act* to allot reservation land to individual Indians. The lands and income generated therefrom are held in trust by the United States. It was found by Justice Lamberth of the United States District Court for the District of Columbia that the government had a duty to provide an accounting of the funds to the beneficiaries. In his judgment, he specifically rejected the plaintiffs' common-law claim for breach of trust. In his view, the rights of the plaintiffs had to be based on statute: "[e]ven though the IIM [Individual Indian Monies] trust is a trust, as that term is used in *Mitchell II*, plaintiffs must point to rights granted by statute if they are to be enforced against the government. There is simply no persuasive basis for doing so on a purely common-law basis."[15] In reaching this conclusion, he relied upon the statement of the United States Supreme Court in *Nevada v. United States* that "the government is simply not in the position of a private litigant or a private party under traditional rules of common law or statute."[16] He also relied upon the dissenting judgment of Justice Powell in *Mitchell II*.

The United States Court of Appeals for the District of Columbia Circuit upheld the judgment generally.[17] Although it did not expressly reject Justice Lamberth's opinion on the common-law basis of liability, it based the fiduciary duty partly on the existence of a "general trust relationship" which *Mitchell II* had held to impose "distinctive obligations" in addition to those established by statute. It was at some pains to reject the government's assumption that the 1994 *Indian Trust Fund Management Reform Act* formed the basis for its fiduciary obligations. Those obligations existed prior to that Act and arose out of the government's elaborate control over Indian assets. In its view, the 1994 Act "reaffirmed and clarified pre-existing duties, it did not create them." It traced those duties back to the early decisions of the United States Supreme Court in *Cherokee Nation v. Georgia*,[18] *Kagama*,[19] and *Seminole Nation*.[20]

The judgment made it clear that fiduciary duties do not need to be expressly set out in the statute or treaty or executive order:[21]

> It is well understood that "[t]he extent of a trustee's duties and powers is determined by the trust instrument and the rules of law which are applicable." *Restatement (Second) of Trusts* s. 201 at 442 (1959). It is the nature of any instrument that establishes a trust relationship that many of the duties and powers are implied therein. They

arise from the nature of the relationship established.

> While the government's obligations are rooted in and out-lined by the relevant statutes and treaties, they are largely defined in traditional equitable terms.

The Court later noted "[t]he general 'contours' of the government's obligations may be defined by statute, but the interstices must be filled in through reference to general trust law."[22]

Confederated Tribes of The Warm Springs Reservation of Oregon v. United States[23] involved a claim for mismanagement of the sale of timber from the tribes' reservation. The Court of Federal Claims found that the government had mismanaged the sale in several ways and, in particular, by obtaining the domestic rather than the export price. However, the court held that the tribes were not entitled to any damages because they had received the full domestic price and it was too speculative to determine the export price. The United States Court of Appeals for the Federal Circuit reversed and applied the principles of trust law that a beneficiary is entitled to recover damages for the improper management of the trust's assets, a court should attempt to place the beneficiary in the position in which it would have been absent the breach and the risk of uncertainty as to the amount of the loss falls on the trustee. The court concluded:[24]

> [T]here is no question that the Tribes have established both a breach and some loss. The only question is whether the proof of loss was too speculative to support any recovery at all, as the trial court held. Under the foregoing principles of trust law, the Tribes should not have borne the risk of uncertainty as to precisely how much the green timber would have sold for if it had not been prematurely harvested. That is particularly true on the facts of this case, where resolving the issue of damages does not require unguided speculation.

White Mountain Apache Tribe v. United States[25] was decided by the United States Court of Appeals for the Federal Circuit in 2001. A 1960 Act of Congress declared that Fort Apache was "held by the United States in trust for the White Mountain Apache Tribe subject to the right of the Secretary of the Interior to use any part of the land and improvements for administrative or school purposes for as long as they are needed for that purpose."[26] At issue was the government's obligation to maintain and restore the buildings on the site. The tribe claimed $14 million in damages for breach of this alleged duty. The Court of Federal Claims had agreed with the government that the tribe had failed to prove the existence of a fiduciary obligation on the part of the United States that would, if breached, give rise to a claim for money damages, and dismissed the complaint for failure to state a claim.[27] It applied *Mitchell I* to hold that the 1960 Act created only a bare trust which did not impose fiduciary duties.

On appeal, the United States Court of Appeal for the Federal Circuit applied its decision in *Brown*[28] to find that control alone sufficed to establish a fiduciary relationship. It was not necessary for the government to also manage the Indian asset. Having found a fiduciary relationship, the court turned to the common law of trusts to define the nature of the obligations imposed by that relationship:[29]

> Once we have determined that a fiduciary obligation exists by virtue of the governing statute or regulations, it is well established that we then look to the common law of trusts, particularly as reflected in the *Restatement (Second) of Trusts*, for assistance in defining the nature of that obligation. . . .
>
>   Under the common law of trusts, it is indisputable that a trustee has an affirmative duty to act reasonably to preserve the trust property.

The Court then considered whether the tribe had a claim for damages:[30]

> It remains only to be determined whether breach of the government's obligations, if proven by the Tribe on remand, gives rise to a presently cognizable claim for money damages. We hold that it does. As the Supreme Court held in *Mitchell II*: "Given the existence of a trust relationship, it naturally follows that the Government should be liable in damages for the breach of its fiduciary duties. It is well established that a trustee is accountable in damages for breaches of trust." *Mitchell II*, 463 U.S. at 226. The *Restatement of Trusts* provides further support for this proposition. *Restatement (Second) of Trusts* § 205 (1959) ("If the trustee commits a breach of trust, he is chargeable with (a) any loss or depreciation in value of the trust estate resulting from the breach of trust").

It rejected the suggestion of the Court of Federal Claims that no compensation should be awarded for the past breach but that, at most, an injunction might be granted ordering compliance in the future. The United States appealed this decision to the United States Supreme Court.

The facts of *Navajo Nation v. United States*,[31] the companion case decided by the Supreme Court with the *White Mountain Apache* case, are striking. The Navajo reservation, which is the largest in the United States, has reserves of coal. Pursuant to the *Indian Mineral Leasing Act of 1938*,[32] the Bureau of Indian Affairs (BIA) supervises and regulates the development and sale of mineral resources on reservations. In 1964, the Navajo Nation entered into a lease agreement with a mining company at rates well below market rates, but containing a provision that the royalty rates could be adjusted by the Secretary of the Interior to a reasonable rate. Negotiations proceeded between the Navajo and the mining company for some time and no agreement was reached. The Navajo asked the Bureau of Indian Affairs to exercise the power to fix the rate. A BIA official issued an initial decision to fix the rate at 20 percent and the mining company was notified of this initial decision. They appealed to the deputy assistant secretary for Indian Affairs, pursuant to the regulations. He reached a decision affirming the 20 percent rate. Before it was formally issued, it was leaked to the mining company. They hired an old friend of the Secretary of the Interior who lobbied on their behalf. The secretary then issued a memorandum, substantially drafted by the mining company, to the deputy assistant secretary telling him to advise the parties that a decision on the appeal was not imminent and they should continue to negotiate. He complied with this instruction and, under financial pressure, the nation agreed to a rate of 12-1/2 percent. The nation was not told of the decision awarding them a 20 percent increase.

The Navajo Nation brought this action for breach of fiduciary duty claiming damages of approximately $600 million. The Court of Federal Claims characterized the actions of the Secretary of the Interior in favouring the interests of the mining company over those of the Nation as "violat[ing] the most basic common law fiduciary duties."[33] However, that court ruled that the breach was not actionable because the United States did not have a trust relationship with the Navajo Nation and monetary relief was not available. The United States Court of Appeals for the Federal Circuit reversed the dismissal of the claim and remanded it for further proceedings, including determination of damages. The court held that the *Indian Mineral Leasing Act* and its regulations were similar to those governing resources that were the subject of *Mitchell II* insofar as federal authority is retained. The statute and regulations left no significant authority in the hands of the Nation. Therefore, the Court of Federal Claims had erred in holding that there was no authorization for a trust relationship between the United States and the Navajo Nation as to the coal resources. As in the *White Mountain Apache* case, an appeal was brought by the United States to the United States Supreme Court.

Decisions in both the *White Mountain Apache*[34] and *Navajo*[35] cases were handed down by the United States Supreme Court on March 4, 2003. In *White Mountain Apache*, a majority of the Court upheld the decision of the United States Court of Appeals for the Federal Circuit but, in *Navajo Nation,* a majority reversed. Justice Souter delivered the opinion of the Court in *White Mountain Apache*, in which four other justices joined. Justice Thomas filed a dissenting opinion in which three other justices joined. Justice Souter noted that "the two seminal cases of tribal trust claims for damages,"[36] *Mitchell I* and *Mitchell II*, "give a sense of when it is fair to infer a fiduciary duty qualifying under the Indian Tucker Act and when it is not."[37] In *Mitchell I,* the characterization of the trust as "limited" or "bare" had distinguished the *General Allotment Act*'s trust-in-name from one with hallmarks of a more conventional fiduciary relationship. There was no functional obligation to manage the timber. In contrast, in *Mitchell II*, the government had full responsibility to manage the Indian resource and land and this led to the imposition of an enforceable fiduciary duty.

Turning to the statute before the Court, Justice Souter declared that the 1960 Act relating to Fort Apache went beyond a bare trust and "permits a fair inference that the Government is subject to duties as a trustee and liable in damages."[38] The statutory language expressly defined a fiduciary relationship in the provision that Fort Apache be "held by the United States in trust for the White Mountain Apache Tribe." Unlike the *General Allotment Act*, however, the statute proceeds to invest the United States with discretionary authority to make direct use of portions of the trust corpus. The United States was in actual occupation of the fort on a daily basis and so had at least as much control over the fort as it had over the timber in *Mitchell II*. He noted:[39]

> While it is true that the 1960 Act does not, like the statute cited in that case, expressly subject the Government to duties of management and conservation, the fact that the property occupied by the United States is expressly subject to a trust supports a fair inference that an obligation to preserve the property improvements was incumbent on the United States as trustee. This is so because elementary trust law, after all, confirms the commonsense assumption that a fiduciary administering trust property may not allow it to fall into ruin on his watch. . . . Given this duty on the part of the trustee to preserve corpus [the trust property], it naturally follows that the Government should be liable in damages for the breach of its fiduciary duties. *Mitchell II* , *supra*, at 226.

In a note, he pointed out that:

> Where, as in *Mitchell II*, 463 206, 225 (1983), the relevant sources of substantive law create "[a]ll of the necessary elements of a common-law trust," there is no need to look elsewhere for the source of a trust relationship. We have recognized a general trust relationship since 1831. *Cherokee Nation v. Georgia*, 5 Pet. 1, 16 (1831) (characterizing the relationship between Indian tribes and the United States as "a ward to his guardian"); *Mitchell II*, *supra*, at 225 (discussing "the undisputed existence of a general trust relationship between the United States and the Indian people").

He then considered and rejected the arguments raised by the United States against this conclusion. The government's interpretation of the statute as not even creating a bare trust was at odds with a plain reading of it. The government's argument that there had to be an explicit provision for money damages was also rejected. A fair inference sufficed and this was found in general trust law. Finally, the Court rejected the government's argument that it should not have to pay any compensation for past breaches of its fiduciary obligations and that an injunction to prevent future breaches was the only appropriate remedy. Justice Souter said:

> We think this is clearly wrong. If the Government is suggesting that the recompense for run-down buildings should be an affirmative order to repair them, it is merely

proposing the economic (but perhaps cumbersome) equivalent of damages. But if it is suggesting that relief must be limited to an injunction to toe the fiduciary mark in the future, it would bar the courts from making the Tribe whole for deterioration already suffered, and shield the Government against the remedy whose very availability would deter it from wasting trust property in the period before a Tribe has gone to court for injunctive relief.

Justice Ginsburg wrote a concurring opinion in which she was joined by Justice Breyer. She said that she was satisfied that the Court's opinion was not inconsistent with the opinion that she wrote in *Navajo Nation*. The decision in *Mitchell I* applied to that case, while the instant case was governed by *Mitchell II*.

In his dissenting opinion, Justice Thomas said the majority had changed the test to determine if Congress has conferred a substantive right enforceable against the government to money damages from one of fair interpretation to one of fair inference. But even under this new test, the 1960 *Act* only created a bare trust as in *Mitchell I* and did not mandate compensation. In concluding otherwise, the majority gave far too much weight to the government's factual "control" over the Fort Apache property, which was all that distinguished the instant case from *Mitchell I*:[40]

> [U]ntil now, the Court has never held the United States liable for money damages under the *Tucker Act* or *Indian Tucker Act* based on notions of factual control that have no foundation in the actual text of the relevant statutes.

The Court's focus on control rendered the inquiry open-ended, with questions of jurisdiction determined by murky principles of the common law of trusts, and a parcel-by-parcel determination whether portions of the property were under United States control.

Justice Ginsburg gave the opinion of the Court in *Navajo Nation*.[41] Chief Justice Rehnquist and four justices joined in the opinion. Justice Souter delivered a dissenting opinion in which two other justices joined. Justice Ginsburg commenced her judgment by saying:[42]

> This Court's decisions in *United States v. Mitchell*, 445 U.S. 535 (1980) (*Mitchell I*), and *United States v. Mitchell*, 463 U.S. 206 (1983) (*Mitchell II*), control this case. Concluding that the controversy here falls within *Mitchell I*'s domain, we hold that the Tribe's claim for compensation from the Federal Government fails, for it does not derive from any liability-imposing provision of the [*Indian Mineral Leasing Act (IMLA)*] or its implementing regulations.

In her review of the *IMLA* she noted that it was designed to advance tribal independence and empowered tribes to negotiate mining leases themselves and, as to coal leasing, assigns primarily an approving role to the secretary.

After giving an account of the facts and the *Mitchell* cases, she summarized the legal position resulting from those decisions:[43]

> To state a claim cognizable under *Indian Tucker Act*, *Mitchell I* and *Mitchell II* thus instruct, a Tribe must identify a substantive source of law that establishes specific fiduciary or other duties, and allege that the Government has failed faithfully to perform those duties. . . . If that threshold is passed, the court must then determine whether the relevant source of substantive law can fairly be interpreted as mandating compensation for damages sustained as a result of a breach of the duties [the governing law] impose[s]. . . . Although the undisputed existence of a general trust relationship between the United States and the Indian people can reinforc[e] the conclusion that the relevant statute or regulation imposes fiduciary duties, that relationship alone is insufficient to support jurisdiction under the *Indian Tucker Act*. Instead, the analysis must train on specific rights-creating or duty-imposing statutory or regulatory prescriptions. Those prescriptions need not, however, expressly provide for money damages; the availability of such damages may be inferred. . . . [T]he substantive source of law may grant the claimant a right to recover damages either expressly or by implication. [Internal quotation marks and citations omitted.]

She next considered whether the *IMLA* and its implementing regulations could fairly be interpreted as mandating compensation for the government's alleged breach of trust and concluded that they could not. They did not impose obligations resembling the detailed fiduciary responsibilities that *Mitchell II* found adequate to support a claim for money damages. The attempt in the dissent to align this case with *Mitchell II* rather than *Mitchell I*, however valiant, fell short of the mark. The secretary did not have a comprehensive managerial role nor was he expressly invested with responsibility to secure the best interests of the Indians. There was not even a limited trust relationship as in *Mitchell I*. Imposing a fiduciary duty on the government to negotiate mining leases would be out of line with Indian self-determination.

In his dissenting opinion, Justice Souter said that he parted with the majority because he took the secretary's obligation to approve mineral leases under the statute as "raising a substantive fiduciary obligation to the Navajo Nation (Tribe) which has pleaded and shown enough to survive the Government's motion for summary judgment."[44] He criticized the majority for giving too much weight to the *IMLA*'s objective of tribal autonomy and not enough to its objective of maximizing tribal revenues through the secretary's approval obligation.

Issues that Have Arisen Under the United States Law

Termination of Trust Relationship

It has been held that the Congress may validly terminate the trust relationship with particular tribes. In *Menominee Tribe v. United States*,[45] the United States Court of Appeals, Federal Circuit, held that application of a *Termination Act* gave rise to no justiciable claim for breach of trust. The *Termination* statutes reflected the policy of the government between 1943 to 1961 to terminate the special relationship between the federal government and the tribe in question.[46] Congress has terminated its trust relationship with over a hundred tribes.[47] *Termination* laws forbade a tribe from exercising governmental powers and require the tribe's property and assets to be distributed to tribal members. Once the tribe and its reservation have been abolished in this manner, the tribe's trust relationship with the United States government ceases to exist. However, the Supreme Court of the United States has held that termination of the relationship by Congress must be express and will not be implied.[48]

Responsible Departments

Although the trust responsibility of the United States government is primarily administered by the Bureau of Indian Affairs, other agencies of that government are also subject to fiduciary standards. In *Ute Indian Tribe v. Utah*,[49] the district court held that the actions of the U.S. Forest Service in its dealings with Indians had to be judged by such standards and quoted in support the statement of the Court of Appeals for the Ninth Circuit in *Nance v. Environmental Protection Agency*: "[i]t is fairly clear that *any* federal government action is subject to the United States' fiduciary responsibilities towards the Indian tribes."[50]

Applicable Rules

Although courts have recognized that not all the rules that govern private fiduciary relationship apply fully to claims by an Indian group against the government, the general rule is that:[51]

> Where a trust relationship between Indians and the Government is established, the Government's actions normally are judged according to standards established in traditional trust law doctrine. The standard of duty as trustee for Indians is not mere reasonableness, but the highest fiduciary standards.

In *United States v. Mason*, the United States Supreme Court referred to *Scott on Trusts* for standards governing the United States as trustee, stating that the government's duty is "to exercise such care and skill as a man of ordinary prudence would exercise in dealing with his own property."[52] The United States Supreme Court applied well-established trust principles in *Mitchell II*[53] to find the government accountable in damages for breach of its fiduciary duty. In doing so, it cited standard texts on trust law. One example of the application of traditional trust rules to the relationship is the requirement of the United States to make a proper accounting of the trust funds in its custody and to keep accurate records.[54] In *Cobell*,[55] the United States Court of Appeal for the District of Columbia Circuit affirmed the district court's conclusion that the United States was required—both by the terms of the relevant legislation and by general trust principles—to provide beneficiaries of individual Indian monies accounts with a complete historical accounting of their funds. It also affirmed the district court's order requiring the government to provide periodic reports on its progress in providing the required accounting.

Conflict of Interest

The United States Supreme Court has also recognized that the government is no ordinary fiduciary, and statute may relieve it from some obligations normally owed by a fiduciary. This is illustrated by the decision of the Court in *Nevada v. United States*[56] where the Court rejected an argument that the government had a conflict of interest and could not represent both a reservation and a reclamation project. Holding that the Indians' interest would not be compromised, the Court said:

> [T]he Government cannot follow the fastidious standards of a private fiduciary, who would breach his duties to a single beneficiary solely by representing potentially conflicting interests without the beneficiary's consent.

In *Three Affiliated Tribes of Fort Berthold Reservation v. United States*,[57] the United States Court of Claims formulated the "good faith effort" test to resolve the potential conflict between the fiduciary duty owed to Indians and the power of the government to expropriate Indian property for the wider public good. The test, which was adopted by the United States Supreme Court in *United States v. Sioux Nation*,[58] requires Congress to make a good-faith effort to give the Indians the full value of the land taken.

Scope of Fiduciary Duty

The fiduciary duty is not limited to property but extends to services provided by federal agencies to Indians.[59] An example is *White v. Califano*,[60] which held that the United States has a trust responsibility to ensure that Indians have access to health care where other agencies are unwilling or unable to provide such care. Likewise, in *McNabb v. Bowen*,[61] the ninth circuit held that the Indian Health Service was obligated to provide necessary health care to an indigent Indian child. However, as noted above, the United States Supreme Court held in *Lincoln v. Virgil*[62] that the government could re-allocate funds in its discretion to provide services to a broader group of Indians.

Consultation

The fiduciary duty has also been held to be the basis of a duty to consult with tribes or Indians where federal action may affect their rights.[63]

Australia [64]

The Australian law relating to Aboriginal peoples has not been applied as often by Canadian courts as the United States law. In part, this may reflect the fact that the Australian law is also in an early stage of development. For example, it was not until the decision of the Australian High Court in 1992 in *Mabo v. Queensland (No. 2)*[65] that the Australian law recognized Aboriginal title. A more fundamental reason may be that Australian law lacks any equivalent to the Royal Proclamation of 1763 and has a different constitutional history. As noted by Philippa Homer, First Assistant Secretary of the Native Title Division in Australia's Commonwealth Attorney-General Department, in a recent paper:[66]

> Australia has no equivalent of the *Royal Proclamation*, no history of negotiating treaties with indigenous inhabitants, no equivalent to the *Indian Act*, 1876, no Comprehensive Claims policy, no equivalent of the *Canada Act, 1982* and no equivalent of the British Columbia Treaty Commission.

She points out that it was exactly one hundred years after section 91(24) of the *Constitution Act, 1867* gave exclusive authority to the Canadian federal government to legislate for "Indians, and Lands reserved for the Indians" that the Australian Commonwealth Parliament gained power for the first time to make general laws with respect to Aboriginal peoples after a national referendum approved conferring such power upon it. Until that time, the Aboriginal reserves set up in Australia were generally created and administered under colonial, state, and territorial legislation.

Despite these differences, as observed by Lamer C.J.C. in *R. v. Van der Peet*, Australian law is still persuasive in the Canadian context:[67]

> The High Court of Australia has also considered the question of the basis and nature of aboriginal rights. Like that of the United States, Australia's aboriginal law differs in significant respects from that of Canada. . . . Despite these relevant differences, the analysis of the basis of aboriginal title in the landmark decision of the High Court in *Mabo v. Queensland (No.2)* (1992), 175 C.L.R. 1 is persuasive in the Canadian context.

With regard to the fiduciary obligations owed to Aboriginal peoples, the Australian law is still not clear whether such obligations are recognized. A major reason for this uncertainty is that the High Court of Australia has been less willing than the Supreme Court of Canada to find the existence of fiduciary relationships generally. In an article published in 1994, Chief Justice Mason of the High Court of Australia commented:[68]

> My impression is that there has been in Canada a greater willingness to find a fiduciary relationship than in Australia and New Zealand, reluctance to do being

perhaps even more marked in England. As yet, we in Australia have no counterpart to *Guerin v. The Queen*. The decision has been relied upon in aboriginal land claim cases but so far it has not formed the basis of a decision.

This reluctance is indicated by the decision of the High Court in *Breen v. Williams*.[69] Like the decision of the Supreme Court of Canada in *McInerney v. MacDonald*,[70] it involved the right of a patient to obtain access to medical records from the patient's doctor. However, the High Court of Australia declined to follow *McInerney* and held that the doctor had no fiduciary duty to provide such records. The Court was unanimous in its approach. Some of the comments on the Canadian law are quite sharp. In their joint judgment, Dawson and Toohey J.J. said La Forest J.'s judgment in *McInerney* was perhaps reflective of a tendency not found in Australia but to be seen in the United States and to a lesser extent Canada, to view a fiduciary relationship as imposing obligations which go beyond the exaction of loyalty and as displacing the role of contract and tort by becoming an independent source of obligations and creating new forms of civil wrong. They comment, "But, with respect, that is achieved by assertion rather than analysis and, whilst it may effectuate a preference for a particular result, it does not involve the development or elucidation of any accepted doctrine."[71]

In words approved by Gummow J. in his judgment, Gaudron and McHugh JJ. also criticized the tendency of Canadian courts to apply fiduciary principles in an expansive manner so as to supplement tort law and provide a basis for the creation of new forms of civil wrongs. They went further in saying:[72]

> The Canadian cases also reveal a tendency to view fiduciary obligations as both proscriptive and prescriptive. However, Australian courts only recognize proscriptive fiduciary duties. This is not the place to explore the differences between the law of Canada and the law of Australia on this topic. With great respect to the Canadian courts, however, many cases in that jurisdiction pay insufficient regard to the effect that the imposition of fiduciary duties on particular relationships has on the law of negligence, contract, agency, trusts and companies in their application to those relationships. Further, many of the Canadian cases pay insufficient, if any, regard to the fact that the imposition of fiduciary duties often gives rise to proprietary remedies that affect the distribution of assets in bankruptcies and insolvencies.

Given this general reluctance of Australian courts to find fiduciary relationships, it may be expected that the doctrine of fiduciary obligations is not as valuable a tool to achieve justice for Australian Aboriginal peoples as it has been for Canadian Aboriginal peoples, and this expectation is confirmed in a review of the relevant case law.

Northern Land Council v. The Commonwealth[73] was an early case on the possible existence of a fiduciary duty owed by the Australian government to

Aboriginal people, and was decided in 1987, just three years after *Guerin* was decided by the Supreme Court of Canada. The case concerned an agreement requiring compensation payments from a mining company which operated a uranium mine on Aboriginal land. The Northern Land Council, representing an Aboriginal group, claimed breach of fiduciary duty, duress, undue influence, and unconscionable conduct on the part of the government. The dispute came before the High Court of Australia by way of a stated case, and the Court decided that the "question of fundamental importance" of whether a fiduciary obligation was owed should not be determined in the abstract but in the light of the facts as found at the trial. The question was, therefore, left open for a later decision.[74]

Mabo (No. 2),[75] decided in 1992, is the seminal decision on Aboriginal (or Native) title in Australian law. It was brought by the Meriam people, who asserted an exclusive right to occupy the Murray Islands in Queensland. Existing law would have denied this claim on the basis that, prior to European settlement, Australia was *terra nullius*—it belonged to nobody—and so it became the absolute property of the Crown, free of any Native title: *Milirrpum v. Nabalco Property Ltd. and The Commonwealth of Australia*.[76] A majority of six out of seven of the High Court of Australia justices rejected this traditional doctrine and found that Native title survived the acquisition of sovereignty by the British Crown and was recognized by the common law of Australia. However, such title is vulnerable to extinguishment by the valid exercise of sovereign power and, in particular, by the making of an inconsistent grant. It may be noted that subsequent decisions of the Court have held that Native title is extinguished by grants of freehold title and of leases giving exclusive possession.[77] It may also be noted that in 1993, the Commonwealth government passed the *Native Title Act* that sets up a framework to govern the establishment and extinguishment of Native title. Significant and controversial amendments were made in 1998 which made it easier for Native title to be extinguished.

The decision in *Mabo (No. 2)* did not rest on any fiduciary duty owed by the Crown to the Indigenous peoples of Australia. Indeed, only two of the justices (Toohey and Dawson J.J.) considered the claim for breach of fiduciary duty in detail. The others made only passing reference in their otherwise comprehensive accounts of the relevant law.[78] The fiduciary duty played a significant role in the judgment of Toohey J. Relying on *Guerin*,[79] he said:[80]

> [I]f the Crown in right of Queensland has the power to alienate land the subject of the Meriam people's traditional rights and interests and the result of that alienation is the loss of traditional title, and if the Meriam people's power to deal with their title is restricted in so far as it is inalienable, except to the Crown, then this power and corresponding vulnerability give rise to a fiduciary obligation on the part of the Crown. The power to destroy or impair a people's interests in this way

is extraordinary and is sufficient to attract regulation by Equity to ensure that the position is not abused. The fiduciary relationship arises, therefore, out of the *power* of the Crown to extinguish traditional title by alienating the land or otherwise; it does not depend on an exercise of that power.

He also found an alternative basis for the fiduciary duty:[81]

Moreover if, contrary to the view I have expressed, the relationship between the Crown and the Meriam people with respect to traditional title alone were insufficient to give rise to a fiduciary obligation, both the course of dealings by the Queensland Government with respect to the Islands since annexation . . . and the exercise of control over or regulation of the Islanders themselves by welfare legislation . . . would certainly create such an obligation.

Dawson J. was the sole dissenting member of the Court in *Mabo (No. 2)* in not acknowledging the existence of Native title on the part of the Meriam people. This rejection of Native title was the basis of his rejection of a fiduciary duty on the part of the Crown. He summarized his conclusion on this point as follows:[82]

In the absence of any native title and in the light of the detailed legislative provisions which govern the relationship of the Crown with the aboriginal inhabitants of the State upon the basis that there is no native title or (if there is a difference) traditional rights in the land, there is, in my view, no foundation for the imposition of a fiduciary duty upon the Crown to deal with the lands comprising the Murray Islands in a manner involving the recognition of any of the rights which the plaintiffs claim. Of course, it was not suggested, nor could it be, that the Queensland legislature which, subject to any paramount Commonwealth legislation, has plenary power to deal with those lands, is under any fiduciary duty in the exercise of that power.

It may be noted that, since he alone denied the existence of Native title and saw such title as the foundation for the imposition of a fiduciary duty, his judgment on this point was clearly not one that finds any support in the other judgments.

The decision of the Australian High Court in *Mabo (No. 2)* and the United States, Canadian, and New Zealand law on the fiduciary obligations owed to Aboriginal peoples were reviewed by Finch J., president of the National Native Title Tribunal, in the 1995 case of *Wadi Wadi People Native Title Application*.[83] The members of the Wadi Wadi People lodged a Native title determination application with the registrar of the tribunal, who formed the opinion that it could not succeed. In the registrar's opinion, the applicants had failed to show a *prima facie* case of Native title as required by the *Native Title Act 1993* because there had been a grant in fee simple of the lands in 1817. Finch J. upheld the registrar's determination. The argument for the applicants included a submission that the grant was invalid on the grounds that there had been a breach by the Crown of its fiduciary duty by failing to satisfy itself that no one else had ownership of the land and by transferring the land without notice to the traditional owners. This argument was rejected on the grounds that, whatever may be the scope of any fiduciary duty, "it could not limit legislative power even if the particular legislation were a breach of the obligation."[84]

The High Court of Australia decided *Wik Peoples v. Queensland*[85] in 1996 without resolving the issue of whether a fiduciary obligation was owed to the Indigenous people concerned. The major issue in the case was whether the grant of a pastoral lease not conferring a right of exclusive possession extinguished Native title. The Court held that the answer depends upon whether the lease and the Native title are legally compatible and so able to co-exist. The Aboriginal plaintiffs submitted, as part of their argument, that the Crown owed them a fiduciary duty. As observed by Brennan C.J. (with whom McHugh and Dawson J.J. agreed), the duty was said to arise from the vulnerability of Native title, the Crown's power to extinguish it, and the position occupied for many years by the Indigenous inhabitants vis-à-vis the government of the state. He rejected these submissions. There had to be some reasonable basis for the beneficiary of a fiduciary duty to expect that the fiduciary will act in his interest.[86] In the case before him, the only function performed by the Crown was to alienate the land. He said that he "was unable to accept that a fiduciary duty can be owed by the Crown to the holders of native title in the exercise of a statutory power to alienate land whereby their native title in or over that land is liable to be extinguished without their consent and contrary to their interests."[87] He concluded that the power of alienation conferred on the Crown was inherently inconsistent with the notion that it should be exercised as agent for or on behalf of the Indigenous inhabitants of the land to be alienated. "Accordingly, there is no foundation for imputing to the Crown a fiduciary duty governing the exercise of the power."[88] This finding led him to reject the further submission that the Crown held its reversionary interest in the leased land as a constructive trustee for the holders of Native title. The other justices delivering separate opinions did not find it necessary to consider the submissions on fiduciary duty and constructive trust.[89]

The current status of any fiduciary duty of the Commonwealth of Australia to the Aboriginal peoples of Australia was described "as an open question" by Kirby J. of the High Court of Australia in the 1997 case of *Thorpe v. Commonwealth of Australia (No. 3).*[90] In that case, the plaintiff, an Aboriginal Australian, sought the following declarations:

1. That, as the result of genocide and illegal invasion, the Commonwealth of Australia owes a fiduciary duty to the original peoples of Australia

2. That the Commonwealth ought to move the United Nations General Assembly for an advisory opinion of the International Court of Justice as to the separate rights and legal status of the original peoples

3. That the Commonwealth ought to negotiate with the plaintiff about the terms of the application to the International Court of Justice.

Kirby J. held that he did not have jurisdiction to make these declarations. The second and third declarations covered matters that were for the executive government to determine, not the Court. It could not control the way in which the Commonwealth conducts Australia's international relations.

With regard to the first declaration regarding the fiduciary duty, Kirby J. said it could not stand alone. It either survived or fell depending upon the fate of the two succeeding declarations, which he dismissed. Therefore, he did not deal in detail with the merits of the requested declaration although he did note that there were difficulties in its specific wording. It was a general declaration of law not a matter for judicial decision because courts usually only determine legal questions in the context of a particular dispute and do not give rulings in the abstract. Also, the foundation for the fiduciary obligation identified in the writ included events such as "the illegal invasion" of Australia by Europeans which occurred long before the establishment of the Commonwealth. It was not clear how the Commonwealth would be liable for such acts.

Despite the rejection of this particular application for a declaration of the existence of a fiduciary duty owed by the Commonwealth of Australia to Australian Aboriginal peoples, Kirby J. made it clear that he was not rejecting the existence of such a duty if correctly brought before the Court. He referred to the law of the United States which, as we saw earlier in this chapter, has held that a fiduciary relationship exists in certain circumstances between the United States and the Indian tribes. He also observed that "[a] fiduciary duty with respect to the lands of indigenous peoples has also received a measure of acceptance in Canada."[91] *Guerin*[92] was cited in support of this statement. Referring to the decision of the Supreme Court of Canada in *Sparrow*,[93] he commented:[94]

> Indeed, in Canada it has been suggested that the Crown has a broader responsibility to act in a fiduciary way towards indigenous peoples arising out of the Crown's historical powers over, and assumption of responsibility for, such peoples within its protection. The recognition of Aboriginal rights within the Canadian Constitution has also been invoked as a foundation for a fiduciary relationship.

Having summarized the law of the United States and Canada, he then turned to the Australian law. He first commented that the approach followed in the United States and Canada "has not gathered the support of a majority in this Court."[95] He next reviewed the *Mabo (No. 2)*[96] case and observed that the holding in that case "did not rest upon any fiduciary obligation owed by the Crown to the indigenous peoples of Australia"[97] and that, as discussed above,[98] only Toohey J. found a fiduciary relationship. He also mentioned Toohey J.'s acknowledgment that any fiduciary relationship did not limit the legislative power of the Parliaments of Australia to derogate from that relationship. However, "any such legislation (and presumably any rule of common law) in derogation would be a breach of the fiduciary obligation if its effect is adverse to the interests of Aboriginal title-holders or does not take account of those interests." Kirby J. then referred to the judgment of Dawson J. in *Mabo (No. 2)*, which is also discussed above, who had concluded that any fiduciary obligation of the kind that had been recognized in Canada was dependent upon the subsistence of an Aboriginal interest existing in or over land. Neither Toohey J. nor Dawson J. considered whether a fiduciary relationship existed *in abstracto*. Continuing his review of Australian law, Kirby J. pointed out that, although in *Wik Peoples v. Queensland*[99] arguments were advanced based on an alleged fiduciary obligation owed by the Crown to the Indigenous peoples, the Court disposed of the matter without resolving whether such an obligation existed and, if it did, whether it entitled the Aboriginal claimants to relief in that case.

Concluding this review of the relevant decisions of the Australian High Court, Kirby J. summarized the status of the law in 1997:[100]

> The result is that whether a fiduciary duty is owed by the Crown to the indigenous peoples of Australia remains an open question. This Court has simply not determined it. Certainly it has not determined it adversely to the proposition. On the other hand, there is no holding endorsing such a fiduciary duty, still less for the generality of the claim asserted in the first declaration of Mr. Thorpe's writ."

He mentioned some of the many difficulties in the claim as noted above. One specific difficulty was expressed as follows:[101]

> The notion of a fiduciary duty has developed in Australia along different lines from those taken by the courts in the United States and Canada. Care must therefore be exercised in invoking the authority of such courts to establish a fiduciary relationship in Australia where this is contested.

In support of this cautionary comment, he referred to the judgment of the Court in *Breen v. Williams*[102] which is considered above.[103]

Bodney v. Westralia Airports Corporation Pty. Ltd.[104] was a decision of the Federal Court of Australia in November 2000. It involved a claim of Native title to lands adjoining the Perth airport held by the Commonwealth of Australia and leased to Westralia Airports Corporation. One of the claimant groups contended that the Crown, in its dealings with Indigenous people in relation to land in Western Australia, owed fiduciary duties and, in acquiring and disposing of land including lands in the claim area, had breached those duties.[105] Therefore, in their submission, the land should be declared to be subject to a constructive trust for those Aboriginal peoples who would, if none of the grants had been made, have held Native title to the land. Counsel for the claimant group relied on United States, New Zealand, and Canadian authorities in support of these propositions as well as the judgments in *Mabo (No. 2)*.

Lehane J. rejected the claim of breach of fiduciary duty and constructive trust.[106] His conclusions on this issue were stated as follows:[107]

> But the second applicant's pleading does not, in my view, allege facts which would establish a fiduciary duty, on the part of the State or of the Commonwealth, requiring either the State or the Commonwealth not to participate as they did (or in the manner in which they did) in the transactions as a result of which the Commonwealth obtained title to the land incorporating the claim area.

In conclusion, the analysis by Kirby J. in *Thorpe* seems to remain an accurate reflection of the current state of the Australian law. None of the major decisions of the High Court of Australia on Aboriginal rights since *Thorpe* have revisited the question of whether there is a fiduciary relationship between the Crown and Aboriginal Australians.[108] It cannot be said that the Court has either rejected or accepted the existence of such a relationship between the Crown and Aboriginal Australians. However, that Court has clearly been more reluctant than the Supreme Courts of Canada and of the United States to find a fiduciary relationship. A major reason for this reluctance is that, as noted by Kirby J. in *Thorpe*, "the notion of a fiduciary duty has developed in Australia along different lines from those taken by the courts in the United States and Canada."[109] In other words, the reluctance in the context of Aboriginal peoples is a reflection of a more general reluctance to embrace fiduciary obligations.

The New Zealand Law

Aboriginal law in New Zealand is a complex interplay of treaty, case law, settlement, and statutory extinguishment.[110] The sovereignty of the New Zealand government is derived from the *Treaty of Waitangi* in 1840.[111] Early cases recognized the validity of Maori property rights as confirmed and guaranteed by the treaty.[112] However, later cases gave less weight to Maori rights as recognized by the treaty, and they were often denied the protection of the law. In *Hoani Te Heuheu Tukino v. Aotea District Maori Land Board*,[113] Viscount Simon L.C. said that any rights purported to be conferred by the treaty could not be enforced by the courts except in so far as they had been incorporated in the municipal law.[114] The treaty had become almost a dead letter.

A turning point was the enactment in 1975 of the *Treaty of Waitangi Act*,[115] which established the Waitangi Tribunal with the duty to inquire into claims that the treaty has been, or will be, breached. If the tribunal finds the claim well founded it may recommend to the Crown that action be taken to compensate for or remove the breach.

Paul McHugh has written extensively on the topic of New Zealand law and the *Treaty of Waitangi*. He points out that "the evidence clearly shows that there was a gulf between the tribal signatures and the Pakeha [non-Maori] who encouraged Maori adhesion to the pact."[116] He also points out that the treaty cannot be fully understood simply by reference to the English version.[117] The Maori version has concepts such as "rangatiratanga" (the authority of the chiefs over their own people) and "taonga" (treasured things) which are not reflected in the English version. It is, therefore, incorrect to see the treaty as a simple ceding of sovereignty by the Maori chiefs in return for a guarantee of their lands, forests, fisheries, and other property. The approach followed in recent years by the Waitangi Tribunal and the courts of New Zealand has been to go beyond the literal meaning of the English version and develop certain "principles" of the treaty to determine its application to specific situations.[118] A key principle has been that of the fiduciary duty owed by the New Zealand government to the Maori people.

In a series of recent cases, the New Zealand Court of Appeal has developed a doctrine of fiduciary duty owed by the government of New Zealand to the Maori. As acknowledged by the Court,[119] this doctrine is similar to that established by the Supreme Court of Canada in *Guerin*.

The first case to recognize the fiduciary duty was the 1987 decision of the New Zealand Court of Appeal in *New Zealand Maori Council v. Attorney General*.[120] The issue before the Court was whether the government could transfer land to non-Crown ownership under the *State-Owned Enterprises Act*. Section 9 of the Act provided that nothing in the Act would permit the Crown "to act in a manner that is inconsistent with the principles of the Treaty of Waitangi." The Maori Council sought a declaration to prevent the transfer of land in a manner that would put it outside the power of the Crown to return it to the Maori if the Treaty of Waitangi Tribunal made such a recommendation. The Court granted a declaration which required the Crown to establish a scheme of safeguards to give reasonable assurance that Maori claims would not be prejudiced. It also granted leave for the parties to apply for further orders.

The Court reached its conclusion that a fiduciary duty exists by analogy to the fiduciary duty owed by one partner to another after finding that the treaty reflected a partnership between the Maori and the Pakeha. Cooke P. explained his reasoning as follows:[121]

What has already been said amounts to acceptance of the submission for the applicants that the relationship between the Treaty partners creates responsibilities analogous to fiduciary duties. Counsel were also right, in my opinion, in saying that the duty of the Crown is not merely passive but extends to active protection of Maori people in the use of their lands and waters to the fullest extent practicable . . . that the duty to act reasonably and in the utmost good faith is not one-sided. For their part the Maori people have undertaken a duty of loyalty to the Queen, full acceptance of her Government through her responsible Ministers, and reasonable co-operation.

He also noted that the other members of the Court had reached similar conclusions:[122]

At the outset I mentioned that each member of the Court was writing a separate judgment. It will be seen that approaching the case independently we have all reached two major conclusions. First that the principles of the Treaty of Waitangi override everything else in the *State-Owned Enterprises Act*. Second that those principles require the Pakeha and Maori Treaty partners to act towards each other reasonably and with the utmost good faith.

That duty is no light one. It is infinitely more than a formality. If a breach of the duty is demonstrated at any time, the duty of the Court will be to insist that it be honoured.

Two years later, in *New Zealand Maori Council v. Attorney General*,[123] the Court restated and expanded upon its position. The fiduciary duty was held to include a duty of consultation. The case was a follow-up to the 1987 decision. The government had announced a plan to transfer forestry assets without ownership of the land itself. The Court found a possible breach of the duty to consult and ordered a further hearing:[124]

It may be as well to add some observations, in the hope of helping resolution of the problem. In the judgments in 1987 this Court stressed the concept of partnership. We think it right to say that the good faith owed to each other by the parties to the Treaty must extend to consultation on truly major issues. That is really clear beyond argument. . . .

The case of *Te Runanga o Muriwhenua Inc. v. Attorney General*,[125] decided in 1990, concerned the fishing rights of Maori tribes and a report of the Waitangi Tribunal. The Court's ruling covered the jurisdiction of the tribunal and related matters. In the course of the judgment, the Court commented on the analogy between the Canadian and the New Zealand law on the fiduciary duty owed to Aboriginal peoples:[126]

More recently in Canada Indian rights have been identified as pre-existing legal rights not created by Royal proclamation, statute or executive order. It has been recognised that, in some circumstances at least, the Crown is under a fiduciary duty to holders of such rights in dealings relating to their extinction. The judgments in *Guerin*, cited earlier, delivered by Dickson J and Wilson J seem likely to be found of major guidance when such matters come finally to be decided in New Zealand. The approach of this Court in the *Maori Council* case to the principles of the Treaty of Waitangi and the partnership and fiduciary analogies there drawn are consistent with them. Her Majesty the Queen's Waitangi Day speech gives the ideal a scope much wider than legal proceedings. There are constitutional differences between Canada and New Zealand, but the *Guerin* judgments do not appear to turn on these. Moreover, in interpreting New Zealand parliamentary and common law it must be right for New Zealand Courts to lean against any inference that in this democracy the rights of the Maori people are less respected than the rights of aboriginal peoples are in North America.

The 1993 decision of the Court in *Te Runanga o Wharekauri Rekahu Inc. v. Attorney General*[127] was another case on fishing rights. It was brought by Maori opposed to a surrender of those rights in exchange for shares in a fishing company. Their claim was dismissed as disclosing no reasonable cause of action. Again, the Court commented on the law in Canada as well as that in Australia, which it thought strengthened its own opinion that fiduciary duties and "a relationship akin to partnership" existed between the Maori and the Pakeha. In the words of the Court:[128]

[C]learly there is now a substantial body of Commonwealth case law pointing to a fiduciary duty.

In New Zealand the Treaty of Waitangi is major support for such a duty. The New Zealand judgments are part of widespread international recognition that the rights of indigenous peoples are entitled to some effective protection and advancement. The only real difference is that, whereas the Canadian Supreme Court required more than 18 months before delivery of its decision in *Sparrow* and the High Court of Australia slightly more than a year before delivery of its decision in *Mabo*, in New Zealand circumstances this Court has had to move more quickly—possibly at the cost of some public and other understanding of the complexity of the task.

Until recently, the highest court in the New Zealand legal system was the Privy Council in London. In *New Zealand Maori Council v. Attorney General [1994]*,[129] that Court also considered section 9 of the *State-Owned Enterprises Act*. As already noted, that section provides that nothing in the *Act* shall permit the Crown to act in a manner that is inconsistent with the principles of the *Treaty of Waitangi*. The government had made a proposal to transfer assets of the broadcasting corporation and the Maori were concerned that this would further weaken the Maori language. The New Zealand Court of Appeal had upheld the judgment of the trial judge permitting the transfer and the Privy Council dismissed the further appeal. In its view, the transfer would have little, if any, effect on the Crown's ability to fulfil its obligation under the treaty. Giving the judgment of the Privy Council, Lord Woolf explained the nature of the Crown's obligation under the treaty to protect "taonga," or Maori treasures such as the Maori language, as being "solemn." He continued:[130]

It does not however mean that the obligation is absolute and unqualified. This would be inconsistent with the Crown's other responsibilities as the government of New Zealand and the relationship between Maori and the Crown. This relationship the Treaty envisages should be founded on reasonableness, mutual cooperation and trust. It is therefore accepted by both parties that the Crown in carrying out its obligations is not required in protecting taonga to go beyond taking such action as is reasonable in the prevailing circumstances.

The question of Aboriginal or Maori customary title formed the subject matter of the decision of the New Zealand Court of Appeal in *Te Runanganui o Te Ika Whenua Inc. Society v. Attorney General*,[131] also decided in 1994. The Court recognized that Crown title is subject to existing Aboriginal rights. It also said that extinguishment of Aboriginal title has to be consistent with the Crown's fiduciary duty and to include proper compensation. Cooke P. referred to the decision of Chapman J. in *R. v. Symonds*[132] and continued:[133]

> Chapman J. also spoke of the practice of extinguishing native titles by fair purchase. An extinguishment by less than fair conduct or on less than fair terms would be likely to be a breach of the fiduciary duty widely and increasingly recognised as falling on the colonising power.

The Court concluded, however, that no matter how liberally Maori customary title and treaty rights may be construed, it cannot be thought that they were ever conceived as including the right to generate electricity. Accordingly, the Court rejected the claim that Maori property rights in a river would be prejudiced by a transfer of certain dams to energy companies.

Ngai Tahu Maori Trust Board v. Director General of Conservation,[134] which was decided the following year, includes an interesting discussion of the application of fiduciary duties in the context of consultation and accommodation.[135] A Maori tribe had a permit enabling it to engage in the whale-watching business. The government issued a permit for the same purpose to a competitor. The Maori tribe claimed that the principles of the treaty had been breached. The Court held that the tribe had pitched its claim too high. However liberally Maori customary title and treaty rights might be construed, tourism and whale-watching were remote from anything contemplated by the original parties and the claim of a veto had to be rejected. The matter was referred back to the director-general to take into account the protection of Maori interests in accordance with the principles of the treaty. The Court noted:[136]

> The view that Maori has customary or aboriginal title or treaty rights (it being unnecessary to distinguish between them in the context) and that the Crown has fiduciary duties extending to its treatment of those rights may be further supported by the judgment of this Court in *Te Runanga o Wharekauri Rekahu Inc. v. Attorney General* [1993] 2 NZLR 301, 303–306, and the authorities there cited.

It rejected the Crown's argument that it only had a duty of consultation and held that treaty principles required active protection of Maori interests:[137]

> Although a commercial whale-watching business is not taonga or the enjoyment of a fishery within the contemplation of the treaty, certainly it is so linked to taonga and fisheries that a reasonable treaty partner would recognize that treaty principles are relevant. Such issues are not to be approached narrowly. The Crown is right to accept in this case that treaty principles apply, at least if not inconsistent with the particular legislation. On the other hand, the Crown is not right to trying to limit those principles to consultation. Since the lands case, *New Zealand Maori Council v. Attorney General* (see especially pp 664, 674, 682, 693, 703, 717), it has been established that the principles require active protection of Maori interests. To restrict this to consultation would be hollow. . . .
>
> In altogether rejecting protection of Ngai Tahu interests as a relevant factor, and in confining treaty principles to an empty obligation to consult, the argument for the Director-General goes too far.

A 2002 decision of the Privy Council on appeal from the New Zealand Court of Appeal is of note for its recognition of a "political trust." *Te Waka Hi Ika o Te Arawa v. Treaty of Waitangi Fisheries Commission*[138] was part of the complicated story of the settlement of Maori commercial fishing rights. The questions before the Court concerned the meaning of "iwi" (tribe) in the settlement legislation. Part of the settlement included a memorandum of understanding providing for a trust "for the ultimate benefit of all Maori." Giving the judgment of the Privy Council, Lord Hoffman commented on the nature of the trust:[139]

> Their Lordships would also observe, without wishing to preempt what may be further argument in the Courts of New Zealand, that the trust for the ultimate benefit of the Maori people would appear to be a concept of public law which uses the term "trust" only by analogy with the more familiar trust of private law. (See the discussion by Megarry V-C in *Tito v. Waddell (No 2)* [1977] 1 Ch 106 at pp 210–219).

Conclusion: Lessons for Canada

This chapter has summarized the laws of the United States, Australia, and New Zealand on the fiduciary obligations owed to the Aboriginal peoples of those countries. It has shown that the law of the United States has long recognized such obligations and generally applies traditional principles of trust and fiduciary law to the relationship.[140] In Canada, there has been much confusion as to the application of such principles due to the repeated use of the unhelpful description of the relationship and of Aboriginal rights as *sui generis* or unique. As discussed in chapter 8, the use of this term adds nothing to explaining the relationship and frustrates the orderly development of the law.[141] The United States law shows that it can be abandoned and the general trust and fiduciary principles applied without such confusion.

Australian law has been reluctant to embrace any expansion of fiduciary relationships from the traditional categories, and this reluctance has been reflected in the discussion in this chapter of the position of Aboriginal Australians.[142] The lack of any Australian equivalent to section 35 of the *Constitution Act, 1982* recognizing and affirming existing Aboriginal and treaty rights in Canada has certainly been a major factor in the sorry state of Aboriginal rights in that country.[143] However, as pointed out by one Australian writer, "[d]espite the many flaws and the impotence of the fiduciary doctrine from Canada, Australia offers sobering reflection of what can happen if there is no recognition of the doctrine."[144] Also, as demonstrated in chapter 5, the fiduciary relationship gave substance to the constitutional protection found in section 35.[145] The Australian law demonstrates the critical role played by the fiduciary doctrine in protecting Aboriginal rights.

New Zealand has not received the attention that it deserves from Canadian courts and legal scholars. Its early recognition of Aboriginal title,[146] its experience with the *Treaty of Waitangi,*[147] the Waitangi Tribunal[148] and the statutory settlement of Maori commercial fishing rights in exchange for shares in a major fishing company[149] all offer lessons that may prove valuable in Canada as we seek to reconcile the interests of Aboriginal people with those of the rest of Canadian society.[150] Of most value for present purposes is the concept of a partnership between the Maori and the non-Maori of New Zealand and the corresponding fiduciary duties imposed on both parties.[151] This recognizes the general obligation of Aboriginal groups to take part in the process of reconciliation of their interests with the rest of Canadian society and more specific obligations such as participating in the consultation process where Aboriginal interests might be infringed.[152] It also removes the implication that some find troubling that the fiduciary relationship is not between equals.[153]

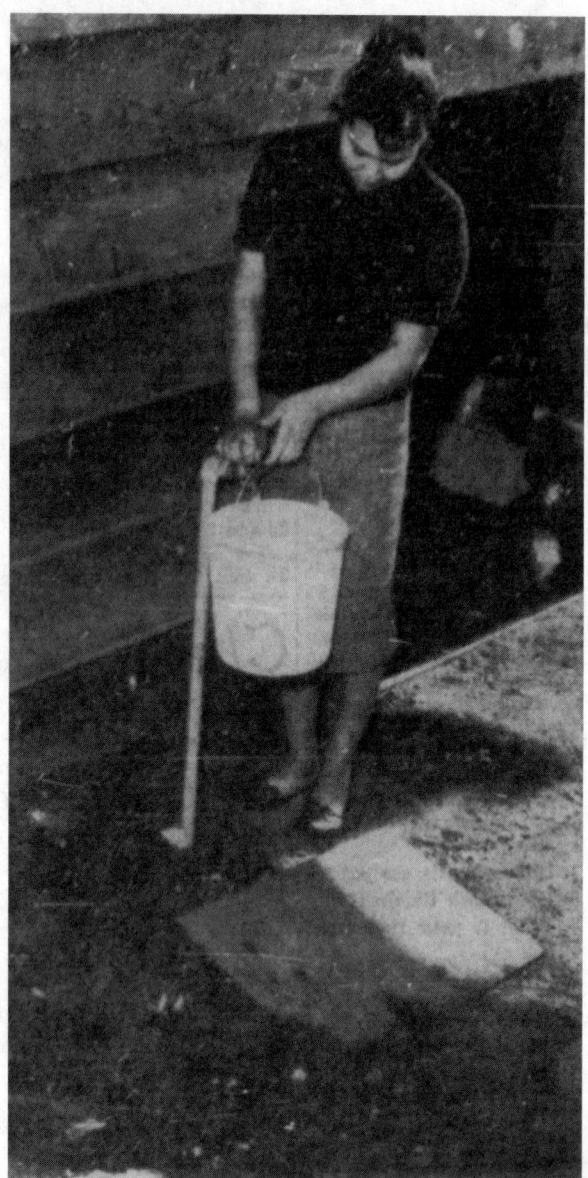

"No running water indoors forces Mrs. Larry Sparrow to draw water from outdoor tap. Indians claim they have no money for improvements. . . . Women wash their clothes in buckets after carrying water from outside taps near their homes. The wooden houses are badly in need of repair and they're overcrowded. There's no drainage system, few families have bathroom facilities and the only toilets are ramshackle shacks behind the houses. Garbage is piled everywhere and four-foot high undergrowth and swamp can be seen near most of the buildings." (Courtesy *Vancouver Sun,* Wednesday, Feb. 21, 1962, p. 29. Caption quotes text from both the original caption and news article.)

Chapter 8

Questions Raised by *Guerin*

The *Guerin* case[1] clearly established that the Crown has a fiduciary relationship with Aboriginal peoples in Canada and firmly rejected the view that this relationship was beyond the powers of courts to enforce and merely imposed political obligations. However, there are several important questions raised but left unanswered by the decision. This chapter examines a number of them in the light of subsequent developments.[2]

Can the fiduciary relationship between the Crown and Aboriginal peoples be terminated?
As Lewis Harvey and I suggested should be the case in a paper presented a couple of months after the *Guerin* decision,[3] it was subsequently decided by the Supreme Court of Canada in *Sparrow*[4] that the fiduciary relationship is incorporated in the Constitution by the recognition and affirmation of existing Aboriginal and treaty rights in section 35 of the *Constitution Act, 1982*.[5] Given this constitutional protection, the relationship can only be terminated with the consent of the Aboriginal peoples involved or by a constitutional amendment passed pursuant to the demanding requirements of section 38 of that Act. This section requires resolutions of both the Senate and the House of Commons and of the legislative assemblies of at least two-thirds of the provinces that have, in the aggregate, at least 50 percent of the population of all the provinces.[6]

Although the Crown cannot unilaterally terminate the fiduciary relationship in the absence of a constitutional amendment, it will be seen from the discussion below that it may reduce its fiduciary obligations by reducing the extent of its power over the interests of Aboriginal peoples.

Which government departments owe fiduciary obligations to Aboriginal peoples?
As discussed in chapter 5, there is authority for the proposition that fiduciary

obligations are owed by all federal departments and not just the Department of Indian Affairs.[7] On the other hand, in the *Blueberry River* case, McLachlin J. suggested that the Director of Veterans Land did not share the fiduciary obligation owed by the Department of Indian Affairs as it would be "problematic" if this was the case.[8] However, as also discussed in chapter 5,[9] the relationship is with the Crown and not any particular government department. Therefore, all government departments must be mindful of the fiduciary relationship between the Crown and Aboriginal peoples and ensure that they discharge their mandates in a manner that respects that relationship and reconciles any competing obligations.[10]

Do the provincial governments have a fiduciary relationship with Aboriginal peoples?

Also for the reasons given in chapter 5,[11] each provincial Crown has a fiduciary relationship with Aboriginal people to the extent of its constitutional power to affect their interests as Aboriginal people. As discussed in that chapter, the following cases support this submission: *Gitanyow,*[12] *Halfway River,*[13] *Cree School Board,*[14] *Kelly Lake Cree Nation,*[15] and *Haida Nation.*[16] The comment by Laskin J.A. of the Ontario Court of Appeal in *Bear Island*[17] that it is doubtful if the province owes a fiduciary duty to Aboriginal peoples would seem to be incorrect.

Does the existence of a public law duty exclude a fiduciary obligation?

Prior to the decision of the Supreme Court of Canada in *Wewaykum,*[18] there was some doubt whether the Crown could owe a fiduciary obligation to Aboriginal peoples if it was acting pursuant to a public law duty. This doubt was evident in some comments made by the Federal Court in the *Fairford First Nation,*[19] *Chippewas of Nawash,*[20] *Scrimbitt*[21] and *Tuplin*[22] cases. In *Wewaykum,*[23] the Supreme Court of Canada explained that, in order for a fiduciary duty to arise, there had to be both "a cognizable Indian interest" and discretionary control by the Crown in relation to that interest. However, the Court expressly held that the existence of a public law duty did not necessarily exclude the creation of a fiduciary duty.

It is difficult to understand the supposed distinction between the public and private law duties owed by the government to Aboriginal peoples. Dickson J. was far from clear in making this distinction in *Guerin.*[24] Referring to the Crown's duty with respect to the interest of Indians in their reserve land, he noted that:[25]

> The Crown's obligation to the Indians with respect to that interest is therefore not a public law duty. While it is not a private law duty in the strict sense either, it is nonetheless in the nature of a private law duty.

Further, his judgment points out that public law duties do not necessarily exclude the application of a fiduciary duty, although they typically do:[26]

> It should be noted that fiduciary duties generally arise only with regard to obligations originating in a private law context. Public law duties, the performance of which requires the exercise of discretion, do not *typically* give rise to a fiduciary relationship.

Since governments deal with Aboriginal peoples in a public and not a private capacity, it might be thought that all of their duties towards Aboriginal peoples are public law duties. More generally, in considering the application of the *Canadian Charter of Rights and Freedoms*,[27] the Supreme Court of Canada has cast doubt on any rigid distinction between the government's traditional role of governing in a public law sense and its private or "non-public" activities.[28]

In any event, the *Sparrow*,[29] *Adams*,[30] *Badger*,[31] *Delgamuukw*,[32] and *Marshall*[33] decisions of the Supreme Court of Canada are all clear authorities for saying that the Crown does owe a fiduciary duty towards Aboriginal peoples in discharging public law duties such as regulating fishing or limiting Aboriginal title for a valid legislative objective. It is difficult to see how these regulations and limitations could be seen to be anything but an exercise of a public law duty, yet the Court still held that the government owed a fiduciary duty to the Aboriginal people affected. In *R. v. Marshall*,[34] the Court referred with approval to the rule in *Sparrow*,[35] repeated in *Badger*,[36] that "[t]he special trust relationship and the responsibility of the government *vis à vis* Aboriginals must be the first consideration in determining whether the legislation or action in question can be justified." This statement was made in the context of a discussion of regulations to control fishing.

Given the attempt to restrict the application of the fiduciary duty in so-called "public law" areas, it is appropriate to note the comment of Professor Finn that equity exposes fiduciaries to a system of judicial review and that:[37]

> Perhaps not surprisingly, given the close resemblance which the fiduciary officer bears to the public official, this system of review reflects in a very large measure that described by the late Professor de Smith in *Judicial Review of Administrative Action*.

This opinion was echoed by Chief Justice Mason of the High Court of Australia:[38] "Modern administrative law—from its earliest days, has mirrored the way in which equity has regulated the exercise of fiduciary powers."

In his judgment in the case of the *Wadi Wadi People*,[39] Finch J. of the Australian National Native Title Tribunal observed that in *Fares Rural Meat and Livestock Co. Pty. Ltd. v. Australian Meat and Live-stock Corporation*, Gummow

J. of the High Court of Australia (and co-author of the leading Australian text on equity law[40]) viewed the unreasonableness ground of judicial review enunciated by Lord Green in *Associated Provincial Picture v. Wednesbury Corporation*[41] as "rooted in the law as to misuse of fiduciary powers."[42]

There is also English authority that likens the duty of public officials to that of a fiduciary. In *Roberts v. Hopwood*,[43] Lords Atkinson and Sumner said that the duty of local authorities in England to their ratepayers was similar to that of trustees or managers of the property of others. More recently, in *Bromley London Borough Council v. Greater London Council*,[44] Lords Wilberforce and Scarman described the duty as being fiduciary.

In *Wewaykum*,[45] the Supreme Court of Canada explained the relationship between the Crown's public law duties and its fiduciary obligations towards Aboriginal peoples. Giving the unanimous judgment of the Court, Binnie J. said:

> [74] The enduring contribution of *Guerin* was to recognize that the concept of political trust did not exhaust the potential legal character of the multitude of relationships between the Crown and aboriginal people. A quasi-proprietary interest (e.g., reserve land) could not be put on the same footing as a government benefits program. The latter will generally give rise to public law remedies only. The former raises considerations "in the nature of a private law duty" (*Guerin*, at p. 385). Put another way, the existence of a public law duty does not exclude the possibility that the Crown undertook, in the discharge of that public law duty, obligations "in the nature of a private law duty" towards aboriginal peoples.

He referred to the judgment of Dickson J. in *Guerin* and the way in which he had distinguished the political trust cases on the basis that they concerned "essentially the distribution of public funds or other property held by the government. . . . The situation of the Indians is entirely different. Their interest in their lands is a pre-existing legal right" not created by the government.[46]

Dickson J. had observed that the political trust cases had indicated that "the Crown is not normally viewed as a fiduciary in the exercise of its legislative or administrative function." Since the Indians' interest in land was an independent legal interest, "[t]he Crown's obligation to the Indians with respect to that interest is therefore not a public law duty. While it is not a private law duty in the strict sense either, it is nonetheless in the nature of a private law duty."[47] Binnie J. said Dickson J. had pointed out that the fiduciary duty was imposed on the Crown "*despite* rather than *because* of its government functions."[48]

Binnie J. noted that *Guerin* had led to "a flood of 'fiduciary duty' claims by Indian bands across a whole spectrum of possible complaints."[49] He gave several examples including to structure elections; require the provision of social services; rewrite negotiated provisions; cover moving expenses; suppress public access to information about band affairs; require legal aid funding; compel registration of individuals under the *Indian Act* and invalidate a consent signed by an Indian mother to the adoption of her child. He said he would offer no comment about the disposition of the particular cases on their facts, but he hinted that they did not give rise to a fiduciary duty,[50] of which Dickson J. had pointed out in *Guerin*: "[w]hile it is not a private law duty in the strict sense either, it is nonetheless in the nature of a private law duty."[51]

He then stressed that, in order to determine if fiduciary obligation exists between the Crown and Aboriginal peoples, it is necessary to focus on two factors: the subject matter of the particular dispute and whether the Crown had discretionary control in relation to that subject matter. He said:

> [83] I think it desirable for the Court to affirm the principle, already mentioned, that not all obligations existing between the parties to a fiduciary relationship are themselves fiduciary in nature (*Lac Minerals, supra*, at p. 597), and that this principle applies to the relationship between the Crown and aboriginal peoples. It is necessary, then, to focus on the particular obligation or interest that is the subject matter of the particular dispute and whether or not the Crown had assumed discretionary control in relation thereto sufficient to ground a fiduciary obligation.

He noted the comment by Rothstein J.A. in *Chippewas of the Nawash First Nation v. Canada*[52] that the Crown had no fiduciary duty to the appellant First Nation with respect to disclosure of information under the *Access to Information Act* and said:

> [85] I do not suggest that the existence of a public law duty necessarily excludes the creation of a fiduciary relationship. The latter, however, depends on identification of a cognizable Indian interest, and the Crown's undertaking of discretionary control in relation thereto in a way that invokes responsibility "in the nature of a private law duty", as discussed below.

Later in his judgment, Binnie J. discussed how the fiduciary duty adds to the obligations of the Crown and the remedies available at public law to the Aboriginal group:

> [94] Insofar as the appellant bands contend for a broad application of a fiduciary duty at the stage of reserve creation in non–s. 35(1) lands (as distinguished from their other arguments concerning existing reserves and reserve disposition), it is necessary to determine what the imposition of a fiduciary duty adds at that stage to the remedies already available at public law. The answer, I think, is twofold. In a substantive sense the imposition of a fiduciary duty attaches to the Crown's intervention the additional obligations of loyalty, good faith, full disclosure appropriate to the matter at hand and acting in what it reasonably and with diligence regards as the best interest of the beneficiary. In *Blueberry River* McLachlin J. (as she then was), at para. 104, said that "[t]he duty on the Crown as fiduciary was 'that of a man of ordinary prudence in managing his own affairs'". See also D.W.M. Waters,

Law of Trusts in Canada (2nd ed. 1984), at pp. 32–33; *Fales v. Canada Permanent Trust Co.*, [1977] 2 S.C.R. 302, at p. 315. Secondly, and perhaps more importantly, the imposition of a fiduciary duty opens access to an array of equitable remedies, about which more will be said below.

What is the effect of transferring powers to Aboriginal peoples upon the Crown's fiduciary relationship?

Although it is taking place very slowly, there has been a gradual process of transferring some of the powers of the federal government to Aboriginal peoples. Part of the motivation behind this transfer appears to be a desire to limit the government's liability for breach of its fiduciary obligations arising out of the exercise of such powers. The transfer is often silent on the effect of the transfer on the Crown's fiduciary relationship with the Aboriginal peoples involved. Sometimes, there may be an express provision preserving the fiduciary or "special" relationship. For example, under the *First Nations Land Management Act*,[53] certain First Nations have assumed the management of reserve lands. The *Framework Agreement* between the Government of Canada and fourteen First Nations signed February 12, 1996, on which the Act is based, provides in clause 1.4 that "the parties acknowledge that the Crown's special relationship with the First Nations will continue." Does this mean that the Crown continues to have a fiduciary duty to provide assistance to a First Nation that has assumed such management powers or to supervise the exercise of those powers by the First Nation?[54] If a First Nation negotiates a self-government agreement or self-government arrangements in a treaty as in the case of the Sechelt and the Nisga'a first nations of British Columbia, is there any basis for imposing a fiduciary duty on the Crown?

The answer would appear to depend upon the extent to which the Crown still retains discretionary control over "a cognizable Indian interest." In *Wewaykum*,[55] Binnie J. of the Supreme Court of Canada referred to the Court's decision in *Sparrow*[56] in which Justices Dickson and La Forest had said that "the *sui generis* nature of Indian title, and the historic powers and responsibility assumed by the Crown constituted the source of such a fiduciary obligation."[57] These powers and responsibility had led, in his words, to a "high degree of discretionary control gradually assumed by the Crown over the lives of aboriginal peoples."[58] This control had "its positive aspects in protecting the interests of aboriginal peoples historically" from abuses.[59] On the other hand, "the degree of economic, social and proprietary control and discretion asserted by the Crown also left aboriginal populations vulnerable to the risks of government misconduct or ineptitude."[60] This discretionary control was a basic ingredient of the fiduciary relationship. He noted:[61]

The importance of such discretionary control as a basic ingredient in Professor E. Weinrib's statement, quoted in *Guerin, supra*, at p. 384, that: "the hallmark of a fiduciary relation is that the relative legal positions are such that one party is at the mercy of the other's discretion."

Therefore, it will be necessary to examine the particular facts on a case-by-case basis to see if the Crown retained the required discretionary control despite the self-government arrangement.

Professor Rotman has suggested that the Crown retains an obligation to ensure a harmonious transition to the Aboriginal group:[62]

> [I]t is insufficient for the Crown to attempt to dispose of its obligations by dumping them unceremoniously on the Native people without providing for their harmonious transition to the aboriginal authority. By virtue of the length of time that the Crown has assumed jurisdiction and responsibility for Indian affairs while simultaneously preventing the Native people from exercising self-determination, it would be unconscionable to allow the Crown to be instantaneously free of its fiduciary responsibilities without providing for a period of adjustment.
>
> Accordingly, the Crown must be duty-bound to facilitate the transfer of control over certain powers to the aboriginal peoples, to supervise their assumption by the aboriginal peoples during the transition period, and to provide aid where required. . . . Should the Crown fail to perform this supervisory role, it will be liable for a breach of its fiduciary duty to the same extent and in the same fashion as if it had failed to positively exercise the transferred powers prior to their transfer.

It is not clear how this residual obligation would be affected if the Aboriginal group in question refused to submit to the Crown's supervisory role. Presumably, the Crown's obligation would be discharged to the extent that it had made good-faith and reasonable efforts to perform its role and it would not be liable if its efforts were frustrated.

To what extent will the federal Crown's obligation to Aboriginal peoples vary depending upon the province where it carries out its obligations? Are the principles of fiduciary obligation common to all the provinces including the civil law jurisdiction of Quebec? Is the federal Crown bound by, and able to obtain relief under, provincial trust legislation?

The answer to these questions would appear to depend upon the somewhat obscure concept of Canadian federal common law. In *Roberts v. Canada*,[63] the Supreme Court of Canada held that the law of Aboriginal title is federal common law. Lamer C.J.C. considered the concept of federal common law in *R. v. Côté*.[64] In considering a claim of Aboriginal rights in the province of Quebec, he said it was not clear that "the advent of British sovereignty continued the French system of law governing the relations between the British Crown and indigenous societies." He continued:[65]

In short, the common law recognizing aboriginal title was arguably a necessary incident of British Sovereignty which displaced the pre-existing colonial law governing New France. As Professor Slattery argues in "Understanding Aboriginal Rights", *supra* [(1987) 66 Can. Bar Rev. 727], at pp. 737–38:

> "The doctrine of aboriginal rights, like other doctrines of colonial law, applied automatically to a new colony when the colony was acquired. In the same way that colonial law determined whether a colony was deemed to be 'settled' or 'conquered,' and whether English law was automatically introduced or local laws retained, it also supplied the presumptive legal structure governing the position of native peoples. The doctrine of aboriginal rights applied, then, to every British colony that now forms part of Canada, from Newfoundland to British Columbia. Although the doctrine was a species of unwritten British law, it was not part of English common law in the narrow sense, and its application to a colony did not depend on whether or not English common law was introduced there. Rather the doctrine was part of a body of fundamental constitutional law that was logically prior to the introduction of English common law and governed its application in the colony."

> Indeed, this Court has held that the law of aboriginal title represents a distinct species of federal common law rather than a simple subset of the common or civil law or property law operating within the province: *Roberts v. Canada*, [1989] 1 S.C.R. 322, at p. 340. See the views of the Royal Commission on Aboriginal Peoples on the status of aboriginal rights as federal common law in *Partners in Confederation: Aboriginal Peoples, Self-Government, and the Constitution* (1993), at p. 20.

To the extent that the law governing the fiduciary obligations of the Crown to Aboriginal peoples is part of "the doctrine of aboriginal rights," it would appear to be federal common law rather than the law of any particular province. Therefore, common principles should apply throughout Canada, including in the civil law juisdiction of Quebec.

It is not clear if the Crown would be subject to, or able to derive relief under, provincial legislation. Each relevant provision would have to be reviewed to determine its applicability. For example, section 96 of the British Columbia *Trustee Act*[66] gives the court the discretion to relieve a trustee from personal liability if the trustee has acted honestly and reasonably. In *Guerin*,[67] the trial judge held that the reference to "the court" meant the Supreme Court of British Columbia not the Federal Court and would not, in any event, have granted relief on the facts. He did not consider the question of whether such provincial legislation could apply to federal common law. Wilson J. in the Supreme Court of Canada said that the finding of concealed fraud disentitled the Crown to relief.

Is the relationship between the Crown and Aboriginal peoples such that there is a presumption that the Crown's obligations are fiduciary in nature?

Although the law is clear that "not all obligations existing between the parties to a fiduciary relationship are themselves fiduciary in nature,"[68] it is still relevant to ask if the relationship between the Crown and Aboriginal peoples is fiduciary in nature (a "*per se*" fiduciary relationship) so that there is a strong presumption that fiduciary duties are owed by the Crown and the burden of proving that the obligation in question is not fiduciary in nature falls on the Crown. The courts have not given a consistent answer to this question. As seen below,[69] if the relationship itself is fiduciary, there will be a presumption that fiduciary obligations are owed. There are numerous statements that there is a fiduciary relationship between the Crown and Aboriginal peoples.[70] Therefore, it would seem that the presumption should be applied. However, some courts have placed the onus on the Aboriginal plaintiffs to prove the existence of a fiduciary duty and have thereby implicitly denied that the relationship is fiduciary in nature with a presumption of such a duty. [71]

In order to determine whether there is a presumption that the Crown's obligations to Aboriginal peoples are fiduciary in nature, it is necessary to consider which class of fiduciary, as described by the Supreme Court of Canada, the Crown comes within. La Forest J. of the Supreme Court of Canada considered three different classes of fiduciary in *Lac Minerals*[72] and *Hodgkinson*.[73] In the *Lac Minerals* case, he considered first the relationships in which a fiduciary duty is presumed:[74]

> Much of the confusion surrounding the term "fiduciary" stems in my view, from its undifferentiated use in at least three distinct ways. The first is as used by Wilson J. in *Frame v. Smith*, supra [[1987] 2 S.C.R. 99]. There the issue was whether a certain class of relationship, custodial and non-custodial parents, was a category, analogous to directors and corporations, solicitors and clients, trustees and beneficiaries, and agents and principals, the existence of which relationship would give rise to fiduciary obligations. The focus is on the identification of relationships in which, because of their inherent purpose or their presumed factual or legal incidents, the courts will impose a fiduciary obligation on one party to act or refrain from acting in a certain way. The obligation imposed may vary in its specific substance depending on the relationship, though compendiously it can be described as the fiduciary duty and interest and a duty not to profit at the expense of the beneficiary. The presumption that a fiduciary obligation will be owed in the context of such a relationship is not irrefutable, but a strong presumption will exist that such an obligation is present. Further, not every legal claim arising out of a relationship with fiduciary incidents will give rise to a claim for breach of fiduciary duty.
>
> It is only in relation to breaches of the specific obligations imposed because the relationship is one characterized as fiduciary that a claim for breach of fiduciary duty can be founded. In determining whether the categories of relationships which should be presumed to give rise to fiduciary obligations should be extended, the rough and ready guide adopted by Wilson J. [in *Frame v. Smith*[75]] is a useful tool for that evaluation.

He then considered a second class where the fiduciary duty arises out of the specific circumstances of a relationship:[76]

> This brings me to the second usage of fiduciary, one I think more apt to the present case. The imposition of fiduciary obligations is not limited to those relationships in which a presumption of such an obligation arises. Rather, a fiduciary obligation can arise as a matter of fact out of the specific circumstances of a relationship. As such it can arise between parties in a relationship which fiduciary obligations would not normally be expected. ...
>
> It is in this sense, then, that the existence of a fiduciary obligation can be said to be a question of fact to be determined by examining the specific facts and circumstances surrounding each relationship: see Waters, Law of Trusts in Canada (2nd ed. 1984), at p. 405. If the facts give rise to a fiduciary obligation, a breach of the duties thereby imposed will give rise to a claim for equitable relief.

Finally, he considered a third sense in which the term "fiduciary" is used, namely where courts find a fiduciary relationship in order to provide certain remedies. He thought this was a misuse of the term.

The important question for us is into which of the first two classes of fiduciaries does the relationship between the Crown and Aboriginal peoples belong: the first, where a fiduciary obligation is presumed (the *per se* class), or the second, where the plaintiff must be able to prove some specific fact which gives rise to such an obligation (the *ad hoc* class)?

There is certainly authority to support inclusion in the first class. Numerous statements of the Supreme Court of Canada and other courts have referred to the relationship between the Crown and Aboriginal peoples as being fiduciary in nature: e.g., *Wewaykum Indian Band v. Canada,*[77] *Quebec (Attorney-General) v. Canada (National Energy Board).*[78] In *Lac La Ronge Indian Band v. Canada,* Gerein J. of the Saskatchewan Queen's Bench commented: "There is a fiduciary relationship between Canada and Indian peoples. This is beyond dispute and does not warrant a lengthy discussion."[79] He cited many authorities in support of this conclusion, including *Guerin*[80] and *R. v. Sparrow,*[81] which he described as "elemental authorities" in support.

On the other hand, there has been a clear trend in the Federal Court to place the Crown/Aboriginal relationship in the second class of fiduciary relationships and require Aboriginal plaintiffs to prove specific facts which give rise to a fiduciary obligation, i.e., the onus of proof is on the Aboriginal group to prove the existence of a fiduciary duty and not on the Crown to rebut the presumption of such a duty. This trend can be seen in the *Fairford First Nation,*[82] *Chippewas of Nawash,*[83] *Tsartlip Indian Band,*[84] *B.C. (Minister of Forests) v. Wilson*[85] and *Mathias*[86] cases. In these cases, the court rejected the argument of the Aboriginal group that there was a fiduciary duty and required them to prove specific facts which gave rise to such a duty. In *Fairford First*

Nation, Rothstein J. did not even consider if the relationship between the Crown and Aboriginal peoples came into the first class of fiduciary described by La Forest J. He left out of his analysis "the traditionally recognized categories of fiduciary i.e. trustee, agent etc.,"[87] and appears to have overlooked Dickson J.'s comment in *Guerin*[88] that the categories of fiduciary should not be considered closed.

In my view, the relationship between the Crown and Aboriginal peoples falls within the first class of fiduciaries. As noted by La Forest J. in the above quotation from *Lac Minerals*,[89] the following words by Wilson J. in *Frame v. Smith*[90] provide a rough and ready guide to the existence of a relationship which is to be included in the first class:[91]

> Relationships in which a fiduciary obligation have been imposed seem to possess three general characteristics:
>
> (a) The fiduciary has scope for the exercise of some discretion or power.
>
> (b) The fiduciary can unilaterally exercise that power or discretion so as to affect the beneficiary's legal or practical interests.
>
> (c) The beneficiary is peculiarly vulnerable to or at the mercy of the fiduciary holding the discretion of power.

She explained vulnerability as follows:[92]

> This vulnerability arises from the inability of the beneficiary (despite his or her best efforts) to prevent the injurious exercise of the power or discretion combined with the grave inadequacy or absence of other legal or practical remedies to redress the wrongful exercise of the discretion or power.

Professor E. Weinrib has written of the relative legal positions of the two parties to the relationship being such that "one party is at the mercy of the other's discretion."[93] In *Hodgkinson*, La Forest J. said this first class had as "their essence discretion, influence over interest and an inherent vulnerability. In these types of relationships, there is a rebuttable presumption, arising out of the inherent purpose of the relationship, that one party has a duty to act in the best interests of the other party."[94]

In my view, the relationship between the Crown and Aboriginal people satisfies the three-step analysis of Wilson J. in *Frame v. Smith*[95] and the test of inherent vulnerability stipulated by La Forest J. in *Hodgkinson*[96] and so falls within the first class of fiduciary in which a fiduciary obligation is presumed. In his thesis on the doctrine of fiduciary obligation as illustrated by an assessment of obligations owed by Canada to Canadian Indians, Gerald Donegan describes the relationship as follows:[97]

> The Crown/Indian relationship contains an inherent opportunity for the exploitation of natives by the Crown. The opportunity exists because performance of the

Crown's historical commitment of protection requires that the government have a discretionary power to prevent what is considers improvident uses or dispositions of reserve lands by the occupying band or its council. This discretionary power is created by the legislation enacted to regulate the relationship between the Crown and status Indians, chiefly, the *Indian Act* and the regulations made pursuant to it. Neither the legislation itself nor any common law doctrine, provides a means of controlling the Crown's use of this discretionary power. The effect of these extraordinary provisions is to put into the hands of the government sweeping powers of control over the use and disposition of reserve land. The extent of this discretion is summed up in section 18(1), which empowers the Crown to decide for itself whether a proposed use of reserve land is for the benefit of the occupying band.

In *Wewaykum*, Binnie J. referred to the "high degree of discretionary control gradually assumed by the Crown over the lives of aboriginal peoples" which leaves them "vulnerable to the risks of government misconduct or ineptitude."[98]

It should be noted that this discretionary power is by no means limited to reserve land. Under the *Indian Act*,[99] the minister decides who is an Indian (ss. 5–7) and where they may live on reserve (s. 20). The minister can limit the power of an Indian to dispose of his assets by will (s. 46). The Act also gives the minister power to control Indian monies (s. 61) and to disallow by-laws passed by the band council (s. 82). Throughout the Act, the minister has unilateral power to make decisions affecting the lives and property of Indian people. Their lack of control over the minister's exercise of discretion in itself makes them peculiarly vulnerable to, or at the mercy of, the minister. Further, it is well established that Aboriginal communities have higher levels of poverty, lower educational standards, and greater social problems than the population generally. In *Lovelace v. Ontario*, Iacobucci, J. said:[100]

> All Aboriginal peoples have been affected "by the legacy of stereotyping and prejudice against Aboriginal peoples." (*Corbiere* [1999] 2 S.C.R. 203 at para. 66). Aboriginal peoples experience high rates of unemployment and poverty, and face serious disadvantages in the areas of education, health and housing.

This adds to their vulnerability.

In *Wewaykum*,[101] McDonald J.A. of the Federal Court of Appeal provided support for including the relationship between the Crown and Aboriginal peoples within the first class of fiduciary relationships. He said:[102]

> The fiduciary nature of the relationship between the Crown and Aboriginal peoples is well-established in Canadian law. That being said, a fiduciary duty does not arise in every facet of Crown–Native relations nor is the content of the fiduciary responsibilities of the Crown identical in every transaction. As noted by the late Justice Sopinka in *Lac Minerals Ltd. v. International Corona Resources Ltd.*:[103]

"When the Court is dealing with one of the traditional relationships, the characteristics or criteria for a fiduciary relationship are assumed to exist. In special circumstances, if they are shown to be absent, the relationship itself will not suffice."

In other words, not every obligation that exists in a well established fiduciary
relationship will amount to a "fiduciary duty." Accordingly, the circumstances of
the 1907 Resolution must be examined to determine if a fiduciary duty arises. If a
duty does arise, the nature and scope of that duty must be ascertained.

This passage is significant as it would appear to be clear support for the
view that the relationship between the Crown and Aboriginal peoples is to be
considered within the first class of fiduciary relationship noted by La Forest J.
in *Lac Minerals*,[104] i.e., a relationship in which there is a strong presumption
of a fiduciary obligation.

When the case came on appeal to the Supreme Court of Canada in *Wewaykum*,[105] Binnie J., giving the opinion of the Court, did not comment on
the above statement. However, his judgment also supports the view that the
relationship is fiduciary in nature. A specific fiduciary duty will be created
whenever there is "a cognizable Indian interest" over which the Crown has
discretionary control.[106] He noted that "the degree of economic, social and
proprietary control and discretion asserted by the Crown . . . left aboriginal
populations vulnerable to the risks of government misconduct or ineptitude."[107] He commented that the importance of such discretionary control as
a basic ingredient in a fiduciary relationship was underscored by Professor E.
Weinrib's statement, quoted in *Guerin,* that "the hallmark of a fiduciary relation is that the relative legal positions are such that one party is at the mercy
of the other's discretion."[108] Later, Binnie J. referred to *Lac Minerals* for the
principle "that not all obligations existing between the parties to a fiduciary
relationship are themselves fiduciary in nature."[109] He then said that this principle applies to the relationship between the Crown and Aboriginal peoples,
thereby implicitly confirming that the relationship is fiduciary in nature.[110]

Justice Binnie went on to observe that, in order to determine if a specific
obligation owed by the Crown to Aboriginal peoples is fiduciary in nature,
it is necessary "to focus on the particular obligation or interest that is the
subject matter of the particular dispute and whether or not the Crown had
assumed discretionary control in relation thereto sufficient to ground a fiduciary obligation."[111] He had earlier pointed out that there are limits to the
duties imposed on the Crown:

81. But there are limits. The appellants seemed at times to invoke the "fiduciary
duty" as a source of plenary Crown liability covering all aspects of the Crown–Indian
band relationship. This overshoots the mark. The fiduciary duty imposed on the

Crown does not exist at large but in relation to specific Indian interests. In this case we are dealing with land, which has generally played a central role in aboriginal economies and cultures. Land was also the subject matter of *Ross River*[112] ("the lands occupied by the Band"), *Blueberry River*[113] and *Guerin*[114] (disposition of existing reserves). Fiduciary protection accorded to Crown dealings with aboriginal interests in land (including reserve creation) has not to date been recognized by this Court in relation to Indian interests other than land outside the framework of s. 35(1) of the *Constitution Act, 1982*.

Therefore, there is a presumption that a fiduciary obligation exists wherever the Crown has discretionary control over "a cognizable Indian interest."[115] As noted by La Forest J. in *Lac Minerals*, "the presumption that a fiduciary obligation will be owed in the context of such a relationship is not irrefutable, but a strong presumption will exist that such an obligation is present."[116] Given this presumption, the onus is on the Crown to demonstrate that the Crown does not owe fiduciary obligations towards Aboriginal peoples in any such case, and the presumption is not an easy one to rebut. In light of this analysis, in my view, *Fairford First Nation*[117] and the cases following it[118] are not good law to the extent that they deny that there is a general on-going fiduciary relationship between the Crown and Aboriginal peoples.

Is the fiduciary duty merely a "shield and not a sword"?

The Ontario Court of Appeal suggested in the *Ardoch Algonquin First Nation*[119] and the *Bear Island*[120] cases that the fiduciary obligation of the provincial Crown is a "shield and not a sword." In *Ardoch*, the court said section 35(1) of the *Constitution Act, 1982* "including the government's fiduciary obligation implicit therein" is to be applied "as a restraint against regulation affecting aboriginal rights, not an affirmative obligation to initiate negotiations with a view to such regulation."[121] These words were quoted with approval by the British Columbia Supreme Court in the *Jules*[122] case in denying that the Crown owed a specific fiduciary duty to provide for the funding of the legal fees of a band. The British Columbia Court of Appeal upheld this aspect of the judgment, but it is not clear if it accepted the shield-not-a-sword approach. No explanation was given in *Ardoch* or *Bear Island* for this limitation on using the fiduciary duty as a "sword" and it is not justified on a plain reading of section 35(1). Clearly, the Supreme Court of Canada applied it as a "sword" in *Guerin*[123] and *Blueberry River*[124] as did the Federal Court of Appeal in the *Semiahmoo*[125] case, the British Columbia Court of Appeal in *Halfway River*,[126] and the British Columbia Supreme Court in *Gitanyow*.[127] Further, I would argue that s. 35(1) and the fiduciary duty which *Sparrow*[128] found to be incorporated into the Constitution by it should be given the same kind of purposive application that La Forest J. said should be given to the *Canadian*

Charter of Rights and Freedoms[129] in the *Lavigne* case:[130]

> It must be borne in mind that the *Charter* is not intended to serve a simply negative role by preventing the government from acting in certain ways. It has a positive role as well, which might be described as the creation of a society-wide respect for the principles of fairness and tolerance on which the *Charter* is based.

In *Sparrow*, the Supreme Court of Canada expressly indicated that section 35(1) should be purposively applied:[131]

> The nature of s. 35(1) itself suggests that it be construed in a purposive way. When the purposes of the affirmation of aboriginal rights are considered, it is clear that a generous, liberal interpretation of the words in the constitutional provision is demanded.

At the very least, these words of the Supreme Court of Canada remove any suggestion that section 35(1) and the fiduciary obligation incorporated therein are only to be used as a shield and not a sword. This interpretation is not "generous" and "liberal" but restrictive and conservative.

Does a competing Crown obligation provide a justification for breach of a fiduciary duty?

In several cases, it has been suggested that the Crown is not in breach of its fiduciary duty towards Aboriginal peoples if it has some competing obligation. The earliest case to this effect is the decision of the Federal Court of Appeal in *Kruger*[132] where the Department of Transport expropriated reserve land for an airport. Heald J. would have held that "the Federal Crown could not default on its fiduciary obligation to the Indians through a plea of competing considerations by different departments of government."[133] However, the majority held that the Crown could compromise the interests of the Indians to satisfy competing obligations. In *Eastmain Band*,[134] the same Court said the Crown "need not and cannot have only [the interest of Indians] in mind. It must seek a compromise between that interest and the whole society, which it also represents of which the Aboriginals are part, in the land in question."[135] Other cases to similar effect are *Samson Indian Nation*[136] and *Fairford First Nation*.[137] In *Tsartlip Indian Band*,[138] the court referred to the competing interests of a member of a band on the one hand, and of the band as a whole on the other.

In my view, the existence of a competing interest should not be a justification for a breach of a fiduciary duty. Rather, courts should apply the justificatory test established by the Supreme Court of Canada in *Sparrow*,[139] elaborated in *Delgamuukw*,[140] and applied in *Adams*[141] and *Badger*[142] to see, first, if the competing interest serves a valid legislative objective and, if so, as a second part of the test, whether the infringement of the Aboriginal interests is as minimal as possible to effect the desired result and whether there was adequate consultation and compensation. Given the obligations of the Crown to the rest of society, Heald J.'s application of the usual fiduciary duty to act exclusively for the benefit of the beneficiary[143] seems too strict. However, the existence of such competing interests should not in itself effectively displace the fiduciary duty just as the existence of other valid legislative objectives does not in itself justify the infringement of Aboriginal title or rights. Applying the *Sparrow/Delgamuukw* justificatory test, the court must proceed in its analysis of whether there has been a breach of fiduciary duty to the second part of the justification test. This will raise the adequacy of compensation paid by the Crown as well as the adequacy of consultations and whether the interference with the Aboriginal interest is as minimal as required to fulfil the competing interest. This approach is now mandated by the two-step process described by Iacobucci J. in the *Osoyoos*[144] case quoted below. It avoids the competing interest "trumping" the Aboriginal interest and it attempts to reconcile those interests.

In *Mabo v. Queensland (No. 2)*,[145] Toohey J. of the Australian High Court had this to say on the topic of the Crown's fiduciary duty to Aboriginal peoples and conflicts of interest:[146]

> A fiduciary has an obligation not to put himself or herself in a position of conflict of interests. But there are numerous examples of the Crown exercising different powers in different capacities. A fiduciary obligation on the Crown does not limit the legislative power of the Queensland parliament but legislation will be a breach of that obligation if its effect is adverse to the interest of the titleholders, or if the process it establishes does not take account of those interests.

Subject to the application of sections 35 and 52 of the *Constitution Act, 1982* which limit legislative powers in Canada, this approach is equally applicable in Canada. The Crown may indeed serve competing interests to those of Aboriginal peoples, but if in serving those other interests it would breach a fiduciary duty it owes to Aboriginal peoples, it must be prepared to pay compensation or provide other accommodation to justify its actions.

This approach is supported by the decision of Iacobucci J., giving the opinion of the majority, in the *Osoyoos Indian Band v. Oliver (Town)*, in which he said:[147]

> [52] In my view, the fiduciary duty of the Crown is not restricted to instances of surrender. Section 35 [of the *Indian Act*] clearly permits the Governor in Council to allow the use of reserve land for public purposes. However, once it has been determined that an expropriation of Indian lands is in the public interest, a fiduciary duty arises on the part of the Crown to expropriate or grant only the minimum interest required in order to fulfill that public purpose, thus ensuring a minimal impairment of the use and enjoyment of Indian lands by the band. This is consistent with the

provisions of s. 35 which give the Governor in Council the absolute discretion to prescribe the terms to which the expropriation or transfer is to be subject. In this way, instead of having the public interest trump the Indian interests, the approach I advocate attempts to reconcile the two interests involved.

[53] This two-step process minimizes any inconsistency between the Crown's public duty to expropriate lands and its fiduciary duty to Indians whose lands are affected by the expropriation. In the first stage, the Crown acts in the public interest in determining that an expropriation involving Indian lands is required in order to fulfill some public purpose. At this stage, no fiduciary duty exists. However, once the general decision to expropriate has been made, the fiduciary obligations of the Crown arise, requiring the Crown to expropriate an interest that will fulfill the public purpose while preserving the Indian interest in the land to the greatest extent practicable.

The Supreme Court of Canada also considered the question of a conflict of interest in the *Wewaykum*[148] case. The Court noted that "the content of the Crown's fiduciary duty towards aboriginal peoples varies with the nature and importance of the interest sought to be protected."[149] One example of this was the difference between the fiduciary duty owed prior to creation of a reserve and that owed after creation with respect to consideration of third-party interests. In discussing the duty prior to reserve creation, the Court said that the Crown could consider such interests:[150]

[96] When exercising ordinary government powers in matters involving disputes between Indians and non-Indians, the Crown was (and is) obliged to have regard to the interest of all affected parties, not just the Indian interest. The Crown can be no ordinary fiduciary; it wears many hats and represents many interests, some of which cannot help but be conflicting: *Samson Indian Nation and Band v. Canada*, [1995] 2 F.C. 762 (C.A.). As the Campbell River Band acknowledged in its factum, "[t]he Crown's position as fiduciary is necessarily unique" (para. 96). In resolving the dispute between Campbell River Band members and the non-Indian settlers named Nunns, for example, the Crown was not solely concerned with the band interest, nor should it have been. The Indians were "vulnerable" to the adverse exercise of the government's discretion, but so too were the settlers, and each looked to the Crown for a fair resolution of their dispute. At that stage, *prior to reserve creation,* the Court cannot ignore the reality of the conflicting demands confronting the government, asserted both by the competing bands themselves and by non-Indians.

However, after the creation of the reserve, the Crown's fiduciary duty could not be shirked by invoking competing interests:[151]

104. [T]he trial judge and the Federal Court of Appeal adopted, with respect, too restricted a view of the content of the fiduciary duty owed by the Crown to the Indian bands with respect to their existing quasi-proprietary interest in their respective reserves. In their view, the Crown discharged its fiduciary duty with respect to existing reserves by balancing "the interests of both the Cape Mudge Indians and the Campbell River Indians and to resolve their conflict regarding the

use and occupation of the [Laich-kwil-tach] reserves . . . [without favouring] the interests of one Band over the interest of the other" (para. 493 F.T.R. and para. 121 N.R.). With respect, the role of honest referee does not exhaust the Crown's fiduciary obligation here. The Crown could not, merely by invoking competing interests, shirk its fiduciary duty. The Crown was obliged to preserve and protect each band's legal interest in the reserve which, on a true interpretation of events, had been allocated to it. In my view it did so.

The United States law has resolved the question of reconciling the fiduciary duty to tribes and the government's duty to the public generally by adopting the "good faith effort" test. This test was developed by the Court of Claims in *Three Affiliated Tribes of Fort Berthold Reservation v. United States*[152] and endorsed by the United States Supreme Court in *United States v. Sioux Nation*.[153] Delivering the opinion of the court in *Sioux Nation*, Justice Blackmun noted that the Court of Claims had relied upon the "good faith effort" test developed in its earlier decision in *Fort Berthold*. The *Fort Berthold* test had been designed to reconcile two lines of cases decided by the U.S. Supreme Court that seemingly were in conflict:[154]

> The first line, exemplified by *Lone Wolf v. Hitchcock*, 187 U.S. 553 (1903), recognizes "that Congress possesse[s] a paramount power over the property of the Indians, by reason of its exercise of guardianship over their interests, and that such authority might be implied, even though opposed to the strict letter of a treaty with the Indians." Id., at 565. The second line, exemplified by the more recent decision in *Shoshone Tribe v. United States*, 299 U.S. 476 (1937), concedes Congress' paramount power over Indian property, but holds, nonetheless, that "[t]he power does not extend so far as to enable the Government 'to give the tribal lands to others, or to appropriate them to its own purposes, without rendering, or assuming an obligation to render, just compensation.'" Id., at 497 (quoting *United States v. Creek Nation*, 295 U.S. 103, 110 (1935)). In *Shoshone Tribe*, Mr. Justice Cardozo, in speaking for the Court, expressed the distinction between the conflicting principles in a characteristically pithy phrase: "Spoliation is not management." 299 U.S., at 498.

He also noted:[155]

> The Fort Berthold test distinguishes between cases in which one or the other principle is applicable:
> "It is obvious that Congress cannot simultaneously (1) act as trustee for the benefit of the Indians, exercising its plenary powers over the Indians and their property, as it thinks is in their best interests, and (2) exercise its sovereign power of eminent domain, taking the Indians' property within the meaning of the *Fifth Amendment* to the *Constitution*. In any given situation in which Congress has acted with regard to Indian people, it must have acted either in one capacity or the other. Congress can own two hats, but it cannot wear them both at the same time.
> "Some guideline must be established so that a court can identify in which capacity Congress is acting. The following guideline would best give recognition to the basic distinction between the two types of congressional action: Where Congress makes

a good faith effort to give the Indians the full value of the land and thus merely transmutes the property from land to money, there is no taking. This is a mere substitution of assets or change of form and is a traditional function of a trustee." 182 Ct. Cl., at 553, 390 F.2d, at 691.

Applying the *Fort Berthold* test to the facts of the case before it, the Court of Claims held that, in passing an Act in 1877 which abrogated the Fort Laramie Treaty of 1868 and terminated the rights of the Sioux to the Black Hills, Congress had not made a good-faith effort to give them the full value of the Black Hills. The U.S. Supreme Court upheld this conclusion and said just compensation, including an award of interest, "must now, at last, be paid."

Is the relationship based on strict trust, a trust-like relationship, or a sui generis fiduciary relationship?

Although the fiduciary concept arose out of the relationship between a trustee and the beneficiary of the trust, that relationship is now but one example of a fiduciary relationship. There are many other examples, such as that between partner and partner, parent and child, agent and principal, solicitor and client, director and company, and doctor and patient.[156] Thus, every trustee is a fiduciary but not every fiduciary is a trustee. However, every fiduciary does owe trust-like obligations to the beneficiary or principal. This was explained by Fry J. in *West of England and South Wales District Bank, Ex parte Dale and Co.*: "What is a fiduciary relationship? It is one in respect of which if a wrong arise, the same remedy exists against the wrong-doer on behalf of the principal as would exist against a trustee on behalf of the *cestui que trust*."[157]

In *Guerin*, the members of the Supreme Court of Canada disagreed on the legal basis of the liability of the Crown.[158] Dickson J. and Wilson J. in their judgments both agreed that the government was in breach of a fiduciary obligation towards the Musqueam Band in entering into the lease with the Shaughnessy Heights Golf Club although they differed on whether that obligation "crystallized into a trust upon surrender of the lands." Dickson J. said that the obligation did "not amount to a trust in the private law sense," but Wilson J. thought that "the fiduciary duty which existed at large under [section 18 of the *Indian Act*] to hold the land in the reserve for the use and benefit of the Band crystallized upon the surrender into an express trust of specific land for a specific purpose."[159] Estey J. thought that the action "should be disposed of on the very simple basis of the law of agency"[160] and hesitated "to resort to the more technical and far-reaching doctrines of the law of trusts and the concomitant law attaching to the fiduciary."[161] (This attempt to avoid the application of fiduciary law seems misguided since an agent is also a fiduciary.) In subsequent cases, courts have generally referred to a fiduciary relationship but, on occasion, have referred to a trust. For example, in *Sparrow,* Dickson C.J.C. and La Forest J. of the Supreme Court of Canada alluded to "the special trust relationship and the responsibility of the government *vis a vis* Aboriginals"[162] and these words were subsequently quoted by the Court in *Nikal,*[163] *Badger,*[164] and *Marshall.*[165] In *Blueberry River,* Gonthier J. deliberately left the point open.[166] As Desjardin J.A. of the Federal Court of Appeal observed in the *Samson Indian Nation* case,[167] the Supreme Court of Canada applied principles of trust law in the *Blueberry River* case. He commented that "[i]t would appear, therefore, that in the context of a trust in Indian law, the effects of a 'true' trust are generally applicable." However, in the *Haida Nation* case, decided in 2004, Chief Justice McLachlin commented that in *Guerin,* the Court "made it clear that the 'trust-like' relationship between the Crown and Aboriginal peoples is not a true 'trust' noting that "[t]he law of trusts is a highly developed, specialized branch of the law."[168]

From a practical point of view, nothing in *Guerin* turned on whether the Crown was described as a fiduciary, trustee, or agent, and this will be so in most cases. Trustees and agents are particular classes of fiduciary.[169] The Crown was held to be in breach of its obligation to the band by all the judges of the Supreme Court of Canada whether they saw that obligation as being based on a general fiduciary relationship or on the more specific fiduciary obligations of a trustee or agent. Dickson J. expressly stated that "[i]f . . . the Crown breaches this fiduciary duty it will be liable to the Indians in the same way and to the same extent as if such a trust were in effect."[170]

What rules govern the fiduciary obligation?

In *Guerin,*[171] Dickson J. took some pains to emphasize the *sui generis* nature of the Crown's fiduciary duty. Later cases have repeated the unique nature of the Crown's duty. In *Samson Indian Nation,* the Federal Court of Appeal said that "it does not necessarily follow that the rules and practices developed with respect to private trusts apply automatically to Crown 'trusts' such as those alleged in the present proceedings. . . . The Crown can be no ordinary 'trustee.'"[172] The Supreme Court of Canada echoed this statement in *Wewaykum*: "[w]hen exercising ordinary government powers in matters involving disputes between Indians and non-Indians, the Crown was (and is) obliged to have regard to the interest of all affected parties, not just the Indian interest. The Crown can be no ordinary fiduciary; it wears many hats and represents many interests, some of which cannot help but be conflicting."[173] Since the fiduciary relationship is said to be *sui generis*, it is still not clear what rules ordinarily applicable to fiduciaries will be excluded from, and what new rules will evolve for, this unique fiduciary relationship.

The description of the Crown's fiduciary relationship to Aboriginal peoples as *sui generis* adds nothing to the explanation of the relationship[174] and serves to confuse and frustrate the orderly development of the law by discouraging the application, where appropriate, of principles common to all fiduciary relationships. It is time to abandon it. All fiduciary relationships are *sui generis* in the sense that they are "situation-specific."[175] As Professor Rotman explains, this means "that the law of fiduciaries is not properly implemented without regard to the context within which it is to be applied."[176] Sir Eric Sachs pointed out in *Lloyd's Bank v. Bundy* that "[e]verything depends on the particular facts."[177] In *Wewaykum*,[178] Binnie J. noted that La Forest J. had pointed out in *McInerney v. MacDonald* that not all fiduciary relationships and not all fiduciary obligations are the same: "[t]hese are shaped by the demands of the situation."[179] He went on to give the example of the fiduciary relationship between solicitor and client where the singular demands of the administration of justice drive and "shape" the content of the relationship.[180] It is difficult to understand why the relationship between the Crown and Aboriginal peoples is any more in a class of its own than that of doctor to patient, director to company, parent to child, or lawyer to client. Each type of fiduciary relationship has special rules applicable to it reflecting the unique aspects of that relationship. However, the situation-specific nature of fiduciary relationships does not generally preclude the application of certain common principles. We have examined such principles in an earlier chapter.[181] To pursue the taxonomic analysis, the Crown's fiduciary relationship to Aboriginal peoples may be *sui generis* or in a genus of its own but so are other fiduciary relationships and this does not prevent them forming part of a family of genera sharing common characteristics. Rather than foreclose further analysis by invoking the mantra of *sui generis,* it would be more profitable for courts to explain why the rules that are common to fiduciary relationships generally should not apply to this particular fiduciary relationship. In the absence of such an explanation, those rules should apply.

What is the relationship between the honour of the Crown and the Crown's fiduciary relationship with Aboriginal peoples?

The recent decision of the Supreme Court of Canada in *Haida Nation v. British Columbia (Minister of Forests)*[182] has raised the question of the relationship between the honour of the Crown and the Crown's fiduciary relationship with Aboriginal peoples. In that case, the Court declined to find a fiduciary obligation on the part of the Crown to consult and to accommodate asserted Aboriginal rights and title before a determination of their existence. Instead, it based this duty on the "honour of the Crown," which it said derives from the assertion by the British Crown of sovereignty in the face of prior Aboriginal occupation of North America.[183] It said that the Aboriginal interest in question was insufficiently specific for the honour of the Crown to mandate that the Crown act in the Aboriginal group's best interest, as a fiduciary, in exercising discretionary control over the subject of the right or title.[184] The honour of the Crown only gave rise to a fiduciary duty in situations to which the Crown had assumed discretionary control over specific Aboriginal interests.[185]

The attempt by the Court to distinguish between the honour of the Crown and its fiduciary obligations adds a further level of confusion to the question discussed above of which rules are to govern. We have seen that, in *Guerin*, Dickson J. declined to find a "trust in the private law sense" because he could not identify trust property.[186] However, he went on to find that the Crown owed a fiduciary obligation which would render it liable in the same way and to the same extent as if a trust had were in effect.[187] Now, in *Haida Nation*, we have the same Court saying that the lack of a specific subject matter prevents a fiduciary obligation being owed but still finding a duty to consult and, if appropriate, accommodate the asserted Aboriginal interest which, as found by the British Columbia Court of Appeal, is the same duty that would arisen on the facts if a fiduciary obligation had been found.[188] The Supreme Court explained the distinction on the grounds that, where the Aboriginal interest had not yet been determined, the honour of the Crown did not mandate that the Crown act as a fiduciary in the best interest of the Aboriginal group. Yet, just a year before, in *K.L.B.* v. *British Columbia*, the Court had been at pains to point out that the fiduciary obligation of a parent did not require that the parent always act in the best interests of the child.[189] No reference is made in *Haida Nation* to this earlier ruling. Unfortunately, the Court's thin analysis in *Haida Nation* adds yet another layer of confusion onto an already confused analysis and gives ammunition to those who would reverse the recent developments in general fiduciary law and take it back to the pre-*Guerin* era.[190]

Previous decisions had treated the honour of the Crown as synonymous with the fiduciary relationship. In *Sparrow*,[191] writing for the Court, Dickson C.J.C. and La Forest J. referred to the decision of the Ontario Court of Appeal in *R. v. Taylor and Williams* in which that Court had said that "the honour of the Crown was involved in the interpretation of Indian treaties."[192] They then referred to *Guerin* and said, "[i]n our view, *Guerin*, together with *R. v. Taylor and Williams* . . . ground a general guiding principle for s. 35(1). That is, the government has the responsibility to act in a fiduciary capacity with respect to aboriginal peoples." Subsequently, they referred to "the concept of holding the Crown to a high standard of honourable dealing with respect to the Aboriginal peoples of Canada as suggested in *Guerin v. The Queen*."[193] These statements indicate that the honour of the Crown is synonymous with the fiduciary relationship rather than distinct from it. Likewise, in *R. v. Van Der Peet*, Lamer C.J.C. explained the relationship between the fiduciary relationship and the honour of the Crown as follows, "[t]he Crown has fiduciary obligations to aboriginal peoples with the result that in dealings between the government and aboriginals the honour of the Crown is at stake. Because of this fiduciary relationship, and its implication of the honour of the Crown, treaties, s. 35(1), and other statutory and constititutional provisions must be given a generous and liberal interpretation."[194] Again, in *Mitchell v. M.N.R.*, speaking for the Court, McLachlin C.J.C. said, "with this assertion of [sovereignty by the Crown] arose an obligation to treat aboriginal peoples fairly and honourably, and to protect them from exploitation, a duty characterized as 'fiduciary' in *Guerin v. The Queen*."[195]

The first indication that the Court was creating a distinction between the honour of the Crown and its fiduciary obligations appears to have been the following curious comment by Binnie J. in *Wewaykum*, "[s]omewhat associated with the ethical standards required of a fiduciary in the context of the Crown and aboriginal peoples is the need to uphold the 'honour of the Crown.'"[196] As Professor Rotman has commented, it is very uncertain what is meant by this comment, "the ethical standards of a fiduciary in the context of Crown–Native relations require, at a minimum, the upholding of the Crown's honour. Such an assertion is, indeed, axiomatic. Describing the Crown's ethical standards as a fiduciary as 'somewhat associated' with the 'honour of the Crown' is akin to saying that a corpse is 'somewhat dead.'"[197]

We must await future cases to see how this new distinction will influence the law. In my view, it is a further unnecessary complication. Any attempt to distinguish between a duty to discharge fiduciary duties and to act honourably is inconsistent with basic law applying to fiduciaries. In *Guerin*, Dickson J. referred to "the fiduciary's strict standard of conduct."[198] It was said by La Forest J. in *Hodgkinson* that "the presence of loyalty, trust and confidence" distinguishes the fiduciary relationship from other relationships.[199] It seems to me that these qualities could be summed up by saying that all fiduciaries, including the Crown, have a duty to act honourably.[200] The eminent American jurist, Justice Cardozo, said in *Meinhard v. Salmon*, that the standard of behaviour for a fiduciary is "not honesty alone, but the punctilio of an honor the most sensitive."[201] The Court's attempt to distinguish between a fiduciary duty and a duty to act honourably seems misguided and is likely to create further, and unnecessary, confusion.

The Four Chiefs—Taken on the steps of the Supreme Court of Canada Building during the *Guerin* hearing, June 13 & 14, 1983: *(l to r)* Chief Ernest Campbell, former Chiefs Gertrude Guerin, Ed Sparrow, and Delbert Guerin. Chief Ernest Campbell, the current chief, was chief at the time of the hearing. Former chiefs Gertrude Guerin and Ed Sparrow were on the Band Council in 1958 at the time the lease with the Shaughnessy Heights Golf Club was signed by the federal government (see pp. 40–41). Former chief Delbert Guerin discovered the terms of the lease in 1970 and commenced action on behalf of the Band in 1975 (see pp. 47–52). (Courtesy of the archives of the Musqueam Indian Band.)

Chapter 9

Procedure, Defences, and Remedies

This chapter sets out some of the procedural matters that are relevant to bringing an action for breach of a fiduciary obligation. It also discusses the defences that may be available to a defendant in a breach of fiduciary duty action and, in particular, defences based upon the length of time since the breach took place. For various reasons discussed below, in the case of a claim brought by an Aboriginal group, a considerable period of time may have elapsed since the breach occurred and the legal effects of this passage of time is often a major issue in the litigation. This chapter also describes the remedies available if the plaintiff is successful in demonstrating that a breach of fiduciary duty has taken place and the defendant has failed to establish a valid defence.

Pleadings

As with any litigation, great care should be taken in preparing the pleadings for a breach of fiduciary duty action. The plaintiff should specifically plead the breach of fiduciary duty and set out the facts that give rise to the duty: *Immocreek Corp. v. Petriosa Enterprises Ltd.*[1] It is not necessary to allege any loss or damages since they are not essential elements of the cause of action: *Clarke v. Perrick.*[2] In *Obonsawin v. Canada,*[3] the Crown was not successful on a motion for particulars of a claim that it had breached its fiduciary duty toward Aboriginal peoples. The claim related to the way in which the Crown administered tax exemptions. The court held that it was sufficient for the statement of claim to indicate that the source of the duty was the historic relationship between the Crown and Aboriginal peoples as protected by section 35 of the *Constitution Act, 1982.*

Trial

In appropriate circumstances, the existence of a fiduciary duty can be determined in a summary trial.[4] Although in *Dopf v. Royal Bank*[5] the British Columbia Court of Appeal expressed doubt whether juries are appropriate for cases involving breach of fiduciary duty, they have been used in such cases: *Mustaji v. Tjin*;[6] The existence of the duty is a question of law for the judge, but the jury may determine the relevant facts.

Class Proceedings

In *Elms v. Laurentian Bank of Canada*,[7] the Supreme Court of British Columbia held that allegations of breach of fiduciary duty could form part of a class proceeding. Writing for the Supreme Court of Canada, Chief Justice McLachlin said in *Western Canadian Shopping Centres Ltd v. Dutton*:[8]

> [55] The defendants' contention that the investors should not be permitted to sue as a class because each must show actual reliance to establish breach of fiduciary duty also fails to convince. In recent decades, fiduciary obligations have been applied in new contexts, and the full scope of their application remains to be precisely defined. The fiduciary duty issues raised here are common to all the investors. A class action should not be foreclosed on the ground that there is uncertainty as to the resolution of issues common to all class members. If it determined that the investors must show individual reliance, the court may then consider whether the class action should continue.

Failure to Prosecute Action

A breach of fiduciary obligation is considered to be one of the more serious forms of civil liability, and the stigma traditionally associated with a claim of breach of fiduciary duty may be a factor in a court dismissing a claim for want of prosecution. This was the case in *Rhyolite Resources Ltd. v. Conquest Resources Corp.*[9] A claim was dismissed after seven years for failure to prosecute the action. The British Columbia Court of Appeal upheld the dismissal on the grounds that the chambers judge was entitled to take the view that the allegation of breach of fiduciary duty was an unpleasant one to have hanging over the head of the respondent.

Onus of Proof

The onus of proof in a breach of fiduciary obligation claim generally operates to the advantage of plaintiffs in that it can involve a reverse onus on the defendant. According to Professor Rotman,[10] the onus on the beneficiary in a fiduciary relationship is restricted to establishing the existence of a fiduciary relationship and a *prima facie* breach of fiduciary duty. He argues that the latter can be established by juxtaposing the nature of the fiduciary obligations under the relationship in question against the fiduciary's impugned actions. The onus then shifts to the fiduciary, who must demonstrate that no breach occurred, either by satisfying the court that no fiduciary relationship existed in the first place, or that no breach of fiduciary duty actually occurred. He also argues that a fiduciary cannot rebut the allegation of breach simply by showing that the beneficiary benefitted from the impugned transaction, that the fiduciary's actions were done in good faith, or that the beneficiary's loss would have occurred notwithstanding the breach.

However, the onus on the defendant to prove that no breach of fiduciary duty took place may only exist if the defendant is in a conflict of interest. The trial judge in *Wewaykum*,[11] involving a breach of fiduciary duty claim against the Crown by two bands, found that the reverse onus on the defendant only arises where a *prima facie* case exists of a true conflict of interest. Only then will the defendant be required to prove it was acting in the best interests of the plaintiff. Where no such conflict of interest exists, the onus remains on the plaintiff to show the defendant did not exercise its discretion honestly, prudently, and for the plaintiff's benefit.[12] The decision of the Federal Court Trial Division in *Lower Kootenay*[13] also supports this approach. In that case, the trial judge found that, because there was no conflict of interest, the onus was on the plaintiff band to show the Crown did not act prudently and reasonably in the negotiations leading up to the impugned lease and in the years that followed.

The reluctance of courts to place the onus of proof on Crown defendants in Aboriginal cases is also evident from the willingness to draw inferences from the evidence which support the Crown's position.[14] In upholding the trial judge's finding that the Crown had provided full disclosure and was not in breach of its fiduciary duty, the Federal Court of Appeal in the *Wewaykum* case[15] rejected the argument that the onus is on the Crown (in that case, ninety years after the fact) to prove that all the facts involved in a transaction were disclosed and fully explained to the First Nation. Rather, the Court of Appeal found it was sufficient if it can be reasonably inferred from the evidence that full disclosure had taken place.[16] In its decision in the case, the Supreme Court of Canada did not comment on the point.[17]

Defences Based on Delay in Bringing Claim

The law provides defences to a defendant to deal with the difficulties presented by delays on the part of the plaintiff in bringing a claim. The basis for these defences was summarized by Binnie J. in *Wewaykum* as follows:[18]

> Witnesses are no longer available, historical documents are lost and difficult to contextualize, and expectations of fair practices change. Evolving standards of conduct and new standards of liability eventually make it unfair to judge actions of the past by the standards of today.

Speaking for the Supreme Court of Canada, he held that "[t]here is nothing in the circumstances of this case to relieve the appellants of the general obligation imposed on all litigants either to sue in a timely way or to forever hold their peace."[19] On the other hand, it may be unfair to the plaintiff to deny a remedy for a breach of fiduciary duty on the grounds of delay in bringing the claim. This has also been recognized by the Supreme Court of Canada. In *M.(K.) v. M.(H.),*[20] the Court said it would be unfair for the victim of a sexual assault to be denied a remedy given the difficulties experienced in discovering the existence of a cause of action and bringing a claim against the defendant. In such cases, the defendant had no right to repose.

In many cases, it is clearly unjust to deny Aboriginal plaintiffs their cause of action because of delay. There are several reasons for this. Until recently, Aboriginal people could not easily obtain legal representation. This is illustrated by the *Chisholm* case[21] discussed in chapter 1. In that case, the widow of a solicitor brought action against the Crown to recover payment of her husband's account for legal services rendered to an Indian band. It was held that the action could not continue partly on the grounds that the written approval of the superintendent-general of Indian Affairs was required for the contract of legal services. Clearly, this requirement would have been a serious deterrent to claims against the Crown for breach of fiduciary duty. In *Guerin*, the trial judge observed, "There was testimony before me which I accept, that the Musqueam Band Council had asked for their own appraisers and lawyers, but [the Indian agent] had told them those matters would be looked after by the Indian Affairs branch."[22] Also, to the extent that the claims involved land claims, they may have violated the restriction on such claims under the *Indian Acts* from 1927 to 1951.[23] Apart from bureaucratic and legal constraints on access to legal representation, lack of funding and knowledge of the legal system also prevented Aboriginal peoples from pursuing their legal claims until recent years.

Even if legal representation could be found, Aboriginal peoples lacked access to the relevant records until comparatively recently. This is again illustrated by the facts of *Guerin*.[24] The lease was signed in 1958, but it was not until 1970 that the Musqueam Band obtained a copy of it because of the refusal of the Department of Indian Affairs to provide a copy. Having obtained a copy of the lease, the band then had to obtain legal advice on what, if anything, could be done about the unfavourable terms that they had discovered in it. This proved to be difficult given the reluctance of most lawyers to take the case and the lack of relevant law in support of such a claim, as discussed in chapter 3. Not until they were ultimately successful could it be said that a cause of action existed. This lack of precedent also explained the failure of bands to bring claims.

In trying to do justice, courts must balance the competing interests of the plaintiff and the defendant when many years have gone by since a claim arose.

Statutes of Limitations[25]

Each province has legislation to deal with stale claims. However, they vary in their details and may not expressly deal with breach of a fiduciary duty. The particulars of the applicable statute must be considered in each case. For example, in Ontario until recently, there was no statutory limitation period for breach of fiduciary duty: *M.(K.) v. M.(H.)*.[26] The British Columbia *Limitation Act*[27] does not specifically address claims for fiduciary duty. However, section 3(5) provides for a six year limitation for causes of action that are not specifically mentioned.[28] If a fraudulent breach of trust or conversion of trust property is shown, the relevant limitation period is ten years under section 3(3).[29] As discussed below, the running of the period may be postponed or "tolled" by a finding of equitable fraud or lack of knowledge of a cause of action. There is also an "ultimate limitation period" of thirty years in section 8 of the *Act* which was held by the Supreme Court of Canada to apply on the facts of *Wewaykum*.[30]

It should be noted that, in actions in the Federal Court, the applicable limitation period is also to be found in provincial law. Section 39(1) of the *Federal Court Act* provides:[31]

> 39(1) Except as expressly provided by any other Act, the laws relating to prescription and the limitation of actions in force in any province between subject and subject apply to any proceedings in the court in respect of any cause of action arising in that province.

The Supreme Court of Canada has held that section 39(1) effectively incorporates by reference the applicable provincial limitation legislation but the relevant provisions will apply as federal law not as provincial law: *Blueberry River*[32] and *Wewaykum*.[33] In the latter case, the Court upheld the constitutionality of the provision.

Equitable Limitations

Even if, as was the case in Ontario, there is no statutory limitation period for a claim of breach of fiduciary duty, the claim is still subject to the possible application of equitable limitations.[34] These limitations are of two types: statutory limitations by analogy and laches/acquiescence.

It may first be noted that statutes of limitations may expressly preserve such equitable limitations. Section 2 of the former *Ontario Limitations Act*[35] was an example. In *M.(K.) v. M.(H.)*, La Forest J. of the Supreme Court of Canada said[36]

> This section makes it clear that the Act does not exhaust the defences available to a defendant because of the passage of time. Thus, certain actions expressly made subject to the *Limitations Act* may not yet be out of time under the terms of that statute, but may be precluded by equitable defences that apply notwithstanding the terms of the Act. The section also gives rise to the inference that there is a category of equitable claims not subject to the Act at all, and that the equitable defences survive in those cases. Such is the case here. The Act does not apply to fiduciary obligations, but the respondent may nonetheless argue that the equitable defence of laches is available to the respondent.

Even if a statutory limitation has no direct application to a claim because the limitation only applies to common law claims rather than equitable claims (such as a breach of a fiduciary duty), a court hearing the claim may still exercise a discretion to apply the limitation by analogy. The doctrine of statutory limitations by analogy can be traced back to the 1806 case of *Hovenden v. Annesley*.[37] However, it must be kept in mind that a court need not exercise its discretion in favour of applying the statutory limitation and may decline to do so if it considers that applying the limitation is not appropriate in the circumstances. The doctrine of statutory limitation by analogy was discussed by La Forest J. in *M.(K.) v. M.(H.)*.[38] He quoted with approval from J. Brunyate, *Limitation of Actions in Equity*,[39] to support the proposition that "equity in this instance is not bound to follow the law."[40] He concluded that even if an analogy could be drawn to a statutory period for a common law action, it would not be appropriate to apply it given the facts of the case. Professor Rotman has pointed out that "the applicability by analogy must be precise."[41] He argues that the only possible analogy to a fiduciary relationship commonly included in statutory limitation acts are those sections relating to trusts and trustees.[42] He notes that references to trusts and trustees in such statutes are generally confined to express or statutory trusts which, he argues, are not analogous to fiduciary relationships.[43]

La Forest J. also explained the test for the defences of laches and acquiescence in *M.(K.) v. M.(H.)*.[44] He gave this explanation in the context of a discussion of the liability of a parent for breach of fiduciary duty arising out of incest. As the Ontario Court of Appeal pointed out in *Chippewas of Sarnia Band v. Canada*,[45] the defences have been applied to bar the claims of Indian bands:

> [298] The doctrine of laches has been applied to bar the claims of an Indian band asserting aboriginal land rights: *Ontario (A.G.) v. Bear Island Foundation* (1984), 49 O.R. (2d) 353 (H.C.) at 447 (aff'd on other grounds (1989), 68 O.R. (2d) 394

(C.A.); [1991] 2 S.C.R. 570); *Wewaykum Indian Band v. Canada* (1995), 99 F.T.R. 1 at 77 and 79. There are also dicta in two decisions of the Supreme Court of Canada considering without rejecting, arguments that laches may bar claims to aboriginal title: *Smith v. The Queen*, [1983] 1 S.C.R. 554 at 570; *Guerin, supra* at 390.

The relevant passages from the judgment of La Forest J. in *M.(K.) v. M.(H.)* dealing with laches and acquiescence are set out below. They commence with reference to the decision of the Privy Council in *Lindsay Petroleum Co. v. Hurd*:[46]

> "[Laches] . . . is a defence which requires that a defendant can successfully resist an equitable (although not a legal) claim made against him if he can demonstrate that the plaintiff, by delaying the institution or prosecution of his case, has *either* (a) acquiesced in the defendant's conduct *or* (b) caused the defendant to alter his position in reasonable reliance on the plaintiff's acceptance of the status quo, or otherwise permitted a situation to arise which it would be unjust to disturb. . . ."
>
> Thus there are two distinct branches to the laches doctrine, and either will suffice as a defence to a claim in equity. What is immediately obvious from all of the authorities is that mere delay is insufficient to trigger laches under either of its two branches. Rather, the doctrine considers whether the delay of the plaintiff constitutes acquiescence or results in circumstances that make the prosecution of the action unreasonable. Ultimately, laches must be resolved as a matter of justice as between the parties, as in the case with any equitable doctrine.
>
> . . . As the primary and secondary definitions of acquiescence suggest, an important aspect of the concept is the plaintiff's knowledge of her rights. It is not enough that the plaintiff knows of the facts that support a claim in equity; she must also know that the facts give rise to that claim: *Re Howelett*, [1949] Ch. 767.

Acquiescence can apply even if the defendant has not altered his or her position in reliance on the plaintiff's delay. Acquiescence in this sense is a waiver of the plaintiff's rights by delay after the plaintiff has knowledge of the facts and that the facts give rise to a claim in equity. However, as emphasized by Justice La Forest, neither laches nor acquiescence can apply unless the plaintiff had knowledge of his or her legal right to bring a claim. Therefore, the plaintiff's absence of legal advice may be relevant to the availability of the defence to the defendant. The question of the effect of the plaintiff's lack of knowledge of a cause of action is discussed below.

In *Wewaykum*,[47] the Supreme Court of Canada held that the defences of laches and acquiescence were applicable to the claims made by the two bands involved in that case against the Crown. They had acted in a manner that could fairly be regarded as a waiver of any rights and that would make any prosecution of their claims unreasonable. Giving the judgment of the Court, Binnie J. said:[48]

> It seems to me both branches of the doctrine of laches and acquiescence apply here, namely: (i) where "the party has by his conduct done that which might fairly be

regarded as equivalent to a waiver" and (ii) such conduct "results in circumstances that make the prosecution of the action unreasonable" (*M.(K.) v. M.(H.)*, *supra*, at pp 76 and 78), conduct equivalent to a waiver is found in the declaration, representations and failure to assert "rights" in circumstances that required assertion, as previously set out.

All of this was done with sufficient knowledge "of the underlying facts relevant to a possible legal claim" (*M.(K.) v. M.(H.)*, *supra*, at p.79).

Limitations: Continuing Breach and Continuing Obligation Arguments

The continuing breach argument has been one method used in an attempt to overcome the defences of statutory limitations and laches. Some Aboriginal plaintiffs have maintained that, until remedied, the Crown's breach of its fiduciary obligation is a continuing breach, thus extending the running of time. However, courts have rejected this "continuing breach" argument. In *Wewaykum*,[49] Binnie J. speaking for the Supreme Court of Canada said "[a]cceptance of such a position would, of course, defeat the legislative purpose of limitation periods." Instead, courts have effectively extended the running of limitation defences by holding that the Crown is under a "continuing obligation" and then considering whether a breach of this continuing obligation has occurred at specific points in time.[50]

In *Semiahmoo*,[51] the Federal Court of Appeal held that the Crown committed a second breach of fiduciary obligation in 1969 when it refused to reconvey the lands to the band despite a band council resolution requesting that the lands be returned. Unlike its earlier breach at the time of the surrender in 1951, this second breach was not barred by the defence of limitations.

A similar result was reached in *Blueberry River*.[52] The Supreme Court of Canada held that the Crown's fiduciary duty continued after the date when the band's mineral rights were sold by the Department of Indian Affairs (the "DIA") to the Department of Veterans Affairs. Gonthier J., for the majority, stated:[53]

> So long as the DIA has the power, whether under the terms of the surrender instrument or under the *Indian Act*, to reserve the mineral rights through a leasing arrangement, the DIA was under a fiduciary duty to exercise this power.

The DIA not only had the power necessary to rectify the inadvertent error that had occurred but it was aware of the error and the potentially negative consequences for the band. Therefore, the Court held that the DIA had committed a second, distinct breach of fiduciary duty in not recovering the mineral rights. The original breach which resulted in the mineral rights being sold was defeated by the limitations defence but this second breach was not time-barred.

Effect of Equitable Fraud

Since the *Guerin* case, the doctrine of equitable fraud has been successfully used by Aboriginal plaintiffs against the Crown in breach of fiduciary duty cases in order to overcome statutory limitations defences and the equitable defences of laches and acquiescence.

As held in *Guerin*, equitable fraud refers to conduct which, having regard to some special relationship between the parties concerned, is an unconscionable thing for one to do to the other.[54] The equitable fraud in that case was the Crown's concealment of a cause of action by not disclosing the terms of the Shaughnessy lease which were substantially different from those approved by the band members.[55] This "fraud" delayed the running of time until the band discovered the fraud or, with reasonable diligence, ought to have discovered it. The word "fraud" is misleading since there is no requirement that the fiduciary act in an intentionally wrongful manner. As Dickson J. said in *Guerin*:[56]

> Although the [Indian Affairs] Branch officials did not act dishonestly or for improper motives in concealing the terms of the lease from the Band, in my view their conduct was nevertheless unconscionable, having regard to the fiduciary relationship between the Branch and the Band.

Therefore, equitable fraud is not the same as deceit or common law fraud.

Equitable fraud was also found by the Federal Court of Appeal in *Semiahmoo*.[57] The Crown did not conceal any of the terms of the surrender and the band was fully aware that it had consented to an absolute surrender. However, the Crown's conduct was held to be unconscionable and to amount to equitable fraud.[58] Goverment officials were aware of the band's reliance on them for all post-surrender information regarding the current and intended use of its land, but they put off answering the band's inquiries for four decades by telling it that development of the land was planned, or that studies would be conducted to determine the best uses of the land. Their conduct constituted equitable fraud.

Effect of Absence of Knowledge of Cause of Action

The running of time with respect to a limitation period may also be postponed by reason of the plaintiff's lack of knowledge of a cause of action. For example, section 6(4) of the British Columbia *Limitation Act*[59] postpones the running of time for various actions until the plaintiff has knowledge of facts that would cause a reasonable person, having taken appropriate advice, to think that there was a reasonable prospect of success. Breach of trust not based on fraud is within this provision.[60] In the case of fraud, the burden is on the trustee to show that the beneficiary was fully aware of the fraud before time begins to run. This provision replaced the common law doctrine of discoverability that postponed the running of time until the acquisition of knowledge or means of knowledge of the facts giving rise to the cause of action.[61] Other jurisdictions still follow the common law doctrine.[62]

The running of the six-year limitation period for breach of fiduciary duty was postponed for thirty years to 1977 in the *Blueberry River* case.[63] This was when the band became aware of events that took place in the 1940s which would give rise to a cause of action. Giving judgment in the 1997 case of *Semiahmoo*,[64] Isaac C.J. noted it was only in the previous fifteen years that Indian bands have been able to exercise the same degree of diligence regarding their legal rights as non-Aboriginal people are. It was not until the Supreme Court of Canada's decision in *Guerin* in 1984 that courts began to recognize a cause of action against the Crown for breach of fiduciary duty in respect of land surrenders:[65]

> [U]ntil the *Guerin* decision, it could not be said that the reasonable plaintiff would have viewed the Band's cause of action as having "a reasonable prospect of success." Until *Guerin*, most aboriginal peoples believed that their only avenue for redress for unfair treatment in land surrenders was in the political arena.

However, in *Wewaykum*,[66] the Supreme Court of Canada was less receptive to this argument given its finding that the plaintiff band had acquiesced in the alleged breach of fiduciary obligation:

> [124] The Campbell River Band at para. 30 and again at para. 133 of its factum links initiation of these proceedings to a new awareness precipitated by the release of the *Guerin* decision in 1984 of the possibility of financial compensation against the Crown. Awareness of the availability of a claim in equity for financial compensation against the Crown does not, however, turn what the band regarded as an equitable situation into an inequitable situation.

Inapplicability of Defence of Contributory Negligence

In a breach of fiduciary duty claim, the traditional rule is that the defendant will not be permitted to reduce his liability on the basis of the plaintiff's contributory negligence. This is illustrated by the decision of the Supreme Court of Canada in *Carl B. Potter v. Mercantile Bank of Canada*.[67] The Court stated that no reduction of damages for contributory negligence could logically take place:[68]

> In the present case the relationship of Potter to the Bank was that of *cestui que trust* [beneficiary] and trustee and I know of no authority for the proposition that a *cestui que trust* owes a duty to its trustee to ensure that the terms of the trust are observed.

This position was thrown into some doubt by the judgment of La Forest J. in *Canson Enterprises Ltd. v. Boughton & Co.*,[69] where, speaking for himself and three other judges, he approved the decision of the New Zealand Court of Appeal in *Day v. Mead*.[70] In that case, the Court held that contributory fault does apply in cases of fiduciary duty.

Canson did not reverse the traditional rule because the Court was evenly split on the issue, with four of the judges disagreeing with La Forest J.'s analysis. Giving the judgment for herself and two other judges, McLachlin J. said the plaintiff was under no duty to mitigate, although losses resulting from clearly unreasonable behaviour on the part of the plaintiff will be adjudged to flow from that behaviour and not the breach. Stevenson J. referred to the *Carl B. Potter*[71] case and said contributory negligence had not been introduced by the "so-called fusion of law and equity."[72] It may also be noted that courts in both Australia and England have declined to follow the *Day v. Mead* case: *Pilmer v. Duke Group Ltd.*,[73] and *Nationwide Building Society v. Thumbleby & Co.*[74]

Ultimate Limitation Period

In British Columbia, there is an ultimate limitation period of thirty years within which to bring actions with only a few exceptions under section 8 of the *Limitation Act*.[75] This ultimate period is not postponed by equitable fraud nor willful concealment of material facts.[76] It was applied by the Supreme Court of Canada in the *Blueberry River* case to the claim based on the transfer of mineral rights which took place just over thirty years before the action was commenced,[77] and to all the claims in the *Wewaykum* case.[78]

Remedies Available

A range of remedies are available to a plaintiff Aboriginal group in a successful action for breach of a fiduciary obligation, and courts consider a number of factors in fashioning a suitable remedy for the circumstances.

As noted by Mark Ellis, the author of the standard Canadian text on fiduciary duties, the remedies available for breach of fiduciary duty are primarily the remedies traditionally available in equity, bolstered by the remedies available conventionally at common law.[79] He discusses the following possible remedies:[80]

- declaration of trust

- accounting for any profit made by the fiduciary

- tracing the proceeds obtained by the fiduciary from any disposition of any property wrongfully disposed of by him

- constructive trust imposing an obligation on the fiduciary to hold property in trust for the beneficiary

- injunctions

- equitable damages or compensation.

Being a cause of action derived from the law of equity rather than the common law, the remedies available for a breach of fiduciary duty are flexible and generally broader than those for tort or contract.[81] In *Soulos v. Korkontzilas*, McLachlin J. observed that "[e]quitable remedies are flexible: their award is based on what is just in all the circumstances of the case."[82] This is true for breaches of fiduciary obligations.[83] Professor McCamus points out that "[a]n impressive array of remedies is available to the victim of a breach of fiduciary obligation."[84] However, it must also be kept in mind that remedies for breach of an equitable obligation, unlike those for a breach of a common law obligation are always subject to the discretion of the court.[85] The court will use this discretion to fashion a remedy that is appropriate to the nature of the wrong and the nature of the loss. As Lambert J.A. of the British Columbia Court of Appeal said in *Canson v. Boughton & Co.*[86] (in words subsequently quoted by La Forest J. of the Supreme Court of Canada[87]):

> The rubric "breach of fiduciary duty" has come to encompass so many different types of liability that it is not now possible to determine the appropriate remedy by defining the wrong simply as a "breach of fiduciary duty." It is necessary, instead, to look through the categorization of the wrong as a "breach of fiduciary duty" to the true nature of the wrong, and to move from there to the determination of the remedy.

Therefore, courts will look closely at the circumstances of each case to determine an appropriate remedy and not automatically apply the same remedies for all breaches of a fiduciary duty.

The Purpose of Equitable Remedies

The purpose of equitable remedies is restitutionary, namely to put the party who has been wronged in the position that he or she would have been in but for the breach.[88] In *Hodgkinson v. Simms*, La Forest J. stated:[89]

> It is well established that the proper approach to damages for breach of fiduciary duty is restitutionary. On this approach, the appellant is entitled to be put in as good a position as he would have been in had the breach not occurred.

The basic propositions are set out in *Guerin*,[90] where Wilson J. quoted at length from the Australian case of *Re Dawson*:[91]

The obligation of a defaulting trustee is essentially one of effecting a restitution to the estate. The obligation is of a personal character and its extent is not to be limited by common law principles governing remoteness of damage. . . .

   Caffrey v. Darby (1801) 6 Ves. Jun. 488; 31 E.R. 1159 is consistent with the proposition that if a breach has been committed then the trustee is liable to place the trust estate in the same position as it would have been in if no breach had been committed. Considerations of causation, foreseeability and remoteness do not readily enter into the matter. . . .

   The principles embodied in this approach do not appear to involve any inquiry as to whether the loss was caused by or flowed from the breach. Rather the inquiry in each instance would appear to be whether the loss would have happened if there had been no breach. . . .

   The cases to which I have referred demonstrate that the obligation to make restitution, which courts of equity have from very early times imposed on defaulting trustees and other fiduciaries, is of a more absolute nature than the common-law obligation to pay damages for tort or breach of contract. It is on this fundamental ground that I regard the principles in Tomkinson's case (*Tomkinson v. First Pennsylvania Banking-Trust Co.* [1961] A.C. 1007) as distinguishable. Moreover the distinction between common-law damages and relief against a defaulting trustee is strikingly demonstrated by reference to the actual form of relief granted in equity in respect of breaches of trust. The form of relief is couched in terms appropriate to require the defaulting trustee to restore to the estate the assets of which he deprived it. Increases in market values between the date of breach and the date of recoupment are for the trustee's account; the effect of such increase would, at common law, be excluded from the computation of damages but in equity a defaulting trustee must make good the loss by restoring to the estate the assets of which he deprived it notwithstanding that market values may have increased in the meantime. The obligation to restore to the estate the assets of which he deprived it necessarily connotes that, where a monetary compensation is to be paid in lieu of restoring assets the compensation is to be assessed by reference to the value of the assets at the date of restoration and not at the date of deprivation. In this sense the obligation is a continuing one and ordinarily, if the assets are for some reason not restored in specie, it will fall for quantification at the date when recoupment is to be effected, and not before.

Ellis has summarized the law by pointing out that "[it] is clear that the remedy [for breach of a fiduciary obligation] is exercised to attempt to restore the status quo where possible" and that an arsenal of equitable relief is available to a Canadian court to achieve this objective.[92]

Factors to be Considered in Fashioning a Remedy

In fashioning a remedy for a breach of a fiduciary obligation, courts adopt an approach that is favourable to the beneficiary rather than the defaulting fiduciary. For example, where there has been a breach, the plaintiff is entitled to the advantage of any increase in market value to the date of trial.[93] The presumption made in *Guerin* was that the Musqueam Band would have developed its land in the most advantageous way if the breach had not occurred:[94]

> The Band was thereby deprived of its land and any use to which it might have wanted
> to put it. Just as it is to be presumed that a beneficiary would have wished to sell
> his securities at the highest price available during the period they were wrongfully
> withheld from him by the trustee (see *McNeil v. Fultz* (1906), 38 S.C.R. 198), so
> also it should be presumed that the Band would have wished to develop its land in
> the most advantageous way possible during the period covered by the unauthorized
> lease. In this respect also the principles applicable to determine damages for breach
> of trust are to be contrasted with the principles applicable to determine damages
> for breach of contract. In contract it would have been necessary for the Band to
> prove that it would have developed the land; in equity a presumption is made to
> that effect: see Waters, *Law of Trusts in Canada* at p. 845.

This approach was followed by the Federal Court of Appeal in the case
of *Semiahmoo Indian Band v. Canada*[95] as considered below.

If the breach of a fiduciary obligation results in a profit to the fiduciary,
compensation does not depend on whether the profit would otherwise have
been available to the beneficiary or on the beneficiary showing proof of loss.
This was explained by Lord Russell in *Regal (Hastings) Limited v. Gulliver:*[96]

> The rule of equity which insists on those, who by use of a fiduciary position make a
> profit, being liable to account for that profit, in no way depends on fraud, or absence
> of bona fides; or upon such questions or considerations as whether the profit would
> or should otherwise have gone to the plaintiff, or whether the profiteer was under
> a duty to obtain the source of the profit for the plaintiff, or whether he took a risk
> or acted as he did for the benefit of the plaintiff, or whether the plaintiff has in fact
> been damaged or benefitted by his action. The liability arises from the mere fact of a
> profit having, in the stated circumstances, been made. The profiteer, however honest
> and well-intentioned, cannot escape the risk of being called upon to account.

In *Canadian Aero Service Ltd v. O'Malley*, the Supreme Court of Canada
followed *Regal (Hastings) Limited* in stating:[97]

> Liability of O'Malley and Zarzycki for breach of fiduciary duty does not depend
> upon proof by Canaero that, but for their intervention, it would have obtained
> the Guyana contract; nor is it a condition of recovery of damages that Canaero
> establish what its profit would have been or what it had lost by failing to realize the
> corporate opportunity in question. It is entitled to compel the faithless fiduciaries
> to answer for their default according to their gain.

Likewise, the defaulting fiduciary is precluded from arguing the inevita-
bility of loss. As observed by Ellis:[98]

> Perhaps most significant to the calculation of fiduciary damages is the concept of
> inevitability of loss. The Courts have long precluded the defaulting fiduciary from
> arguing that the loss would have occurred in any event: *Island Realty Investments Ltd.
> v. Douglas* (1985), 19 E.T.R. 56 (B.C.S.C.). In that case, the Court acknowledged
> the inevitability of loss, and, absent the equitable position reflected in precedents

cited to it, would have dismissed the action:

"The real estate market declined dramatically. . . . That Lawson would have defaulted in any event is almost certain. If that had happened, the plaintiff could not have forced proceedings. . . . I regard it as highly probable that a similar result would have occurred had there been no breach of trust. It must be admitted that conjecture is involved in the foregoing, but if the remedy available to the plaintiff depended upon proof that loss occurred as a result of the breach of trust I would find for the defendants, and not reluctantly as the investment of the plaintiff was in the higher risk category.

"However, [the plaintiff's counsel] has persuaded me that such a disposition is not open to me because his claim is based on a breach of trust. If a loss follows a breach as in this case I cannot consider the proposition that the loss would have occurred in any event. It is not the same as proving damages following a breach of contract."

Generally,[99] there will be no inquiry into whether the defaulting fiduciary can escape or limit liability by application of the doctrines of causation, remoteness, and foreseeability. Under these doctrines, which apply in other areas of the law governing civil liability, the defendant may demonstrate that his default did not cause the particular form of loss suffered by the plaintiff or that the loss was too remote in that it was not sufficiently connected with the default or could not be reasonably foreseen by the defendant. As Wilson J. said in *Guerin*: "Considerations of causation, foreseeability and remoteness do not readily enter into the matter."[100]

McLachlin J. noted in *Blueberry River*[101] that the trial judge's emphasis on the low value of the mineral rights at the time of the Crown's second breach of fiduciary duty was misplaced because it reflected a concern that the band would unjustly receive a windfall benefit at the expense of the Crown. This was an error in law because it sought to bring foreseeability into the fiduciary analysis by way of the back door.[102] She cited the judgment of La Forest J. in *Hodgkinson*[103] in support of the statement that "[t]he beneficiary of a fiduciary duty is entitled to have his or her property restored or value in its place, even if the value of the property turns out to be much greater than could have been foreseen at the time of the breach."[104]

In granting a remedy, it is appropriate for the court to consider that remedies for breach of fiduciary duty contain an element of deterrence. In *Semiahmoo*, Chief Justice Isaac of the Federal Court of Canada said that "it is well-settled that fiduciary law contains within it an element of deterrence" and that a restitutionary remedy "will signal to [the Crown] that it must act with due regard to the best interests of affected Indian Bands when dealing with land retained by [it]."[105]

In *Soulos*, McLachlin J. said:[106]

> The constructive trust imposed for breach of fiduciary relationship thus serves not only to do the justice between the parties that good conscience requires, but to hold fiduciaries and people in positions of trust to the high standards of trust and probity that commercial and other social institutions require if they are to function effectively.

Punitive damages may be awarded if the conduct of the defendant is especially repugnant to the best interests of the beneficiary.[107]

Constructive Trust

One well established remedy for breach of fiduciary obligation is the imposition of a constructive trust. In a constructive trust, the defaulting fiduciary is required to hold property in trust for the beneficiary. Like all equitable remedies, it is only available when, in the exercise of its discretion, a court considers it an appropriate and just remedy. It may be ordered as an alternative to, or in addition to, compensation for the breach. The leading case on the use of a constructive trust as a remedy for breach of the fiduciary duty owed to Aboriginal people is *Semiahmoo*. In that case, Chief Justice Isaac of the Federal Court of Appeal observed:[108]

> Once it is decided that a restitutionary remedy is appropriate, the next step is to determine *which* restitutionary remedy. The constructive trust is only one of the restitutionary remedies available to a court. One alternative is to award equitable damages.

A constructive trust is the appropriate remedy wherever there is a causal connection between a breach of fiduciary duty and the loss of a property right, and where the property is still in the fiduciary's control. In *Semiahmoo*, in breach of its fiduciary obligations to the band, the Crown had obtained a surrender of reserve lands for use as a customs house but most of the land was not used for that or any other purpose. The Court ordered the Crown to hold the lands on a constructive trust for the benefit of the band. The Court stated:[109]

> The imposition of the constructive trust simply does for the respondent what its fiduciary duty required of it back in 1969; it gives back to the Band an interest in the surrendered land. . . .
>
> By virtue of the respondent's breaches of its fiduciary duty, the Band lost, and was not able to regain, its interest in the surrendered land. Given the unique value placed upon land by the First Nations in general, and upon the surrendered land by the Band in particular, a monetary award simpliciter would be an inadequate remedy for the respondents actual breach of fiduciary duty. In my view, it is appropriate in these circumstances for the Court to create a beneficial interest in the Surrendered Land for the Band by imposing a constructive trust.

In *Lac Minerals*,[110] La Forest J. found that a constructive trust was an appropriate remedy for breach of fiduciary duty resulting in the loss to the beneficiary of rights to a gold mine. He found that, even in a commercial context, a gold mine could be a sufficiently valuable and "unique" property so that:[111]

> To award only a monetary remedy in such circumstances when an alternative remedy is both available and appropriate would . . . be unfair and unjust.
>
> [H]aving specific regard to the uniqueness of the Williams property, to the fact but for Lac's breaches of duty Corona would have acquired it, and recognizing the virtual impossibility of accurately valuing the property, I am of the view that it is appropriate to award Corona a constructive trust over that land.

A further consideration will be the benefit that would be obtained by the fiduciary if the property were to remain in its hands. In *Semiahmoo*, the Court stated:[112]

> As stated by Wilson J. in *Lac Minerals* "the imposition of a constructive trust also ensures, of course, that the wrong doer does not benefit from his wrong doing, an important consideration in equity which may not be achieved by a damage award.

One question that was unclear until the 1997 decision of the Supreme Court of Canada in the *Soulos* case[113] was whether a constructive trust could be made available in the absence of unjust enrichment of the defendant. In *Semiahmoo*, the Court stated:[114]

> It is not entirely clear from the authorities whether, in a case of breach of a fiduciary duty, it is necessary to show an unjust enrichment in order to justify a restitutionary remedy or whether it is sufficient to show that ordinary damages, calculated on common law principles, would not provide adequate compensation to the beneficiary for the impugned breach.

The Court then went on "for the sake of completeness" to consider the decision of the Supreme Court of Canada in *Pettkus v. Becker*,[115] which had suggested three elements in its test for a constructive trust where unjust enrichment is found:

1) enrichment of the defendant

2) corresponding deprivation suffered by the plaintiff

3) absence of a juristic reason for the enrichment.

The Court in *Semiahmoo* had little trouble finding these three elements to be satisfied on the facts of the case:

1) In relation to enrichment of the defendant:[116]

> By refusing to reconvey the surrendered land to the Band, the respondent was

enriched because it retained the land from 1969 to the present without title being fettered by redesignation of the land as part of the Band's Reserve. In my respectful view, a further finding that the respondent used the land productively—for example, by generating a profit or by using it for a public purpose—is not required in order to justify a finding that the respondent has been enriched.

2)   In relation to deprivation of the band:[117]

As a result of the respondent's failure to reconvey the surrendered land to the Band, the Band has been deprived of the opportunity to develop the land themselves. . . . Moreover, the surrendered land has a unique value to the Band, and thus, the fact that they receive market value for the land (as undeveloped property) in the original surrender agreement does not detract from the conclusion that they suffered a deprivation as a result of the respondent's failure to reconvey the land to the Band in 1969.

3)   In relation to the absence of juristic reason:[118]

It is a simple rule of fiduciary law that the fiduciary must disgorge any benefits obtained at the expense of the beneficiary. . . . In this case, the respondent obtained the surrendered land in contravention of its fiduciary duty to the Band. It is a fiduciary duty born out of the "honor of the Crown" and it is the role of the Courts to ensure that the Crown lives up to that duty. In this case, a restitutionary remedy is required in order to redress fully the wrongs committed to the Band by the respondent.

It is now clear that it is no longer necessary to consider the *Pettkus v. Becker* test as a condition of an order of constructive trust. The "lack of clarity" in the authorities which was referred to by the Court in *Semiahmoo* was resolved by the Supreme Court of Canada in *Soulos v. Korkontzilas*.[119] That case dealt with a situation in which a real estate agent breached his fiduciary duty to his client, who wanted to purchase a commercial building, by failing to give him information on the price at which the vendor would sell. It was a case where there was an absence of financial loss since the market value of the building had declined. Giving the opinion of the majority of the Court, McLachlin J. said:[120]

This raises the legal issue of whether a constructive trust over property may be imposed in the absence of enrichment of the defendant and corresponding deprivation of the plaintiff. In my view, this question should be answered in the affirmative.

The Court in *Soulos* adopted "good conscience" as the basis for the imposition of a constructive trust. However, this does not mean that a judge is free to impose a constructive trust whenever he or she feels that it is appropriate to do so based on his or her own notions of good conscience. Rather, as noted by McLachlin J., "good conscience" is based on the following legal considerations:[121]

It thus emerges that a constructive trust may be imposed where good conscience so requires. The inquiry into good conscience is informed by the situations where constructive trusts have been recognized in the past. It is also informed by the dual reasons for which constructive trusts have traditionally been imposed: to do justice between the parties and to maintain the integrity of institutions dependent on trust-like relationships. Finally, it is informed by the absence of an indication that a constructive trust would have an unfair or unjust effect on the defendant or third parties, matters which equity has always taken into account. Equitable remedies are flexible; their award is based on what is just in all the circumstances of the case.

The Court then listed four factors for guidance in this type of constructive trust:[122]

(1) The defendant must have been under an equitable obligation, that is, an obligation of the type that courts of equity have enforced, in relation to the activities giving rise to the assets in his hands [a fiduciary obligation would satisfy this requirement];

(2) The assets in the hands of the defendant must be shown to have resulted from deemed or actual agency activities of the defendant in breach of his equitable obligation to the plaintiff [again, property held by a fiduciary in her capacity as a fiduciary would satisfy this requirement, as would any property acquired by her as the result of a breach of fiduciary obligation];

(3) The plaintiff must show a legitimate reason for seeking a proprietary remedy, either personal or related to the need to ensure that others like the defendant remain faithful to their duties [in many cases, the plaintiff will not be able to satisfy this requirement because monetary compensation will be an adequate remedy and it is not necessary to give the plaintiff a interest in property held by the defaulting fiduciary] and;

(4) There must be no factors which would render imposition of a constructive trust unjust in all the circumstances of the case; e.g., the interests of intervening creditors must be protected [the facts of each case would have to be considered to see if a third party who had an interest in the property in question would be unfairly affected by the imposition of a constructive trust in favour of the plaintiff or if it would be otherwise unjust to impose such a trust].

Compensation

In most actions for breach of a fiduciary obligation, the principal remedy awarded will be compensation for the loss caused to the beneficiary, as was the case in *Guerin*.[123] As noted by Chief Justice Lamer in *Delgamuukw*, "Compensation for breaches of fiduciary duty [is] a well-established part of the landscape of aboriginal rights: *Guerin*."[124]

Where a constructive trust is imposed, equitable damages may also be appropriate to compensate for loss of use in the interim. In *Semiahmoo*, the Federal Court of Appeal stated:[125]

By providing the Band with a beneficial interest in the Surrendered Land, the imposition of a constructive trust allows the Band to capture the appreciation in value of the Surrendered Land as undeveloped land. However, it may be that the constructive trust provides inadequate compensation in this case because, had the Band been able to retain the Surrendered Land (that is, but for the respondent's breaches of its fiduciary duty) the Band could have potentially earned much more by developing the land.

The Court set out the correct approach to the measure of equitable compensation:[126]

> It is well-settled that the proper approach to equitable damages for breach of fiduciary duty is restitutionary. (*Hodgkinson v. Simms, supra* at 440, per La Forest J.) Courts have always imposed on defaulting trustees and other fiduciaries an obligation to make restitution which is "of a more absolute nature than the common law obligation for tort or breach of contract". (*Guerin, supra* at 361.) As stated by Dickson J. (as he then was) in *Fales v. Canada Permanent Trust Co.*, [1977] 2 S.C.R. 302, 70 D.L.R. (3d) 257, the measure of damages is "the actual loss which the acts or omissions have caused to the trust estate." . . . Applying this approach to the case at bar, equitable damages should be calculated based on the presumption that the Band would have used the land in the most advantageous way during the period that it was improperly held by the Crown. . . .
>
> The measure of these damages is, in essence, the incremental value that the Band would have derived from development of the Surrendered Land in the most advantageous way available to them.

The Court further concluded that consequential damages arising from the adverse impact on other parts of the reserve, should also be compensable:[127]

> In order to ensure full restitution, the referee will also have to determine whether the Band suffered any damage to the remainder of the Reserve during the period from 1969 to the date of this Court's judgment and, if yes, the referee will have to quantify that amount. For example, did the loss of the surrendered land impede development on the remainder of the Reserve?

Where the breach has not led to the loss of any property interest, such as failure to collect proper lease revenues, the obligation is to effect restitution through payment of equitable compensation alone.[128] In *Guerin*, compensation was the sole remedy that was appropriate in the circumstances. Since the lands had been leased by the Crown to the golf club, no constructive trust could be imposed on the Crown to hold them for the Musqueam Band.

In appropriate cases, the defaulting fiduciary will be ordered to account to the beneficiary for any profit obtained through the breach. *Halsbury's Laws of England* states:[129] "[w]here a trustee makes a profit by an improper employment of trust money or property, he is liable to make good to the trust estate the amount of that profit in addition to the money or property improperly employed." If the fiduciary has not made any profit, accounting is not appropriate. In *Semiahmoo*,[130] for example, the Federal Court of Appeal held that an accounting would be inappropriate because the Crown had not acquired or used the land for profit. The Court held that equitable compensation for loss of use would be more just in the circumstances.

The fiduciary's liability may be reduced by a set-off of any amount received by the beneficiary. The Court held that the value of compensation received by the band in the 1951 surrender and the interest it would have accumulated must be set off against any equitable damages flowing to the band as a result of the breach of fiduciary duty:[131]

> Finally, the referee will also have to determine the value of the compensation received by the Band in the 1951 surrender agreement, adjusted for compound interest to the date of this Court's judgment. This amount will reduce the net monetary compensation owed to the Band by the Crown, over and above the Band's beneficial interest in the Surrendered Land created by the constructive trust. Alternatively, if the amount of the compensation received by the Band in 1951 plus interest is higher than the equitable damages, the Band will have to repay the net amount to the respondent.

On the other hand, the amount awarded may be increased to include interest. A court of equity can award interest for the period from the date of the breach to the date of the judgment, either as a component of equitable compensation or under a statute such as the British Columbia *Court Order Interest Act*.[132] Courts of equity have jurisdiction to award interest on judgments in appropriate circumstances regardless of the availability of statutory interest.[133] As noted above,[134] equitable compensation is calculated with the full benefit of hindsight and based on the best rate of return that the fiduciary could have reasonably and lawfully obtained for the beneficiary. The best rate of return may include compound interest that would have been earned but for the breach. This principle was recently discussed by Madam Justice Dillon in *B.(K.L.) v. British Columbia*:[135]

> Pre-judgment interest assessed at the real rate of return achieves a fair result by compensating the plaintiffs for loss of use of their money. The justice of the case calls for equity to fully protect the plaintiffs and for a generous, restorative remedial approach to be taken. Courts have used the equitable jurisdiction in the past in cases involving compound interest to compensate a plaintiff for breach of fiduciary duty where to do so is necessary in the interests of justice and fairness despite a statutory ban. It is just and proper in this case to award pre-judgment equitable interest ancillary to equitable compensation. . . .

In *Wewaykum Indian Band v. Canada*,[136] Mr. Justice Teitelbaum was prepared to apply this principle in awarding pre-judgment compound interest against the Crown for loss resulting from a breach of fiduciary duty. Relying on

Dube J.'s decision in *Lower Kootenay Indian Band v. Canada*,[137] he said:[138]

> I also wish to note that in [*Lower Kootenay*], Dubé, J., calculated the compensation owed by the Crown to the Indian Band by adopting the approach taken by Mr. Nilsen (also an expert in the case before me), who assumed that the difference between market rent net deductions and the rent received under the lease could have been invested and would have accumulated compound interest. Dubé, J., was of the opinion, and so am I, that this is a fair and realistic approach to the calculation of compensation.

Mr. Justice Teitelbaum, therefore, would have included compound interest in the compensation for loss of use of the reserve if he had decided that the Crown was liable for breach of fiduciary obligation.

Compensation for Loss of Reserve Lands: The Cases

The following cases provide examples of how compensation may be assessed for a breach of a fiduciary obligation owed by the Crown to Aboriginal peoples:

1. the Supreme Court of Canada[139] and trial decisions[140] in *Guerin*

2. the Federal Court of Appeal decision in *Semiahmoo*[141]

3. the Federal Court trial decision in *Wewaykum*[142]

4. the Federal Court trial decision in *Lower Kootenay*.[143]

These cases all dealt with breaches, or alleged breaches, of fiduciary obligation by the Crown arising out of the surrender of reserve lands.

Guerin

In *Guerin*, the Supreme Court of Canada upheld the global assessment of damages by Collier J., as trial judge, in the sum of $10 million.[144] He said that the aim of the damages was to compensate the band for the actual loss which the Crown's breaches of trust had caused to the "trust estate" (the surrendered reserve lands) on the theory the plaintiffs are entitled to be placed as far as possible in the same position as if there had been no breach of trust,[145] citing *Fales v. Canada Permanent Trust Co.*[146] as authority.

Given his finding that the band would have refused to surrender its lands on the terms of the lease which was signed, Collier J. considered what would likely have occurred if the lease had been turned down. He concluded that the golf club would not have agreed to enter into a lease on the terms approved by the band. As a result, he rejected the Crown's argument that the appropriate measure of the band's damages should be the difference between the lease the band had wanted and the unauthorized lease.

Instead, he looked at other potential uses to which the reserve lands could have been put but for the unauthorized lease. He concluded it was necessary to determine the amount of loss suffered by the band on the assumption a lease for a golf course would not likely have been entered into. He found that, after a period of some delay to take into account time for planning, tenders, and negotiation and a period of initial slow development, the 162 acres in question would have been successfully marketed as prepaid ninety-nine-year leasehold lots for residential development. This conclusion was based on evidence of "economic, business, population and real estate value trends, housing accommodation demand, and raw land shortages, all during the period 1958 to 1973" in Vancouver.[147] He also looked at what the band had done with other portions of its reserve and the timing of this activity, and noted some of its reserve lands had been developed on a ninety-nine-year leasehold basis.

The band called as its chief witness on damages a real estate appraiser whose expertise was as a consultant in matters relating to real estate evaluation and marketing and feasibility studies. The Crown called three real estate appraisers as expert witnesses on damages. All of the experts agreed the 162 acres were prime residential property in Vancouver, both in 1957–58 when they were surrendered and then leased to the golf club, and at the time of trial. Therefore, the highest and best use for these lands was as prime residential property, not a golf course, and the band was entitled to be compensated on that basis.

Collier J. then considered the anticipated return from leasehold residential development as against the actual return from the unauthorized lease, and came up with a global figure of $10 million, a number he acknowledged was not based on a precise rationale, mathematical or otherwise. The figure was more than the $1.6 million loss calculated by one of the Crown's experts and less than the $45 to $71 million loss calculated by the band's expert. He described the amount as "a considered reaction based on the evidence, the opinions, the arguments and, in the end, [his] conclusions of fact."[148] Although he did not indicate their relative importance, he set out a non-exhaustive list of the "factors and contingencies" he "had in mind" in reaching the $10 million figure. These were:[149]

a)   the difficulty in determining when the 162 acres would have been developed, in what way, and at what monetary return (assuming the unauthorized lease had never been entered into);

b)   the contingency that the area might not, even at the time of trial, be satisfactorily developed or provide a realistic economic return;

c)   the astonishing increases in land values, inflation, and interest rates since 1958, and the fact no one could reasonably, in 1958, have envisaged these increases;

d)   contrary to (*c*) above, that those same increases must be taken into account in any damages award;

e)   the possibility that the unauthorized lease would remain in effect until its expiry in 2033;

f)   the "very real contingency" that the lease might be terminated at a future rental review period;

g)   the monies the band had received to date under the unauthorized lease, and what might be received in the future if the lease remained in effect; and

h)   the value of the reversion of the improvements, whether at the end of prepaid ninety-nine-year residential leases, or at the end of the golf club lease.

When the case reached the Supreme Court of Canada, Dickson J. simply affirmed Collier J.'s damages assessment as reflecting no error in principle.[150] The reasons of Wilson J. deal, in slightly more detail, with the issue of damages.[151] She approved his approach on the basis it represented an attempt to put a monetary value, as of the date of trial, on the band's lost opportunity to develop the land for residential purposes for a period of seventy-five years, and then to subtract from this amount the value of the unauthorized golf club lease. She found it was appropriate to compensate the band as of the date of trial, rather than, as the Crown argued, as of the date of the breach, notwithstanding that market values for the lands had increased significantly since the date of the Crown's breach. At common law, such increases would be excluded from the calculation of damages.

Justice Wilson also found that, because the claim was in equity, a presumption operated to the effect that the band would have developed its land in the most advantageous way possible during the period covered by the unauthorized lease. There was no need for the band to prove, as it would have had to do if the claim had been based on breach of contract, that it would in fact have developed the land in the most advantageous manner. The band was entitled to compensation which reflected the increase in the market value of the land since the date of breach and which was based on the presumption that the band, had it retained the lands, would have put them to their most advantageous use.

She did not address, in any detail, Collier J.'s use of contingencies, such as the unforeseen rate of increase in real estate values. However, the affirmation by the Supreme Court of Canada of his $10 million award of damages on the basis it reflected no error in principle supports the use of contingencies to reduce the quantum of damages which an Aboriginal plaintiff might otherwise be entitled to receive from the Crown for breach of fiduciary duty resulting in the loss of use of its reserve lands.

Semiahmoo

In *Semiahmoo*,[152] a band gave an absolute surrender to the Crown in 1951 of part of its reserve on the understanding the lands would be used by the Crown for customs purposes. In exchange it received payment by the Crown of $550 per acre. The Crown retained title to all of the surrendered land and the lands remained, as of the date of the court proceedings, unused for any purpose. As we have seen,[153] the retention of the lands by the Crown enabled the Federal Court of Appeal to make an order that the Crown held them as a constructive trustee for the band. The Court noted that the imposition of a constructive trust allowed the band to capture the appreciation in value of the surrendered land as undeveloped land. In other words, the constructive trust remedy replaced what would otherwise (assuming the Crown was no longer on title) have been compensation for the permanent loss of the land, which would have been calculated based on the present day, unimproved market value of the land.

The Court found that the constructive trust alone might provide inadequate compensation because, had the band been able to retain the land, it could potentially have earned more by developing it. In other words, the constructive trust did not account for past loss based on the revenues the band could have earned from the land. The Court went on to provide guidelines to assist the referee who would be determining the amount of compensation over and above the constructive trust, if any, required to provide the band with full restitution, as well as the amount the band had to repay the Crown for the compensation it had received in 1951.

The Court emphasized that the overriding objective was to place the band, insofar as was possible, in the same position it would have been but for the Crown's breach of its fiduciary duty in 1969 when it failed to reconvey the land to the band.[154] It adopted the approach followed by Wilson J. in *Guerin*[155] and held that damages should be calculated based on the presumption the band would have used the land in the most advantageous way during the period it was improperly held by the Crown. The Court pointed out that the referee should keep in mind that the band had already been compensated, at least in part, for the Crown's actionable breach of fiduciary duty by the imposition of the constructive trust. The focus was to be on providing restitution for the second actionable breach, not the first breach which was time-barred, meaning the band could only collect damages, if any, incurred from 1969 to the date of judgment. These damages were described as "the incremental value that the band would have derived from the development of the Surrendered Land in the most advantageous way available to them."[156]

The Court also directed the referee to determine whether the band had suffered any damage, as a result of losing the disputed lands, to the remainder of its reserve by, for example, impeding its development during the period from 1969 to the date of judgment and, if so, to quantify that damage. The Court referred by analogy to the principle in expropriation law known as "injurious affection" or "consequential damage," which recognizes that where part of an owner's land is expropriated, the owner's remaining land may be made less valuable as a result of its severance from the expropriated portion.[157] Finally, the Court indicated that the referee would have to determine the value of compensation received by the band pursuant to the 1951 surrender agreement, adjusted for compound interest to the date of judgment.

Wewaykum

Mr Justice Teitelbaum, the trial judge in *Wewaykum*,[158] dismissed the claims of the Campbell River and Cape Mudge bands, which were based on the claim of each of the bands that it had been deprived of its right of exclusive use of both the reserve in its own name and the reserve in the name of the other band. His decision was upheld by the Federal Court of Appeal[159] and the Supreme Court of Canada.[160] Notwithstanding his dismissal of the claims, he provisionally assessed damages with respect to each of the bands' claims for compensation in the event he was wrong in finding no breach of fiduciary duty by the Crown.

The bands relied on *Guerin*[161] and argued their damages should be assessed according to the trust principles that La Forest J. suggested in *Canson*[162] were appropriate where a fiduciary has control of property belonging to another, as opposed to where a fiduciary is merely under a duty to perform an obligation. Teitelbaum J., however, rejected this argument, saying he "tend[ed] to favour the view" that this case falls within the second category referred to by La Forest J. in *Canson*.[163] However, in considering what the best approach would be for determining what reasonable compensation should flow from a breach of the Crown's duty to act honestly and impartially in its dealings with the two plaintiff bands, he nonetheless followed the trial judge's approach in *Guerin*, which was based on breach of trust principles. Like the trial judge in *Guerin*, he took into account contingencies, both when assessing the present market value of the reserves and the value of their past loss of use.[164]

The damages claimed by the bands consisted of:

a) compensation in an amount equivalent to the present value of the two reserves (to account for the permanent loss of the reserves); and

b) compensation for past lost potential and actual revenues, together with compound interest, from the use of the two reserves.

The experts called by the parties included real estate appraisers, a forestry engineer, and an economist.

Mr. Justice Teitelbaum accepted as a contingency that the value of certain lands sold by the Campbell River Band as an eighty-acre subdivision should be deducted from the calculation of the present market value of the Campbell River reserve in the event that the Cape Mudge Band was successful in its claim to that reserve. He rejected the Cape Mudge Band's argument that it was entitled to have damages calculated with the full benefit of hindsight and based on the highest and best use of the land. The Cape Mudge Band made this argument to try to defeat the assumption that it would also have sold the eighty-acre subdivision had it been in possession of the reserve, instead of renting it out. This subdivision had been sold by the Campbell River Band in 1921. While Teitelbaum J. acknowledged that the Cape Mudge Band's argument "may be true as a matter of law,"[165] he found there was no evidence from which to draw any inference that the Cape Mudge Band would have treated the subdivision differently. He noted the lack of any evidence that the monies paid in 1921 for the subdivision were less than fair market value.[166] Thus, in calculating compensation for loss of the present value of the reserve, he excluded the value of the eighty acres that had been sold. He also noted it was appropriate for the experts to have provided for contingencies in appraising present value, including for matters such as soil conditions and time for obtaining development permits.

With respect to calculating compensation for past lost use, Teitelbaum J. favoured restricting these to the actual revenue generated by the reserve, rather than its potential revenue. This was because there was no evidence that the Cape Mudge Band would have generated greater revenues from the reserve than the Campbell River Band had done.[167] He concluded it was speculative and inappropriate to consider the rental revenues that might have been earned from the eighty-acre subdivision had it not been sold, or revenues the Cape Mudge Band might have received had it managed and developed the remainder of the reserve more effectively than the Campbell River Band had done.

Given his finding that the claim for historical loss of revenue should be restricted to the revenue actually generated by the Campbell River Band in relation to the reserve, and given that the experts, in estimating the actual revenues received, had only included developments which, in hindsight, had the potential to generate a net gain for the band, Teitelbaum J. took into account contingencies for risk, including that any potential development or investment may have resulted in a net loss for the Cape Mudge Band.[168]

He noted that if his treatment of the eighty-acre subdivision sold in 1921 was wrong and it was necessary to calculate the value of lost rental revenues, then the costs incurred in developing the land to generate the claimed revenues and contingencies, such as vacancy rates and leasing, site preparation, and servicing costs, and when the leasing would likely have occurred and whether parts of the lands would likely not have been leased, would have to be accounted for.[169]

Mr. Justice Teitelbaum found that allowance had to be made for the "unrealized investment income" the bands could have earned on revenues generated by the reserves. A compound interest rate, based on the rate that monies in the band's trust account earned, was the appropriate one to use because it reflected a return on an investment that was readily available to a prudent investor.[170] He pointed out the compound interest included in his calculation of lost past use reflected investment returns only. It was not an award of pre-judgment interest. The latter only applied as of February 1, 1992, when sections 31 and 31.1 of the *Crown Liability and Proceedings Act*[171] came into force. Section 31 of this Act provides that no interest shall be awarded against the Crown for the period before the provision came into force, and thereafter the applicable rate of interest is that which applied in the relevant province.[172]

Teitelbaum J.'s inclusion of compound interest to reflect loss of investment returns in his damages assessment was challenged by the Crown by way of a cross-appeal from the trial decision. However, the Federal Court of Appeal refused to consider the merits of the cross-appeal and dismissed it on procedural grounds.[173] The Supreme Court of Canada did not deal with the question of remedies when the case came before it.[174]

Lower Kootenay[175]

In *Lower Kootenay*, the trial judge, Dube J., calculated damages based on the one breach of fiduciary duty by the Crown which was not statute-barred, namely the failure of the Department of Indian Affairs from 1974 to 1982 to cancel a fifty-year lease of reserve lands which was void because the surrender on which it was premised had never been submitted to the Governor in Council for acceptance.

Mr. Justice Dube accepted the calculations of a senior real estate appraiser called by the band who prepared, based on 1974 being a hypothetical year of abandonment of the lease, a table showing the accumulated rent and interest lost by the band. This expert witness calculated the total amount accumulated up to 1982 (when the term of the lease ended) resulting from investment of the difference between market rent and the rent actually received by the band under the lease. He assumed (*a*) rent was paid annually in advance, in accordance with the terms of the actual lease, and (*b*) the band had possession of the lands and was able to rent it such that the measure of its loss was the market rental value of the lands less appropriate deductions. The expert obtained basic market rental values from documents entered into evidence and then, using these as benchmarks, assumed the rent would rise incrementally by a fixed amount per acre per annum along the same lines as the consumer price index for Canada. He also assumed the lessee would be responsible for maintaining dykes and deducted an allowance of 20 percent of market rent for such maintenance. Lastly, he assumed that the difference between the market rent (net of deductions) and rent received under the lease could have been invested and have accumulated compound interest. In the end, Dube J. granted judgment to the band of $969,166 plus accrued interest from 1982 (at appropriate bank rates) to the date of judgment.[176]

The Specific Claim Option

As an alternative to litigation for breach of fiduciary duty, a plaintiff First Nation has an option to pursue a claim for compensation through the Specific Claims Policy of the federal government for the breach by that government of its "lawful obligations."[177] Although the policy was announced in 1982, prior to the 1984 decision of the Supreme Court of Canada in *Guerin* establishing the enforceability of fiduciary duties owed by the Crown to Aboriginal peoples, a breach of fiduciary duty is often the basis for the allegation of a breach of a "lawful obligation." In their survey of Aboriginal land claims in Canada, William B. Henderson and Derek T. Ground comment that "the concept of the fiduciary relationship between the Crown and Aboriginal peoples must be at the heart of any claims process."[178] They write, "[w]e venture to say that every claim in the process today has an element of fiduciary obligation at its base."[179]

Unfortunately, in practice the Specific Claims Policy has proven to be a poor alternative to litigation. It has been underfunded and understaffed with the result that relatively few claims have been resolved and claims take many years to be reviewed.[180] Further, the review is conducted by Department of Indian Affairs officers and Department of Justice lawyers with an obvious conflict of interests rather than an independent body, and there is no appeal to an independent tribunal. (On the other hand, claimants will not be defeated by technical defences based on limitations or laches.) A joint task force of the Assembly of First Nations and the Department of Indian Affairs recommended reform in 1998.[181] In 2003, the *Specific Claims Resolution Act*[182] was passed to put the specific claims procedure on a statutory footing and make several changes to that procedure. It faced much opposition from the Assembly of First Nations, which said that it failed to implement the recommendations of the joint task force or to deal with their concerns and especially the lack of a truly independent tribunal to review claims.[183] As of December 31, 2004, the federal government had failed to bring the *Act* into force and it is not clear if it will ever be proclaimed in force or what amendments may be made to it to deal with these criticisms.

Chapter 10

Conclusion

There can be no dispute that *Guerin*[1] was a landmark decision that fundamentally changed the Canadian law both with respect to Aboriginal peoples and fiduciary obligations generally.[2] *Guerin*'s major contribution to Canadian law was that it established the fiduciary relationship between the Crown and Aboriginal peoples.[3] In the *Sparrow*[4] case in 1990, the Supreme Court of Canada subsequently used the existence of this relationship to give substance to the then recent weak recognition of existing Aboriginal and treaty rights in section 35(1) of the *Constitution Act, 1982*.[5] *Guerin* has also led directly or indirectly to some improvement in the economic conditions of Aboriginal peoples and has given them greater negotiating power with governments and so improved their political position. More generally, *Guerin* triggered the dramatic expansion of the concept of fiduciary obligations in Canadian law.[6]

Protection of Aboriginal and Treaty Rights

Before discussing the impact of *Guerin* on the legal protection for Aboriginal and treaty rights, it is necessary to observe the lack of legal definition of such rights until recent years. A report prepared for the Indian–Eskimo Association of Canada in 1970 stated:[7]

> The Indians have been very dependent upon the Federal Government, for Indians have, generally speaking, not gone to court to test or enforce their rights. Unfortunately, this has meant that their legal rights and aboriginal claims are very poorly defined in our law. Being poorly defined they could easily be disregarded by the government when the frame of reference changed, and that has happened.

Guerin and subsequent cases have gone a long way to providing the required definition and legal protection of Aboriginal and treaty rights.

Before considering *Guerin*'s impact on the Canadian law, it is also fruitful to ask what would have been the current state of that law if the fiduciary

225

principle did not exist as a key principle of Aboriginal law. We might ask what protection would exist for the Aboriginal peoples of Canada if there had been no appeal in *Guerin* from the decision of the Federal Court of Appeal holding that the government's duty to the Musqueam Band was not legally enforceable[8] or if the Supreme Court of Canada had rejected the appeal.

An answer to these questions may be found in the experience of Aboriginal peoples in Australia. At a conference held in London, Ontario in June 2001, Professor Behrendt from Australia suggested some lessons for Canada from the Australian experience:[9]

> Another reflection from the Australian experience is the implication for the failure to prove a fiduciary duty. In Australia, the lack of a clear court finding that the fiduciary relationship arises has meant that Indigenous peoples are left with little to ensure that the government will consult on policies and actions that may infringe on or extinguish their rights. It has meant that Indigenous peoples, particularly Aboriginal title holders, are captive to the whim of the legislature. If the government is not benevolent and acting in good faith in its dealings with Indigenous peoples, it leaves Aborigines and Torres Strait Island peoples vulnerable to the infringement of fundamental rights. This is not very secure tenure for the recognition and protection of those rights. Despite the many flaws and the impotence of the fiduciary doctrine from Canada, Australia offers sobering reflection of what can happen if there is no recognition of the doctrine.

It is important, of course, to recognize the different constitutional framework in Australia and the lack of constitutional protection for Aboriginal rights as well as the absence of treaties.[10] However, it is equally important to note that, without the application of the fiduciary doctrine to the bald recognition and affirmation of existing Aboriginal and treaty rights in section 35(1) of the *Constitution Act, 1982*,[11] that recognition and affirmation may have amounted to little more than empty words. This has been the fate of the recognition of the principle of the supremacy of God enshrined in the preamble to the *Canadian Charter of Rights and Freedoms*. Courts have said that this is not an enforceable "right" which, if breached, will permit a challenge to legislation.[12] The vaguely worded section 35, which was not even part of the *Charter*, may have suffered a similar fate. On its face, it provided no substantive protection for the rights that it "recognized and affirmed." Unlike the rights and freedoms recognized by the *Charter*, there was no "guarantee" of existing Aboriginal and treaty rights. Indeed, in the view of one leading Aboriginal law scholar, because of the lack of any guarantee or other substantive protection for Aboriginal and treaty rights, "far from protecting or guaranteeing the rights of the aboriginal peoples of Canada, [section 35] provides for the diminution and abrogation of such rights without their consent."[13] How much weaker would this meagre protection for those rights have been if the Crown had been successful in its argument that the Musqueam and other Aboriginal peoples could not legally enforce their rights against the Crown? If existing Aboriginal and treaty "rights" could not be enforced by a court, what would there be to acknowledge and affirm within section 35? The constitutional protection would have been as hollow as the protection provided by the doctrine of political trust that was rejected in *Guerin*.

As noted by Professor Slattery in his influential article "Understanding Aboriginal Rights,"[14] section 35 required courts to confront many of the unresolved issues concerning Aboriginal rights. Writing in 1987, three years after the Supreme Court of Canada decision in *Guerin*, he said that in that case "the Supreme Court has signalled that it is ready for the task. While not dealing directly with the new constitutional provisions[15] the judgment provides the stimulus and much essential material, for reflection on the fundamental nature and origins of aboriginal rights."[16] The decision had "a profound significance for aboriginal land claims."[17] Prior to *Guerin*, the jurisprudence on Aboriginal title had been unclear, as the *Calder*[18] case left room for argument on whether the Canadian law recognized the concept of Aboriginal title. In the view of Professor Slattery, "the *Guerin* decision ends this aspect of the controversy, with seven of the eight judges holding that aboriginal title is a legal right that can be extinguished only by native consent or by legislation."[19] However, he saw the greatest importance of the case in "the fact that in *Guerin* the Supreme Court shows a willingness to consider the topic of aboriginal rights afresh and to initiate a dialogue concerning the broad principles that alone can make sense of the subject."[20] Subsequent decisions of the Court show this prediction was accurate. The law relating to Aboriginal peoples in Canada has been fundamentally rewritten since the *Guerin* decision in 1984.

Writing several years later in 2000, Professor Slattery surveyed the current state of the law:[21]

> Over the past thirty years, the Supreme Court of Canada has begun remapping the neglected territory of aboriginal and treaty rights. It has done so piecemeal, in a series of important decisions extending from *Calder* in 1973 to the recent *Marshall* case. When it started, the Court had little to go on. The results of previous forays into this territory had been uncertain at best and misleading at worst. The leading authority on the subject, the Privy Council decision in *St Catherine's Milling and Lumber Company*, was replete with dubious assumptions and obscure terminology. In effect, the Supreme Court of Canada inherited a sketch map of shadowy coasts and fabulous isles, with monsters at every turn.
>
> Let it be said that the Supreme Court has fared well in its initial ventures. Little-known areas have been brought to light and apocryphal seas dispelled. We now know broadly what is *terra firma* and what is not, and the monsters have been largely tamed or banished to the decorative margins.

We have followed much of the Supreme Court's remapping of Aboriginal law in this book because the law relating to the fiduciary obligations owed to Aboriginal peoples has been central to that process. *Guerin* itself banished the monster of political trust to the margins of the law, and with it, the view that any obligations owed by the Crown to Aboriginal peoples could not be legally enforced.[22] *Guerin* also gave substance to the Aboriginal and treaty rights so recently recognized and affirmed by section 35(1) but in vague language that failed to provide any substantive protection for those rights.[23] The fiduciary principle recognized in *Guerin* was subsequently applied by the Supreme Court of Canada in the *Sparrow* decision to provide such protection.[24] In that case, the Court applied the principle to require the justification of any infringement of existing Aboriginal rights. That test was subsequently extended by the Court to protect treaty rights in *Badger*[25] and Aboriginal title in *Delgamuukw*.[26] The latter case held that any infringement must be "consistent with the special fiduciary relationship between the Crown and aboriginal peoples."[27] This always requires meaningful consultation and, "ordinarily," the payment of fair compensation or some other accommodation such as the grant of a government licence to use or develop resources.[28] This duty to consult and accommodate (which grew directly out of the fiduciary relationship) has resulted in great economic benefits to Aboriginal peoples.[29] It may prove to be a valuable means to ease the poverty that has dominated Aboriginal communities for too long.

Improvement in Economic Conditions

In their factum, or written argument, to the Supreme Court of Canada in *Guerin*, the National Indian Brotherhood submitted that the "desperate economic conditions that Indian people suffer is a source of anguish for most Canadians."[30] Those bands that have shown the ability to overcome their economic condition, by and large, have been those that have enjoyed the full development of reserve resources. In their view, if the Court failed to find an enforceable fiduciary duty, there would be a disincentive for Indian peoples to develop their land and so alter their economic circumstances. To the extent that the Court's decision that the Crown owed legally enforceable fiduciary obligations has caused the government to manage assets under its control in a prudent manner and obtain the return that a prudent trustee in the circumstances would have obtained, it will have improved the economic situation of Aboriginal peoples dependent on such assets. For example, in the *Blueberry River*[31] case, the Supreme Court of Canada held that a prudent trustee would not have surrendered subsurface rights but preserved them for the beneficiaries. To the extent that an Aboriginal group receives compensation for a breach of this duty, its economic situation will be improved. As noted by Chief Justice Lamer in *Delgamuukw*, "Compensation for breaches of fiduciary duty [is] a well-established part of the landscape of aboriginal rights: *Guerin*."[32] The amount of compensation received by Aboriginal peoples since the *Guerin* case for breaches of fiduciary obligations awarded by courts or negotiated in settlement of litigation or under the Specific Claims Process must now amount to many hundreds of millions of dollars.

Of greater long-term significance than the preservation or recovery of what few assets most Aboriginal groups currently possess or compensation for what they have lost is the possibility of increasing those assets through application of the duty to consult and accommodate, which is a particular example of the fiduciary duty.[33] The leading case on the duty to consult and accommodate is *Haida Nation v. British Columbia (Minister of Forests)*[34] discussed in detail in chapter 5. The British Columbia Court of Appeal issued a declaration that the provincial Crown and a forestry company had "legally enforceable duties to the Haida people to consult with them in good faith and to endeavour to seek workable accommodations between the aboriginal interests of the Haida people, on the one hand, and the short-term and the long-term objectives of the Crown and Weyerhaeuser to manage [the licence and the lands in question] in accordance with the public interest, both aboriginal and non-aboriginal, on the other hand."[35] Although the order was varied by the Supreme Court of Canada to remove the reference to the forestry company, it was affirmed with respect to the province, and the Court commented that the province may have to change its policies to accommodate the Aboriginal interest.[36] A number of measures may be suggested to satisfy the duty to accommodate the interests of the Aboriginal group. In *Haida*, Lambert J.A. referred to "the sharing of economic opportunities"[37] while Chief Justice Finch referred to the possibility of the allocation of part of the timber to the Haida.[38] The duty to consult and accommodate in a resource context will require a meaningful discussion of economic sharing as well as compensation for infringement. Some possible measures could include the following:

(a) sharing of royalty payment based on resources extracted

(b) lump sum payment for infringement as compensation

(c) provision of infrastructure to benefit the Aboriginal group

(d) participation by way of joint ventures

(e) subcontracting or employment opportunities

(f) service fees for reviewing proposed activities and development cost charges

(g) the Aboriginal group to get priority in the allocation of licences at reduced fees.

Political Aspects

Guerin and the legal developments to which it led have strengthened the political power of Aboriginal peoples.[39] The existence of legally enforceable obligations owed to Aboriginal peoples means that when they lobby or negotiate with governments, they do so with the alternative of being able to commence litigation if their concerns are not given a proper reception. They are not merely supplicants dependent on the whims of the government of the day. The availability of judicial remedies also reduces the risk of the use of more confrontational approaches such as road blockades or taking physical possession of land to which they assert some rights. The existence of potential liability on the part of the Crown for mismanagement of the assets of Aboriginal peoples is also a powerful incentive for the Crown to transfer some of its powers to them. Although self-government has been slow in coming and is still very limited, there has been a marked increase in the pace of the transfer of power to Aboriginal peoples since the *Guerin* decision.[40] There is little doubt that this process will continue and, one hopes, accelerate in the years to come.

Some of the political aspects of the fiduciary relationship between the Crown and Aboriginal peoples were considered in a series of papers presented at a conference held in June 2001 in London, Ontario, which was co-sponsored by the Law Commission of Canada and the Association of Iroquois and Allied Indians.[41] Some commentators found the description of the relationship between the Crown and Aboriginal peoples as fiduciary to be troubling because it suggested a relationship that was not between equals.[42] One commentator even went so far as to question the continued use of the fiduciary doctrine. In the words of Professor Gordon Christie:[43]

> No matter how twisted, tweaked, or perfected, fiduciary doctrine cannot meaningfully be applied to Crown–Aboriginal relationships. The basic point is clear enough: the Crown cannot be held to the standard principles of fiduciary doctrine, for it cannot act to promote in an appropriate manner the best interests of Aboriginal peoples, given its public duties—in particular given the nature of these duties in its role as what we might term "an intruding and alien sovereign."

These concerns are misplaced. Inequality between the parties is not a necessary requirement for a fiduciary relationship. A beneficiary may be equal in power to, or even more powerful than, the fiduciary but still, in the particular circumstances, be at the mercy of the fiduciary. A man may be wealthy and powerful but he is still owed a fiduciary obligation of loyalty by an errand boy to whom he has has entrusted his money. Partnerships are an example of a fiduciary relationship where, far from being unequal, the parties are presumptively equal.[44] Also, as argued in chapter 8, the Crown's public law duties to Canadians generally *can* be reconciled with its fiduciary duties towards Aboriginal peoples.[45]

Guerin and Fiduciary Obligations

It is now over twenty years since the Supreme Court of Canada decided *Guerin,* but the fiduciary relationship between the Crown and Aboriginal peoples is, in some ways, still in its adolescence. One can see its essential characteristics and its potential but, to quote Hargrave P. in *B.C. Native Women's Society v. Canada*, it is still "in a state of flux and evolution."[46] Like a young adult, it is sometimes confused and confusing. It is also threatening to some and has received its share of criticism. Indeed, in *A(C) v. Critchley*, Chief Justice McEachern of the British Columbia Court of Appeal even suggested that it should be "confined to its particular facts" as something of a misfit born of a flawed "experiment."[47] Like an adolescent, its apparent strength may conceal its vulnerability. The fiduciary relationship is well established as a key concept in Canadian Aboriginal law, but its strength cannot be taken for granted.

Some commentators have praised the work of the Supreme Court of Canada in developing this area of the law. For example, Clea Parfitt and Melinda Munro have commented that "the Court has led the commonwealth in recognizing the value of fiduciary duty in protecting the interests of the weak and/or the powerless in our society."[48] Other commentators have been less impressed. For example, Chief Justice McEachern was critical of the whole fiduciary obligation "experiment" in giving his reasons in *Critchley*.[49] This case involved a claim against the provincial government for sexual abuse suffered by the plaintiffs when they were children in the care of the province. He said:

> [75] Our Supreme Court of Canada has led the way in the common law world of extending fiduciary responsibilities and remedies but it has not provided as much guidance as it usually does in emerging areas of law. The law in this respect has been extended by our highest court not predictably or incrementally but in quantum leaps so that judges, lawyers and citizens alike are often unable to know whether a given situation is governed by the usual laws of contract, negligence or other torts, or by fiduciary obligations whose limits are difficult to discern. . . .

> [79] . . . [C]ases in the Supreme Court of Canada . . . have failed to make the law as clear as it should be. . . .

> [81] . . . In delivering its judgments in these cases, the Court has written hundreds of pages. Yet it is difficult to find a comprehensive statement of the law. In some cases, there are multiple sets of reasons, and, as already mentioned, the Court was

divided in some cases on whether the conduct in question amounted to a breach of a fiduciary duty. In other cases, the Court was as concerned to explain the differences, usually on the question of damages, between conduct that might sound in either tort or fiduciary damages, thus raising once again the spectre of the result depending upon the cause of action in which the case is framed. Moreover, in a number of lower court cases, where liability might be decided in tort, the outrage of the judge seems to elevate the case to one in fiduciary duty. With respect, this is no way to decide important legal questions since some judges have higher (or lower) outrage levels than others.

[82] We have no way of knowing how the learned judges of the Supreme Court of Canada might view this case. History suggests they may have a number of different views.

In his view, all the cases decided by the Supreme Court of Canada except *Guerin* could be explained on the grounds that the defendants personally failed to discharge a legal duty for their own benefit.

Guerin was the odd man out, and McEachern C.J. suggested that it should not be followed or, to use legalese, should be "confined to its particular facts":[50]

Thus, only in *Guerin* was the defendant held to have breached a fiduciary duty without personal wrongdoing beyond possible carelessness or negligence. *Guerin* may be regarded as a case where a fiduciary disobeyed the instructions of the beneficiary, although even on that basis, there was no personal advantage accruing to the fiduciary. *Guerin*, however, was a special case where the aboriginal right in question was said to be unique. In that respect *Guerin* is obviously a case that should be confined to its particular facts and we should not be timid just because one case does not fit a useful pattern. Experience, rather than logic, governs the development of the law.

He went on to hold that recovery for breach of fiduciary duty should be confined to cases where, in addition to the other usual requirements such as vulnerability and the exercise of discretion, the defendant personally takes advantage of a relationship of trust or confidence for his or her direct or indirect personal advantage. In effect this would turn the clock back to the pre-*Guerin* era and redirect "fiduciary law back towards where it was before this experiment began but with much broader remedies, such as damages, when fiduciary duties are actually breached."[51]

In my opinion, the contribution of the Supreme Court of Canada to this area of the law is to be applauded. The Court can certainly be fairly criticised for a lack of clarity and some inconsistency on occasion, but the general thrust of the jurisprudence has been positive in requiring a higher standard of conduct on the part of fiduciaries than other areas of law such as tort or administrative law would impose. As Chief Justice McLachlin observed extra-judicially with respect to the broader doctrine of restitution, of which fiduciary law can be seen to form a part:[52]

> As might be expected in unchartered waters, we sometimes flounder. Sometimes, we take a wrong step, find ourselves in too deep, and have to step back. Sometimes we start out one way, run up against a rock, and find we must backtrack and take a different course. To those observing from safer shores, the sight may not be elegant or even edifying. Yet in Canada, lawyers, academics and the public (to the extent this can be gauged) seem to approve of the venture, if not every step the courts take. There seems to be a general acceptance that we are headed in the right direction.

While the law may need to be consolidated and simplified, any attempt to turn back the clock to the pre-*Guerin* era is unjustified.

Guerin and the developments in Aboriginal and fiduciary law to which it led[53] have been outstanding examples of the use of law to bring about greater justice. In the words of one writer: [54]

> By using fiduciary principles to govern Crown–aboriginal relations and incorporating those principles into constitutional protections, the Supreme Court of Canada adopted the most compelling and effective means within existing law to achieve justice in the area of aboriginal rights. There is no other mechanism currently operating in law or equity that contains the breadth and flexibility—at least with respect to establishing and enforcing an obligation—to respond adequately to the *sui generis* relationship between the Crown and Aboriginal peoples.

The law of equity, of which fiduciary principles form a part, can be traced to the England of the late fifteenth century.[55] It arose as an attempt to moderate the rigour of the common law and to achieve greater justice. A former justice of the High Court of Australia has described how the principles of equity have been applied "at the ends of the earth as in England" and thereby ensured "the enduring influence of English jurisprudence . . . in the history of civilisation."[56] Although Vancouver may not fairly be described as at "the end of the earth," the English feudal ecclesiastical chancellors who first gave voice to those principles cannot have begun to imagine their application to a dispute over the leasing of lands on an Indian reserve in that city in order to achieve justice.[57] Nor could they have imagined that those principles would be incorporated into the protection for Aboriginal and treaty rights which forms part of the Canadian Constitution or that they would become an integral part of the unique intersocietal law, derived from both the English common law and Aboriginal legal systems, which constitutes Canadian Aboriginal law.[58] This application of ancient principles may be seen as an impressive example of the ability of the law to continue to grow and adapt to new situations. The application of fiduciary law to the relationship between governments and Aboriginal peoples is at the growing point, the meristem, of legal developments in Canada.

Although some have criticized the *Guerin* decision, it is an outstanding example of the development of law to bring about a just result to people who have historically been denied their day in court.[59] It may be seen as a tribute to the Canadian legal system and its highest court. Above all, it is a tribute to the determination of the Musqueam people to achieve some measure of justice for the wrong done to them.

Notes

Notes to Preface

[1] [1984] 2 S.C.R. 335.

[2] Jordan Furlong, "Our Legal Century" (Dec., 2000) *National Magazine,* Canadian Bar Assoc. at 17. The January/February 2000 issue of *Aboriginal Times* noted its importance not only for fiduciary duty but also for what it said about Aboriginal title and included it as one of the ten milestones in Aboriginal law since the Royal Proclamation of 1763.

[3] [2002] 4 S.C.R. 245 at para. 73.

[4] (2002), 215 D.L.R. (4th) 496 at para. 61. According to Tom Berger, a leading Aboriginal rights practitioner, until the *Guerin* decision, it was most unlikely that a lawyer of ordinary competence would have advised an Indian band to bring an action for a breach of a fiduciary obligation: *Mathias v. Canada* [1998], F.C.J. No. 330 (T.D.) (Q.L.). Professor Leonard Rotman refers to *Guerin* as a landmark case which "blazed a new path in Canadian aboriginal rights jurisprudence" and resulted in "a complete overruling of the principles which had shaped judicial considerations of aboriginal rights in Canada for almost a hundred years: Leonard I. Rotman, *Parallel Paths: Fiduciary Doctrine and the Crown–Native Relationship on Canada* (Toronto: University of Toronto Press, 1996) at 3–8; see also Leonard I. Rotman, "Crown–Native Relations As Fiduciary" in *Aboriginal Ownership and Management of Resources in Canada: An Analysis of Litigation and Negotiation: Getting to a Win–Win?* (Halifax: Canadian Bar Association, 2003) at 9; Leonard Rotman, "Developments in Aboriginal Law: The 2002–2003 Term" (2003) 22 Sup. Ct. L. Rev. (2d) 1 at 18.

[5] Donovan W.M. Waters, "New Directions in the Employment of Equitable Doctrines: The Canadian Experience" in T.G. Youdan, ed., *Equity, Fiduciaries and Trusts* (Toronto: Carswell, 1989) at 414. In a review of Canada's Comprehensive Claims Policy conducted in 2002, lawyers for the Assembly of First Nations commented that "the decision in *R. v. Guerin* changed forever the legal relationship between First Nations and the Crown" and was partly responsible for changes made to that policy: Mark Stevenson and Albert Peeling, "Legal Review of Canada's Comprehensive Land Claims Policy" prepared for Assembly of First Nations, 15 February 2002 at 3, online: Turtle Island Native Network <http://www.turtleisland.org/news/disc.pdf>.

[6] P. Hogg, *Constitutional Law of Canada,* looseleaf (Toronto: Carswell, 1997) at s. 27.5; J.E. Magnet, *Constitutional Law of Canada,* 8th ed. (Edmonton: Juriliber, 2001), part 4, c. 2.

[7] Judge D. Arnot, "Treaties As a Bridge to the Future" (2001) 50 U.N.B.L.J. 57 at 66.

[8] Brian Slattery, "Understanding Aboriginal Rights" (1987) 66 Can. Bar Rev. 727 at 728–31. See also William B. Henderson & Derek T. Ground, "Survey of Aboriginal Land Claims" (1994) 26 Ottawa L. Rev. 187 at 225.

[9] Paul Tennant, *Aboriginal Peoples and Politics* (Vancouver: University of British Columbia Press, 1990) at 222.

[10] *Ibid.*

[11] W.F. Flanagan, "Fiduciary Duties in Commercial Relationships: When Does the Marketplace Set the Rules?" in A. Anand & W.F. Flanagan, *Selected Topics in Corporate Litigation* (Kingston: Queen's Annual Business Law Symposium, 2001) at 3, 17; see also Donovan W.M. Waters, "The Reception of Equity in the Supreme Court of Canada (1875–2000)" (2001) 80 Can. Bar Rev. 620 at 678.

[12] *Supra* note 4 at para. 70.

[13] B.A. Keon-Cohen, "The *Mabo* Litigation: A Personal and Procedural Account" (2000) 24 Melbourne U.L. Rev. 35. One parallel between the two cases was the determined effort of the respective governments to prevent the Aboriginal claimants from having their claims adjudicated on the merits. In the *Mabo* litigation, the Queensland government passed special legislation to nullify

the claim of Native title, which was declared invalid by a bare majority of the High Court of Australia as being contrary to the *Racial Discrimination Act 1975* (Cth.) in *Mabo (No.1)* (1988), 166 C.L.R. 186. In *Guerin*, the government of Canada raised the even more fundamental defence that the government was only under a political obligation towards Aboriginal people which could not be enforced by the courts, an argument that would be destructive of the most basic requirement of equality before the law; see chapter 3, text following note 148. For a discussion of *Mabo (No. 2)* (1992), 175 C.L.R. 1 (H.C.A.) as it relates to the fiduciary obligations owed to Aboriginal peoples, see chapter 7, text accompanying note 75 *et seq.*

[14] It should be noted that this book deals with that obligation under domestic rather than international law. For a discussion of Canada's fiduciary duty to Aboriginal peoples under international law, see S. James Anaya, Richard Falk & Donat Pharand, "Canada's Fiduciary Obligation to Aboriginal Peoples in the Context of Accession to Sovereignty by Quebec," vol. 2, International Dimensions, prepared for Royal Commission on Aboriginal Peoples (Ottawa: Supply and Services Canada, 1995). (It has been suggested that international law on trust territories can be traced back to the relationship between North American Indians and colonial powers: Douglas Sanders, *The Friendly Care and Directing Hand of the Government: A Study of Government Trusteeship of Indians in Canada*, 22 February 1977 [unpublished, archived at Musqueam Band Office] at 6–8.) Nor does this book deal with fiduciary concepts under Aboriginal legal systems or customary law. In the case of the Musqueam and other Coast Salish peoples, the head of an extended family might hold property on a form of trust: Homer G. Barnett, *The Coast Salish of British Columbia* (Eugene, Oreg.: Univ. of Oregon, 1955) at 244. Compare S.K.B. Asante, "Fiduciary Principles in Anglo-American Law and the Customary Law of Ghana—A Comparative Study" (1969) 14 I.C.L.Q. 1144. For an analysis of fiduciary obligations based on "*sui generis* Aboriginal orders" and a rejection of common law standards of fiduciary obligations, see James Sákéj Youngblood Henderson, "Commentary" in *In Whom We Trust* (Toronto: Irwin for Law Commission of Canada and Association of Iroquois and Allied Indians, 2002) at 81. For a study of Coast Salish concepts of justice, see Bruce G. Miller, *The Problem of Justice: Tradition and Law in the Coast Salish World* (Lincoln, Nebr.: Univ. of Nebraska Press, 2001). For an in-depth examination of the continued existence of First Nations laws in Canada, see John Borrows, *Recovering Canada: The Resurgence of Indigenous Law* (Toronto: Univ. of Toronto Press, 2002).

[15] Thomas R. Berger, *One Man's Justice: A Life in the Law* (Toronto: Douglas & McIntyre, 2002) at 257–58.

[16] Professor Sossin has described the Crown's fiduciary obligations as "one of the most vibrant fields of scholarship and litigation in Canadian public law": Lorne Sossin, Book Review of *Liability of the Crown* by Peter W. Hogg & Patrick J. Monahan (2003) 82 Can. Bar Rev. 551 at 553; the Ontario Court of Appeal recently described it as "an important and expanding area": *Bonaparte v. Canada (Attorney General)*, [2003] 3 C.N.L.R. 43 (Ont. C.A.) at para. 32.

[17] See chapter 10.

[18] See Berger, *supra* note 15 at 4.

Notes to Chapter 1

[1] This was also true for British Columbia, the province from which *Guerin v. The Queen*, [1984] 2 S.C.R. 335 came: see *Calder v. Attorney-General for British Columbia* (1973), 34 D.L.R. (3d) 145 (S.C.C.) at 156, Judson J.

[2] See generally J.R. Miller, *Skyscrapers Hide the Heavens: A History of Indian–White Relations in Canada* (Toronto: Univ. of Toronto Press, 1991) at 23–80.

[3] *R. v. Sioui*, [1990] 1 S.C.R. 1025 at 1054 per Lamer J. for the Court. See for example the *Treaty of Albany*, 1664, with the Iroquois, *infra* text accompanying note 17, and the *Treaty of Peace and Friendship*, 10 March 1760, with the Mi'kmaq, which was considered by the Supreme Court of Canada in *R. v. Marshall*, [1999] 3 S.C.R. 456 and by the New Brunswick Court of Appeal in *Bernard v. The Queen*, [2003] 4 C.N.L.R. 48.

[4] See the Royal Proclamation 1763, George R., Proclamation, 7 October 1763 (3 Geo. III), reprinted in R.S.C. 1985, App. II, No. 1, *infra* note 18.

[5] See *infra* text accompanying note 49 *et seq.* One writer has summarized the development of the relationship as follows: ". . . through a period of three centuries [the various Indian nations] have by degrees acquiesced in a change from their original status as allies of the King to subjects under the special protection of the King, specially exempt from many of the duties and burdens of the ordinary subjects, holding a peculiar personal relation with the King . . . based originally upon military service and in its nature feudal." Canada, Parliament, "Report on the Indian Title in Canada with Special

Reference to British Columbia," 20 August 1909, by T.R.E. MacInnes in House of Commons, Sessional Paper No. 47, Ottawa, 1914 at 1–2 [typescript at Main Library, University of British Columbia].

[6] (1990), 71 D.L.R. (4th) 193 at 209 (S.C.C.).

[7] [1990] 1 S.C.R 1075.

[8] *Ibid.* at 1108.

[9] Brian Slattery, "Understanding Aboriginal Rights" (1987) 66 Can. Bar Rev. 727.

[10] *Wewaykum Indian Band v. Canada*, [2002] 4 S.C.R. 245 at para. 79. See also *Mitchell v. Peguis Indian Band*, *supra* note 6 at 225, La Forest J.

[11] *Supra* note 9 at 753.

[12] (2004), 245 D.L.R. (4th) 33, 2004 SCC 73.

[13] *Ibid* at para. 18. See further chapter 5, text accompanying note 129 *et seq.*

[14] *Ibid* at para. 17.

[15] (2004), 245 D.L.R. (4th) 193, 2004 SCC 74.

[16] *Ibid* at para. 24.

[17] See Leonard Rotman, "Conceptualizing Crown–Aboriginal Fiduciary Relations" in *In Whom We Trust* (Toronto: Irwin Books for Law Commission of Canada and Association of Iroquois and Allied Indians, 2002) at 28–43. See also Peter Hutchins, "Benefits and Burdens: When Do Fiduciary Obligations Arise?" in *UFO's—Unidentified Fiduciary Obligations* (Winnipeg: Canadian Bar Association, 28 May 1994); Renee Dupluis & Kent McNeil, "Canada's Fiduciary Obligation to Aboriginal Peoples in the Context of Accession to Sovereignty by Quebec," vol. 2, Domestic Dimensions, prepared for Royal Commission on Aboriginal Peoples, (Ottawa: Supply and Services Canada, 1995) at 4–47; David C. Nahwegahbow, Michael W. Posluns, Don Allen & Douglas Sanders, "The First Nations and the Crown: A Study of Trust Relationships," Research Report prepared for the Special Committee of the House of Commons on Indian Self-Government, April 1983 [unpublished] at 72–173.

[18] *Supra* note 4. See J. Borrows, "Constitutional Law from a First Nation Perspective: Self Government and the Royal Proclamation" (1994), 28 U.B.C. L. Rev. 1; B. Slattery, *The Land Rights of Indigenous Canadian Peoples* (Saskatoon: University of Saskatchewan Native Law Centre, 1979); Alan Lafontaine, "Coexistence of the Fiduciary Obligation of the Crown and the Aboriginal Right to Self-Government" in *In Whom We Trust*, *supra* note 17.

[19] (1887), 13 S.C.R. 577.

[20] *Ibid.* at 608–10.

[21] *Ibid.*

[22] (1774) 1 Cowp. 204, 98 E.R. 848. See *Easterbrook v. The King*, [1931] S.C.R. 210 at 217–18, Newcombe J. holding that a lease "was ineffective and void . . . for non-compliance with the preemptory requirements of the proclamation, which have the force of statute"; *Calder v. Attorney-General of British Columbia*, *supra* note 1 at 203, Hall J.; *R. v. Secretary of State for Foreign & Commonwealth Affairs*, [1982] 2 All E.R. 118 at 124–25 (Eng. C.A.), Lord Denning: "To my mind, the royal proclamation of 1763 was equivalent to an entrenched provision in the constitutions of the colonies in North America."

[23] *Supra* note 1 at 203. As noted by Mr. Justice Dickson in *Guerin*, *supra* note 1 at 376, it is the surrender requirement in the *Indian Act* derived from the Royal Proclamation that, in part, gave rise to the fiduciary relationship, see chapter 4 note 47 *et seq.*

[24] *Ontario (Attorney-General) v. Bear Island Foundation* (1989), 68 O.R. 394 (Ont. C.A), appeal dismissed, [1991] 2 S.C.R. 570; *Chippewas of Sarnia Band v. Canada* (2000), 195 D.L.R. (4th) 135 (Ont. C.A.), application for leave to appeal dismissed, [2001] 4 C.N.L.R. iv (note); application for reconsideration dismissed, [2002] 3 C.N.L.R. iv (note). See James I. Reynolds, "Aboriginal Title: The Chippewas of Sarnia" (2002) 81 Can. Bar Rev. 97 at 100–102.

[25] 14 Geo. III, c. 83 (U.K.), reprinted in R.S.C. 1985, App. 2, No. 2.

[26] *Supra* note 1 at 383.

[27] See chapter 2, text accompanying note 18.

[28] See, for example, the decision in *Degamuukw v. British Columbia*, [1997] 3 S.C.R. 1010.

[29] Wilson Duff, *The Indian History of British Columbia: The Impact of the White Man* (Victoria: Provincial Museum of Natural History and Anthropology, 1965) at 43; Robin Fisher, *Contact and Conflict*, 2d ed. (Vancouver: University of British Columbia Press, 1992) at 12–17, 98–100, 106–9; David R. Williams, *The Man for a New Country: Sir Matthew Baillie Begbie* (Sidney, B.C.: Gray's, 1977) at 100–18. Early settlers seem to have established generally good relationships with

the Aboriginal population including the Musqueam, trading with them and visiting their villages. See, for example, Fitzgerald McCleery, *Diary: Fitzgerald McCleery Earliest Settler (North Arm, Fraser River), Vancouver 1862–1866* (Vancouver: City Archives, 1940), *passim*. In 1927, Senator McLennan described settlement in the province as a "peaceful penetration": *Report and Evidence of the Special Joint Committee of the Senate and House of Commons Appointed to Inquire into the Claims of the Allied Indian Tribes of British Columbia*, Journals of the Senate of Canada 1926–27 at 156.

[30] For an early example of armed conflict, see Morag MacLachlan, ed., *The Fort Langley Journals 1827–30*, (Vancouver: University of British Columbia Press, 1998) at 102–3 describing a battle between Hudson's Bay Company employees and raiding Lekwiltok Indians. In 1861, Indians from Lamalchi Village on Kuper Island killed a settler and his daughter, leading to a bombardment of the village and the execution of the Indian leaders by way of reprisal: see Barry M. Gough, *Gunboat Frontier: British Maritime Authority and the Northwest Coast Indians, 1846–1890* (Vancouver: University of British Columbia Press, 1984) at 129–47; Chris Arnett, *The Terror of the Coast* (Burnaby, B.C.: Talon, 1999). See generally B.A. McKelvie, *Tales of Conflict* (Vancouver: Daily Province, 1949).

[31] Quoted in John Adams, *Old Square-Toes and His Lady: The Life of James and Amelia Douglas* (Victoria: Horsdal & Schubart, 2001) at 110. See also his letter to the Colonial Secretary of 14 March 1859: "[a]s friends and allies, the native races are capable of rendering the most valuable assistance to the Colony, while their enmity would entail on the settlers a greater amount of wretchedness and physical suffering, and more seriously retard the growth and material development of the Colony than any other calamity to which, in the ordinary course of events, it would be exposed." *Papers Connected with the Indian Land Question 1850–1875* (Victoria: Government Printing Office, 1875), reprinted 1987, at 16.

[32] Williams, *supra* note 29 at 102.

[33] *Ibid.*

[34] See chapter 10, text accompanying note 21 *et seq*. In *Wewaykum Indian Band v. Canada* [2003] 2 S.C.R. 259, 2003 SCC 45, the Supreme Court of Canada referred at para. 90 to "the significant transformations of the law as it relates to aboriginal issues that we have all witnessed since 1985." Hugesson J. noted in *Shubenacadie Indian Band v. Canada (Attorney-General)*, 2001 FCT 181 at para. 54 (T.D.) that Aboriginal law "had been in a state of rapid evolution and change. Claims which might have been considered outlandish or outrageous only a few years ago are now being accepted." For an account of Aboriginal law as it existed in 1972, see Peter A. Cuming & Neil H. Mickenberg, eds., *Native Rights in Canada*, 2d ed. (Toronto: The Indian-Eskimo Association, 1972). See also Thomas Berger, *One Man's Justice: A Life in the Law* (Toronto: Douglas & McIntyre, 2002) at 113; Justice LaForme, "Commentary" in *In Whom We Trust*, *supra* note 17 at 305–6.

[35] *Supra* note 1; see K.M. Lysyk, "The Indian Title Question in Canada: An Appraisal in the Light of *Calder*" (1973) 51 Can. Bar Rev. 450; Berger, *supra* note 34 at 107–39.

[36] Department of Indian Affairs and Northern Development, *In All Fairness: A Native Claims Policy. Comprehensive Claims* (1981). In *Wewaykum Indian Band v. Canada*, *supra* note 10, Binnie J. observed at para. 75: "In *Calder v. Attorney-General of British Columbia*, [1973] S.C.R. 313, the [Supreme Court of Canada] had recognized for the first time in the modern era that the Indian interest in their ancestral lands constituted a *legal* interest that predated European settlement. Recognition of aboriginal rights could not, therefore, be treated merely as an act of grace and favour on the part of the Crown" [emphasis in original].

[37] *Supra* note 7 at 1105, see chapter 5, text accompanying note 68 *et seq*.

[38] M. Gautreau, "Demystifying the Fiduciary Mystique" (1989) 68 Can. Bar Rev. 1 at 1–2. This article has been relied on *inter alia* by the Supreme Court of Canada in *Lac Minerals Ltd. v. International Corona Resources Ltd.*, [1989] 2 S.C.R. 574 [*Lac Minerals*] and by the Federal Court, Trial Division in *Alexander Band No. 134 v. Canada*, [1991] 2 F.C. 3.

[39] For a history of equity, see W. Holdsworth, *History of English Law*, 3d ed. (London: Methuen, 1923), vol. 1 at 445–69, vol. 4 at 275–83, 417–43, vol. 5 at 215–338, vol. 6 at 523–51, 640–71, vol. 9 at 335–408, vol. 12 at 178–330, 583–605, vol. 13 at 574–668; G.B. Adams, "The Origins of English Equity" (1916) 16 Colum. L. Rev. 87. For its influence in English law, see C.K. Allen, *Law in the Making*, 7th ed. (London: Oxford University Press, 1964) at 399–425. For the history of equity in Canada, see D.W.M. Waters, "The Reception of Equity in the Supreme Court of Canada (1875–2000)" (2001) 80 Can. Bar Rev. 620. For some comments on the history of the fiduciary obligation, see Robert Megarry, "Historical Development" in *Special Lectures of the Law Society of Upper Canada, 1990* (Scarborough, Ont.: De Boo, 1991) at 1; W.F. Flanagan, "Fiduciary Duties in

Commercial Relationships: When Does the Marketplace Set the Rules?" in A. Anand & W.F. Flanagan, eds., *Selected Topics in Corporate Litigation* (Kingston: Queen's Annual Business Law Symposium, 2001) at 3–17. One of the earliest cases to discuss the fiduciary duty was *Keech v. Sandford* (1726), 25 E.R. 223.

[40] John McGhee, *Snell's Equity*, 30th ed. (London: Sweet & Maxwell, 2000) at para. 1 03.

[41] On the fusion of the administration of law and equity in Canada, see *Canadian Encyclopedic Digest*, looseleaf (Toronto: Carswell, 2001) title 55 (Ontario), title 56 (Western) at paras. 1–2; P.M. Perell, "A Legal History of the Fusion of Law and Equity in the Supreme Court of Ontario" (1988) 9 Advocates' Q. 472; Reynolds, *supra* note 24 at 103–11.

[42] L.S. Sealy, "Fiduciary Relationships" [1962] Camb. L.J. 69 at 69–72.

[43] *Halsbury's Laws of England*, 4th ed., reissue vol. 16(2) (London: Butterworths, 2003) at para. 404.

[44] (1994), 117 D.L.R. (4th) 161.

[45] *Ibid.* at 174

[46] *Ibid.* at 186.

[47] [2002] 3 S.C.R. 631 at para. 16.

[48] L.C. Green, "North America's Indians and the Trusteeship Concept" (1975) 4 Anglo-Am. L. Rev. 137 at 149. See also his article "Trusteeship and Canada's Indians" (1976) 3 Dal. L.J. 104 at 118.

[49] 12 Vict. 1849, c. 9. For an account of trust arrangements that were established for Indian property in pre-Confederation Upper and Lower Canada, see Nahwegahbow *et al., supra* note 17 at 104–33 .

[50] 1850, (13–14 Vict.), c. 42, s. 1; see also *An Act Respecting Management of the Indian Lands and Property*, 1860, (23 Vict.) c. 151, s. 8.

[51] *Terms of the Union of British Columbia With Canada*, Order of Her Majesty The Queen in Council, 16 May 1871 (U.K.) reproduced in R.S.C. 1985, App. II, No. 10. The transfer of reserve lands from the province to the federal government did not take place until British Columbia *Order in Council No. 1036*, approved and ordered 29 July 1938, which referred to "the lands set out in the schedule attached hereto to be conveyed to His Majesty the King in right of the Dominion of Canada in trust for the use and benefit of the Indians of the Province of British Columbia." Musqueam Reserve No. 2 (the reserve in question in the *Guerin* case) was included in the schedule as part of those lands.

[52] *Indian Act*, S.C. 1876, c. 18, s. 4. For a review of references to trusts in provisions of the federal Indian Acts from 1868 to 1950, see Nahwegahbow *et al., supra* note 17 at 146–56.

[53] S.C. 1912, c. 40, s. 2.

[54] *Quebec Boundaries Extension Act*, S.C. 1912, c. 45.

[55] (1905), 4 Ex. C.R. 417. Earlier cases contain non-binding or "obiter" statements that the trust was not a "true" trust: see *Church v. Fenton* (1878), 28 U.C.C.P. 384 at 388, Gwynne J. to the effect that the use of the word "trust" was "not . . . strictly accurate," aff'd without comment on this point: (1879), 4 O.A.R. 159, (1880), 5 S.C.R. 239; *Quirt v. The Queen* (1890), 17 O.A.R. 421 at 444, Osler J.A. saying that the expression in the *Ontario Assessment Act*, R.S.O. 1887, c. 193, s. 7, referring to lands being vested in the Crown in trust for Indians "does not denote a real trust but merely a restriction which the Crown has imposed upon itself," and (1891), 19 S.C.R. 510 at 519, Strong J. who described the rights of the Crown as regards Indian lands as being of an "anomalous and peculiar nature" and "different from a right of property either as a fiduciary or beneficial owner"; *St. Catherine's Milling and Lumber Co. v. The Queen, supra* note 19 at 649. See also Taschereau J., *infra* note 92.

[56] *Ibid.* at 438.

[57] *Ibid.* at 443. [Emphasis added.]

[58] (1916), 53 S.C.R. 172. See also *Ontario v. Dominion of Canada and Quebec: In Re Indian Claims* (1895), 25 S.C.R. 434 at 511–12 in which Gwynne J. (dissenting) said, "the terms and conditions expressed in those instruments [i.e., treaties] as to be performed by or on behalf of the Crown, have always been regarded as involving a trust graciously assumed by the Crown to the fulfilment of which with the Indians the faith and honour of the Crown is pledged, and which trust has always been most faithfully fulfilled as a treaty obligation of the Crown"; quoted with approval by Binnie J. in *R. v. Marshall, supra* note 3 at para. 50.

[59] *Ibid.* at 196 [emphasis added.].

[60] [1921] A.C. 401.

[61] *Ibid.* at 411.

⁶² (1935), 5 C.N.L.C. 92.

⁶³ [1940] 1 D.L.R. 390 (N.S. Co. Ct.).

⁶⁴ *Ibid.* at 397.

⁶⁵ [1948] 3 D.L.R. 797 (Exch.).

⁶⁶ [1950] S.C.R. 168. *Miller* has been cited as authority for the proposition that "the relationship between the Crown and the Indians is obviously one of trust in respect to both reserve lands and Indian funds held by the Government": Cuming & Mickenberg, *supra* note 34 at 237. With respect, this overstates the significance of the decision, which dealt with a procedural issue related to the availability of a Petition of Right rather than whether a fiduciary relationship exists between the Crown and Aboriginal peoples.

⁶⁷ *Ibid.* at 174.

⁶⁸ (1979), 102 D.L.R. (3d) 602.

⁶⁹ See chapter 3, text accompanying note 133 *et seq.* For a discussion of the political trust doctrine, see Lorne Sossin, "Public Fiduciary Obligations, Political Trusts and the Equitable Duty of Reasonableness in Administrative Law" (2003) 66 Sask. L. Rev. 129 at 159–69.

⁷⁰ It may be noted that the political trust doctrine is still mentioned from time to time. For example, the Privy Council suggested in the recent case of *Te Waka Hi Ika o Te Arawa v. Treaty of Waitangi Fisheries Commission*, [2002] 2 N.Z.L.R. 17 that a particular trust for the benefit of Maori people may not be a trust in the private law sense and referred to the *Tito* case, *infra* note 74.

⁷¹ (1881–82), 7 A.C. 619 at 625–26 (H.L.).

⁷² [1876] 1 Q.B.D. 69 (Eng. C.A.).

⁷³ Cockburn C.J. at 492

⁷⁴ [1977] 3 All E.R. 129 (Ch.).

⁷⁵ *Ibid.* at 216–17.

⁷⁶ [1978] A.C. 359 (H.L.).

⁷⁷ *Ibid.* at 397.

⁷⁸ *Supra* note 71.

⁷⁹ [1925] A.C. 578, [1925] All E.R. 24 (H.L.).

⁸⁰ *Ibid.* at 33.

⁸¹ [1983] 1 A.C. 768, [1982] 1 All E.R. 129 (H.L.). Considered in *Harris v. Canada*, [2000] 4 F.C.R. 37 (C.A.) at paras. 41–47, in which the court refused to dismiss a claim that the Minister of National Revenue owed fiduciary duties to taxpayers generally. (In subsequent proceedings reported at [2002] 2 F.C. 484, Dawson J. held that no fiduciary duty was owed by the Crown in providing advance tax rulings.) In *Duplesis v. Canada*, [2000] F.C. No. 1917 (F.C.T.D.) (QL), appeal dismissed by Lemieux J., 2001 FCT 1038, Prothonotary Aronovitch dismissed the Crown's motion to strike out a claim for breach of fiduciary duty brought by a soldier who alleged that he was denied adequate treatment for post-traumatic stress syndrome. She held that there was "a serious question of law here that is more appropriately left for determination by the trial judge on the merits" (para. 31).

⁸² *Ibid.* at 154.

⁸³ *Ibid.* at 172.

⁸⁴ (1894), 24 S.C.R. 1.

⁸⁵ It was also applied by the Privy Council in the 1902 New Zealand case of *Te Teira Te Paea v. Te Roera Tareha*, [1902] A.C. 56, involving a title allotted to a Maori chief in trust. It was held that no enforceable trust was created for the benefit of the traditional owners. Giving the decision, Lord Lindley observed that the use of the word "trust" is not always sufficient to create an equitable right or obligation which can be enforced by legal proceedings (*ibid.* at 72).

⁸⁶ (1908), 39 S.C.R. 657.

⁸⁷ *Ibid.* at 670.

⁸⁸ (1914), 50 S.C.R. 283, 23 D.L.R. 547.

⁸⁹ (1913), 13 D.L.R. 463 at 465–66, Meredith C.J.O.

⁹⁰ *Ibid.*

⁹¹ *Supra* note 19.

⁹² *Ibid.* at 649.

⁹³ [1950] S.C.R. 211.

⁹⁴ *Ibid.* at 219.

⁹⁵ See generally: Reid Peyton Chambers, "Judicial Enforcement of the Federal Trust Responsibility

to Indians" (1975) 27 Stan. L. Rev. 1213; L.C. Green, "North America's Indian and the Trusteeship Concept" (1975) 4 Anglo-Am. L. Rev. 137; N. Carter, "Race and Power Politics as Aspects of Federal Guardianship over American Indians: Land Related Cases 1887–1924" (1976) 4 Am. Indian L. Rev. 197; D. McNeil, "Trusts: Towards an Effective Indian Remedy for Breach of Trusts" (1980) 8 Am. Indian L. Rev. 429; Felix Cohen, *Handbook of Federal Indian Law* (Washington: United States Goverment Printing Office, 1982) at 220–28; Stephen L. Pevar, *The Rights of Indians and Tribes* (Toronto: Bantam, 1983) at 23–31; James I. Reynolds & Lewis F. Harvey, "The Fiduciary Obligation of the United States and Canadian Governments Towards Indian Peoples" in *Indians and the Law* (Vancouver: Continuing Legal Education Society of British Columbia, 1985); Richard H. Bartlett, *Indian Reserves and Aboriginal Lands: A Homeland* (Saskatoon: University of Saskatchewan Native Law Centre, 1990) at 190–94; William C. Canby, *American Indian Law*, 3d ed. (St. Paul, Minn.: West, 1998) at 33–58; Camilla Hughes, "The Fiduciary Obligations of the Crown to Aborigines: Lessons from the United States and Canada" (1993) U.N.S.W.L.J. 70; David H. Getscher, "Federal Fiduciary Obligations to Indian Tribes in the United States" in *Unidentified Fiduciary Obligations* (Winnipeg: Canadian Bar Association, 1994); David W. Elliott, "Aboriginal Peoples in Canada and the United States and the Scope of the Special Fiduciary Relationship" (1996) 24 Man. L.J. 137; Janice Aitkin, "The Trust Doctrine in Federal Indian Law" (1997) 18 N. Ill. U.L. Rev. 115; Russel Lawrence Barsh, "Trust Responsibility and the Coordination of Aboriginal Issues in the United States: Potential Applications in Canada," report prepared for the Aboriginal Justice Implementation Commission (Manitoba), June 2000, online: Aboriginal Justice Implementation Commission <http://www.ajic.mb.ca/consult.html>; Raymond Cross, "The Future of International Indigenous Trusts and Fiduciary Law: A Comparative Analysis" in *In Whom We Trust* (Toronto: Irwin Law for Law Commission of Canada, 2002); Reid Peyton Chambers & Douglas B.L. Endreson, *Testimony to Senate Committee on Indian Affairs Oversight Hearings on the Management of Indian Funds* (26 February 2002); Neil Jessup Newton *et al*, "Symposium: The Indian Trust Doctrine after the 2002–2003 Supreme Court Term" (2003) 39 Tulsa L. Rev. 237; (1991) 42 C.J.S., ss. 38–48.

[96] Berger, *supra* note 34.

[97] *Johnson v. McIntosh*, 21 U.S. 543 (1823); *Cherokee Nation v. Georgia*, 30 U.S. 1 (1831); *Worcester v. Georgia*, 31 U.S. 515 (1832).

[98] [1984] 2 S.C.R. 335 at 377–78. The Supreme Court of Canada did not discuss the American cases on the fiduciary obligations of the government in *Guerin*. However, Professor Barlett has suggested that the judgment of Dickson J. adopted the language and approach of a student note on the *Mitchell II* decision of the United States Supreme Court (*infra* note 127): Barlett, *supra* note 95 at 197 note 102. See also *Calder v. Attorney-General for British Columbia*, *supra* note 1 at 380, in which Hall J. described *Johnson v. McIntosh*, *supra* note 97, as "the *locus classicus* of the principles governing aboriginal title" and Judson J. *ibid* at 320–21; *R. v. Van Der Peet*, [1996] 2 S.C.R. 507 at 540–44, Lamer C.J.C., and *Nireaha Tamaki v. Baker*, [1901] A.C. 561 at 580 (P.C.).

[99] (1979), 107 D.L.R. (3d) 513 at 545.

[100] *Supra* note 98 at para. 35.

[101] *Supra* note 1 at 383 and chapter 4, text accompanying note 47 *et seq*. See *supra* note 18 *et seq*. for the Royal Proclamation of 1763.

[102] *Supra* note 97.

[103] 25 USCS s. 177; *Joint Tribal Council of the Passamaquoddy Tribe v. Morton*, 528 F.2d 370 (1st Cir. 1975); *Mashpee Tribe v. New Seabury Corp.*, 592 F.2d 575 (1st Cir. 1975); *infra* text accompanying notes 122, 125. Many subsequent enactments of Congress have reaffirmed the trust responsibility in specific areas. For example, the *National Indian Forest Resources Management Act*, 25 U.S.C. s. 3101, states that "the United States has a trust responsibility toward Indian forest lands." See Chambers & Endreson, *supra* note 95 at 34–56; Barsh, *supra* note 95 at 7–8 and Annex I.

[104] Cohen, *supra* note 95 at 221.

[105] Pevar, *supra* note 95 at 23.

[106] *Ibid.* at 24; Chambers, *supra* note 95 at 1215 note 12.

[107] Chambers, *supra* note 95 at 1215–23, see also Green, *supra* note 95 at 137.

[108] *Supra* note 97. See also *Worcester v. Georgia*, *supra* note 97 at 557, in which Chief Justice Marshall said that the right of the Cherokee "to all the lands within those [territorial] boundaries . . . is not only acknowledged but *guaranteed* by the United States" [emphasis added].

[109] Chambers, *supra* note 95 at 1218–19.

[110] *Supra* note 95 at 138.

[111] 118 U.S. 375 (1886) at 383–84 [emphasis added].

[112] 187 U.S. 553 (1903); see also *Cherokee Nation v. Southern Kansas Ry. Co.*, 135 U.S. 614 (1890); *Cherokee Nation v. Hitchcock*, 187 U.S. 294 (1902); *United States v. Sandoval*, 231 U.S. 28 (1913).

[113] Chambers, *supra* note 95 at 1230–34; in addition to cases cited in the text, see *Lane v. Pueblo of Sante Rosa*, 249 U.S. 110 (1919); *Cramer v. United States*, 261 U.S. 219 (1923); *United States v. Creek Nation*, 295 U.S. 103 (1935).

[114] 299 U.S. 476 (1937).

[115] *Ibid.* at 497–98 [citations omitted].

[116] 316 U.S. 286 (1942); applied in *Morton v. Ruiz*, 415 U.S. 199 (1974); see also *United States v. Sioux Nation*, 448 U.S. 371 (1980); *Nevada v. United States*, 463 U.S. 110 (1983).

[117] *Ibid.* at 296–97 [citations omitted].

[118] In addition to the cases cited in the text, see also *Schaghticoke Tribe v. Kent School Corp.*, 423 F.Supp. 780 (D. Conn. 1976); *Navajo Tribe v. United States*, 62 F.2d 981 (Ct.Cl. 1980); *American Indians Residing on the Marikopa-Ak Chin Reservation v. United States*, 667 F.2d 980 (Ct.Cl. 1981).

[119] *Menominee Tribe v. United States*, 101 Ct.Cl. 10 (1944) at 18–19.

[120] 354 F.Supp 252 (D.D.C. 1972).

[121] *Ibid.* at 258.

[122] 477 F.2d 939 (Ct.Cl. 1973) at 942.

[123] 363 F.Supp. 1238 (N.D.Cal. 1973).

[124] *Supra* note 103. See also *Mashpee Tribe v. New Seabury Corp, supra* note 103.

[125] *Ibid.* at 379.

[126] 445 U.S. 535 (1980). See: Gail M. Lambert, "Indian Breach of Trust Suits: Partial Justice in the Court of the Conqueror" (1980) 33 Rutgers L. Rev. 502; Neil Jessup Newton, "Enforcing the Federal–Indian Trust Relationship After *Mitchell* (1982) 31 Cath. U. L. Rev. 635; Richard W. Hughes, "Can the Trustee Be Sued for Its Breach: The Sad Saga of *U.S. v. Mitchell* (1981) 26 S.D.L. Rev. 447; Note, "Whom Can the Indians Trust After *Mitchell*" (1981) 53 U. Colo. L. Rev. 179; Note, "The Re-emergence of the Trust Relationship after *U.S. v. Mitchell*" (1983) 18 Land & Water L. Rev. 491.

[127] 463 U.S. 206 (1983); see Kimberly T. Ellwanger, "Money Damages for Breach of the Federal-Indian Trust Relationship after *Mitchell II*" (1984) 59 Wash. L. Rev. 675; Note, "Rethinking the Trust Doctrine in Federal Indian Law" (1984) 98 Harv. L. Rev. 422.

[128] *Navajo Nation v. United States,* 155 L. Ed. 2d 60 (2003) at 76.

[129] *Ibid.,* quoting *Mitchell II, supra* note 127 at 212.

[130] 28 U.S.C. s. 1505.

[131] 591 F.2d 1300 (Ct.Cl. 1979).

[132] 24 Stat. 388, as amended, 25 U.S.C. ss. 331 *et seq.* (1976).

[133] *Supra* note 126.

[134] *Ibid.* at 542.

[135] *Ibid.* at 542–43.

[136] *Ibid.* at 545.

[137] *Ibid.* at 546.

[138] 664 F.2d 265 (Ct.Cl. 1981).

[139] *Ibid.* at 270.

[140] *Supra* note 127. The decision of the U.S. Supreme Court in *Mitchell II* was handed down a couple of weeks after *Guerin* was argued in the Supreme Court of Canada. Therefore, it was not included as part of the argument.

[141] *Ibid.* at 224.

[142] *Ibid.* at 225–26.

[143] *Ibid.* at 225.

[144] *Supra* note 68.

[145] It may be noted that the decision of the Supreme Court of Canada in *Guerin, supra* note 1, did

not completely eradicate the political trust doctrine in Canada. It still re-emerges from time to time: see *R. v. Vincent* (1993), 12 O.R. (3d) 427 at 440 (Ont. C.A.); see also *Authorson v. Canada* (2002), 215 D.L.R. (4th) 496 at para. 62 (Ont. C.A.), rev'd by the Supreme Court of Canada on another point, [2003] 2 S.C.R. 40.

[146] Douglas Sanders, *First Nations and Canadian Law—Supplementary Materials* (2 October 2000) [unpublished], Vancouver: University of British Columbia Faculty of Law, 2000] at 1.

[147] Richard H. Bartlett, *Indian Reserves and Aboriginal Lands in Canada: A Homeland* (Saskatoon: Univ. of Saskatchewan Native Law Centre, 1990) at 189.

Notes to Chapter 2

[1] For accounts of the pre-contact period, see: Homer G. Barnett, *The Coast Salish of British Columbia* (Eugene, Oreg.: Univ. of Oregon Press, 1955); J.E.M. Kew, *Coast Salish Ceremonial Life: Status and Identity in a Modern Village* (Ph.D. thesis, University of Washington, 1970) [unpublished] [Kew, *The Coast Salish*]; J.E.M. Kew, *A Synopsis of Musqueam Culture and History*, unpublished exhibit dated 14 August 1979, entered at trial of *Guerin v. The Queen* [1982] 2 F.C. 385 [Kew, *Synopsis*]; Musqueam Band, *Musqueam Comprehensive Land Claim—Preliminary Report on Musqueam Land Use and Occupancy*, presented to the Office of Native Claims, June 1984 at 11–38; William C. Sturtevant, general ed., & Wayne Suttles, volume ed., *Handbook of North American Indians*, vol. 7: Northwest Coast (Washington, D.C.: Smithsonian Instituation, 1990), [*Handbook*] esp. Wayne Suttles, "Central Coast Salish" at 453–75; Wayne Suttles, *Coast Salish Essays* (Vancouver: Talonbooks, 1987) [Suttles, *Essays*]; Reg Ashwell, *Coast Salish* (Surrey, B.C.: Hancock House, 1978); Cole Harris, *The Resettlement of British Columbia* (Vancouver: U.B.C. Press, 1992) at 68–76 (especially on seasonal movements and resource use); Dorothy Irene Kennedy, *Looking for Tribes in all the Wrong Places: An Examination of the Central Coast Salish Social Network* (M.A. Thesis, Univ. of Victoria, 1995) [unpublished]; Raymond Hull, Gordon Soules & Christine Soules, *Vancouver's Past* (Seattle: Univ. of Washington, 1974) at 5–10; Nick Russell, "The Indian People of the Vancouver Area when the First Europeans Arrived" in Chuck Davis, ed., *The Vancouver Book* (Vancouver: J.J. Douglas, 1976) at 18–19; R.G. Matson & Gary Coupland, *The Prehistory of the Northwest Coast* (San Diego: Academic, 1995) at 154–77; 200–225; Bruce G. Miller, *The Problem of Justice: Tradition and Law in the Coast Salish World* (Lincoln, Nebr.: Univ. of Nebraska Press, 2001). For a comprehensive account of the Musqueam language, see Wayne Suttles, *Musqueam Reference Grammar* (Vancouver: U.B.C. Press, 2004) [Suttles, *Grammar*].

[2] Kew, *Synopsis*, *supra* note 1 at 1.

[3] W. Kaye Lamb, ed., *The Letters and Journals of Simon Fraser, 1806–1808* (Toronto: MacMillan, 1960) at 106.

[4] For accounts of the post-contact period, see Robin Fisher, *Contact and Conflict*, 2d ed. (Vancouver: U.B.C. Press, 1992); Wilson Duff, *The Indian History of British Columbia: The Impact of the White Man* (Victoria: Provincial Museum, 1964); Douglas Cole & David Darling, "History of the Early Period" in *Handbook*, *supra* note 1 at 119; J.E. Michael Kew, "History of Coastal British Columbia Since 1846" in *Handbook*, *supra* note 1 at 159. For accounts of the history of Aboriginal title in British Columbia, see *Papers Connected with the Indian Land Question 1850–1875* (Victoria: Government Printing Office, 1875), reprinted 1987 [*Papers*]; Canada, Parliament, "Report on the Indian Title in Canada with Special Reference to British Columbia," 20 August 1909, by T.R.E. MacInnes, House of Commons, Sessional Paper No. 47, 1914; G.M. Matheson, *Resume of the British Columbia Indian Land Question*, Memorandum of the Department of Justice, 30 December 1921 [unpublished, copy in library of Ratcliff & Company, North Vancouver]; *Report and Evidence of the Senate and House of Commons Appointed to Inquire into the Claims of the Allied Tribes of British Columbia*, Journal of the Senate of Canada 1926–27 ["*Special Joint Committee Report*"]; George Edgar Shankel, *The Development of Indian Policy in British Columbia* (Ph.D. Thesis, Univ. of Washington, 1945) [unpublished]; Forest E. La Violette, *The Struggle for Survival* (Toronto: Univ. of Toronto Press, 1961) at 98–144; Peter A. Cumming & Neil H. Mickenberg, *Native Rights in Canada*, 2d ed. (Toronto: The Indian-Eskimo Association, 1972) at 171–93; Robert Excell, "History of Land Claims in B.C." (1990) 48 The Advocate (B.C.) 866; Paul Tennant, *Aboriginal Peoples and Politics: The Indian Land Question in British Columbia 1849–1989* (Vancouver: U.B.C. Press, 1990). For an account of the creation of reserves across Canada, see Richard H. Bartlett, *Indian Reserves and Aboriginal Lands in Canada: A Homeland* (Saskatoon: Univ. of Saskatchewan Native Law Centre, 1990).

[5] Henry R. Wagner, *Spanish Explorations in the Strait of Juan De Fuca* (Santa Ana, Calif.: Fine Arts Press, 1933); F.M. Padron *et al.*, *To the Totem Shores: The Spanish Presence on the Northwest Coast* (Madrid: Ediciones El Viso, 1986); Wayne Suttles, "They Recognize No Superior Chief: The Strait of Juan De Fuca in the 1790s" in Josa Luis Peset, ed., *Culturas de la Costa Noroesta de America* (Madrid: Turner, 1989); Tomas Bartroli, *Genesis of Vancouver City: Explorations of its site 1791, 1792 & 1808* (Vancouver: Tomas Bartroli, 1997); Nick Russell, *supra* note 1 at 18–20. The first Europeans to see the Musqueam were probably those on board the *Santa Saturnina* with Jose Maria Narvaez, who saw Musqueam villages from his vessel in 1791: Wagner at 38.

[6] *Supra* note 3. The Musqueam oral history is that their ancesters refused access by Fraser to the ocean because he had stolen canoes futher up the river now named after him. This oral history is supported to some extent by Fraser's own account. He notes that the chief from whom he had borrowed the canoe was reluctant for him to use it and that eventually he had "to force it away from the owner leaving a blanket in its place": *ibid* at 108. The records kept by Fraser and his companions were used by David Thompson to draw the earliest known map of the region, which included the location of "Musquiam Village": Bartroli, *supra* note 5 at 146.

[7] Jose Espinosa y Tello, *Relacion Del Viage Hecho Par Las Goletas "Sutil" y "Mexicana" En El Ano 1792* (Madrid, 1802), translated in Wagner, *supra* note 5 at 260. See Bartroli, *supra* note 5 at 87–92.

[8] George Vancouver, *A Voyage of Discovery to the North Pacific Ocean and Round the World, 1791–1795,* ed. by W. Kaye Lamb, vol. 2 (London: Hakluyt Society, 1984) at 581. Another British naval officer who accompanied Vancouver, Peter Puget, also recorded a friendly welcome: "the conduct of these people was friendly and inoffensive": Bartroli, *supra* note 5 at 70.

[9] Barnett, *supra* note 1 at 1–2. The Musqueam and other Coast Salish traded with the Hudson's Bay Company at Fort Langley from 1827 onwards: see Morag Maclachlan, ed., *The Fort Langley Journals 1827–30*, (Vancouver: University of British Columbia Press, 1998). One of the company's employees complained that "the Musquaims are rather impudent when they come to the Fort": *ibid.* at 71.

[10] See generally Robert T. Boyd "Demographic History, 1774–1874" in *Handbook, supra* note 1 at 135.

[11] See especially Fisher, *supra* note 4 at 102–6, 162–67, 175–205; Cole Harris, *Making Native Space* (Vancouver: University of British Columbia Press, 2002); Harris, *supra* note 1 at 85–92.

[12] "Petition of the Chiefs of the Fraser River to the Superintendent of Indian Affairs," 14 July 1874 in *Papers, supra* note 4 at 137.

[13] Harris, *supra* note 1 at 86–88; for details of pre-emption during the 1860s, see Bruce Macdonald, *Vancouver: A Visual History* (Vancouver: Talonbooks, 1992) at 14–15.

[14] Fitzgerald McCleery, *Diary, Fitzgerald McCleery, Earliest Settler (North Arm, Fraser River),* (Vancouver: City Archives, 1940) at 65–66.

[15] Fisher, *supra* note 4 at 196.

[16] See Barnett, *supra* note 1 at 244, 250–51; Suttles, *Essays, supra* note 1, at 20–21.

[17] Harris, *supra* note 1 at 101.

[18] *Ibid.* at 171; Harris, *supra* note 11 at 17–69; *Papers, supra* note 4 at 5–11; chapter 1, text accompanying note 27 *et seq.* On 25 March 1861, Governor Douglas requested an advance from the imperial government to "purchase the native rights in the land," noting that "the native Indian population of Vancouver Island have distinct ideas of property in land, and mutually recognize their several exclusive possessory rights in certain districts." Lord Newcastle, the Secretary of State for the Colonies, wrote back on 19 October 1861 referring to "the great importance of purchasing without loss of time the native title to the soil of Vancouver Island" which was "essential to the interest of the people of Vancouver Island," but that it was a purely colonial matter and he would not burden the British taxpayer to supply the funds (*Papers, ibid.* at 17–18). By 1870, Joseph Trutch, the Commissioner of Lands and Works in the colonial government and the man in effective charge of Aboriginal affairs, was saying "the title of the Indians in the fee of the public lands, or any portion thereof, has never been acknowledged by Government, but, on the contrary, is distinctly denied." He dismissed the Douglas Treaties as "made for the purpose of securing friendly relations between those Indians and the settlement of Victoria, then in its infancy, and certainly not in acknowledgment of any general title of the Indians to the land they occupy" (*ibid.,* Supplement at 11). The provincial government refused to participate in the hearing of the Special Joint Committee of the House of Commons and the Senate in 1927 to consider Aboriginal title in British Columbia: see *Special Joint Committee Report, supra* note 4. This policy of denial was the official position of the provincial government until 1990

and still reflects to a large extent the approach of the government.

[19] Harris, *supra* note 11 at 75, 351 note 13. The original size of the reserve is unclear. Harris suggests 342 acres but notes that there is uncertainty.

[20] *Papers, supra* note 4 at 41–43; for the view that the policy of Douglas was less generous than is usually thought, see Tennant, *supra* note 4 at 26–38.

[21] See Harris, *supra* note 11 at 75. It also appears that the size of the original reserve was decreased on a second occasion: *infra* note 36. By 1874, the reserve consisted of 314 acres: *infra* text accompanying note 26.

[22] *British North America Act* (now the *Constitution Act*), *1867*, (U.K.), 30 & 31 Vict., c. 3 s. 91(24). See Harris, *supra* note 11 at 70–103, for federal–provincial relations during this period on the so-called "Indian Land Question."

[23] *Terms of Union of British Columbia with Canada,* Order of Her Majesty The Queen In Council, 16 May 1871 (U.K.), reprinted in R.S.C. 1985, App. II, No. 10.

[24] Fisher, *supra* note 4 at 182–83; *Papers, supra* note 4 at 116–43.

[25] Fisher, *ibid*; *Papers, ibid.* at 119. The agreement of the province to allot "twenty acres of land to each head of an Indian family" was formally recorded in an order in council dated 15 June 1874, see *Papers, ibid.* at 133. As noted by Shankel, it is surprising that the federal government so readily agreed to this allotment, asking only that there should be no restriction on the number of family members: *supra* Shankel, note 4 at 105.

[26] *Papers, ibid.* at 134.

[27] *Ibid.*

[28] *Ibid.* at 139 [emphasis in original].

[29] *Ibid.* at 143; *supra* note 25.

[30] *Papers, ibid.* at 152; see Harris, *supra* note 11 at 91–98 for the federal position.

[31] *Papers, ibid.* at 152–54.

[32] *Ibid.* at 161–63, 169–70. Ottawa would later repeat this pattern of not supporting its own officials on Aboriginal affairs by its abandonment of its representative to the 1876 joint reserve commission, Gilbert Sproat: Harris, *supra* note 11 at 102–3, 163–64.

[33] Shankel, *supra* note 4 at 108.

[34] Fisher, *supra* note 4 at 190; Harris, *supra* note 11 at 104–66.

[35] Fisher, *ibid.* The reserve was shown in the 1913 Schedule of Indian Reserves as having 392.5 acres. The McKenna-McBride Commission, which visited the reserve on 24 June 1913, had it re-surveyed and confirmed it at 416.82 acres: *Report of the Royal Commission on Indian Affairs for the Province of British Columbia,* vol. 3 (Victoria: Province of British Columbia, 1916) at 632, 658, 671, 685 [McKenna-McBride Report]. There was another reserve of 60.75 acres confirmed on neighbouring Sea Island and one in Langley of 5.16 acres used with other bands as a fishing station (*ibid.*).

[36] Harris, *supra* note 1 at 91.

[37] *Ibid.* at 92. In 1874, the Musqueam complained to Dr. Powell that they did not have enough grass for their cattle and had lost fifteen head the previous winter: Harris, *supra* note 11 at 75. Part of the future Shaughnessy golf course was once used for farming and market (or "Chinese") gardening and provided some employment: Leona Marie Sparrow, *Work History of a Coast Salish Couple* (M.A. Thesis, University of British Columbia, 1976) [unpublished] at 43, 108.

[38] *Supra* note 35 at 632.

[39] *Ibid.* at 623.

[40] See Harris, *supra* note 11 at xxv.

[41] *Supra* text accompanying note 26.

[42] *Supra* note 35 at 643. The 1876 joint reserve commission thought that "the Musqueam reserve may be considerably increased by reclamation of land from the sea": Harris, *supra* note 11 at 356 note 16. As Harris points out, this was an extraordinary proposal that only shows the power of the surrounding white properties (*ibid.*).

[43] Kew, *Synopsis, supra* note 1 at 7. For a map of Musqueam territory with names of places, see Suttles, *Grammar, supra* note 1 at 566–74.

[44] Fisher, *supra* note 4 at 165; *Papers, supra* note 4 at 25, 147; Harris, *supra* note 11 at 35–36, 68, 87–88.

[45] Fisher, *supra* note 4 at 165. Trutch was appointed as the first lieutenant governor of the province of British Columbia in 1871.

[46] *Ibid.*

[47] *The Pre-Emption Ordinance,* Ordinance No. 13, 31 March 1866, s. 1. This provision was subsequently re-enacted in provincial *Land Acts* including s. 12 of the *Land Act* of 1948, R.S.B.C. 1948, c. 175 and was not repealed until 1953: *Land Act Amendment Act,* S.B.C. 1953, c. 23, s. 3.

[48] Fisher, *supra* note 4 at 165.

[49] *Report of the Government of British Columbia on the Subject of Indian Reserves,* 18 August 1875 at 4 in *Papers, supra* note 4.

[50] *Land Ordinance (British Columbia) 1865,* Ordinance No. 27, 11 April 1865, s. 20. In 1874, Father Grandidier protested the inequity and the impact on the living standards of Indians of the pre-emption policy in a letter to the *Victoria Standard:* "Children and owners of the soil, they want a sufficient share of it to get a living from it. They do not think that when a white man can pre-empt 320 acres and buy as much more, besides the facility of leasing more, that they are unreasonable in asking 80 acres of their own land per family: and in that they are supported by the example of the Dominion Government's conduct towards the other Indians": *Papers, supra* note 4 at 146.

[51] Barnett, *supra* note 1 at 2. In the same year, Professor Drucker gave an equally pessimistic assessment of the culture of Northwest Coast Indians generally as having disappeared except for a few fragments: Philip Drucker, *Indians of the Northwest Coast* (Garden City, N.Y.: The Natural History Press, 1955) at viii.

[52] Kew, *Synopsis, supra* note 1 at 7; see *infra* text accompanying notes 107–9.

[53] *British Columbia Fisheries Regulations,* 26 November 1888. See Diane Newell, *Tangled Webs of History: Indians and the Law in Canada's Pacific Coast Fisheries* (Toronto: Univ. of Toronto Press, 1993); Douglas C. Harris, *Fish, Law, and Colonialism: The Legal Capture of Salmon in British Columbia* (Toronto: Univ. of Toronto Press, 2001). The Musqueam were successful in *R.* v. *Sparrow,* [1990] 1 S.C.R. 1075 in asserting their Aboriginal right to fish and placing an obligation on the government to justify any infringement; see chapter 5, text accompanying note 68.

[54] Kew, *Synopsis, supra* note 1 at 8–11; Kew in *Handbook, supra* note 1 at 162–64; Harris, *supra* note 1 at 92–96. For the work history of one Musqueam couple, see Sparrow, *supra* note 37. See generally Rolf Knight, *Indians at Work: An Informal History of Native Indian Labour in British Columbia 1858–1930* (Vancouver: New Star Books, 1978).

[55] Kew, *Synopsis, supra* note 1 at 10–11.

[56] *Ibid.* at 11. In the 1870s, Methodist missionary Rev. Charles M. Tate made visits to Musqueam by trails and canoe from New Westminister over what was then swampy land: J.S. Matthews, *Conversations with Khahtsahlano 1932–1954* (Vancouver: City Archives, 1955) at 156–60. A Catholic church was subsequently built on the Musqueam Reserve.

[57] Kew, *ibid.* at 11–12. Section 160 of the *Public Schools Act,* S.B.C. 1958, c. 42 permitted school boards to enter into agreements with the Government of Canada for the education of Indian children. The chief of the Musqueam at the time of the negotiation of the Shaughnessy Lease, Ed Sparrow, started residential school at the age of eleven and reached the eighth grade. During that time, he worked on the school farm to pay for his keep. He described his experience: "[r]esidentials, you've got to work. You only have a few hours school each day and the rest of the day you're working for the school whether it was Catholic or Protestant. . . . At least I learned how to work you know. I didn't get much education but I know how to work": Sparrow, *supra* note 37 at 56–57.

[58] Duff, *supra* note 4 at 105. In some northern British Columbia towns, the prejudice was so bad that Indians were segregated and not even permitted to walk with a white man: La Violette, *supra* note 4 at 170–71. A more subtle prejudice against the original inhabitants of the province is revealed in the book by Margaret Ormsby commissioned by the Centennial Committee as part of its programme to mark the centenary of the province in 1958. There are only a couple of passing references to the Aboriginal peoples. Apparently only the history of the European settlers was considered worthy of being recorded, and nothing is said of the dramatic impact of European settlement on the Aboriginal way of life: Margaret A. Ormsby, *British Columbia: A History* (Toronto: MacMillan, 1958). Racial discrimination against Indian peoples was reflected in provincial legislation such as s. 92 of the *Public Schools Act,* R.S.B.C. 1948, c. 297 stating that Indians were not permitted to vote at any school meeting, and restrictions on voting in elections: see chapter 3, text accompanying note 109.

[59] *The Province* (5 June 1941) at 4. The relationship between the settlers and the Musqueam was not always strained. The first settler in the area got on well with his neighbours: see McCleery, *supra* note 14 *passim.* The daughter of another early settler, Joseph Silvey, who came to the province in

the 1860s, told of his experiences, "the Musqueams treated them with kindness, and they sure were good (with emphasis) to my father and his companions": Matthews, *supra* note 56 at 196. Her father subsequently married the daughter of the Musqueam chief: *ibid* at 197–99.

⁶⁰ *Vancouver v. Chow Chee*, [1942] 1 W.W.R. 72 (B.C.C.A.). The threat to abolish the reserve was not hollow. It may be noted that the Songhees reserve in the city of Victoria was destroyed and the people moved to a new reserve outside of the city in 1911: *Songhees Indian Reserve Act*, S.C. 1911, c. 24. The *Indian Act* was also amended in 1911 to give a general power to the federal government to remove Indians from reserve lands in or adjacent to towns and to sell such lands without a surrender: S.C. 1911, c. 14, s. 2; see *Re Indian Reserve, City of Sydney, Nova Scotia* (1916), 4 C.N.L.C. 246 at 249 (Ex. Ct.) referring to the "racial inequalities of the Indian" as a check on social development. As Professor Bartlett commented, "The amendment is a clear instance of the federal government's failure to protect Indian interests that conflicted with local interests": Bartlett, *supra* note 4 at 28. The provision was not repealed until 1951.

⁶¹ See generally on spirit dancing: Pamela Amoss, *Coast Salish Spirit Dancing: The Survival of an Ancestral Religion* (Seattle: Univ. of Washington Press, 1978); Barnett, *supra* note 1 at 272–310; Diamond Jenness, *The Faith of a Coast Salish Indian* (Victoria, Provincial Museum, 1955); G. Jilek, *Indian Healing: Shamonic Ceremonalism in the Pacific Northwest Today* (Surrey, B.C.: Hancock House, 1982); Kew, *The Coast Salish, supra* note 1. For the potlach and attempts to suppress it, see Douglas Cole & Ira Chaikin, *An Iron Hand Upon the People* (Vancouver: Douglas & McIntyre, 1990); Christopher Bracken, *The Potlach Papers* (Chicago: Univ. of Chicago Press, 1997).

⁶² Kew, *Synopsis, supra* note 1 at 16; see also Kew, "Central and Southern Coast Salish Ceremonies" in *Handbook, supra* note 1 at 476–80; Suttles, *Essays, supra* note 1 at 199–208, 223–28.

⁶³ Kew, *The Coast Salish, supra* note 1 at 2.

⁶⁴ *Supra* note 22.

⁶⁵ *Department of Secretary of State Act*, S.C. 1868, c. 42. See generally on the development of Indian administration in Canada: Duff, *supra* note 4 at 63–65; J.G. McGilp, "The Relations of Canadian Indians and Canadian Governments" (1963) 6 Can. Pub. Admin. R. 299. For the history of Indian agents in British Columbia, see Shankel, *supra* note 4 at 37–38, 168–72. The first agent was appointed by Governor Douglas in 1859.

⁶⁶ The following account is based on the transcript of the *Guerin* trial.

⁶⁷ Kew, *Synopsis, supra* note 1 at 17. For an account of the *Indian Act*, both historically and as it was substantially in force during the 1950s, see Richard H. Bartlett, *The Indian Act of Canada* (Saskatoon: Univ. of Saskatchewan Native Law Centre, 1980). See Robin Jarvis Brownlie, *A Fatherly Eye: Indian Agents, Government Power and Aboriginal Resistance in Ontario 1918–1939* (Don Mills, Ont.: Oxford Univ. Press, 2003) at 29–40 for a general discussion of the role of the Indian agent during the interwar period. That role had not fundamentally changed by the 1950s.

⁶⁸ Kew, *ibid.* at 16. Rolf Knight has summed up the department and the Indian agent as follows: "Cast in a strongly colonial mould, the Department of Indian Affairs, however, was never marked with the deceit and corruption of its counterpart south of the border. While its field officers (the Indian Agents) were often patronizing, arbitrary and autocratic, their main failing was that they were ineffectual in protecting Indian interests": Knight, *supra* note 54 at 266.

⁶⁹ Kew, *ibid.* at 21–22. For one account of the role of an Indian agent, see W.M. Halliday, *Potlach and Totem: The Recollections of an Indian Agent* (Toronto: J.M. Dent, 1935). His attitude towards Indians was racist and patronizing. For example, he states baldly, "[a]n Indian is naturally tricky and cunning" (*ibid.* at 146). His attitude was also somewhat contradictory and superficial. On the one hand, he recognized that "[t]he Indian was the original possessor and owner of the county in which we live. We came in, and without force, or without argument, absorbed his country and called it our own" (*ibid.* at 239). Yet on the other hand, he dismisses the Aboriginal title movement of the early decades of the 1900s (see *infra* notes 98–103) as being based on selfishness and somehow answered by the argument "that the greatest boon and the greatest blessing that has come to [Indians] was the advent of the white man": Halliday at 134–40. In his book on Aboriginal rights, Donald Purich quotes an official with the Department of Indian Affairs as saying: "Here I was a young kid in his early twenties and I was absolutely astounded at the power I had over the life of these people. . . . I was really wet behind the ears and here I was telling all these people two and three times older how they should live": Donald Purich, *Our Land: Native Rights in Canada* (Toronto: Lorimer, 1986) at 122.

⁷⁰ J.R. Miller, *Shingwauk's Vision: A History of Native Residential Schools* (Toronto: Univ. of Toronto Press, 1996) at 205–6. He quotes hereditary Nisga'a chief Bert McKay as saying that, as a teacher in Alert Bay, Anfield recognized that the local people were not farmers but seafarers: *ibid.* at 159; see also J.R. Miller, "The State, the Church, and Residential Schools in Canada" (Paper presented at a

conference on Religion and Public Life: Historical and Comparative Themes, Queen's University, 13–15 May 1999) [unpublished]; text accompanying note 41, which was based on an interview with Mrs. M. Anfield, widow of Earl Anfield available on-line: <http:// generalsynod.anglican.ca/ ministry.rs/resources/miller.html> . In his autobiography, Chief Simon Baker describes how, as senior teacher of the St. George's Residential School in Lytton, British Columbia in the 1920s, Anfield took an interest in what he did and always seemed to help and encourage him. He was invited to be a pallbearer at Anfield's funeral: Vera J. Kirkness, ed., *Khot-La-Cha: The Autobigraphy of Chief Simon Baker* (Vancouver/Toronto: Douglas & McIntyre, 1994) at 41. In her account of her experiences as a teacher/nurse on Village Island, the winter home of the Mamalilikulla people, Hughina Hughes refers to Earl Anfield in his role as principal of St. Michael's Residential School in nearby Alert Bay. She describes how he announced the prize-winners at the celebrations in Alert Bay to mark the coronation of King George VI in 1936 and helped to install a radio. She also says that he was instrumental in helping James Sewid to become the first Native fish captain to buy his boat. She comments: "Principal of the residential school, Earl Anfield, was widely respected by both his peers and annual enrolment of 150–200 students": Hughina Harold, *Totem Poles and Tea* (Surrey, B.C.: Heritage House, 1996) at 218. The residential school has now been closed, and there is a proposal to re-open it as an economic and cultural base. A cleansing ceremony was held by Aboriginal people in February, 2003 to take away the memories of the abuse that many Aboriginal students suffered: *The Province* (24 February 2003). For a description of Anfield by one of his assistants, see chapter 3, text accompanying notes 45–51.

[71] Cole & Chaikin, *supra* note 61 at 152. In his autobiography, Chief Simon Baker credits Anfield with changing the practice at the Squamish Nation so that a member of the band council rather than the Indian agent chaired meetings: *supra* note 70 at 100–101.

[72] Quoted by the trial judge, Mr. Justice Collier, [1982] 2 F.C. 385 at 390. Professor Brownlie has noted that, during the 1950s, there were few formal qualifications for Indian agents and those hired were simply expected to be familiar with the office procedures and filing system of the Indian Affairs Branch: Brownlie, *supra* note 67 at 33–34.

[73] Collier J., *ibid.* at 400.

[74] *Ibid.* at 401.

[75] *Ibid.* at 395.

[76] *Ibid.* at 392.

[77] *Case on Appeal,* vol. 6 at 1156, vol. 18 at 3590.

[78] See chapter 1, text accompanying note 18.

[79] Collier J., *supra* note 72 at 425.

[80] *Ibid.* at 419. See chapter 3, text accompanying note 2 *et seq.* for an account of how the band obtained a copy of the lease.

[81] *Ibid.* at 425. His widow vigorously defended his reputation and her solicitor wrote a letter to the Crown's lawyers rejecting the "unfounded and scurrilous attacks on his character" made during the trial. The trial judge refused to allow it to be included in the trial record but said he would have had some concern at the press report of the allegations made against Anfield if there had been a jury: *Vancouver Sun* (19 September 1979).

[82] *Case on Appeal,* vol. 9 at 1640.

[83] *Ibid.*, vol. 13 at 2457–59.

[84] Collier J., *supra* note 72 at 397. Under the *Indian Advancement Act,* which was in force from 1884 to 1951, the Indian agent had the sole legal power to call and preside over band council meetings: S.C. 1884, c. 28, s. 9. In 1966, the Hawthorne Committee commented that "[a]gain and again one is reminded of the insignificance of official band councils as decision-making bodies": *Survey of Contemporary Indians of Canada,* vol. 2 (Ottawa: Indian Affairs Branch, 1966) at 193. The first elections for the Musqueam band council took place in 1952: "History Made at Point Grey Reserve: Musqueam Indians Elect Council," *The Province* (1 December 1952) at 5.

[85] Kew, *Synopsis, supra* note 1 at 20.

[86] *Ibid.*

[87] H.B. Hawthorn, C.S. Belshaw & S.M. Jamieson, *The Indians of British Columbia: A Study of Contemporary Social Adjustment* (Toronto: University of Toronto, 1958) at 458–60.

[88] Betty Walsh, "Shaughnessy and Adjacent Areas" in *The Vancouver Book, supra* note 1 at 102–3. See also the following undated booklets produced by the club: *Clubhouse Opening, October 1, 1983* and *Shaughnessy Golf and Country Club, Founded in 1911.*

[89] *Case on Appeal,* vol. 8 at 1590–91.

[90] Given the evidence in the case on this point, it is somewhat ironic that Justice Binnie, who was counsel for the Crown during the appeals, should refer to the case as involving the lease of land in "suburban Vancouver" in *Wewaykum Indian Band v. Canada,* [2002] 4 S.C.R. 245 at para. 76. The restriction on having alcohol was removed by order in council, P.C. 1956–1607.

[91] *Case on Appeal,* vol. 9 at 1638.

[92] *Ibid.,* vol. 2 at 390.

[93] *Ibid.,* vol. 9 at 1641.

[94] *Ibid.,* vol. 2 at 326, 389.

[95] This account is based, in part, on information provided by Delbert Guerin to the author.

[96] *Case on Appeal,* vol. 7 at 1795.

[97] *Ibid.* at 1285.

[98] See Duff, *supra* note 4 at 69–70; Harris, *supra* note 11 at 217–61. On the history of Indian organizations in the province, see Tennant, *supra* note 4. It may be noted that in 1906, three Salish chiefs went to London to seek an audience with King Edward VII to pursue their claim to Aboriginal title and were told to "go back to Canada and take the matter up with the Canadian Government, and, if you cannot get satisfaction there, come back to us, and we will take it up": *Special Joint Committee Report, supra* note 4, evidence of Andrew Paull; see generally on this attempt to raise the question of Aboriginal title: Daniel P. Marshall, *Those Who Fell from the Sky* (Duncan, B.C.: Cowichan Tribes, 1999) at 146–61. For the role of Andrew Paull in the campaign for recognition of Aboriginal title in the early decades of the 1900s, see Herbert Francis Dunlop, *Andy Paull—As I Knew Him and Understood His Times* (Vancouver: Order of the O.M.I. of St. Paul's Province, 1989) at 124–72.

[99] *Special Joint Committee Report, ibid.*

[100] Duff, *supra* note 4 at 57; see Shankel, *supra* note 4 at 267–80; Tennant, *supra* note 4 at 104–13; and E. Brian Titley, *A Narrow Vision* (Vancouver: U.B.C. Press, 1986) at 135–61 for accounts of the hearing and the *Special Joint Committee Report.*

[101] *Special Joint Committee Report, supra* note 4 at vii–x.

[102] *An Act to Amend the Indian Act,* S.C. 1926–27, c. 32, s. 6, which was reproduced as s. 141 of the *Indian Act 1927,* R.S.C. 1927, c. 98. The restrictions were not repealed until 1951. They brought the federal government into line with the position of the provincial government, which had "always consistently refused to allow the question of land title to come up for judicial decision either before a Dominion court or the Privy Council in London": Shankel, *supra* note 4 at 7. The rejection of the *Petition* and the legal restrictions set back the resolution of the issue of Aboriginal title until the *Calder* case [1973] S.C.R. 313 put it back on the political agenda: see chapter 1 at note 35. In that case, the Supreme Court of Canada was split equally on whether Aboriginal title still existed in the province of British Columbia. The decision of the Court in *Guerin* would go a long way to answering that question (see preface, text accompanying note 8) but it was the decision of the Court in *Delgamuukw v. British Columbia* [1997] 3 S.C.R. 1010 (see chapter 4 at note 45) that clearly recognized such title.

[103] For an account of some of these experiences, see Tennant, *supra* note 4 *passim,* and Dunlop, *supra* note 98.

[104] See Miller, *supra* note 70; Law Commission of Canada, *Restoring Dignity: Responding to Child Abuse in Canadian Instutions* (Ottawa: Minister of Public Works, 2000).

[105] *The Native Voice* (January 1958) at 4–5.

[106] One Musqueam member, Rose Sparrow, who was married to Ed Sparrow, the chief at the time of the Shaughnessy Lease negotiations, described the situation before running water came to the reserve: "The city was far up, up there and we had no money to put in water pipes or anything to get water. Our drinking water was up in the spring up here, the spring water up here. In the early evening the boys would go pack water. Send the boys and they'd go up there, get pails of water. We'd always send them up there. That's for cooking and drinking. But for washing clothes we used to come to this well over here. We didn't want to drink that in the well that was up there. We just use that for washing.": Sparrow, *supra* note 37 at 20.

[107] The chief of the band in 1962, Mrs. Gertrude Guerin, was quoted as saying that only 10 of the 250 band members had regular employment: *Vancouver Sun* (21 February 1962) at 29. A report prepared for the Department of Indian Affairs by Professor Donald B. Fields and William T. Stanbury in 1968 estimated that, based on 1961 statistics, the average income for wage earners living on reserves in British Columbia was only $1,856, and only one wage earner in twenty-two earned more than $5,000 in a year. It described these incomes as "abysmally low" compared with the rest of British Columbians

and not sufficient to support an individual let alone a family: John Kirkwood, "Hidden Report—Raw Deal for Indians," *The Province* (1 April 1972) at 5.

[108] Rose Sparrow remembered digging for cedar roots, splitting them into the right length, and then making baskets which were bartered for second-hand clothing, shoes, and household items by going door to door to the non-Indian people of Vancouver: Sparrow, *supra* note 37 at 16–17, 137, 205–7.

[109] Rose Sparrow also described the whole band going down to Wreck Beach near the reserve in the spring to pick seaweed (before log booms ruined the harvest) and selling it to Chinese merchants: *ibid.* at 211–12.

[110] *Case on Appeal*, vol. 10 at 1814, see chapter 3, text accompanying note 45 *et seq.*

[111] See chapter 3.

[112] *Supra* text accompanying note 59.

[113] The amount of taxes being paid by lessees of reserve lands to municipalities and the province was a widespread cause of concern: Kirkwood, *supra* note 107.

[114] *Vancouver Sun* (15 June 1967).

[115] For details of the band's negotiations with the city over taxes and services, see articles in the *Vancouver Sun* of 13, 22 February 1969; 7, 19 March 1969; and 23 June 1970.

Notes to Chapter 3

[1] This chapter is based on the transcript of the trial as contained within the *Case on Appeal* filed in the Supreme Court of Canada in *Guerin v. The Queen*, [1984] 2 S.C.R. 335 [*Case on Appeal*], the factums of the parties filed in the Federal Court of Appeal and the Supreme Court of Canada, the reported decisions, the Davis & Company files, and the recollections of Delbert Guerin, other members of the Musqueam, and members of their legal team, including the author.

[2] John Kirkwood, "Hidden Report—Raw Deal For Indians," *The Province* (1 April 1972) at 5.

[3] *Case on Appeal* (Exhibit 86).

[4] *Case on Appeal*, vol. 10 at 1814, evidence of William Grant, witness for the Crown.

[5] See chapter 9, text accompanying note 25 *et seq.*

[6] *Ibid.*, text accompanying note 34 *et seq.*

[7] See chapter 1, text accompanying note 55 *et seq.* for the Canadian and English cases, and text accompanying note 95 *et seq.* for the United States cases.

[8] One writer has summed up his legal skill as an advocate as follows: "perhaps his greatest skill is not strictly derived from the law books but from his ability to get along with and 'read' people, including judges at every level of the system": Jim Tobler, "The Legal Sorcery of Marvin Storrow" (Summer 2002) 5:2 *Nuvo* 38 at 40.

[9] Gunnar Eggertson (1928–1999) practised with the Department of Justice in Vancouver from 1970 to 1995. His obituary in *The Advocate* noted that "[h]e conducted a wide range of litigation and was counsel at the trial level in the *Guerin* case which, of course, later went on to the Supreme Court of Canada and set an important precedent in the area of aboriginal law." It also notes that he was "a kind, considerate and caring man without a mean bone in his body" and "the antithesis of aggressiveness, yet through his tireless hard work, his compassion and stubbornness he was indeed a successful litigator": (1999) 57 Advocate (B.C.) 760.

[10] From 1986 to 1998, he was a senior partner at a large Toronto law firm from which he was himself appointed directly to the Supreme Court of Canada, where he now sits. It was somewhat unusual, although not unprecedented, for a Supreme Court justice to be appointed directly from practice to that Court without serving as a judge on another court. His judgments include *Wewaykum Indian Band v. Canada*, [2002] 4 S.C.R. 245, chapter 5, note 52 *et seq.*, which was the first case since *Guerin* in 1984 in which the Court reviewed the fiduciary duty of the Crown to Aboriginal people in any significant detail. One of his early judgments, *R. v. Marshall*, [1999] 3 S.C.R. 456, involving treaty rights, aroused considerable controversy among non-Aboriginal fishers. His judgments have received praise for their clarity and reasoning: Kirk Makin, "Five Years On, Binnie Settles into the Bench" *Globe and Mail* (10 February 2003) A3.

[11] Mr. Justice Frank Collier (1922–1996) had been primarily an insurance defence counsel prior to his appointment in 1971 to the Federal Court of Canada, Trial Division, where he served for twenty-one years. Perhaps as the result of his insurance background, he suggested that the Musqueam take out

insurance on his life to cover the costs of a rehearing if he should die before giving judgment. Coverage of $300,000 was obtained: *Vancouver Sun* (22 May 1981). He was known as a courtroom lawyer with a scholarly bent. He is described in his obituary as a "gentle, austere and very private person." (During the *Guerin* trial, his sense of humour and love of sports became apparent. He kept control of what were sometimes spirited exchanges between the lawyers with firmness, humour, and occasional sporting analogies.) His obituary also notes that he "became known for the clarity and precision of his reasons (if not always for their timeliness) and for the breadth and depth of his knowledge of the law," see (1996) 54 Advocate (B.C.) 947; (1971) 29 Advocate (B.C.) 292. On the timeliness of his judgments, it may be noted that his decision in *Guerin* was delivered fifteen months after the close of argument and ended with his expression of regret over the delay.

[12] *Guerin v. The Queen*, [1984] 2 S.C.R. 335, *Case on Appeal*, vol. 1 at 27–33. See chapter 1, text accompanying note 55 *et seq.* for the case law as it stood at the time of the trial.

[13] *Case on Appeal, ibid.* at 36–38.

[14] *Ibid.*

[15] *Ibid.* at 40–67. His report is referred to in chapter 2 *passim.*

[16] *Ibid.* at 79–111.

[17] *Ibid.* at 111–200; vol. 2 at 201–311.

[18] *Case on Appeal*, vol. 1. at 120. Withholding documents seems to have been a common practice of the department. During the hearings of the Special Joint Committee of the Senate and the House of Commons to inquire into the claims of the Allied Indian Tribes of British Columbia in 1927 (see chapter 2, text accompanying note 98 *et seq.*), the Committee refused to allow the representatives of the Tribes to have access to relevant documents: Paul Tennant, *Aboriginal Peoples and Politics* (Vancouver: U.B.C. Press, 1990) at 106–8. Professor Brownlie notes that the Indian agent for the Parry Island Band in the 1930s kept copies of important documents relating to a treaty away from the chief to prevent "unrest": Robin Jarvis Brownlie, *A Fatherly Eye:Indian Agents, Government Power and Aboriginal Resistance in Ontario, 1918–1939* (Don Mills, Ont: Oxford U. Press, 2003) at 69.

[19] *Case on Appeal, ibid.* at 143. For the difficulties of Aboriginal peoples in obtaining legal advice, see chapter 9, text accompanying notes 21–23.

[20] *Case on Appeal, ibid.* vol. 2 at 311–400; vol. 3 at 401–507. For something of the varied background of Ed Sparrow and his wife, Rose, see the following account by his granddaughter: Leona Sparrow, *Work History of a Coast Salish Couple* (M.A. Thesis, University of British Columbia 1976) [unpublished]. He died in August 1998 at the age of ninety-nine: see *Vancouver Sun* (6 August 1998) at B7 for his obituary.

[21] See chapter 2, text accompanying note 92 *et seq.*

[22] *Case on Appeal*, vol. 6 at 1147–1206.

[23] *Ibid.* at 1156.

[24] *Ibid.*, vol. 7 at 1282–87.

[25] *Ibid.* at 1297–1355, see *supra* note 3 *et seq.*

[26] *Ibid.* at 1287–97.

[27] *Ibid.* at 1296.

[28] *Ibid.* at 1293–94.

[29] *Ibid.* at 1295.

[30] *Ibid.* at 1297.

[31] *Ibid.*, vol. 5 at 906–74.

[32] *Ibid.* at 938.

[33] *Ibid.*, vol. 3 at 509–600; vol. 4 at 601–800; vol. 5 at 801–905.

[34] *Ibid.*, vol. 8 at 1464–1506; vol. 12 at 2201–35.

[35] *Ibid.* (Exhibit 148).

[36] *Ibid.*, vol. 12 at 2211.

[37] *Ibid.*, vol. 8 at 1508–40.

[38] *Ibid.*, vol. 9 at 1627.

[39] *Ibid.* at 1641.

[40] *Ibid.* at 1638.

[41] *Ibid.* at 1640.

[42] *Ibid.* at 1647–48.

[43] *Ibid.*, vol. 9 at 1691–1753.

[44] *Ibid.* at 1719.

[45] *Ibid.* at 1756–1800; vol. 10 at 1801–39.

[46] *Ibid.*, vol. 10 at 1814.

[47] *Ibid.* at 1819.

[48] *Ibid.* at 1826.

[49] *Ibid.* at 1820. See chapter 2, text accompanying note 70 *et seq.* for more information on Earl Anfield.

[50] *Ibid.*

[51] *Ibid.* at 1824.

[52] [1982] 2 F.C. 385 at 411.

[53] *Ibid.* at 419. See *supra,* text accompanying notes 2–4.

[54] *Supra* note 46 at 1874–1921.

[55] *Ibid.* at 1898.

[56] *Ibid.* (Exhibit 166).

[57] *Ibid.*, vol. 12 at 2297-BB. For the political trust doctrine, see chapter 1, text accompanying note 69 *et seq.*

[58] *Ibid.* at 2297-PP.

[59] The Crown's reliance on the political trust defence was criticized in the press and by the local Member of Parliament. The minister of Justice, Jacques Flynn, ordered the withdrawal of the defence on 20 November 1979: *Vancouver Sun* (20 and 21 November 1979). Despite this withdrawal, the defence was raised on the appeal, thereby earning this rebuke from Madam Justice Wilson in the Supreme Court of Canada:

> I agree with the appellant's submission that the Crown's tactics in this regard left a lot to be desired. It is quite apparent that when the trial judge indicated a willingness to permit an amendment at trial but went on to order discovery on the issue, the Crown renounced the defence both at trial and through ministerial statements made out of court. It nevertheless went ahead and sought leave to raise it in the Federal Court of Appeal. Even though, as the Court of Appeal pointed out, the defence is a strictly legal one and the Band was probably not prejudiced by the absence of discovery, the Crown's behaviour does not, in my view, exemplify the high standard of professionalism we have come to expect in the conduct of litigation.

[1984] 2 S.C.R. 335 at 353.

[60] *Case on Appeal,* vol. 24 at 2298–2339.

[61] *Ibid.* at 2316.

[62] [1982] 2 F.C. 385 at 421.

[63] *Ibid.* at 393.

[64] *Ibid.* at 392.

[65] *Ibid.* at 395.

[66] *Ibid.* at 398.

[67] *Ibid.* at 399.

[68] *Ibid.* at 400.

[69] *Ibid.* at 401.

[70] *Ibid.* at 405–6.

[71] *Ibid.* at 406–7.

[72] *Ibid.* at 409–10.

[73] *Ibid.* at 413.

[74] *Ibid.*

[75] *Ibid.* at 419.

[76] *Ibid.* at 425.

[77] *Ibid.* at 415.

[78] *Ibid.*

[79] *Ibid.* at 416; see *supra,* text accompanying notes 58 and 59.

80 *Ibid.* at 417–18.

81 *Ibid.* at 418.

82 *Ibid.* at 418–29. For a discussion of these defences, see chapter 9, text accompanying note 18 *et seq.*

83 *Ibid.* at 425.

84 *Ibid.*

85 *Ibid.* at 429–30.

86 *Ibid.* at 430–43. See chapter 9 for a discussion of remedies generally, and chapter 9, text accompanying note 144 *et seq.* for an account of the compensation awarded in *Guerin.*

87 *Ibid.* at 437.

88 *Ibid.* at 439.

89 *Ibid.*

90 *Ibid.*

91 *Ibid.* at 440–41.

92 *Ibid.* at 441.

93 *Ibid.* at 441–42.

94 *Ibid.* at 443.

95 *Supra,* text accompanying note 89.

96 *Supra,* text accompanying notes 26–32.

97 *Case on Appeal,* vol. 8 at 1590–91.

98 [1982] 2 F.C. 445. Sections 31 and 31.1 of the *Crown Liability and Proceedings Act*, R.S.C. 1985, c.C-50 (in force from 1 February 1992) provide that, generally speaking, the provincial laws on pre-judgment and post-judgment interest apply to the Federal Court. For a review of the development of the law relating to payment of interest by the federal Crown on judgments, see *Beattie v. Canada*, [2004] 3 C.N.L.R. 18, 2004 FC 674 at paras. 80–97.

99 *Ibid.* at 452. This decision was overruled two years later by the Federal Court of Appeal, which held that s. 40 of the *Federal Court Act*, R.S.C. 1970 (2d Supp.), c. 10 gave a discretion to the court to vary the rate of post-judgment interest: *Domestic Converters Corp. v. Artic S.S. Line*, [1984] 1 F.C. 211 at 229 (C.A.); see also *CAE Industries Ltd. v. R.*, [1986] 1 F.C. 129 at 179–80, leave to appeal ref'd, (1985), 20 D.L.R. (4th) 347 n. (S.C.C.).

100 See Appellant's Memorandum of Fact and Law filed in the appeal *Guerin v. The Queen* (1983), 143 D.L.R. (3d) 416 (F.C.A.).

101 See text accompanying note 59 and Appellant's Memorandum of Fact and Law, *supra* note 100 at 30–37; see chapter 1, text accompanying note 69 *et seq.* for a discussion of this doctrine.

102 (1882), 7 App. Cas. 619 (H.L.); see chapter 1, text accompanying note 71.

103 [1977] W.L.R. 323 (Ch.); see chapter 1, text accompanying note 74.

104 [1950] S.C.R. 211; see chapter 1, text accompanying note 93.

105 Respondents' Memorandum of Fact and Law at 45–66, filed in the appeal *Guerin v. The Queen*, *supra* note 100.

106 [1950] S.C.R. 168; see chapter 1, text accompanying note 66.

107 (1935), 5 C.N.L.C. 92 (Ex.); see chapter 1, text accompanying note 62.

108 (1982), 125 D.L.R. (3d) 513 (F.C.T.D.).

109 *Canada Elections Act*, R.S.C. 1952, c. 23, s. 14(2)(e). The restriction on voting in federal elections was imposed by section 11 of the *Electoral Franchise Act*, S.C. 1885, c.40 and not removed until *An Act To Amend The Canada Elections Act*, S.C. 1960, c.7, s.1. Indians were also denied the right to vote in provincial elections until s. 2 of the *Elections Act Amendment Act 1949*, S.B.C. 1949, c. 19. s. 2 removed the restriction. The provincial restriction was first introduced in 1875 by *An Act To Amend The Qualification And Registration Of Voters Amendment Act 1871*, 1872, 35–38 Vict., c. 39, s. 13.

110 Respondents' Memorandum of Fact and Law, *supra* note 105 at 42.

111 S.C. 1960, c. 44, s. 1.

112 Part 1 of the *Constitution Act, 1982*, being Schedule B to the *Canada Act 1982* (U.K.), 1982, c. 11, s. 15, not in effect until 1985 (see s. 32(2)).

113 Appellant's Memorandum of Fact and Law, *supra* note 100 at 22–26.

114 See Respondents' Memorandum of Fact and Law, *supra* note 105 at 36–37.

[115] *Ibid.*

[116] Citing Judson J. in *Calder v. Attorney-General of British Columbia,* [1973] S.C.R. 313 at 328.

[117] *Shoshone Tribe v. United States,* 299 U.S. 476 (1937); *United States v. Sioux Nation,* 448 U.S. 371 (1980); see chapter 1, text accompanying note 95 *et seq.* for the United States law as it was at the time of the *Guerin* case.

[118] *Supra* note 100 at 50–52.

[119] Respondents' Memorandum of Fact and Law, *supra* note 105 at 81–83.

[120] See, for example, *The Trust and Loan Company of Upper Canada v. Ruttan,* [1877] 1 S.C.R. 564.

[121] (1983), 143 D.L.R. (3d) 416; see comment by T.C. Youdan (1983) 13 E.T.R. 248.

[122] (1888), 14 A.C. 46 (P.C.).

[123] [1921] 1 A.C. 401.

[124] *Supra* note 116. See chapter 1, text accompanying note 35.

[125] *Shoshone Tribe v. United States, supra* note 117; *United States v. Sioux Nation, supra* note 117.

[126] [1921] 1 A.C. 399.

[127] *The Queen v. Devereux,* [1965] 1 Ex. C.R. 602, [1965] S.C.R. 567; *Joe v. Findlay* (1978), 87 D.L.R. (3d) 239 (B.C.S.C.), 122 D.L.R. (3d) 377 (B.C.C.A.); *Brick Cartage Ltd. v. The Queen,* [1965] 1 Ex. C.R. 102.

[128] K. Lysyk, 'The Indian Title Question in Canada: An Appraisal in the Light of *Calder*" (1973) 51 Can. Bar Rev. 450.

[129] *Supra* note 121 at 462.

[130] *Indian Act,* R.S.C. 1970, c. I-6, ss. 37–41.

[131] *Ibid.,* s. 39(1)(c).

[132] (1981), 62 C.C.C. (2d) 227.

[133] *Supra* note 121 at 442.

[134] Citing *Rustomjee v. The Queen,* [1876] 2 Q.B.D. 69 (Eng. C.A.) at 74, see chapter 1, text accompanying note 72; *Civilian War Claimants Association Limited v. The King,* [1932] A.C. 14 (H.L.) at 27; *Miller v. The King, supra* note 106 at 175; *Tito v. Waddell, supra* note 103 at 217.

[135] *Supra* note 102.

[136] (1894), 24 S.C.R. 1; see chapter 1, text accompanying note 84.

[137] *Supra* note 103.

[138] [1978] A.C. 359 (H.L.); see chapter 1, text accompanying note 76.

[139] *Supra* note 106.

[140] *Supra* note 102.

[141] *Supra* note 136.

[142] *Supra* note 103.

[143] *Supra* note 121 at 467.

[144] Section 18(1) provides: "Subject to this Act, reserves are held by Her Majesty for the use and benefit of the respective bands for which they were set aside; and subject to this Act and to the terms of any treaty or surrender, the Governor in Council may determine whether any purpose for which lands in a reserve are used or are to be used is for the use and benefit of the band."

[145] *Supra* note 121 at 467.

[146] *Ibid.* at 469.

[147] See chapter 1, text accompanying note 51, and chapter 2, text accompanying note 23. For the provincial order in council, see chapter 1 at note 51.

[148] *Supra* note 121 at 470.

[149] See *R. v. Hampden* (1637), 3 St. Tr. 825 (Exch.); cf. *Reference Re Language Rights under s. 23 of the Manitoba Act and s. 133 of the Constitution Act 1876,* [1985] 1 S.C.R 721 at 748 for the rule of law.

[150] *Constitution Act, 1982,* being Schedule B to the *Canada Act 1982* (U.K.), 1982, c. 11, s. 35(1); see chapter 1, text accompanying note 37, and chapter 5, text accompanying note 66 *et seq.* Leading constitutional scholars Professors Hogg and Monihan have dismissed a non-enforceable trust as "a nothing": P. Hogg & P. Monihan, *Liability of the Crown,* 3d ed. (Toronto: Carswell, 2000) at 259. The idea of non-enforceable "rights" raises serious jurisprudential questions: H.L.A. Hart, "Definition and Theory in Jurisprudence" (1954) 70 Law Q. Rev. 37 esp. at 49.

Notes to Chapter 4

[1] *Guerin v. The Queen*, [1984] 2 S.C.R. 335, *Case on Appeal*, vol. 1 at 20–69.

[2] *Ibid.* at 20–60 to 20–63.

[3] *Ibid.* at 20–76.

[4] Appellant's Factum at 42–45. See chapter 3, text accompanying note 58 for this ruling. The facum is available on-line at the website of the Native Law Centre, University of Saskatchewan: <www.usask.ca/nativelaw/factums>.

[5] *Ibid.* at 58–62. It was contended that the doctrine of political trust was part of the act of state doctrine, which cannot be used by the Crown against a citizen: *Walker v. Baird*, [1892] A.C. 491 (P.C.); *Attorney-General v. Nissan*, [1970] A.C. 179 (H.L.).

[6] *Ibid.* at 68–77.

[7] *Ibid.* at 45–52. See chapter 1, text accompanying note 66 for *Miller v. The King*, [1950] S.C.R. 168.

[8] *Ibid.* at 52–54.

[9] Reliance was placed on *Fales v. Canada Permanent Trust Co.*, [1977] 2 S.C.R. 302; see M. Cullity, "Judicial Control of Trustees' Discretions" (1975) 25 U.T.L.J. 99.

[10] See *The Queen v. Nowegijick* (1983), 46 N.R. 41 (S.C.C.) at 48, Dickson J., cf. *Northern Cheyenne Tribe v. Hollowbreast*, 425 U.S. 649 (1976) at 655 note 7. See chapter 1, text accompanying note 95 *et seq.* for discussion of the United States law.

[11] Factum of National Indian Brotherhood. The applications to intervene of the Union of Ontario Indians, the Union of British Columbia Indian Chiefs, the Treaty 8 Tribal Association, the Gitksan-Carrier Tribal Council, the Carrier-Sekani Tribal Council, and the Association of Iroquois and Allied Indians were dismissed on 14 April 1983.

[12] *Ibid.* at 4–6.

[13] Factum of the Crown at 67–72.

[14] *Ibid.* at 77–78.

[15] *Ibid.* at 79–82.

[16] *Ibid.* at 82–83, relying upon *Ontario Mining Company v. Seybold*, [1903] A.C. 73 at 83–84, Lord Davey.

[17] *Ibid.* at 55–64.

[18] I left some papers in the courtroom that I needed to refer to overnight. The security guard let me into the courtroom through the entrance used by the judges which is immediately behind their chairs. I could not resist the temptation to sit in the Chief Justice's chair and so had a view of the Court that few lawyers will ever see.

[19] [1984] 2 S.C.R. 335. In their biography of Dickson C.J.C., Robert J. Sharpe and Kent Roach describe the process by which the Court reached its decision. Dickson J.'s conference notes indicate that all members of the Court agreed that the terms of the lease were "disgraceful" and that the Musqueam appeal should be allowed. He believed that Le Dain J. had taken "a very technical view of things." Despite this agreement on the outcome of the appeal, his attempt to get the Court to speak with one voice was unsuccessful. Wilson J. and Estey J. insisted on writing separate reasons. Wilson J. had written the first draft of the reasons for consideration by the other members of the Court. She based the decision on a breach of an express trust. Dickson J. agreed with clerk Martin Freiman that it was "entirely unnecessary to stretch and, with respect, deform the law of trusts to this extent to achieve an equitable solution": Robert J. Sharpe & Kent Roach, *Brian Dickson: A Judge's Journey* (Toronto: Osgoode Society for Canadian Legal History, 2003) at 446–48.

[20] *Kinloch v. Secretary of State for India* (1881–82) 7 A.C. 619 at 625–26 (H.L.); see chapter 1, text accompanying note 71.

[21] *Supra* note 19 at 375.

[22] *Ibid.* at 376.

[23] George R., Proclamation, 7 October 1763 (3 Geo. III), reprinted in R.S.C. 1985, App. II, No. 1; see chapter 1, text accompanying note 18 *et seq.*

[24] *Supra* note 19 at 376.

[25] *Calder v. Attorney-General of British Columbia*, [1973] S.C.R. 313; see chapter 1, text accompanying note 35.

[26] (1888), 14 App. Cas. 46

[27] 21 U.S. (8 Wheat.) 543 (1823).

[28] 31 U.S. (6 Peters) 515 (1832).

[29] *Amodu Tijani v. Secretary of State, Southern Nigeria*, [1921] 2 A.C. 399 (P.C.).

[30] [1921] 1 A.C. 401.

[31] *Supra* note 19 at 378.

[32] *Ibid.* at 379. See chapter 1, text accompanying note 67 *et seq.* for the political trust doctrine.

[33] *Ibid.* The distinction between recognized and unrecognized Aboriginal title is not one that is made in Canadian law, and Dickson J. seems to have adopted without acknowledgement the terminology from United States law; see *Northwestern Bands of Shoshone Indians v. United States*, 324 U.S. 335 (1945). See also chapter 8, note 171 for another example of the unacknowledged influence of United States law on the judgment of Dickson J.

[34] *Supra* note 26.

[35] *Supra* note 27.

[36] *Supra* note 29.

[37] *Supra* note 30.

[38] In the *St. Catherine's Milling* case, Lord Watson described the Indian title as "a mere burden" on the Crown's proprietary estate in the land, *supra* note 26 at 58.

[39] *Supra* note 25.

[40] (1916), 53 S.C.R. 172; see chapter 1, text accompanying note 58.

[41] [1974] S.C.R. 695, Laskin J.

[42] *Western International Contractors Ltd v. Sarcee Development Ltd*, [1979] 3 W.W.R. 631.

[43] *Supra* note 7.

[44] *Supra* note 19 at 382.

[45] *Ibid.* In *Delgamuukw v. British Columbia*, [1997] 3 S.C.R. 1010 at para. 117, Lamer C.J.C. said that the content of Aboriginal title can be summarized by two propositions: "first, that aboriginal title encompasses the right to exclusive use and occupation of the land held pursuant to that title for a variety of practices which need not be aspects of those aboriginal practices which are integral to distinctive aboriginal cultures; and second, that those protected uses must not be irreconciliable with the nature of the group's attachment to that land."

[46] *Supra* note 19 at 383. See chapter 1, text accompanying note 38 *et seq.* for the origin of fiduciary obligations.

[47] *Ibid.*

[48] *Ibid.* For a discussion of the Royal Proclamation of 1763, see chapter 1, text accompanying note 18 *et seq.*

[49] *Supra* note 19 at 384. See chapter 3, text accompanying note 145 for the decision of the Federal Court of Appeal on this point.

[50] E. Weinrib, "The Fiduciary Obligation" (1975) 25 U.T.L.J. 1 at 4.

[51] *Supra* note 19 at 384; see chapter 6 for a discussion of fiduciary obligations generally. In *Authorson v. Canada* (2000), 215 D.L.R. (4th) 496 at para. 26, the Ontario Court of Appeal referred to these words as Dickson J.'s "most famous passage."

[52] *Ibid.*

[53] *Ibid.* at 385. See chapter 8, text accompanying note 18 *et seq.* for a discussion of whether the existence of a public law duty excludes a fiduciary obligation.

[54] *Ibid.*

[55] *Ibid.* at 386. See *infra* text accompanying note 75 for the view of Wilson J. that the Crown became "a full-blown trustee by virtue of the surrender." For a discussion of the relationship between fiduciary and trust obligations, see chapter 8, text accompanying note 156 *et seq.*

[56] *Ibid.* It may be noted that this passage overlooks the fact that the surrender in question was not an unconditional surrender as in the *Smith* case [1983] 1 S.C.R. 554. The surrender was for the purpose of lease not for sale as in *Smith*. See James I. Reynolds & Lew F. Harvey, "The Fiduciary Obligation of the United States and Canadian Governments" in Continuing Legal Education Society of British Columbia ("C.L.E.), *Indians and the Law II* (Vancouver: C.L.E., 1985) at 24–25; see also Richard H. Bartlett, *Indian Reserves and Aboriginal Lands: A Homeland* (Saskatoon: Univ. of Saskatchewan Native Law Centre, 1990) at 198–99. In the view of Professor Waters, there was a sufficient interest for the purposes of a trust: Donovan Waters, "New Directions in the Employment of Equitable Doctrines: The Canadian Experience"

in Timothy G. Youdan, ed., *Equity, Ficuciaries and Trusts* (Toronto: Carswell, 1989) at 423.

[57] *Ibid* at 386 citing *Pettkus v. Becker*, [1980] 2 S.C.R. 834 at 847 and *Rathwell v. Rathwell,* [1978] 2 S.C.R. 436. See chapter 9, text accompanying note 119 for the Court's subsequent clarification in *Soulos v. Korkontzilas*, [1997] 2 S.C.R. 217 that a constructive trust can be found even in the absence of unjust enrichment.

[58] *Ibid.* at 386–87.

[59] *Ibid.* at 387. See *infra* text accompanying note 80 *et seq.* for the judgment of Estey J. based on agency, and chapter 8, text accompanying note 171 *et seq.* for a criticism of this emphasis on the *sui generis* nature of the Crown's fiduciary obligations to Aboriginal peoples.

[60] *Ibid.* at 388–90.

[61] *Ibid.* at 388–89.

[62] *Ibid.* at 389.

[63] *Ibid.* at 389–90; see chapter 9 for a discussion of these defences.

[64] *Ibid.* at 390.

[65] *Ibid.* at 390–91. See chapter 3, text accompanying note 86, and chapter 9, text accompanying note 144 *et seq.* for the judgment of the trial judge on damages.

[66] *Ibid.* at 341.

[67] *Ibid.* at 341–48. See chapter 3, text accompanying note 64 *et seq.*

[68] *Ibid.* at 348–52.

[69] *Supra* note 25.

[70] *Supra* note 19 at 349–50.

[71] *Ibid.* at 350–52. See chapter 3, text accompanying note 133 *et seq.* See chapter 1, text accompanying note 67 *et seq.* for the political trust doctrine.

[72] *Ibid.* at 351.

[73] *Ibid.* at 353–55.

[74] *Ibid.* at 354.

[75] *Ibid.* at 355.

[76] *Ibid.*

[77] *Ibid.* at 356.

[78] R.S.B.C. 1960, c. 390; see chapter 9, text accompanying note 54 *et seq.* for a discussion of equitable fraud.

[79] *Supra* note 19 at 356–64. For more information on this part of her judgment, see chapter 9, text accompanying notes 90 and 150 *et seq.* For a criticism of the trial judge's decision on the compensation awarded, see chapter 3, text accompanying note 95 *et seq.* An action to declare the lease void was unsuccessful: *Musqueam Indian Band v. Canada,* [1990] 2 F.C. 351 (F.C.T.D.).

[80] *Ibid.* at 391.

[81] *Ibid.* at 393.

[82] *Ibid.* at 394.

[83] Bartlett, *supra* note 56 at 202. See also Dickson J., *supra* at note 59 and accompanying text.

[84] See chapter 1, text accompanying note 35, and chapter 5, text accompanying note 66 *et seq.*

[85] (1990), 70 D.L.R. (4th) 385 at 406 (S.C.C.).

Notes to Chapter 5

[1] *Wewaykum Indian Band v. Canada*, [2002] 4 S.C.R. 245 at para. 82 [*Wewaykum*].

[2] See Leonard I. Rotman, *Parallel Paths: Fiduciary Doctrine and the Crown–Native Relationship in Canada* (Toronto: Univ. of Toronto Press, 1996) at 112.

[3] [1990] 1 S.C.R. 1075.

[4] [1995] 4 S.C.R. 344.

[5] See chapter 8, text accompanying notes 82–86.

[6] [2001] 3 S.C.R. 746.

[7] [2002] 2 S.C.R. 816.

[8] *Supra* note 1.

[9] See Leonard I. Rotman, "Crown–Native Relations As Fiduciary" in *Aboriginal Ownership and*

Management of Resources in Canada: An Analysis of Litigation and Negotiation. Getting to a Win–Win?" (Halifax: Canadian Bar Association, 2003).

[10] *Wewaykum, supra* note 1 at para. 83; see chapter 6, text accompanying note 78.

[11] See Rotman, *supra* note 9.

[12] *Supra* note 3 at 1108.

[13] [1994] 1 S.C.R. 159 at 183. In *R. v. Van der Peet*, [1996] 2 S.C.R. 507, Lamer C.J.C. said at para. 24: "The Crown has a fiduciary obligation to aboriginal peoples with the result that in dealings between the government and aboriginals the honour of the Crown is at stake."

[14] *Supra* note 7 at para. 68 [emphasis added]. In *Mitchell v. M.N.R.*, [2001] 1 S.C.R. 911, speaking for the Court, Chief Justice McLachlin said at para. 9: "with this assertion of [sovereignty by the Crown] arose an obligation to treat aboriginal peoples fairly and honourably, and to protect them from exploitation, a duty characterized as 'fiduciary' in *Guerin v. The Queen.*"

[15] [2000] 1 C.N.L.R. 245 at paras. 344–45. But see chapter 8, text accompanying notes 82–86 for a contrary trend in the Federal Court of Canada.

[16] *Report of the the Royal Commission on Aboriginal Peoples: Restructuring the Relationship*, vol. 2 (Ottawa: Supply and Services Canada, 1996) at 24–25.

[17] *Supra* note 1 at para. 81.

[18] [1988] 2 S.C.R. 654 at para. 39. With respect to lands allocated to a particular member of the band rather than the band itself, see: *Boyer v. R.* (1986), 26 D.L.R. (4th) 284 (F.C.A.) and *Tsartlip Indian Band v. Canada (Minister of Indian Affairs)* (2000), 181 D.L.R. (4th) 730 (F.C.A.), discussed *infra* text accompanying note 43.

[19] *Supra* note 7 at para. 77. In *Chingee v. British Columbia* (2002), 8 B.C.L.R. (4th) 149 at para. 78 (B.C.S.C.), Cohen J. said that the historical protection of Indians from improvident bargains "was a hallmark of the Crown's traditional fiduciary duty, one of the most basic principles of Indian land law." See also *Mannpar Enterprises v. The Queen* (1999), 173 D.L.R. (4th) 243 at para. 62 (B.C.C.A.) in which the Crown refused to renew a licence to extract gravel from reserve lands because of the concerns by band members over the extent of environmental degradation. Giving the judgment of the Court, Hall J.A. said, "I believe that the Crown is entitled to invoke its fiduciary duty to the Skyway Band in this case to meet any suggestion that it was in 1993 acting in 'bad faith towards [the licensor].'"

[20] (1985), 17 D.L.R. (4th) 591(F.C.A.), leave to appeal to S.C.C. refused, [1985] 2 S.C.R. viii.

[21] (1993), 109 D.L.R. (4th) 449 (Ont. C.A.), leave to appeal refused (1994), 110 D.L.R. (4th) vii 16 (S.C.C.).

[22] *Ibid.* at 459–60.

[23] [1992] 2 C.N.L.R. 54 (F.C.T.D.).

[24] *Ibid.* at 105–8.

[25] *Supra* note 4. For case commentary, see Owen B. Griffiths, "Case Commentary on *Blueberry River*: Is the Crown's Fiduciary Obligation in the Currents of Change?" [1996] 3 C.N.L.R. 25; J. Paul Selembier, "Crown Fiduciary Duty, Indian Title: Legacy of *Apsassin v. The Queen*" [1996] 3 C.N.L.R. 1; David Knoll, "Improvident Surrenders and the Crown's Fiduciary Obligations: *Blueberry River Band v. Canada*" (1996) 54 The Advocate (B.C.) 715. For an account of the case by the counsel for the band, see Thomas R. Berger, *One Man's Justice—A Life in the Law* (Vancouver: Douglas & McIntyre, 2002) at 243–71.

[26] *Supra* note 4 at 363.

[27] *Ibid.* at 364.

[28] *Ibid.* at 365.

[29] *Ibid.* at 365–66.

[30] *Ibid.* at 366.

[31] *Ibid.* at 371.

[32] *Ibid.* at 401.

[33] *Ibid.* at 371–72.

[34] *Ibid.* at 379–80.

[35] *Ibid.* at 382.

[36] *Ibid.* at 398.

[37] *Ibid.* at 401.

[38] *Ibid.* at 405–6.

[39] (1997), 148 DLR (4th) 523, [1998] 1 C.N.L.R. 250, (F.C.A.). For commentary, see case note by

Bob Freedman, (1997) 36 Alta. L.R. 218. See also chapter 9, text accompanying note 108 *et seq.* and note 152 *et seq.* for the discussion of remedies in this case.

⁴⁰ *Supra* note 31.

⁴¹ *Supra* note 39 at 536.

⁴² [1999] 2 C.N.L.R. 60 (F.C.T.D.). For a criticism of this judgment to the extent that it required the First Nation to prove specific facts giving rise to a fiduciary duty, see chapter 8, text accompanying note 82 *et seq.*

⁴³ [2000] 2 F.C. 314; [2000] 3 C.N.L.R. 386, 181 D.L.R. (4th) 730 (F.C.A.).

⁴⁴ (1986), 26 D.L.R. (4th) 284

⁴⁵ *Ibid.* at 292–93.

⁴⁶ [2000] F.C.J. No. 1568 (T.D.). For a criticism of the excessive attention attributed in this and other cases to the *sui generis* nature of the Crown's fiduciary obligations to Aboriginal peoples and the supposed distinction with "private law" fiduciary duties, see chapter 8, text accompanying note 171 *et seq.*

⁴⁷ [2000] 1 C.N.L.R. 245 (Sask. Q.B), aff'd [2001] 4 C.N.L.R. 120, (2001), 206 D.L.R. (4th) 683 (Sask. C.A.).

⁴⁸ *Ibid.* at para. 348.

⁴⁹ *Supra* note 6.

⁵⁰ *Supra* note 7.

⁵¹ *Ibid.* at para. 62. See *infra* note accompanying note 66 *et seq.* for s. 35 of the *Constitution Act, 1982.*

⁵² *Supra* note 1. For case comments, see Kent McNeil, "Culturally Modified Trees, Indian Reserves and the Crown's Fiduciary Obligations" (2003) 21 Sup. Ct. L. Rev. (2d) 105; David E. Elliott, "Much Ado About Dittos: *Wewaykum* and the Fiduciary Obligation of the Crown" (2003) 29 Queen's L.J. 1; Fred Fenwick, "Narrowing the Crown's Fiduciary Obligations" (2003) 27 Law Now 42; Leonard I. Rotman, "*Wewaykum*: A New Spin on the Crown's Fiduciary Obligations to Aboriginal Peoples" (2004) 37 U.B.C. L. Rev. 219.

⁵³ *Ibid.* at para. 71.

⁵⁴ *Ibid.* at para. 73.

⁵⁵ *Ibid.* at para. 86.

⁵⁶ *Ibid.* at para. 89.

⁵⁷ *Ibid.* at para. 91.

⁵⁸ *Ibid.* at para. 94.

⁵⁹ [1984] 2 S.C.R. 335 at 350.

⁶⁰ *Supra* note 1 at para. 100.

⁶¹ *Ibid.* at para. 102.

⁶² *Ibid.* at para. 103.

⁶³ *Ibid.* at para. 104. On the question of the Crown's obligation to balance competing interests, see chapter 8, text acompanying note 132 *et seq.*

⁶⁴ *Ibid.* at para. 106.

⁶⁵ *Ibid.* at paras. 107–37. See chapter 9, text accompanying note 18 *et seq.*

⁶⁶ *Constitution Act, 1982,* being Schedule B to the *Canada Act 1982* (U.K.), 1982, c. 11, s. 35(1). For judicial and academic commentary on the impact of this section, see *R. v. Agawa* (1988), 53 D.L.R. (4th) 101 (Ont. C.A.); Brian Slattery, "The Constitutional Guarantee of Aboriginal and Treaty Rights" (1983) 8 Queen's L.J. 232; Kent McNeil, "The *Constitution Act, 1982,* Sections 25 and 35" [1988] 1 C.N.L.R. 1; William Pentney, "The Rights of the Aboriginal Peoples of Canada and the *Constitution Act:* Part II – Section 35: The Substantive Guaranteee" (1988), 22 U.B.C. L. Rev. 207. For a discussion of Aboriginal rights as they existed prior to the section, see Peter A. Cumming & Neil H. Mickenberg, eds., *Native Rights in Canada,* 2d ed. (Toronto: The Indian-Eskimo Association of Canada, 1972) at 13–50.

⁶⁷ Richard H. Bartlett, "Survey of Canadian Law—Indian and Native Law" (1983) 15 Ottawa L. Rev. 431 at 500. Some Indian groups were so concerned that they applied, without success, to the English courts to prevent passage of the English legislation implementing the Act: *R. v. Secretary of State for Foreign and Commonwealth Affairs* [1982] 2 All E.R. 118, [1982] Q.B. 892 (Eng. C.A.); *Manuel v. Attorney-General,* [1982] 3 All E.R. 786 (Ch.), aff'd [1982] 3 All E.R. 822 (Eng. C.A.). This concern was not without some foundation. See, for example, the decisions of the Saskatchewan Court of Appeal

in *R. v. Eninew and R. v. Bear,* [1984] 2 C.N.L.R. 126. The original intent was that Aboriginal and treaty rights would be identified and defined at constitutional conferences (see *Constitution Act, 1982, supra* note 66, s. 37(2)) but these failed to make any substantial progress: Kent McNeil, *Emerging Justice? Essays on Indigenous Rights in Canada and Australia* (Saskatoon: Univ. of Saskatchewan Native Law Centre, 2001) at 167–73. For an account of the background to the constitutional amendments, see Donald Purich, *Our Land: Native Rights in Canada* (Toronto: Lorimer, 1986) at 183–202.

[68] [1990] 1 S.C.R. 1075. For commentary, see W.I.C. Binnie, "The *Sparrow* Doctrine: Beginning of the End or End of the Beginning?" (1990) 15 Queen's L. J. 217; Michael Asch & Patrick Maclem, "Aboriginal Rights and Canadian Sovereignty: An Essay on *R. v. Sparrow*" (1991) 29 Alta. L. Rev. 498. In *Wewaykum, supra* note 1, Binnie J. observed at para. 78 that "[t]he *Guerin* concept of a *sui generis* fiduciary duty was expanded in *R. v. Sparrow* . . . to include protection of the aboriginal peoples' pre-existing and still existing aboriginal and treaty rights within s. 35 of the *Constitution Act, 1982.*"

[69] *Sparrow, ibid.* at 1105, Dickson C.J.C. and La Forest J.

[70] *Ibid.* at 1108.

[71] *Ibid.* at 1109.

[72] See *infra* text accompanying note 77.

[73] [1996] 2 S.C.R. 507, Lamer C.J.C.

[74] *Supra* note 68 at 1099.

[75] [1996] 2 S.C.R. 723 at 797.

[76] *Supra* note 68 at 1110, Dickson C.J.C. and La Forest J. It should be noted that provincial infringement of Aboriginal and treaty rights raises serious constitutional issues: see Nigel Bankes, "*Delgamuukw*, Division of Powers and Provincial Land and Resource Laws: Some Implications for Provincial Resource Rights" (1998) 32 U.B.C. L. Rev. 317; Kent McNeil, "Aboriginal Title and the Division of Powers: Rethinking Federal and Provincial Jurisdiction" (1998) 61 Sask. L. Rev. 431; Kerry Wilkins, "Of Provinces and Section 35 Rights" (1999) 22 Dal. L. J. 185; *Haida Nation v. British Columbia (Minister of Forests)* (2002), 5 B.C.L.R. (4th) 33 at paras. 77–79, Lambert J.A.

[77] [1996] 2 C.N.L.R. 113 (B.C.C.A.) at 115–16.

[78] *Ibid.*

[79] [1996] 2 C.N.L.R. 136 (B.C.C.A.); see also the decision of the Court in *R. v. Alphonse,* [1993] 4 C.N.L.R. 19.

[80] [1996] 2 C.N.L.R. 184 (B.C.C.A.).

[81] [1996] 3 S.C.R. 101.

[82] *Ibid.* at para. 54, Lamer C.J.C. See also *R. v. Côté,* [1996] 3 S.C.R. 139 at para. 76 and *R. v. Marshall,* [1999] 3 S.C.R. 456 at para. 64, Binnie J. applying this analysis. See also *Liidlii Kue First Nation v. Canada,* [2000] 4 C.N.L.R. 123 at para. 25 (F.C.T.D.) and *Apsassin v. British Columbia Oil and Gas,* 2004 BCSC 92, [2004] 4 C.N.L.R. 284 (*sub nom. Saulteau First Nation v. British Columbia Oil and Gas Commission*) at paras. 188–92, aff'd [2004] 4 C.N.L.R. 340, 2004 BCCA 286, finding the test to be satisfied by the legislation in question.

[83] *Supra* note 75.

[84] [2003] 2 S.C.R. 207; see also *R. v. McPherson,* [1993] 1 W.W.R. 415 (Man. Prov. Ct.), rev'd (1994), 111 D.L.R. (4th) 278 (Man. Q.B.).

[85] [1997] 1 F.C. 325 (F.C.T.D.).

[86] [1998] 4 C.N.L.R. 68 (F.C.T.D.). See *infra* note 125 *et seq.* for a general discussion of the obligation to consult and accommodate.

[87] (2002), 98 B.C.L.R. (3d) 16 (B.C.C.A.), rev'd on the facts (2004), 245 D.L.R. (4th) 193, 2004 SCC 74.

[88] *Westbank First Nation v. British Columbia (Minister of Forests)* (2001), 191 D.L.R. (4th) 180, [2001] 1 C.N.L.R. 361 (B.C.S.C.); *British Columbia (Minister of Forests) v. Wilson,* 2000 BCSC 1135; *Soowahlie Indian Band v. Canada (Attorney-General)* (2001), 1 FCT 1258 (F.C.T.D.), aff'd (2001), 209 D.L.R. (4th) 677 (F.C.A.). In *TransCanada Pipelines Ltd. v. Beardmore (Township)* (2000), 186 D.L.R. (4th) 403, the Ontario Court of Appeal held that "it is only after the First Nation has established . . . infringement through an appropriate hearing that the duty of the Crown to consult with First Nations becomes engaged as a factor for the court to consider in the justificatory phase of the proceeding."

[89] *Supra* note 87 at paras. 173, 194, Rowles J.A. See also *Haida Nation v. British Columbia (Minister of Forests)* (2002), 99 B.C.L.R. (3d) 209 at paras. 29, 31, 37 (B.C.C.A.) in which this "timing fallacy" is exposed; aff'd (2004), 245 D.L.R. (4th) 33, 2004 SCC 73.

[90] *Supra* note 87.

[91] [1997] 3 S.C.R. 1010 at paras. 167–69.

[92] *R. v. Sikyea* (1964), 43 D.L.R. (2d) 150 (N.W.T.C.A.), aff'd [1964] S.C.R. 642. For a discussion of the law relating to treaties prior to section 35(1) of the *Constitution Act, 1982*, see Cumming & Mickenberg, *supra* note 66 at 53–62, 207–26.

[93] See *supra* text accompanying note 76 *et seq.* For the argument that it is inappropriate to extend the *Sparrow* test to permit justification of the infringement of treaty rights, see L.I. Rotman, *Parallel Paths*, *supra* note 2 at 125–26; L.I. Rotman, "Defining Parameters: Aboriginal Rights, Treaty Rights and the *Sparrow* Justificatory Test" (1996) 36 Alta. L. Rev. 149.

[94] [1995] 4 C.N.L.R. 78 (N.W.T. Terr. Ct.).

[95] [1996] 1 S.C.R. 771.

[96] *Ibid.* at para. 75. See also *R. v. Sundown,* [1999] 1 S.C.R. 393; *R. v. Marshall, supra* note 82, further reasons [1999] 3 S.C.R. 533.

[97] [1999] 4 C.N.L.R. 1 (B.C.C.A.).

[98] [2002] 1 C.N.L.R. 169 (F.C.T.D.) [*Mikisew Cree-F.C.T.D.*]; rev'd [2004] 2 C.N.L.R. 74, 2004 FCA 66.

[99] (1999), 66 B.C.L.R. (3d) 165 (B.C.S.C.). On the duty to negotiate generally, see *infra* text accompanying note 171 *et seq.*

[100] *Supra* note 86.

[101] [1993] 3 C.N.L.R. 55 (F.C.A.). On the question whether a competing Crown obligation provides a justification for breach of a fiduciary duty, see chapter 8, text accompanying note 132 *et seq.*

[102] (2001), 206 D.L.R. (4th) 638 at para. 194 (Sask. C.A.).

[103] [1987] 3 F.C. 174 (F.C.T.D.). See also *Derrickson v. Canada* (1991), 49 F.T.R. 295 (F.C.T.D.) in which Teitelbaum J. refused the Crown's motion to strike out a claim for breach of fiduciary duty based on the Crown's failure to provide funding for legal counsel for a former chief accused of wrongdoing.

[104] (2001), 95 B.C.L.R. (3d) 273 (B.C.C.A.), aff'd (*sub nom. British Columbia (Minister of Forests) v. Okanagan Indian Band)*, [2004] 3 S.C.R. 371, [2004] 1 C.N.L.R. 7. In *Xeni Gwet'in First Nation v. British Columbia*, [2004] 2 C.N.L.R. 391, the British Columbia Court of Appeal rejected a claim that s. 35 of the *Constitution Act, 1982* required the province to fund a land claim, noting at para. 22 that "[t]here is no authority for a general proposition of law that a fiduciary relationship requires the fiduciary to spend his money to further the interests of the beneficiary."

[105] *Ibid.* at para. 29.

[106] *Ibid.* at paras. 29, 37.

[107] *Ibid.* at para. 37.

[108] *Supra* note 59 at 353; see chapter 3, note 59.

[109] [1993] 1 C.N.L.R. 50 (F.C.T.D.); see also *Enoch Band of Stony Plain Indians v. Canada*, [1994] 3 C.N.L.R. 41 (F.C.A.). In *Stoney Band v. Canada*, [2004] 4 C.N.L.R. 348, 2004 FC 122, Gibson J. allowed the Band's appeal from a dismissal of an action against the Crown for want of prosecution. The Crown had chosen to "lie in the weeds" and took no steps to defend the action or seek a stay of action. Although not considering if a fiduciary duty existed in the circumstances, Gibson J. held that the Crown's actions were not consistent with the "honour of the Crown."

[110] *Ibid.* at 54.

[111] [1999] 4 C.N.L.R. 65 at para. 12 (F.C.T.D.).

[112] [1995] 125 D.L.R. (4th) 294 (F.C.A.), see subsequent proceedings at [1998] 2 F.C. 60 (F.C.A.). Followed in *Harry v. R.*, 2003 BCSC 533 at paras. 39–65.

[113] *Ibid.* at para. 30.

[114] (1997), 138 F.T.R. 109 (F.C.T.D.), aff'd (1998), 234 N.R. 24 (F.C.A.), leave to appeal refused, [1998] S.C.C.A. No. 579.

[115] *Ibid.* at para. 20.

[116] [1988] 2 C.N.L.R. 62 (F.C.T.D.).

[117] [1998] 3 C.N.L.R. 24 (Que. Sup. Ct.).

[118] *Ibid.* at para. 116.

[119] [1997] 9 W.W.R. 236 (Man. Q.B.), aff'd [1998] 9 W.W.R. 583 (Man. C.A.).

[120] [1988] 1 C.N.L.R. 69 (F.C.T.D.).

[121] (1997), 148 D.L.R. (4th) 356 (F.C.T.D.).

[122] [1997] 1 C.N.L.R. 1 (F.C.T.D.), aff'd (1999), 251 N.R. 220 (F.C.A.).

[123] *Ibid.* at para. 6, Rothstein J.A. For the rejection by the Supreme Court of Canada of the proposition that fiduciary obligations do not arise if the Crown is acting pursuant to a "public law" duty, see *infra* chapter 8, text accompanying note 18 *et seq.*

[124] [1995] 4 C.N.L.R. 18 (F.C.T.D.), aff'd [1997] 3 C.N.L.R. 62 (F.C.A.).

[125] There are a great number of papers on the duty to consult and accommodate. See the following: B. Fisher, "The Constitutional and Fiduciary Duties of the Provincial Crown: The Impact of Recent Decisions on the Duty to Consult & the Determination of Aboriginal Rights" in *Aboriginal Law Conference 2002* (Vancouver: Continuing Legal Education Society of British Columbia, 2002); P.G. Foy, "Communication, Consultation, Accommodation: Parsing the Haida and Taku Duties" in *Aboriginal Law Conference 2004* (Vancouver: Continuing Legal Education Society of British Columbia, 2004); W. S. Garton, "Negotiations and Consultation of Disputes with First Nations" in *Aboriginal Law Conference 1999* (Vancouver: Continuing Legal Education Society of British Columbia, 1999); J. Hunter, "Consultation with First Nations. When Does the Obligation Arise?" in *Canadian Aboriginal Law 2000* (Vancouver: Pacific Business & Law Institute, 2000); T. Isaac, "The Crown's Duty to Accommodate & Consult Aboriginal People" in *Aboriginal Law Conference 2003* (Vancouver: Continuing Legal Education Society of British Columbia, 2003), reprinted (2003) 61 The Advocate (B.C.) 865; T. Isaac & A. Knox, "The Crown's Duty to Consult Aboriginal Peoples" (2003) 41 Alta. L. Rev. 49; S. Lawrence & P. Maclem, "From Consultation to Reconciliation: Aboriginal Rights and the Crown's Duty to Consult" (2002) 79 Can. Bar Rev. 252; Pacific Business & Law Institute, *Consultation with First Nations After Delgamuukw* (Vancouver: PBLI, 1998); Pacific Business & Law Institute, *Consultations After the Taku River Tlingit and Haida Decisions* (Vancouver: PBLI, 2002); S. Rush, "Aboriginal Title In British Columbia: An Update on the Duty to Consult and the Duty to Bargain in Good Faith" in *Canadian Aboriginal Law 1999* (Vancouver: Pacific Business & Law Institute, 1999); S. Rush, "Negotiation and Consultation in British Columbia: Two Years After *Delgamuukw*" in *Aboriginal Law Conference 1999* (Vancouver: Continuing Legal Education Society of British Columbia, 1999).

[126] *Supra* note 59 at 389; chapter 4, text accompanying notes 61–62 . See also *Skerryvore Ratepayers Assoc. v. Shawanga Indian Band, supra* note 21.

[127] (2002), 5 B.C.L.R. (4th) 33 at para. 62 (B.C.C.A.) [*Haida II*], aff'd in part and rev'd in part (2004), 245 D.L.R. (4th) 33, 2004 SCC 73 [*Haida-SCC*] without reference to this point.

[128] (2002), 99 B.C.L.R. (3d) 209 at para. 55 (B.C.C.A.) [*Haida I*], aff'd *Haida-SCC, supra* note 127 without reference to this point.

[129] *Haida-SCC, supra* note 127 at para 18. See chapter 8, text accompanying note 182 *et seq* for a discussion of the relationship between the honour of the Crown and the Crown's fiduciary relationship with Aboriginal peoples.

[130] *Ibid.*

[131] *Supra* note 91 at para. 168.

[132] [1999] 3 S.C.R. 533 at para. 43.

[133] *Infra* text accompanying note 182 *et seq.*

[134] *Supra* note 91 at para. 168.

[135] *Supra* note 97; see also *Haida II, supra* note 127 at paras. 23, 34, 36, quoted *infra* text accompanying note 194, and the discussion *infra* text accompanying note 183 *et seq.* It may be noted that the obligation of accommodation does not fall on any particular ministry or person: *Lax Kw'Alaams Indian Band v. British Columbia (Ministry of Sustainable Resource Management),* 2002 B.C.S.C. 1075 at para. 34.

[136] *Haida-SCC, supra* note 127 at paras. 57–59.

[137] *Ibid* at para. 53. Consultation with third parties can be taken into account in considering the adequacy of the Crown's process of consultation: *Kelly Lake Cree Nation v. British Columbia (Minister of Energy and Mines),* [1999] 3 C.N.L.R. 126 at para. 154 (B.C.S.C.).

[138] *Haida II, supra* note 127 at para. 72, Lambert J.A. See further *infra* text accompanying note 205 *et seq.*

[139] *Haida-SCC, supra* note 127 at paras. 52–56, see *infra* text accompanying note 214 *et seq.*

[140] *Haida-SCC, ibid.* at para 42. See also *Halfway River, supra* note 97 at para. 161 per Finch J.A.; *Heiltsuk Tribal Council v. British Columbia (Minister of Sustainable Resource Management)* (2003), 19 B.C.L.R. (4th) 107, 2003 BCSC 1422 at paras. 103–18 holding that the Heiltsuk had been unwilling to avail themselves of

the consultation process and had frustrated that process and *Lax Kw'Alaams Indian Band v. Minister of Forests and West Fraser Mills Ltd*, 2004 BCSC 420 at paras. 45–49 rejecting the Band's submission of inadequate consultation because they chose not to participate in the process to approve a Forest Development Plan.

[141] *Supra* note 91 at paras. 155–59.

[142] *Mikisew Cree-F.C.T.D.*, *supra* note 98 at para. 161. In *Nunavik Inuit v. Canada*, *supra* note 86, Richard A.C.J. of the Trial Division of the Federal Court of Canada said at para. 110 that "[a]ny negotiations should also include other Aboriginal nations which have a stake in the territory claimed."

[143] *Supra* text accompanying note 130.

[144] *Haida-SCC*, *supra* note 127 at para. 35. See also *Gitxsan and other First Nations v. British Columbia (Minister of Forests)* (2002), 10 B.C.L.R. (4th) 126 at para. 86. In *Pictou v. Canada*, [2003] 2 F.C. 738 (F.C.A.), the Federal Court of Appeal held that the Mi'kmaq had failed to show they had a strong *prima facie* case of a treaty right to trade goods which they claimed were exempt from sales tax. Therefore, the Crown had no duty to consult with them before assessing them for failure to collect and remit the tax.

[145] *Mikisew Cree-F.C.T.D.*, *supra* note 98 at para 154, Hansen J. See also *Squamish Nation v. British Columbia (Minister of Sustainable Resource Management)*, 2004 BCSC 1320 at paras. 73–74.

[146] *Ibid.*

[147] *Haida II*, *supra* note 127 at para. 91. In *Musqueam Indian Band v. British Columbia (Minister of Sustainable Resource Management)*, [2004] 3 C.N.L.R. 224 at paras. 68–70, Warren J. held that subsequent consultation and accommodation may cure an earlier breach. The British Columbia Court of Appeal reversed this decision: 2005 BCCA 128.

[148] *Supra* note 98 at paras. 141, 153.

[149] *Supra* note 77 at para. 77. See also: *Halfway River*, *supra* note 97 at para. 160; *Gitxsan*, *supra* note 144 at para. 88; *Haida Nation v. British Columbia (Minister of Forests)*, [2004] 4 C.N.L.R. 56 at paras. 10, 39. In *R. v. Nikal*, [1996] 3 S.C.R. 1013, Cory J. said at para. 110: "the need for dissemination of information and a request for consultations cannot simply be denied."

[150] *Supra* note 97 at para. 161, Finch J.A.

[151] *Supra* note 80 at para. 100.

[152] *Supra* note 91 at para. 168.

[153] *Haida-SCC*, *supra* note 127 at para. 39. In *Husby Forest Products v. Minister of Forests* (2004), 25 B.C.L.R. (4th) 289, 2004 BCSC 142, additional reasons 2004 BCSC 734, Madam Justice Garson explained the steps involved in applying the consultation principles.

[154] *Haida-SCC*, *ibid.* at para. 43.

[155] *Ibid* at para. 44.

[156] *Ibid.*

[157] *Ibid* at para. 45.

[158] *Ibid.* at para. 47.

[159] *Ibid.* at para. 11. For subsequent decisions applying the decision of the Supreme Court of Canada in *Haida Nation*, see *Gitanyow First Nation v. British Columbia (Minister of Forests)*, 2004 BCSC 1734; *Blaney v. British Columbia (Minister of Agriculture, Food and Fisheries)*, 2005 BCSC 283, and *Musqueam v. British Columbia (Minister of Sustainable Resources)*, 2005 BCCA 128.

[160] *Delgamuukw*, *supra* note 91 at para. 169; *Gitxsan*, *supra* note 144 at para. 88.

[161] *Haida-SCC*, *supra* note 127 at para. 41, McLachlin C.J.C.; see also *Halfway River*, *supra* note 97 at para. 146. In *Musqueam Indian Band v. British Columbia (Minister of Sustainable Resource Management)*, *supra* note 147 at para. 68, Warren J. commented that "[d]esultory communications and lack of transparency, in my view, cannot amount to fulfilment of the Province's weighty obligations of consultation and accommodation towards Musqueam."

[162] *Gladstone*, *supra* note 75 at para. 62.

[163] *Mikisew Cree-F.C.T.D.*, *supra* note 98 at para 157. But see *Lax Kw'Alaams Indian Band v. British Columbia (Minister of Sustainable Resource Management)*, *supra* note 135 at para. 37.

[164] *Supra* note 128 at para. 48.

[165] *Supra* note 91 at para. 169.

[166] *Supra* note 127 at para. 101.

[167] *Mikisew Cree-F.C.T.D.*, *supra* note 98. In *Musqueam Indian Band v. British Columbia*, *supra* note 147 at paras. 74–76, Warren J. held that he could not determine in summary proceedings for a declaration and injunction if the duty to accommodate could be satisfied by compensation or if it required the grant of

interests in lands that the Musqueam claimed were being transferred in infringement of their Aboriginal title. He also held at paras. 81–87 that the duty did not amount to an obligation to "freeze" dispositions of all Crown-held lands pending a final determination of claims of Aboriginal title and rights.

[168] *Supra* note 68 at 1116.

[169] *Supra* note 75 at para. 62, Lamer C.J.C.

[170] *Supra* note 91 at paras. 162–69.

[171] (1997), 148 D.L.R. (4th) 96 (Ont. C.A.), leave to appeal to appeal to S.C.C. refused, (*sub nom. Perry v. Ontario)* (1997), 48 C.R.R. (2d) 376 note.

[172] *Ibid.* at 125.

[173] *Supra* note 86. See also *Musqueam Indian Band v. Canada,* [2004] 3 C.N.L.R. 252 at paras. 24–38, in which Phelan J. held that the federal Crown had a duty to negotiate with the band prior to transferring Crown lands which might be used to accommodate an infringement of their Aboriginal title and granted an interlocatory injunction to prevent the transfer.

[174] *Nunavik Inuit, ibid.* at para. 110.

[175] *Supra* note 99.

[176] *Ibid.* at para. 44.

[177] *Haida-SCC, supra* note 127 at para. 25.

[178] [1991] 2 C.N.L.R. 22 (F.C.T.D.) at 29. In *Ahenakew v. Canada,* [2003] 2 C.N.L.R. 131, 2003 FCT 306, McKay J. refused to strike out a statement of claim insofar as it sought a declaration that the Crown owed fiduciary duties to Aboriginal peoples in the development of legislation which may affect their Aboriginal, treaty, or constitutional rights.

[179] *Supra* note 1. In *Chippewas of Nawash First Nation v. Canada (Minister of Fisheries and Oceans),* [2003] 2 C.N.L.R. 78 (F.C.A.), the Federal Court of Appeal affirmed a decision that the federal government was not in breach of a fiduciary obligation in not extending the Aboriginal Fisheries Strategy from coastal communities to First Nations in Ontario. See also *Treaty Eight First Nations v. Canada (Attorney-General),* [2003] 4 C.N.L.R. 349 (F.C.T.D.) holding that there was no fiduciary obligation with respect to amending election and referendum regulations, and *Perron v. Canada,* (April 4, 2003), 01-CV-219938CP (Ont. Sup. Ct.) rejecting a claim that section 6 of the *Indian Act* regulating Indian status was a violation of the fiduciary duty owed to Aboriginal peoples by the Crown.

[180] *Ibid.* at para. 85.

[181] *Ibid.* at para. 81. It should be noted that Binnie J. had earlier stated at para. 79 that "[a]ll members of the Court accepted in *Ross River* [*supra* note 7] that potential relief by way of fiduciary remedies is not limited to s. 35 rights (*Sparrow*) [*supra* note 68], or existing reserves (*Guerin*)." It has been submitted by Professor McNeil that the "cognizable Indian interest" need not be a legal interest and may be a social or economic interest: Kent McNeil, "Aboriginal Autonomy and the Crown's Fiduciary Obligation," paper presented at the Canadian Bar Association's 2004 Canadian Legal Conference and Expo (Winnipeg, 15–17 August 2004) at 2–3.

[182] *Supra* chapter 4; see also *Blueberry River, supra* note 4.

[183] *Infra* text accompanying note 187 *et seq.* See B. Fisher, "The Constitutional and Fiduciary Duties of the Provincial Crown: The Impact of Recent Decisions on the Duty to Consult and the Determination of Aboriginal Rights" and Kathryn Kickbush, "The Provincial Crown's Fiduciary Relationship with Aboriginal Peoples" in *Aboriginal Law Conference – 2002* (Vancouver: Continuing Legal Education Society of British Columbia, 2002); see also L.I. Rotman, *Parallel Paths: Fiduciary Doctrine and the Crown–Native Relationship in Canada* (Toronto: Univ. of Toronto Press, 1996) at 221–54. For an argument that the British Crown still has a fiduciary relationship with Canada's Aboriginal peoples, see *ibid.* at 203–20; see, however, *R. v. Secretary of State for Foreign and Commonwealth Affairs, ex parte Indian Association of Alberta,* [1982] 2 All E.R. 118 (Eng. C.A.); *Manuel v. Attorney General,* [1982] 3 All E.R. 786 (Ch.), aff'd [1982] 3 All E.R. 822 (Eng. C.A.); *Noltcho v. Attorney General,* [1982] 3 All E.R. 786 (Ch.).

[184] *Haida-SCC, supra* note 127 at paras. 57–59.

[185] [2000] 2 C.N.L.R. 13.

[186] [1991] 2 S.C.R. 570 at 575. See Rotman, *supra* note 183 at 241–43.

[187] *Supra* note 95. In *R. v. Côté,* [1996] 3 S.C.R. 139 at para. 74, Chief Justice Lamer said: "The majority of recent cases which have subsequently invoked the *Sparrow* framework have similarly done so against the backdrop of a federal statute or regulation. . . . But it is quite clear that the *Sparrow* test

applies where a provincial law is alleged to have infringed an aboriginal or treaty right in a manner which cannot be justified—The text and purpose of s.35(1) do not distinguish between federal and provincial laws which restrict aboriginal or treaty rights, and they should both be subject to the same standard of constitutional scrutiny." See also *Delgamuukw, supra* note 91 at para. 186, specifically referring to provincial hunting and fishing regulations.

[188] *Supra* note 77.

[189] *Supra* note 97.

[190] *Supra* note 87.

[191] *Supra* note 99. In *Kelly Lake Cree Nation v. British Columbia (Minister of Energy & Mines), supra* note 137, Taylor J. held that the province had a duty to consult in a meaningful manner: "[t]hat obligation of the Province is no more or less than the duty enunciated in the cases that follow *Guerin v. The Queen* culminating in *Delgamuukw.*" See also *Cree School Board v. Canada (Attorney General)*, [1998] 3 C.N.L.R. 24 at para. 116–17, in which Croteau S.C.J. of the Quebec Superior Court referred to "Canada and Quebec's fiduciary duty towards the Cree."

[192] *Gitanyow, ibid.* at 101–2. The historic obligations of the colonial and provincial governments towards Aboriginal peoples was described by one writer in 1909 as follows: "just as the Dominion Government was charged by the Imperial Government under the *British North America Act* [now *Constitution Act, 1867*, s. 91(24)] with the care of the Indians and the trusteeship of lands reserved for them, so the Provincial and Colonial Governments before Confederation stood in the same position as guardians and trustees of the Indians under direction and ultimate control of the Imperial Government": Canada, Parliament, "Report on the Indian Title in Canada with Special Reference to British Columbia," 20 August 1909, by T.R.E. MacInnes, House of Commons Sessional Paper No. 47, Ottawa, 1914 at 9 [typescript at Main Library, University of British Columbia].

[193] [1990] 2 S.C.R. 85 at 108–9 [emphasis in original]. The judgment of Dickson C.J.C. is a dissenting judgment. La Forest J. said that he "questioned his conclusion that it is realistic, in this day and age, to proceed on the assumption that, from the aboriginal perspective, any federal–provincial divisions that the Crown has imposed upon itself are simply internal to itself, such that the Crown might be considered what one might style an 'indivisible entity.'"

[194] *Supra* note 128 [emphasis added]. See also *Haida-SCC, supra* note 127 at paras. 57–59, McLachlin C.J.C., and *Haida II, supra* note 127 at para. 61: "In *Halfway River First Nation v. British Columbia (Ministry of Forests)* (1999), 178 D.L.R. (4th) 666 (B.C.C.A.) this Court confirmed that the fiduciary duty is owed to the Indian people equally by the provincial Crown as by the federal Crown," Lambert J.A.; *Taku River Tlingit First Nation v. British Columbia (Project Assessment Director), supra* note 87 at paras. 161–62, 173, 194; Renee Dupuis & Kent McNeil, "Canada's Fiduciary Obligation to Aboriginal Peoples in the Context of Accession to Sovereignty by Quebec," vol. 2, Domestic Dimensions, report prepared for the Royal Commission on Aboriginal Peoples (Ottawa, Supply and Services Canada, 1995) at 24–25, 48–49; Leonard I. Rotman, "Provincial Fiduciary Obligations to First Nations: The Nexus Between Governmental Powers and Responsibility" (1994) 32 Osgoode Hall L.J. 735.

[195] *Supra* note 4.

[196] *Ibid.* at para. 111.

[197] See *supra* chapter 1, text accompanying note 6 *et seq.*

[198] *Supra* note 193.

[199] *Supra* note 20 at 608.

[200] *Supra* note 85.

[201] *Supra* note 13. In *Apsassin v. British Columbia Oil and Gas Commission, supra* note 82, the Court rejected an argument by the commission that it owed no fiduciary duties to the First Nations involved in the case because it was independent decision-making body, similar to the National Energy Board. The Court held that, unlike the NEB, the commission is an administrative decision-maker, and it must fulfil the Crown's constitutional obligations to engage in good faith consultations with First Nations with a view to accommodating their interests.

[202] *Ibid.* at 183–84.

[203] (1991), 84 D.L.R. (4th) 562.

[204] *Ibid.* at 566. See *Westbank First Nation v. British Columbia Hydro and Power Authority*, [1999] 3 S.C.R. 134 on the status of the authority as an agent of the Crown.

[205] *Supra* notes 127, 128. For commentary on this case, see J. Aldridge, "The First Nation Perspective" and J. Howard, "The Industry Perspective" in *"Haida Nation v. British Columbia and Weyerhaeuser:*

Differing Perspectives" (2003) 61 Advocate (B.C.) 177. Of course, non-Crown parties may owe fiduciary duties to Aboriginal peoples in the same circumstances in which they would owe fiduciary duties to non-Aboriginal peoples such as a lawyer to a client or an employee to an employer. For an example, see *Olsen v. Dick and Cape Mudge Band,* 2000 BCSC 220.

206 See *Haida I, supra* note 128 at para. 60. In *Musqueam Indian Band v. British Columbia (Minister of Sustainable Resource Management), supra* note 147 at paras. 77–79, Warren J. held that a third party was entitled to rely on a contractual representation by the Crown that it had met its duties of consultation. However, it ran the risk of having the contract abrogated if those duties were not, in fact, met by the Crown.

207 *Haida II, supra* note 127 at para. 138 [emphasis added].

208 *Ibid.* at paras. 118–23. In subsequent proceedings reported at [2004] 4 C.N.L.R. 56, Kelleher J. held that Weyerhaeuser's defect of title would apply to a transferee: see para. 35.

209 See *Haida II, ibid.* at paras. 99–101 for a summary of his conclusions.

210 *Ibid.* at para. 100.

211 *Ibid.* at para. 65. The cases cited in support of this principle were: *Syncrude Canada Ltd. v. Hunter Engineering Co.,* [1987] 1 S.C.R. 426; *Air Canada v. M. & L. Travel Ltd,* [1993] 3 S.C.R. 787; *Royal Bank v. Fogler, Rubinoff* (1991), 84 D.L.R. (4th) 724 (Ont. C.A.); *Gold v. Rosenberg* (1997), 152 D.L.R. (4th) 385 (S.C.C.); *Citadel General Assurance Co. v. Lloyd's Bank Canada* (1997), 152 D.L.R. (4th) 411 (S.C.C.). The doctrine of "knowing receipt" is discussed in the following: M. Bryan, "The Receipt-Based Constructive Trust" (1999) 37 Alta. L. Rev. 73; Bradley Crawford, "Constructive Thinking? The Supreme Court's Extension of Constructive Trusts to Banks on the Basis of Constructive Notice of a Breach of Trust by a Customer" (1998) 31 Can. Bus. L.J. 1; M. Ellis, *Fiduciary Duties in Canada,* looseleaf (Toronto: Carswell, 2002) at 1–8; Paul A. Finn, "The Liability of Third Parties for Knowing Receipt of Assistance" in Donovan W.M. Waters, ed., *Equity, Fiduciaries and Trusts 1993* (Toronto: Carswell, 1993); Simon Gardner, "Knowing Assistance and Knowing Receipt: Taking Stock" (1996) 112 Law Q.Rev. 56; C. Harpum, "The Stranger as Constructive Trustee" (1986) 102 Law Q. Rev. 114, 267; S.F. Hartley, "Third Party Liability for 'Knowing Assistance' and 'Knowing Receipt' on Breach of Trust" (1999) 19 E.&T. J. 71; P.D. Maddaugh & J.D. McCamus, *The Law of Restitution* (Aurora, Ont.: Canada Law Book, 1990) at 84–86; Mitchell McInnes, "Reflections on the Canadian Law of Unjust Enrichment: Lessons from Abroad" (1999) 78 Can. Bar Rev. 416; Mitchell McInnes, "Knowing Receipt and the Protection of Trust Property: *Banton v. C.I.B.C.*" (2002) 81 Can. Bar Rev. 171; Michael Ng, *Fiduciary Duties,* looseleaf (Aurora, Ont.: Canada Law Book, 2003) at 2:20.30 and chapter 11; Lord Nicholls, "Knowing Receipt: Need for a New Landmark" in W.R. Cornish et al., eds., *Restitution Past, Present and Future* (Oxford: Hart, 1998); P.M. Perell, "Intermeddlers or Strangers to the Breach of Trust or Fiduciary Duty" (1999) 21 Advocates' Q. 94; James I. Reynolds, "Aboriginal Title and the Transmission of Fiduciary Obligations from the Crown to Business—Is the Leap of Logic Galactic or Synaptic?" in *Fiduciary Obligations – 2003* (Vancouver: Continuing Legal Education Society of British Columbia, 2003); Lionel Smith, "W[h]ither Knowing Receipt?" (1998) 114 Law Q. Rev. 394; Ruth Sullivan, "Strangers to the Trust" (1984) 8 E. & T. Q. 217; D.W.M. Waters, *Law of Trusts in Canada,* 2d ed. (Toronto: Carswell, 1984) at 409.

212 *Supra* note 77 *et seq.*

213 *Haida II, supra* note 127 at paras. 77–80. For a discussion of the constitutional difficulties posed by provincial infringement of Aboriginal title, see *supra* note 76.

214 *Haida-SCC supra* note 127.

215 *Supra* text accompanying notes 129–30.

216 *Haida-SCC, supra* note 127 at paras. 52–56.

217 *Supra* text accompanying notes 212–13.

218 *Haida-SCC, supra* note 128 at para. 53.

219 *Ibid* at para. 54. See *supra* text accompanying note 211 *et seq.*

220 *Haida-SCC, ibid* at para. 18.

221 See chapter 8, text accompanying notes 156–70 for a discussion of this distinction.

222 *Haida-SCC, supra* note 127 at para. 54. For a contrary view, see Reynolds, *supra* note 211.

223 See Darwin I. Hanna, "The Fiduciary Obligations of the Chief and Council" in *Managing Aboriginal Community Assets* (Vancouver: Continuing Legal Education Society of British Columbia, 2002).

224 [1992] 4 C.N.L.R. 21 (B.C.S.C.) at 23. In *Nicola Band v. Trans-Can. Displays,* 2000 BCSC 1209, it was held that a band council has a fiduciary obligation to its members to make decisions regarding the use of band lands in the best interests of all the members. This responsibility requires it to balance competing interests in a procedurally fair process. A band council may owe a fiduciary duty to those

who are not members but may be entitled to become members: *Hodgson v. Ermineskin Indian Band,* [2000] F.C.J. No. 313 (F.C.T.D.) (QL), aff'd [2001] F.C.J. No. 2042 (F.C.A.) (QL).

225 *Ibid.* at 24.

226 *Ibid; Leonard v. Gottfriedson,* [1982] 1 C.N.L.R. 60 (B.C.S.C.).

227 [2002] 4 C.N.L.R. 280, 2002 BCSC 944.

228 [1999] 1 C.N.L.R. 14 (B.C.S.C.).

229 [2003] 3 C.N.L.R. 130 (B.C.S.C.).

230 (1997), 147 D.L.R. (4th) 615 (Ont. C.A.). See also *Buffalo v. Canada (Minister of Indian Affairs & Northern Development),* [2003] 1 C.N.L.R. 1 at para. 11 (F.C.T.D.). In *Williams v. Squamish Indian Band,* [2003] 2 C.N.L.R. 390 (F.C.T.D.), the Court held that the fiduciary duty of a band council to an infant band member did not extend to the investing of his distribution funds in an interest-bearing account to be held for his benefit until he reached the age of majority. The council could release the funds to his grandmother for his maintenance and upbringing while he was a child in her care.

231 (1996), 136 D.L.R. (4th) 383 (F.C.T.D.), aff'd (1999), 176 D.L.R. (4th) 254 (F.C.A.).

232 *Ibid.* at 398. On the relevance of the distinction, see chapter 8, text accompanying note 156 *et seq.*

233 *Supra* note 59.

234 *Supra* note 86.

235 [1993] 1 W.W.R. 415 (Man. Prov. Ct.); rev'd (1994), 111 D.L.R. (4th) 278 (Man. Q.B.).

236 [2001] 2 C.N.L.R. 291 (Ont. C.A.). See also *Report of the Royal Commission on Aboriginal Peoples: Perspectives and Realities,* vol. 4 (Ottawa: Supply and Services Canada, 1996) at 224; Dale Gibson, "When Is a Métis an Indian?" in Paul L.A.H. Chartrand, *Who Are Canada's Aboriginal Peoples?* (Saskatoon: Purich, 2003) at 262–63.

237 *Ibid.* at 338.

238 *Supra* note 77 *et seq.*

239 *Supra* note 84.

240 [1986] 3 F.C. 249 (F.C.T.D.). See also *Tuplin v. Canada (Indian & Northern Affairs),* [2002] 1 C.N.L.R. 350, in which Jenkins J. of the Supreme Court of Prince Edward Island held that the registrar of Indian and Northern Affairs did not owe a fiduciary duty in considering an individual's request to change his registration under the *Indian Act.* He did so on the basis that this was a public law duty only; see chapter 8, text accompanying note 18 *et seq.* For the United States law, see chapter 7, text accompanying notes 13–22.

241 See *Blackfoot Indian Band No. 146 (Members) v. Canada and Blackfoot Band, No. 146 (Chief and Councillors),* [1987] 2 C.N.L.R. 63 (F.C.T.D.); *Deer v. Kahnawake Indian Band* (1990), 41 F.T.R. 306 (F.C.T.D.); *B.C. Native Women's Society v. Canada,* [2000] 1 F.C. 304 (F.C.T.D.); *Bonaparte v. Canada (Attorney General),* [2003] 3 C.N.L.R. 43 (Ont. C.A.).

242 (1991), 49 F.T.R. 295 (F.C.T.D.).

243 R.S.C. 1985, c. I-5.

244 *Beattie v. Canada* (2000), 197 F.T.R. 209 (F.C.T.D.), aff'd (2001), 207 D.L.R. (4th) 374 (F.C.A.); *Blueberry River Indian Band v. Canada* (2001), 201 D.L.R. (4th) 35 (F.C.A.).

245 *Anishinaabeg of Kabapikotawangag Resource Council Inc. v. A.G. Canada,* [1998] 4 C.N.L.R. 1 (Ont. C.J. (G.D.)).

Notes to Chapter 6

1 [1984] 2 S.C.R. 335.

2 See the following texts on fiduciary law generally: Continuing Legal Education Society of British Columbia ("C.L.E."), *Fiduciary Obligations – 1998,* (Vancouver: C.L.E., 1998); C.L.E., *Fiduciary Obligations – 2003* (Vancouver: C.L.E., 2003); M.V. Ellis, *Fiduciary Duties in Canada,* looseleaf (Toronto: Carswell, 2002); P.D. Finn, *Fiduciary Obligations* (Sydney: Law Book Company, 1977); P.D. Maddough & J.D. McCamus, *The Law of Restitution,* c. 25 (Aurora, Ont: Canada Law Book, 1990); Michael Ng, *Fiduciary Duties: Obligations of Loyalty and Faithfulness,* looseleaf (Aurora, Ont.: Canada Law Book, 2003); L.I. Rotman, *Parellel Paths: Fiduciary Doctrine and the Crown–Native Relationship in Canada* (Toronto: Univ. of Toronto Press, 1996) at 149–99; J.C. Shepherd, *The Law of Fiduciaries* (Toronto: Carswell, 1981); T.G. Youdan, ed., *Equity, Fiduciaries and Trusts* (Toronto: Carswell, 1989); *Special Lectures of the Law Society of Upper Canada 1990: Fiduciary Duties* (Scarborough, Ont.: De Boo,

1991) [*Special Lectures*]; Donovan W.M. Waters, ed., *Equity, Fiduciaries and Trusts 1993* (Toronto: Carswell, 1993); A. MacInnes & B.M. Hamilton, eds., *Fiduciary Duties/Conflicts of Law*, Isaac Pitblado Lectures (Winnipeg: Law Society of Manitoba, 1993).

　　There are a large number of articles on fiduciary duties including the following: A.W. Scott, "The Fiduciary Principle" (1949) 37 Cal. L. Rev. 521; L.S. Sealy, "Fiduciary Relationships" (1962) Cambridge L.J. 69; L.S. Sealy, "Some Principles of Fiduciary Obligation" (1963) Cambridge L.J. 119; E.J. Weinrib, "The Fiduciary Obligation" (1975) 25 U.T.L.J. 1; J.C. Shepherd, "Towards a Unified Concept of Fiduciary Relationships" (1981) 97 Law Q. Rev. 51; T. Frankel. "Fiduciary Law" (1983) 71 Cal. L. Rev. 795; J.D. McCamus, "The Recent Expansion of Fiduciary Obligation" (1987) 23 E.T.R. 301; R. Flannigan, "The Fiduciary Obligation" (1989) 9 Oxford J. Legal Stud. 285; M. Gautreau, "Demystifying the Fiduciary Mystique" (1989) 68 Can. Bar Rev. 1; J. Giles, "Fiduciary Duties—The New Reach of Equity" in Frank E. McArdle, ed., *1987 Cambridge Lectures* (Montreal: Yvon Blais, 1989); R. Flannigan, "Fiduciary Obligation in the Supreme Court" (1990) 54 Sask. L. Rev. 45; Dennis Klinck, "'Things of Confidence': Loyalty, Secrecy, and Fiduciary Obligation" (1990) 54 Sask. L. Rev. 73; Leonard I. Rotman, "Fiduciary Doctrine: A Concept in Need of Understanding" (1996) 34 Alta. L. Rev. 821; Robert Flannigan, "The Boundaries of Fiduciary Accountability" (2004) 83 Can. Bar Rev. 35 [Flannigan, "Boundaries"].

[3] Flannigan, "Boundaries," *supra* note 2 at 56.

[4] Flannigan, "Boundaries," *supra* note 2 at 69, citing *Midcon Oil & Gas Limited v. New British Dominion Oil Company Limited,* [1958] S.C.R. 314; *Peso Silver Mines Limited (N.P.L.) v. Cropper,* [1966] S.C.R. 673; *Jirna Limited v. Mister Donut of Canada Ltd,* [1975] 1 S.C.R. 2; *Hawrelak v. City of Edmonton,* [1976] 1 S.C.R. 387. For accounts of the development of the law, see Justice Peter Cory, "Recent Decisions of the Supreme Court of Canada on the Fiduciary Relationship" in Continuing Legal Education Society of British Columbia, *Fiduciary Obligations – 1998, supra* note 2; Justice Beverley McLachlin, "Restitution in Canada" in W.R. Cornish, ed., *Restitution, Past, Present and Future* (Oxford: Hart, 1998); J.D. McCamus, "Promethius Unbound: Fiduciary Obligation in the Supreme Court of Canada" (1997) 28 Can. Bus. L.J. 107; Ng, *supra* note 2 at 3-1 *et seq.*

[5] (1994), 117 D.L.R. (4th) 161 at 175. See also his judgment in *M.(K.) v. M.(H.),* [1992] 3 S.C.R. 6 at 62–69. Writing extrajudicially, Justice McLachlin has also traced the modern law of fiduciary obligations to the judgment of Dickson J. in *Guerin*: Justice Beverly McLachlin, *supra* note 4 at 278–79. Both Professor W.F. Flanagan and Professor Donovan Waters have likewise traced the development of the modern law of fiduciary duty by the Supreme Court of Canada to *Guerin*: preface, text accompanying note 11. See also Flannigan, "Boundaries," *supra* note 2 at 69–70.

[6] (2002), 215 D.L.R. (4th) 496 at para. 70.

[7] In *Western Canadian Shopping Centres Inc. v. Dutton,* [2001] 2 S.C.R. 534 at para. 55, Chief Justice McLachlin noted that "[i]n recent decades fiduciary obligations have been applied in new contexts and the full scope of their application remains to be precisely defined."

[8] [1987] 2 S.C.R. 99.

[9] *Infra* note 47.

[10] *Supra* note 8 at para. 77.

[11] [1989] 2 S.C.R. 574 [*Lac Minerals*]; see case notes by Donovan W.M. Waters (1990) 69 Can. Bar Rev. 455, and Peter D. Maddough (1990) 16 C.B.L.J. 198.

[12] [1991] 3 S.C.R. 534; see P.M. Perell, "The Aftermath of Fusion: *Canson Enterprises Ltd. v. Broughton & Co*" (1993) 14 Advocates' Q. 488.

[13] [1992] 2 S.C.R. 138.

[14] [1992] 2 S.C.R. 226.

[15] *Ibid.* at 289

[16] *Supra* note 5.

[17] *Ibid.* at 61–62.

[18] *Supra* note 5.

[19] [2002] 3 S.C.R. 631.

[20] See *B.(P.A.) v. Curry* (1997), 30 B.C.L.R. (3d) 1 (B.C.C.A.), aff'd 174 D.L.R. (4th) 45 (S.C.C.).

[21] [2003] 2 S.C.R. 403; see John J.L. Hunter & Kimberly-Ann Knapp, "The *KLB* Trilogy: A Second Look at No-fault Liability" (2004) 62 Advocate (B.C.) 511.

[22] A similar result was reached in the companion case of *E.D.G. v. Hammer,* [2003] 2 S.C.R. 459.

[23] (2000), 215 D.L.R. (4th) 496 (Ont. C.A.), rev'd [2003] 2 S.C.R. 40; see S.A. Clements & J.T. Park, "*Authorson v. Canada*: Opportunity Lost?" (2003) 82 Can. Bar Rev. 535 for a case comment. In *Caille v. R.* (1991), 4 F.T.R. 59 (F.C.T.D.) involving similar facts, the Court distinguished *Guerin*.

[24] (1881), 7 A.C. 619 (H.L.); see chapter 1, text accompanying note 71.

[25] [1977] 3 All E.R. 129 (Ch.); see chapter 1, text accompanying note 74.

[26] *Supra* text accompanying note 5.

[27] *Supra* note 23 at para. 69.

[28] *Ibid.* at para. 70.

[29] *Ibid.* at paras. 72–73.

[30] [2003] 2 S.C.R. 40.

[31] See chapter 1, text accompanying note 38 *et seq.* for the history of fiduciary obligations.

[32] Justice Beverly McLachlin, *supra* note 4 at 278. For a recent, highly critical account of the Canadian law which he perceives to be in "analytical turmoil," see Flannigan, "Boundaries," *supra* note 2.

[33] L.S. Sealy, "Fiduciary Relationships" (1962) Cambridge L.J. 69 at 73. In *Lac Minerals,supra* note 11 at para. 145, La Forest J. commented that there are "few legal concepts more frequently invoked but less conceptually certain than the fiduciary relationship"; see generally: R. Flannigan, "Fiduciary Obligation in the Supreme Court" (1990) 54 Sask. L. Rev. 45; L.I. Rotman, "The Vulnerable Position of Fiduciary Doctrine in the Supreme Court of Canada" (1996) 24 Man. L.J. 60; Ng, *supra* note 2 at chapter 4.

[34] *Lac Minerals*, *supra* note 11 at 646–48, La Forest J. See chapter 8, text accompanying note 68 *et seq.* for a discussion of whether the relationship between the Crown and Aboriginal peoples is in this first class of fiduciary relationship. See Ng, *supra* note 2 at chapter 5 for a discussion of *per se* relationships generally.

[35] *Lac Minerals, ibid.* at 597; *Wewaykum Indian Band v. Canada*, [2002] 4 S.C.R. 245 at para. 83; see *infra* note 78 *et seq.*

[36] *Lac Minerals, ibid.* at 646–47; *Hodgkinson v. Simms, supra* note 5 at 176. See Ng, *supra* note 2 at chapter 6 for a discussion of *ad hoc* fiduciary relationships and below chapter 8, text accompanying note 68 *et seq.* for further discussion of the classes of fiduciary.

[37] [1975] 1 Q.B. 326 at 341.

[38] *Laskin v. Bache & Co. Inc.* (1972), 23 D.L.R. (3d) 385 at 392 (Ont. C.A.); *Goldex Mines Ltd. v. Revill* (1974), 7 O.R. 216 at 224 (Ont. C.A.).

[39] *Supra* note 1 at 384.

[40] Finn, *supra* note 2 at 8–14; Weinrib, *supra* note 2 at 4.

[41] *Supra* note 1 at 384.

[42] Weinrib, *supra* note 2 at 4.

[43] Finn, *supra* note 2 at 13.

[44] (1983), 143 D.L.R. (3d) 416 at 467; see chapter 3, text accompanying note 145.

[45] *Supra* note 1 at 384; see chapter 4, text accompanying note 49.

[46] *Supra* note 8.

[47] *Ibid.* at 136.

[48] *Supra* note 11.

[49] *Ibid.* at 599.

[50] *Supra* note 14.

[51] *Ibid.* at 292.

[52] *Supra* note 5 at 62–66.

[53] *Supra* note 5 at 178.

[54] (1996), 130 D.L.R. (4th) 193 at 209, see chapter 5, text accompanying note 25 *et seq.* On the requirements for a fiduciary relationship, see also *Cadbury Schweppes Inc. v. F.B.I. Foods Ltd*, [1999] 1 S.C.R. 142; *Fairford First Nation v. Canada (Attorney General)*, [1999] 2 C.N.L.R. 60 (F.C.T.D.); *Visagie v. TVX Gold Inc.* (2000), 49 O.R. (3d) 198 (Ont. C.A.).

[55] *Ibid.* at 232. On the requirement for vulnerability, see Rotman, *supra* note 33 and chapter 8, text accompanying note 91 *et seq.*

[56] *Supra* note 19 at para. 16.

[57] D.W.M. Waters, "The Development of Fiduciary Obligations" in R. Johnstone et al., eds., *Gerald V. La Forest at the Supreme Court of Canada 1985–1997* (Winnipeg: Canadian Legal History Project,

Faculty of Law, University of Manitoba, 2000), 81 at 83.

[58] *Supra* note 1 at 384.

[59] *Ibid.* at 386.

[60] See Finn, *supra* note 2 at 15. See also *Haida Nation v. British Columbia (Minister of Forests)* (2002), 5 B.C.L.R. (4th) 33 at para. 34 (B.C.C.A.), Lambert J.A.: "Whenever that fiduciary duty arises [i.e., the duty of both the federal and provincial Crowns to Aboriginal peoples], and to the extent of its operation, it is a duty of utmost good faith."

[61] (1973), 40 D.L.R. (3d) 371 at 381–82 (S.C.C.).

[62] *Supra* note 11 at 646–47.

[63] *Supra* note 5 at 173; see also McLachlin J. in *Norberg v. Wynrib, supra* note 14 at 272. For a discussion of fiduciary obligations and other causes of action, see *infra* text accompanying note 84 *et seq.*

[64] *Ibid.* at 214.

[65] *Supra* note 1 at 334

[66] *Supra* note 54 at 203. See also *Norberg v. Wynrib, supra* note 14 at 230, McLachlin J., and *Wewaykum, supra* note 35 at paras. 86 and 94, Binnie J. In *Haida Nation v. British Columbia (Minister of Forests)* (2004), 245 D.L.R. (4th) 33, 2004 SCC 73 at para. 18, Chief Justice McLachlin said that the Crown's fiduciary duty "requires that the Crown act with reference to the Aboriginal group's best interests."

[67] *K.L.B. v. British Columbia, supra* note 21 at para. 49. It may be noted that, subsequent to this case, the Court affirmed in *Haida Nation* the duty of the Crown to act in the best interests of Aboriginal peoples, *supra* note 66.

[68] (1990), 70 D.L.R. (4th) 385 at 409 (S.C.C.).

[69] Maddaugh & McCamus, *supra* note 2 at 588, quoting from *Meinhard v. Salmon*, 249 N.Y. 458 at 464 (C.A. 1928).

[70] (1986), 56 O.R. (2d) 274 at 286 (Ont. Div. Ct.).

[71] Finn, *supra* note 2 at 15–16, 78–81.

[72] *Ibid.* at 2; Sealy, "Fiduciary Relations," *supra* note 2 at 81; *Re Coomber*, [1911] 1 Ch. 723 at 728.

[73] Finn, *ibid.* at 1. See also Frankfurter J. in *Securities & Exchange Commission v. Cheney Corp.*, 318 U.S. 80 (1943) at 85–86: "To say that a man is a fiduciary only begins analysis. It gives direction to further inquiry: To whom is he a fiduciary? What obligations does he owe as a fiduciary? In what regard has he failed to discharge these obligations? And what are the consequences of his deviation from duty?"

[74] *Supra* note 61.

[75] *Supra* note 1 at 385. See chapter 8, text accompanying note 171 *et seq.* for a discussion of this description of the Crown's fiduciary obligations.

[76] [2001] 3 S.C.R. 746.

[77] *Ibid.* at para. 135.

[78] *Supra* note 11 at 597.

[79] *Giradet v. Crease & Company* (1987), 11 B.C.L.R. (2d) 361 at 362, Southin J.A. See *infra* text accompanying note 84 *et seq.* for the relationship between breach of fiduciary obligations and other causes of action.

[80] [2000] 3 C.N.L.R. 303 (*sub nom. Roberts v. Dick*), see also decision of the Supreme Court of Canada, *supra* note 35 at para. 83.

[81] *Ibid.* at para. 120.

[82] [1994] 1 S.C.R. 159.

[83] *Ibid.* at 183.

[84] (1998), 166 D.L.R. (4th) 475.

[85] For the relationship between breaches of fiduciary obligations and torts, see Joost Blom, "Breach of Fiduciary Obligation and Other Emerging Torts" in *Torts—1998 Update* (Vancouver: Continuing Legal Education Society of British Columbia, 1998); S.A. Clements & J.T. Park, "*Authorson v. Canada*: Opportunity Lost?" (2003) 82 Can. Bar Rev. 535; Ng, *supra* note 2 at :20.20, 7:20.30. In *Bristol and West Building Society v. Mothew*, [1996] 4 All E.R. 698 at 712, Lord Millet stated, "Breach of fiduciary obligation, therefore, connotes disloyalty or infidelity. Mere incompetence is not enough."

[86] *Supra* note 84 at para. 150.

[87] *Ibid.* at para. 154. Prof. Donovan Waters has criticized the approach taken by the British Columbia Court of Appeal in *Critchley*, noting that breach of fiduciary duty case law, including decisions by courts in the United Kingdom, supports the imposition of a broader duty that incorporates deterrent aspects rather than one which simply requires a fiduciary to avoid intentional, unauthorized self-profiting and placing

itself in a conflict situation: Donovan W.M. Waters, "The Reception of Equity in the Supreme Court of Canada (1875–2000)" (2001) 80 Can. Bar Rev. 620 at 683–84. See chapter 10, text accompanying note 47 *et seq.* for a discussion of the judgment of McEachern C.J. in the *Critchley* case.

[88] (1995), 99 F.T.R. 1.

[89] *Ibid.* at 498.

[90] (1993), 100 D.L.R. (4th) 504. See *infra* note 95 for decision of Supreme Court of Canada.

[91] See *supra* note 78.

[92] *Supra* note 80.

[93] *Supra* note 35.

[94] *Supra* note 63.

[95] *Supra* note 54 at 230.

[96] *Supra* note 35 at paras. 86 and 94. In *K.L.B. v. British Columbia, supra* note 21 at para. 40, McLachlin C.J.C. commented that the fiduciary obligations of the Crown towards Aboriginal peoples "have been held to include a requirement to use due diligence in advancing particular interests of aboriginal peoples."

[97] This view is also supported by *Lower Kootenay Indian Band v. Canada*, [1992] 2 C.N.L.R. 54 (F.C.T.D.), chapter 5, text accompanying note 23, where the Crown's "neglectful omission" in failing to ever submit a surrender for lease to the Governor in Council for acceptance constituted a breach of the Crown's fiduciary obligation to the plaintiff band. See generally Ng, *supra* note 2 at 1:20.20.

[98] See generally chapter 9 dealing with procedure, defences, and remedies.

[99] See Blom, *supra* note 85 at 9, 18.

[100] See generally Maddough & McCamus, *supra* note 2.

[101] *Supra* note 1.

[102] *Supra* note 54.

[103] *Supra* note 4 at 277. For a criticism of this "conflation of unjust enrichment and fiduciary obligations," see Mitchell McInnes, "Reflections on the Canadian Law of Unjust Enrichment: Lessons from Abroad" (1997) 78 Can. Bar Rev. 416 at 421–25.

[104] John McCamus, "Remedies for Breach of Fiduciary Duty" in *Special Lectures, supra* note 2 at 65; see Maddough & McCamus, *supra* note 2 for the Canadian law of unjust enrichment or restitution.

[105] *Supra* note 4 at 275.

[106] *Supra* note 1 at 385. On the fiduciary obligations of governments, see: Arne Peltz & Luningning Alcuitas-Imperial, "Fiduciary Obligations As a Source of Remedies Against Public Officials: The Aboriginal Context and Beyond" in A. MacInnes & B.M. Hamilton, eds., *Fiduciary Duties/Conflicts of Law*, Isaac Pitblado Lectures (Winnipeg: Law Society of Manitoba, 1993); Larissa Behrendt, "Bargaining on More Than Goodwill: Recognising a Fiduciary Obligation in Native Title" in Lisa Streilein, ed., *Land, Rights, Law: Issues of Native Title*, vol. 2:4 (Canberra: Native Title Research Unit, Australian Institute of Aboriginal and Torres Strait Island Series, 1999) at 2–3; L. Sossin, "Public Fiduciary Obligations, Political Trusts, and the Equitable Duty of Reasonableness in Administrative Law" (2003) 66 Sask. L. Rev. 129.

[107] *Supra* note 23 *et seq.* See also chapter 1, text accompanying notes 79–83 and chapter 8, text accompanying notes 18 *et seq.*

[108] Ellis, *supra* note 2 at 19-2.

[109] See *ibid* at chapter 19.

[110] *Re Collins and Pensions Commissioner of Ontario, supra* note 70.

[111] *Toronto v. Bowes* (1854), 4 Gr. 489 (U.C. Ch.), aff'd (1856), 6 Gr. 1 (U.C. C.A.), aff'd (1858), 11 Moo. P.C. 463, 14 E.R. 770.

[112] *Guitierrez v. Jeske*, 2003 ABQB 647 at paras. 110–12.

[113] *D.E. (Guardian ad litem of) v. British Columbia*, 2003 BCSC 1013 at para. 177.

[114] *Supra* note 20.

[115] *Apsassin v. British Columbia Oil and Gas Commission*, 2004 BCSC 92, [2004] 4 C.N.L.R. 284, *(sub nom. Saulteau First Nation v. British Columbia Oil and Gas Commission)* aff'd [2004] 4 C.N.L.R. 340, 2004 BCCA 286.

[116] *Supra* note 35 at para. 94. See chapter 9, text accompanying note 79 *et seq.* for remedies available for breach of fiduciary obligations.

[117] See chapter 10, text accompanying note 49 *et seq.*

[118] Flannigan, *supra* note 2 at 67.

[119] See chapter 10, text accompanying note 51 *et seq.*

Notes to Chapter 7

[1] (1998), 156 A.L.R. 721.

[2] Chapter 1, text accompanying note 95 *et seq.*

[3] 463 U.S. 206 (1983) (see *U.S. v. Mitchell*); see chapter 1, text accompanying note 127 *et seq.*

[4] *Navajo Nation v. United States*, 537 U.S. 488 (2003), 155 L.Ed. 2d 60.

[5] *White Mountain Apache v. United States*, 537 U.S. 465 (2003), 155 L. Ed. 40.

[6] 480 U.S. 700 at 707 (1987).

[7] 508 U.S. 182 (1993). See also *Rice v. Cayetano*, 528 U.S. 495 (2000) in which the majority distinguished the situation of native Hawaiians from that of Indians.

[8] In addition to the cases cited in the text, see *Pawnee v. United States*, 830 F.2d 187 (Fed. Cir. 1987); *Black Hills Inst. v. South Dakota School of Mines and Technology*, 12 F.3d 737 (8th Cir. 1993); *Coosewan v. Meridian Oil Co.*, 25 F.3d 920 (10th Cir. 1994); *Shoshone-Bannock Tribes v. Reno*, 56 F.3d 1476 (D.C. Cir. 1995); *Masayesva on Behalf of Hopi Indian Tribe v. Hale*, 118 F.3d 1371 (9th Cir. 1997).

[9] 50 F.3d 994 (Fed. Cir. 1995)

[10] *Supra* note 3.

[11] 86 F.2d 1554 (Fed. Cir. 1996).

[12] *Ibid.* at 1563.

[13] 103 F.3d 896 (8th Cir. 1997).

[14] 91 F.Supp. 2d 1 (D.D.C. 2000). For complete information on this case, see online: Indian Trust: *Cobell v. Norton*, <http://www.indiantrust.com>, and for a highly critical account of the handling of this complex litigation by the trial judge, see Richard J. Pierce Jr. "Judge Lamberth's Reign of Terror at the Department of Interior" (2004) 56 Admin. L. Rev. 235.

[15] *Ibid.* at 30.

[16] 463 U.S. 110 at 141 (1983).

[17] 240 F.3d 1081 (D.C.Cir. 2001), see also *Cobell v. Norton*, (December 3, 2004), D.C. No. 03-5262, (D.C.Cir. 2004) upholding the jurisdiction of the the District Court to issue an injunction requiring the disconnection of substantially all of the Department of the Interior's computer systems from the Internet but vacating the injunction on procedural grounds.

[18] *Cherokee Nation v. Georgia*, 30 U.S. 1 (1831); chapter 1 accompanying note 108.

[19] *United States v. Kagama*, 118 U.S. 375 (1886); chapter 1, text accompanying note 111.

[20] *Seminole Nation v. United States*, 316 U.S. 286 (1942); chapter 1, text accompanying note 116.

[21] *Supra* note 17 at 1099.

[22] *Ibid.* at 1101. The reference to contours relates back to Justice Marshall's decision in *Mitchell II*, see chapter 1, text accompanying note 141.

[23] 248 F.3d 1365 (Fed. Cir. 2001).

[24] *Ibid.* at 1372.

[25] 249 F.3d 1364 (Fed. Cir. 2001).

[26] Pub. L. No. 86-392, 74 Stat. 8 (1960).

[27] 46 F. Cl. 20 (1999).

[28] *Supra* note 11.

[29] *Supra* note 25 at 1377–78.

[30] *Ibid.* at 1381.

[31] 263 F.3d 1325 (Fed. Cir. 2001).

[32] 25 U.S.C., ss. 2101–8.

[33] 46 Fed. Cl. 217 at 219.

[34] *Supra* note 5, cited to 155 L. Ed. 2d 40. See Nell Jessup Newton, "Symposium: The Indian Trust Doctrine after the 2002–2003 Supreme Court Term: Introduction" (2003) 39 Tulsa L. Rev. 237; Gregory C. Sisk, "Yesterday and Today: of Indians, Breach of Trust, Money and Sovereign Immunity" (2003) 39 Tulsa L. Rev. 313; Raymond Cross, "The Federal Trust Duty in an Age of Indian Self-Determination: An Epitaph for a Dying Doctrine?" (2003) 39 Tulsa L. Rev. 369.

[35] *Supra* note 4, cited to 155 L.Ed. 2d 60.

[36] *Supra* note 34 at 47.

[37] *Ibid.* at 49. See chapter 1, text accompanying note 126 *et seq.* for discussion of the *Mitchell*

decisions.

38 *Ibid.* at 50.

39 *Ibid.* at 51.

40 *Ibid.* at 57.

41 *Supra* note 35.

42 *Ibid.* at 69.

43 *Ibid.* at 77–78.

44 *Ibid.* 83.

45 726 F.2d 712 (Fed. Cir. 1983) applying *Menominee Tribe v. United States*, 391 U.S. 404 (1968).

46 Reid Peyton Chambers, "Judicial Enforcement of the Federal Trust Responsibility to Indians" (1975) 27 Stanford L. Rev. 1213 at 1226 note 66.

47 Stephen L. Pevar, *The Rights of Indians and Tribes* (Toronto: Bantam, 1983) at 26–27; William C. Canby, *American Indian Law*, 3d ed. (St. Paul, Minn.: West, 1998) at 55–58.

48 *Menominee Tribe v. United States, supra* note 45. See chapter 8, text accompanying note 3 *et seq.* for a discussion of whether the fiduciary relationship between the Crown and Canadian Aboriginal peoples can be terminated under Canadian law.

49 521 F.Supp. 1072 (D.Utah 1981); see also *Navajo Tribe v. United States*, 364 F.2d 320, 322–24 (Ct. Cl. 1966) (Federal Bureau of Mines held to fiduciary standards). See chapter 5, text accompanying note 195 *et seq.* for a discussion of which government departments owe fiduciary obligations to Aboriginal peoples under Canadian law.

50 645 F.2d 701 at 711 (9th Cir. 1981) [emphasis in original]. Chambers, *supra* note 46 at 1234 note 101: the trust responsibility "is really a duty of the United States and not exclusively one of a particular department"; Russel Lawrence Barsh, *Trust Responsibility and the Coordination of Aboriginal Issues in the United States: Potential Application in Canada*, report prepared for the Aboriginal Justice Implementation Commission (Manitoba, June 2000) at 7–10, online: Aboriginal Justice Implementation Commission <http://www.ajic.mb.ca/consult.html>; Kevin H. Kono, "The Trust Doctrine and the Clean Water Act: the Environmental Protection Agency's Duty to Enforce Tribal Water Quality Standards Against Upstream Polluters" (2001) 80 Or. L. Rev. 677.

51 *American Indians Residing on the Maricopa – AK Chin Reservation v. United States*, 667 F.2d 980 (Ct.Cl. 1981) at 990; see generally Reid Peyton Chambers & Douglas B.L.Endreson, *Testimony to Senate Committee on Indian Affairs Oversight Hearings on Management of Indian Trust Funds*, 26 February 2002 at 17–27; Rodina Cave, "Simplifying the Indian Trust Responsibility" (2000) 32 Ariz. St. L.J. 1399. See also *Seminole Nation v. United States, supra* note 20 at 296–97: "as trustee of the Indians, the conduct of the United States should . . . be judged by the most exacting fiduciary standards."

52 412 U.S. 391 (1973) at 398.

53 *Supra* note 3 at 225–26, chapter 1, text accompanying note 142. See comments of Souter J. of the United States Supreme Court in *White Mountain Apache, supra* text accompanying note 39 applying "elementary trust law."

54 *Sioux Tribe v. United States*, 64 F.Supp. 312, 331 (Ct.Cl. 1946); *Manchester Band of Pomo Indians, Inc. v. United States*, 363 F.Supp. 1238 at 1248 (N.D.Cal. 1973).

55 *Supra* note 17 at 1102–3.

56 463 U.S. 110 at 128 (1983).

57 390 F.2d 686 (Ct. Cl. 1968). See chapter 8, text accompanying note 152 *et seq.*

58 448 U.S. 371 (1980).

59 Chambers & Endreson, *supra* note 51 at 27–34; Chambers, *supra* note 46 at 1243–46.

60 437 F.Supp. 543 (D.S.D. 1977), aff'd 581 F.2d 697 (8th Cir. 1978).

61 829 F.2d 787 (9th Cir. 1987). See also *Meyers v. Board of Education of San Juan School District*, 905 F.Supp. 1544 (D. Utah 1995), (United States has a trust obligation to meet the education needs of Navajo children).

62 *Supra* note 7.

63 *H.R.I. Inc. v. E.P.A.*, 198 F.3d 1224, 1225 (10th Cir. 2000); *Midwaters Trawlers Cooperative v. United States Department of Commerce*, 139 F.Supp. 2d 1136, 1145–46 (D.Wash. 2000), see chapter 5, text accompanying note 125 *et seq.* for a discussion of the duty to consult and accommodate under Canadian law.

64 For the Australian law see: Robert Blowes, "Governments: Can You Trust Them with Your Traditional

Title?" (1993) 15 Sydney L. Rev. 254, reprinted in *Essays on the Mabo Decision* (Sydney: The Law Book Company, 1993); Frank Brennan, *"Mabo* and the *Racial Discrimination Act*: The Limits of Native Title and Fiduciary Duty under Australia's Sovereign Parliaments" (1993) 15 Sydney L. Rev. 206; Camilla Hughes, "The Fiduciary Obligation of the Crown to Aborigines: Lessons from the United States and Canada" (1993) 16 U.N.S.W.L.J. 70; Lisa Di Marco, "A Critique and Analysis of the Fiduciary Concept in *Mabo v. Queensland*" (1994) 19 Melbourne U.L. Rev. 868; David Tan, "The Fiduciary As an Accordian Term: Can the Crown Play a Different Tune?" (1995) 69 Aust. L.J. 440; H.A. Amankwah, "Is the Limit of the Equitable Doctrine of Fiduciary Liability Determinable?" (1996) 3 J.C.U. L. Rev. 102; Shaunnagh Grace Dorsett, *The Crown's Fiduciary Duties to Indigenous Australians* (LL.M. Thesis, University of Calgary, 1996); Larissa Behrendt, "Bargaining on More than Goodwill: Recognising a Fiduciary Obligation in Native Title" in Lisa Strelein, ed., *Land, Rights, Laws: Issues of Native Title*, vol. 2:4 (Canberra: Native Title Research Unit, Australian Institute of Aboriginal and Torres Strait Island Series, 1999); Stuart Rush, "Aboriginal Title and the State's Fiduciary Obligation" (Paper presented to the Conference on Land and Freedom, 9–11 July 1999, Newcastle, Australia); Richard Bartlett, "Fiduciary Obligation, Traditional Lands and Aboriginal Title in Australia," Larissa Behrendt, "Lacking Good Faith: Australia, Fiduciary Duties and the Lonely Place of Indigenous Rights," and Raymond Cross, "The Future of International Indigenous Trust and Fiduciary Law: A Comparative Analysis" in *In Whom We Trust* (Toronto: Irwin Law for Law Commission of Canada and the Association of Iroquois and Allied Indians, 2002).

[65] (1992), 175 C.L.R. 1 (H.C.A.), [*Mabo (No.2)*].

[66] "Reflections on Issues of Responsibility and Power: Native Title in Australia" (Paper presented at Pacific Business Law Institute, International Indigenous Forum, Vancouver, B.C., 25–26 October 2002) at 6. For the Royal Proclamation, see chapter 1, text accompanying note 18 *et seq*. For detailed reviews and comparisons of the Aboriginal laws of Australia and Canada, see Andrew Larkan, "From Recognition to Reconciliation: The Functions of Aboriginal Law" (1999) 23 Melbourne U.L. Rev. 65; Larissa Behrendt, "The Protection of Indigenous Rights: Contemporary Canadian Comparisons," Department of the Parliamentary Library, Parliament of Australia, Research Paper 27, 1999–2000.

[67] [1996] 2 S.C.R. 507 at para. 38.

[68] Anthony Mason, "The Place of Equity and Equitable Remedies in the Contemporary Common Law World" (1994) 110 Law Q. Rev. 238 at 246–47.

[69] (1996), 138 A.L.R. 259, 186 C.L.R. 71 (H.C.A.). It is also shown by the decision of the High Court of Australia in *Hospital Products Limited v. United States Surgical Corporation* (1984), 156 C.L.R. 41 (H.C.A.) which was decided in the same year as *Guerin*. See also *Paramasivam v. Flynn* (1998), 160 A.L.R. 203 at 220–21 (F.C.A.); *Cubillo v. Commonwealth* (2000), 174 A.L.R. 97 at paras. 1292–94, aff'd (2001) 112 F.C.R. 455 at 577–78 (F.C.A.) (removal of part-Aboriginal child from mother); *Pilmer v. Duke Group Ltd* (2002), 180 A.L.R. 249 at paras. 124–25 (H.C.A.), Kirby J.; *Tusyn v. State of Tasmania*, 2004 TASSC 50 at para. 28. See generally Shaunnagh Dorsett, "Comparing Apples and Oranges: The Fiduciary Principle in Australia and Canada After *Breen v. Williams* (1996) 8 Bond L. Rev. 158; Julie Cassidy, "The Stolen Generation: Canadian and Australian Approaches to Fiduciary Duties" (2002–3) 34 Ottawa L. Rev. 175. For a critical review of the recent Australian jurisprudence on fiduciary law, see Robert Flannigan, "The Boundaries of Fiduciary Accountability" (2004) 83 Can. Bar Rev. 35 at 76–85.

[70] [1992] 2 S.C.R. 138; *supra* chapter 6, text accompanying note 13.

[71] *Supra* note 69 at para. 24.

[72] *Ibid.* at para. 40.

[73] (1987), 61 A.L.J.R. 616 (H.C.A.).

[74] *Ibid.* at paras. 16–17.

[75] *Supra* note 65. The recognition of Native title in *Mabo (No. 2)* has turned out over the last decade to have very limited results for Australian Aboriginal people: see *Western Australia v. Ward* (2002), 191 A.L.R. 1 at paras. 969–70 (H.C.A.), Callinan J. In *Wilson v. Anderson* (2002), 190 A.L.R. 313 (H.C.A.), Kirby J. (who has tended to rule in favour of Aboriginal claimants) said, at para. 126: "The legal advance that commenced with *Mabo v. Queensland [No. 2]*, or perhaps earlier, has now attracted such difficulties that the benefits intended for Australia's indigenous peoples in relation to native title to land and waters are being channelled into costs of administration and litigation that leave everyone dissatisfied and many disappointed." See generally James I. Reynolds, "Recent Developments in Aboriginal Law in the United States, Australia and New Zealand: Lessons for Canada?" (2004) 62 Advocate (B.C.) 59, 177. One of the counsel for the successful Aboriginal claimants in *Mabo (No. 2)*

has expressed his own disappointment with the results of the case: "So what has all this meant? What, in the final analysis, has been achieved from this litigation? It might be argued that the jury is still out, but to my mind, the national response is now clear. It is a sorry picture indeed. . . . [O]pportunities to deliver land justice have been squandered. . . . One is tempted sometimes, to return to the common law and draft a new statement of claim: to endeavour, for example, to establish the existence of a free-standing fiduciary duty owed by the Crown to traditional owners when dealing with their land.": B.A. Keon-Cohen, "The *Mabo* Litigation: A Personal and Procedural Account" (2000) 24 Melbourne U.L. Rev. 35. In fact, as he points out, the pleadings in *Mabo (No. 2)* were amended to raise the existence of the fiduciary duty after the *Guerin* decision (*ibid.* at notes 299–307).

[76] (1971) 17 F.L.R. 141 (N.T.S.C.).

[77] *Fejo v. Northern Territory* (1998), 156 A.L.R. 721; *Western Australia v. Ward, supra* note 75; *Wilson v. Anderson, supra* note 75; see *infra* text accompanying note 85 on the effect of a pastoral lease on Native title.

[78] See Brennan J., *supra* note 65 at 60–61: "If native title were surrendered to the Crown in expectation of a grant of a tenure to the indigenous title holders, there may be a fiduciary duty on the Crown to exercise its discretionary power to grant a tenure so as to satisfy the expectation [see *Guerin.*] but it is unnecessary to consider the existence or extent of such a fiduciary duty in this case." Deane and Gaudron J.J. suggest that actual or threatened interference with the enjoyment of native title can, in appropriate circumstances, "attract the protection of equitable remedies' (*ibid.* at 113).

[79] [1984] 2 S.C.R. 335.

[80] *Supra* note 65 at 203.

[81] *Ibid.*

[82] *Ibid.* at 169–70.

[83] (1998), 129 A.L.R. 167 (National Native Title Trib.).

[84] *Ibid.* at 187.

[85] (1996), 141 A.L.R. 129 (H.C.A.).

[86] *Ibid.* at 160. For the relevance of the expectations of the parties as a factor in the creation of a fiduciary duty, see chapter 6, text accompanying note 53.

[87] *Ibid.*

[88] *Ibid.* at 161.

[89] See judgments of Toohey J., *ibid.* at 182; Gauden J., *ibid.* at 210; and Gummow J., *ibid.* at 200.

[90] (1997), 144 A.L.R. 677 (H.C.A.).

[91] *Ibid.* at 688.

[92] *Supra* note 79.

[93] [1990] 1 S.C.R. 1075. See chapter 5, text accompanying note 68 *et seq.*

[94] *Ibid.* at 688. See chapter 1, text accompanying note 6 *et seq.* for a discussion of the basis of the fiduciary duty in the historical relationship between the Crown and Aboriginal peoples.

[95] *Ibid.*

[96] *Supra* note 65.

[97] *Supra* note 90 at 688.

[98] *Supra* notes 80–81.

[99] *Supra* note 85.

[100] *Supra* note 90 at 688.

[101] *Ibid.* at 689.

[102] *Supra* note 69.

[103] *Ibid.*

[104] (2000), 180 A.L.R. 91 (F.C.A.).

[105] *Ibid.* at para. 18.

[106] *Ibid.* at paras. 46–67.

[107] *Ibid.* at para. 66.

[108] *Fejo v. Northern Territory* (1998), 156 A.L.R. 721 (H.C.A.); *Commonwealth v. Yarmirr* (2001), 184 A.L.R. 113 (H.C.A.); *Western Australia v. Ward* (2002), 191 A.L.R. 1 (H.C.A.); *Wilson v. Anderson* (2002), 190 A.L.R. 313 (H.C.A.); *Yorta Yorta Aboriginal Community, Members of v. Victoria* (2002), 194 A.L.R. 538 (H.C.A.). In *Coe v. The Commonwealth* (1993), 118 A.L.R. 199 (H.C.A.), Mason C.J.

struck out a claim for breach of fiduciary duty on the basis of inadequate pleadings. He said it would not be appropriate in an application to strike out the claim to decide whether Toohey J. was correct in *Mabo (No. 2)* that the duty arose out of the power of the Crown to extinguish traditional title or whether Dawson J. was correct in his suggestion that the subsistence of an Aboriginal interest in land is essential to the creation of a fiduciary relationship. It may be noted that, in *Nulyarimma v. Thompson*, [1999] FCA 1192 at paras. 225–29, the Full Court of the Federal Court of Australia rejected a claim for breach of fiduciary obligation based on the failure to proceed with the listing of lands under the World Heritage Convention, and in *Noble & McBride v. State of Victoria & State of Queensland*, 1999 QCA 110, the Queensland Court of Appeal rejected a claim that a fiduciary duty was owed by the state governments to pay a reward to the descendents of Aboriginal policemen for helping to capture the famous Australian outlaw Ned Kelly; see esp. McPherson J.A. at paras. 22–24.

[109] *Supra* note 90 at 689. Compare the following comment by Professor Flannigan, who suggests the opposite conclusion for the relationship between general fiduciary law and the duties owed by the Crown to Aboriginal peoples: "It may be that the Australians are so concerned to avoid the application of the *Guerin/Sparrow* analysis to their own aboriginal/Crown issues that they are unduly restrictive in their general analysis," Flannigan, *supra* note 69 at 84. He provides no authority for this suggestion.

[110] See generally: Paul McHugh, *The Maori Magna Carta* (Auckland: Oxford Univ. Press, 1991) esp. at 239–64; Katherine S.A. Gordon, "Building Sustainable Relationships: The New Zealand Experience" in *Treaty Making—New Solutions & Innovative Approaches* (Vancouver: Pacific Business & Law Institute, 2000); Donna Hall "The Fiduciary Relationship Between Maori and the Government in New Zealand" in *In Whom We Trust, supra* note 64.

[111] Reproduced in the First Schedule to the *Treaty of Waitangi Act 1975*, 1975/114, reprinted with amendments: R.S.N.Z., 33 RS 907. See generally on the case law under the treaty: *New Zealand Maori Council v. Attorney General*, [1987] 1 N.Z.L.R. 641 (C.A.); *Ngati Apa v. Attorney General*, [2003] 3 N.Z.L.R. 643 at paras. 14–48 (C.A.), Elias C.J.

[112] See *R. v. Symonds*, [1840] N.Z.P.C.C. 387; *Kauwaenga* (1870), reported at (1984) 14 V.U.W.L.R. 227 (Maori Land Ct.). Since 1862, there have been *Native Land Acts* which have established Native (later Maori) Land Courts which investigate traditional ownership of land and convert such ownership into freehold grants. This scheme is still found within the present legislation, *Te Ture Whenua Maori Act 1993*, (N.Z.), 1993/4. See generally, Richard Boast *et al.*, *Maori Land Law* (Wellington: Butterworths, 1999).

[113] [1941] 2 All E.R. 93 (P.C.). In *Wi Parata v. Bishop of Wellington*, (1877) 3 N.Z. Jur. R. (N.S.) S.C. 72, Sir James Prendergast dismissed the treaty as "a simple nullity." The decision was criticized by the Privy Council in *Nireaha Tamaki v. Baker*, [1901] A.C. 561, in which, giving the judgment of Court, Lord Davey referred to the argument that there is no customary law of the Maoris of which the courts of law can take cognizance and said, at 577, the argument went too far and "that it was rather late in the day for such an argument to be addressed by a New Zealand court."

[114] *Ibid.* at 98.

[115] *Supra* note 111.

[116] McHugh, *supra* note 110 at 3.

[117] *Ibid.* at 1–9.

[118] In *New Zealand Maori Council v. Attorney General*, [1994] 1 N.Z.L.R. 513 (P.C.), Lord Woolf, giving the judgement of the Privy Council, noted, at 517, that "[w]ith the passage of time, the 'principles' which underlie the Treaty have become much more important than its precise terms."

[119] See *infra* text accompanying note 126.

[120] [1987] 1 N.Z.L.R. 641 (C.A.).

[121] *Ibid.* at 664.

[122] *Ibid.* at 667.

[123] [1989] 2 N.Z.L.R. 142 (C.A.).

[124] *Ibid.* at 152.

[125] [1990] 2 N.Z.L.R. 641 (C.A.).

[126] *Ibid.* at 655.

[127] [1993] 2 N.Z.L.R. 301 (C.A.).

[128] *Ibid.* at 306.

[129] [1994] 1 N.Z.L.R. 513 (P.C.).

[130] *Ibid.* at 517.

[131] [1994] 2 N.Z.L.R. 20 (C.A.). For a further discussion of such title, see *Ngati Apa v. Attorney General, supra* note 111 and, especially as it relates to claims to the foreshore and sea spaces, C. Rebecca Brown & James I. Reynolds, "Aboriginal Title to Sea Spaces: A Comparative Study" (2004) 37 U.B.C. L. Rev. 459 at 478–91.

[132] *Supra* note 112.

[133] *Supra* note 131 at 24.

[134] [1995] 3 N.Z.L.R. 553 (C.A.).

[135] See generally chapter 5, text accompanying note 125 *et seq.* for the Canadian law on the duty to consult and accommodate.

[136] *Supra* note 134 at 559.

[137] *Ibid.* at 560.

[138] [2002] 2 N.Z.L.R. 17. See chapter 1, text accompanying note 69 *et seq.* for a discussion of the political trust doctrine.

[139] *Ibid.* at para 21.

[140] *Supra* note 51 *et seq.*

[141] Chapter 8, text accompanying note 171 *et seq.*

[142] *Supra* text accompanying note 108 *et seq.*

[143] *Supra* text accompanying note 66 *et seq* and see note 75.

[144] Behrendt, *supra* note 64 at 265; see chapter 10, text accompanying note 9.

[145] See chapter 5, text accompanying note 66 *et seq.*

[146] *Supra* text accompanying note 112.

[147] *Supra* text accompanying note 111.

[148] *Supra* text accompanying note 115.

[149] *Treaty of Waitangi (Fisheries Claims) Settlement Act 1992*, (N.Z.) 1992/121; *supra* text accompanying note 127.

[150] *R. v. Van der Peet, supra* note 67 at para. 31.

[151] *Supra* text accompanying note 121.

[152] See chapter 5, text accompanying note 140.

[153] See chapter 10, text accompanying note 42 *et seq.*

Notes to Chapter 8

[1] [1984] 2 S.C.R. 335.

[2] For further discussion of the questions raised by *Guerin,* see J.I. Reynolds & L. Harvey, "The Fiduciary Obligation of the United States and Canadian Governments Towards Indian Peoples" in *Indians and the Law II* (Vancouver: Continuing Legal Education Society of British Columbia, 1985) at 30–33. See also questions raised by Donovan W.M. Waters, "New Direction in the Employment of the Equitable Doctrines: The Canadian Experience" in T.G. Youdan, ed., *Equity, Fiduciaries and Trusts* (Toronto: Carswell, 1989) at 421–23; Gord Hannon "Benefits and Burdens: A Number of Questions About Fiduciary Duties of the Provincial Crown to Aboriginal People" in *UFO's—Unidentified Fiduciary Obligations* (Winnipeg: Canadian Bar Association, 28 May 1994); Leonard I. Rotman, *Parallel Paths: Fiduciary Doctrine and the Crown–Native Relationship in Canada* (Toronto: Univ. of Toronto Press, 1996) at 203–90; and Charles Pryce, "Commentary" in *In Whom We Trust* (Toronto: Irwin Law for Law Commission of Canada, 2002) at 213.

[3] Reynolds & Havey, *supra* note 2 at 30.

[4] [1990] 1 S.C.R. 1075 at 1110; see chapter 5, text accompanying note 68 *et seq.*

[5] *Constitution Act, 1982,* being Schedule B to the *Canada Act 1982* (U.K.), 1982, c. 11.

[6] It has been suggested by Professor Rotman that it would be "unseemly" to allow the Crown to unilaterally terminate its fiduciary relationship with Aboriginal peoples: *supra* note 2 at 257. He further suggests that, even if *Guerin* were to be overturned, the Crown's duty would continue to exist on an "extralegal plane." He concludes that the relationship "may be seen to exist at the pleasure of the aboriginal peoples" (*ibid.*). See also Renee Dupuis & Kent McNeil, *Canada's Fiduciary Obligation in the Context of Accession to Sovereignty by Quebec,* vol. 2, Domestic Dimensions (Ottawa: Royal Commission on Aboriginal Peoples, 1995) at 2.

[7] See chapter 5, text accompanying note 195 *et seq.*

[8] [1995] 4 S.C.R. 344 at paras. 110–11; see chapter 5, text accompanying note 195 *et seq.*

[9] See chapter 5, text accompanying notes 197–98.

[10] See *infra* text accompanying note 132 *et seq.* See chapter 7, text accompanying note 49 *et seq.* for the position under the laws of the United States.

[11] See text accompanying chapter 5 note 187 *et seq.*

[12] [1999] 3 C.N.L.R. 89 (B.C.S.C.).

[13] [1999] 4 C.N.L.R. 1 (B.C.C.A.).

[14] [1998] 3 C.N.L.R. 24 (Qc. Sup. Ct.).

[15] [1999] 3 C.N.L.R. 126 (B.C.S.C.).

[16] [2002] 2 C.N.L.R. 121, 99 B.C.L.R. (3d) 209; further reasons: (2002), 5 B.C.L.R. (4th) 33 (B.C.C.A.), aff'd (2004), 245 D.L.R. (4th) 33, 2004 SCC 73.

[17] [2000] 2 C.N.L.R. 13 at para. 34 (Ont. C.A.). See chapter 5, text accompanying note 185.

[18] [2002] 4 S.C.R. 245 [*Wewaykum*].

[19] [1999] 2 C.N.L.R. 60 (F.C.T.D.).

[20] (1999), 251 N.R. 220 (F.C.A.).

[21] [2000] 1 C.N.L.R. 205 (F.C.T.D.).

[22] (2001), 207 Nfld. & P.E.I.R. 292 (P.E.I.T.D.).

[23] *Supra* note 18 at para. 85. See *Treaty Eight First Nations v. Canada (Attorney-General)*, [2003] 4 C.N.L.R. 349 at paras. 56–71 (F.C.T.D.).

[24] *Supra* note 1.

[25] *Ibid.* at 385.

[26] *Ibid.* [emphasis added]. See generally on governments as fiduciaries: chapter 6, text accompanying note 106 *et seq.*

[27] Part 1 of the *Constitution Act, 1982, supra* note 5.

[28] *Lavigne v. O.P.S.E.U.*, [1991] 2 S.C.R. 211 at 314, La Forest J. for the majority.

[29] *Supra* note 4.

[30] [1996] 3 S.C.R. 101.

[31] [1996] 1 S.C.R. 771.

[32] [1997] 3 S.C.R. 1010.

[33] [1999] 3 S.C.R. 533 at para. 32 per the Court. See chapter 6, text accompanying note 106 *et seq.* for a general discussion of governments as fiduciaries.

[34] *Ibid.* at 564.

[35] *Supra* note 4 at 1114.

[36] *Supra* note 31 at para. 97, Cory J.; see also *R. v. Nikal*, [1996] 1 S.C.R. 1013 at para. 109, Cory J.

[37] P.D. Finn, *Fiduciary Obligations* (Sydney: Law Book Company, 1977) at 3. See also Lorne Sossin, "Public Fiduciary Obligations, Political Trusts and the Equitable Duty of Reasonableness in Administrative Law" (2003) 66 Sask. L. Rev. 129 at 146–59.

[38] Sir Anthony Mason, "The Place of Equity and Equitable Remedies in Contemporary Common Law," (1994) 110 Law Q. Rev. 238 at 238.

[39] (1995), 129 A.L.R. 167 at 179 (Aust. National Native Trib.); see chapter 7, text accompanying note 83.

[40] R.P. Meagher, W.M.C. Gummow & J.R.F. Lehane, *Equity—Doctrines and Remedies,* 3d ed. (Sydney: Butterworths, 1992).

[41] [1948] 1 K.B. 223 at 230 (Eng. C.A.).

[42] (1990), 96 A.L.R. 153 at 167 (H.C.A.).

[43] [1925] A.C. 578 at 596, 603–4 (H.L.); see chapter 1, text accompanying notes 79–80.

[44] [1983] 1 A.C. 768 at 815, 838 (H.L.); see chapter 1, text accompanying notes 81–83.

[45] *Supra* note 18. See also *K.L.B. v. British Columbia*, [2003] 2 S.C.R. 403 at para. 40, McLachlin C.J.C.; *supra* chapter 6, text accompanying note 21.

[46] *Supra* note 1 at 378–79.

[47] *Ibid.* at 385.

[48] *Supra* note 18 at para. 76.

[49] *Ibid.* at para. 82; see chapter 5, text accompanying note 179 for the full quotation.

[50] *Ibid.* at paras. 83–85.

[51] *Supra* note 1 at 385.

[52] *Supra* note 20 at para. 6.

[53] S.C. 1999, c. 24. The Act has been extended to additional First Nations by *Order Amending the Schedule to the First Nations Land Management Act,* P.C. 2003-714, 15 May 2003.

[54] Clause 50.2 of the Framework Agreement expressly excludes vicarious liability on the part of the Crown for the acts or omissions of a First Nation after the First Nation's land code takes effect. However, this exclusion of liability would not seem broad enough to cover the Crown's liability for its own acts or omissions including any duty to provide assistance to, or supervision of, a First Nation which assumes management of its reserve lands. It may be noted that it is now established that the band council is also under a fiduciary obligation: see chapter 5, text accompanying note 223 *et seq.*

[55] *Supra* note 18.

[56] *Supra* note 4.

[57] *Ibid.* at 1108.

[57] *Supra* note 18 at para. 79.

[58] *Ibid.* at para. 80.

[60] *Ibid.*

[61] *Ibid.*

[62] Rotman, *supra* note 2 at 259–60. See also Kent McNeil, "Aboriginal Autonomy and the Crown's Fiduciary Obligation", a paper presented to the Canadian Bar Association's Canadian Legal Conference and Expo, Winnipeg, Manitoba, 15–17 August 2004, at 8.

[63] [1989] 1 S.C.R. 322. See J.M. Evans & B. Slattery, "Federal Jurisdiction—Pendant Parties—Aboriginal Title and Federal Common Law—Charter Challenges—Reform Proposal: *Roberts v. Canada*" (1989) 66 Can. Bar Rev. 732.

[64] [1996] 3 S.C.R. 139. For a discussion of the federal common law of Aboriginal and treaty rights, see Robert Mainville, *An Overview of Aboriginal and Treaty Rights and Compensation for Their Breach* (Saskatoon: Purich, 2001) at 61–70. On the extent and scope of the fiduciary obligations owed to the Aboriginal peoples of Quebec, see Dupuis & McNeil, *supra* note 6.

[65] *Ibid.* at para. 49.

[66] R.S.B.C. 1996, c. 464.

[67] [1982] 2 F.C. 385 at 429–30; *supra* note 1 at 356.

[68] *Wewaykum, supra* note 18 at para. 83; *Lac Minerals Ltd. v. International Corona Resources Ltd.,* [1989] 2 S.C.R. 574 at 597 [*Lac Minerals*], Sopinka J. See chapter 6, text accompanying note 78 *et seq.*

[69] *Infra* note 74.

[70] *Infra* notes 77–81; see chapter 5, text accompanying notes 10–16.

[71] *Infra* notes 82–86.

[72] *Supra* note 68.

[73] *Hodgkinson v. Simms,* [1994] 3 S.C.R. 377 [*Hodgkinson*].

[74] *Supra* note 68 at 646–47.

[75] [1987] 2 S.C.R. 99; see *infra,* text accompanying note 91 for this "rough and ready guide."

[76] *Supra* note 68 at 648.

[77] [2000] 3 C.N.L.R. 303 at para. 120 (F.C.A.) (*sub nom. Roberts v. Canada*).

[78] [1994] 1 S.C.R. 159 at 183, Iacobucci J. For futher discussion, see chapter 5, text accompanying note 11 *et seq.*

[79] [2000] 1 C.N.L.R. 245 (Sask. Q.B.) at paras. 344–45.

[80] *Supra* note 1.

[81] *Supra* note 4.

[82] *Supra* note 19.

[83] *Supra* note 20.

[84] [2000] 3 C.N.L.R. 386, 181 D.L.R. (4th) 730 (F.C.A.).

[85] 2000 BCSC 1135.

[86] [2000] F.C.J. No. 1568 (F.C.T.D.). Compare S. Ronald Stevenson, "Is the Fiduciary Role of Government Changing?" in *The 2001 Isaac Pitblado Lectures: Practising Law in an Aboriginal Reality*

(Winnipeg: Law Society of Manitoba, 2001) at 88 suggesting, without any detailed analysis, that "this relationship seems closer to the second than the first category. It is necessary to examine the specific facts of any claim to see if it is fiduciary in character."

[87] *Supra* note 19 at para 41.

[88] *Supra* note 1 at 384.

[89] *Supra* note 74.

[90] *Supra* note 75.

[91] *Ibid.* at 136.

[92] *Ibid.* at 137, quoted with approval by Sopinka J. in *Lac Minerals, supra* note 68 at 607. For a discussion of vulnerability as a factor in fiduciary relationships, see Leonard Rotman, "The Vulnerable Position of Fiduciary Doctrine in the Supreme Court of Canada" (1996) 24 Man. L.J. 60.

[93] E. Weinrib, "The Fiduciary Obligation" (1975) 25 U.T.L.J. 1 at 7. See *Lac Minerals, supra* note 68 at 600, Sopinka J.; *Guerin, supra* note 1 at 384, Dickson J; *Wewaykum, supra* note 18 at para. 80, Binnie J.

[94] *Supra* note 73 at 409.

[95] *Supra* note 91.

[96] *Supra* note 94.

[97] Gerald Donegan, *Analysis of the Function and Application of Fiduciary Obligation* (LL.M. Thesis, McGill University, 1996) [unpublished] at 10. See also Michael Hudson, "Crown Fiduciary Duties Under the Indian Act" in Andrea P. Morrison & Irwin Cotler, eds., *Justice for Natives—Searching for Common Ground* (Montreal and Kingston: McGill & Queen's University, 1997) at 257.

[98] *Supra* note 18 at paras. 79–80. The Royal Commission on Aboriginal Peoples commented that "[t]he relationship between Aboriginal peoples and the Crown reflects the classic fiduciary paradigm of one party's vulnerability to another's power and discretion": *Report of the Royal Commission on Aboriginal Peoples: Restructuring the Relationship*, vol. 2 (Ottawa: Supply and Services Canada, 1996) at 43.

[99] R.S.C. 1985, c. I-5.

[100] [2000] 1 S.C.R. 950 at para. 69; see *Report of the Royal Commission of Aboriginal Peoples, supra* note 98, especially vol. 3 for the social conditions of Aboriginal peoples.

[101] *Supra* note 77.

[102] *Ibid.* at para. 120.

[103] *Supra* note 68.

[104] *Supra* note 74.

[105] *Supra* note 18.

[106] *Ibid.* at para. 85.

[107] *Ibid.* at para. 80.

[108] *Supra* note 93.

[109] *Supra* note 68 at 597.

[110] *Supra* note 18 at para. 83.

[111] *Ibid.* See also *Haida Nation v. British Columbia (Minister of Forests)* (2004), 245 D.L.R. (4th) 33, 2004 SCC 73 at para. 18, McLachlin C.J.C.

[112] [2002] 2 S.C.R. 816.

[113] [1995] 4 S.C.R. 344.

[114] *Supra* note 1.

[115] *Wewaykum, supra* note 18 at para. 85. See also Michael Ng, *Fiduciary Duties: Obligation of Loyalty and Faithfulness,* looseleaf (Aurora, Ont.: Canada Law Book, 2003) at 2:20.10: "Thus, a multitude of relationships are fiduciary per se, including those that might be described as . . . political (such as Crown–Indians)," *ibid.* at 5:20.60.20; Peter D. Maddough, "Definition of Fiduciary Duty" in *Fiduciary Obligations—2003* (Vancouver: Continuing Legal Education Society of British Columbia, 2003): "In Canada, for example, we would now have to include among the established categories of fiduciaries the relationship between the Crown and Aboriginal Canadians."

[116] *Supra* text accompanying note 74.

[117] *Supra* note 19.

[118] *Supra* notes 83–86.

[119] (1997), 148 D.L.R. (4th) 96 (Ont. C.A.).

[120] *Supra* note 17.

121 *Supra* note 119 at 124.

122 2000 BCSC 1135 at para. 91, aff'd (2002), 95 B.C.L.R. (3d) 273 at para. 29 (B.C.C.A.); aff'd, without reference to this point, [2003] 2 S.C.R. 371.

123 *Supra* note 1.

124 *Supra* note 8.

125 (1997), 148 D.L.R. (4th) 523.

126 *Supra* note 13.

127 *Supra* note 12.

128 *Supra* note 4.

129 Part I of the *Constitution Act, 1982, supra* note 5.

130 *Supra* note 28 at 315.

131 *Supra* note 4 at 1106.

132 *Kruger v. The Queen* (1985), 17 D.L.R. (4th) 591 (F.C.A.).

133 *Ibid.* at 608.

134 [1993] 3 C.N.L.R. 55 (F.C.A.).

135 *Ibid.* at 63. Professor Parkinson is critical of *Guerin* on the grounds that it "cannot be said that government owes a duty of loyalty to act only in the interests of aboriginal peoples, for the responsibility of government is that balances must be found between different legitimate community interests and needs": P. Parkinson, ed., *The Principles of Equity* (Sydney: Law Book Co., 1996) at 360.

136 [1995] 2 F.C. 762 (F.C.A.).

137 *Supra* note 19.

138 *Supra* note 84.

139 *Supra* note 4, see chapter 5, text accompanying note 77 *et seq.* for a discussion of this test.

140 *Supra* note 32.

141 *Supra* note 30.

142 *Supra* note 31.

143 *Supra* note 133.

144 *Osoyoos Indian Band v. Oliver (Town)*, [2001] 3 S.C.R. 746; *infra* note 147.

145 (1992), 175 C.L.R. 1, see *supra* chapter 7, text accompanying note 75 *et seq.* for a discussion of this judgment.

146 *Ibid.* at 205.

147 *Supra* note 144 at paras. 52–53; see Leonard I. Rotman, "*Wewaykum:* A New Spin on the Crown's Fiduciary Obligations to Aboriginal Peoples?" in *Canadian Aboriginal Law 2003* (Ottawa: Pacific Business & Law Institute, 2003) at 12.8–12.9.

148 *Supra* note 18.

149 *Ibid.* at para. 86.

150 *Ibid.* at para. 96 [emphasis in original].

151 *Ibid.* at para. 104.

152 390 F.2d 686 at 691 (Ct. Cl. 1968).

153 448 U.S. 371 (1980). See J.D. Hurley, "Aboriginal Rights in Modern American Case Law" [1983] 2 C.N.L.R. 9 at 37.

154 *Ibid.* at 408.

155 *Ibid.* at 408–9.

156 See chapter 1, text accompanying note 38 et seq. for the origins of fiduciary obligations and chapter 6 discussing fiduciary relationships in general.

157 (1879), 11 Ch. D. 772 at 778.

158 See chapter 4, text accompanying note 19 *et seq.*

159 Dickson J., *supra* note 1 at 376, Wilson J., *supra* note 1 at 355.

160 *Ibid.* at 391.

161 *Ibid.* at 394–95.

162 *Supra* note 4 at 1107–8, 1114.

163 [1996] 1 S.C.R. 1013 at para. 109, Cory J.

164 *Supra* note 31 at para. 97, Cory J.

[165] [1999] 3 S.C.R. 533 at para. 32 per the Court.

[166] *Supra* note 8 at para. 13. In *Enoch Band of Stony Plain Indians v. Canada*, [1994] 3 C.N.L.R. 41 (F.C.A.), the Federal Court of Appeal upheld a band's appeal from an order that references to a trust or breach of trust should be removed from a statement of claim filed by it. The Court noted, at 42–43, that "we are dealing with an area of the law which cannot be said to be settled with certainty."

[167] [1998] 2 F.C. 60 at 74–75.

[168] *Supra* note 111 at para. 54 quoting *Guerin, supra* note 1 at 386.

[169] Ng, *supra* note 115 at 1:20.10.20. Compare the analysis of the English Court of Appeal in *Bristol and West Building Society v. Mothew*, [1996] 4 All E.R. 698, distinguishing between breach of fiduciary duty and breach of trust. The distinction between a breach of trust and a breach of fiduciary obligation may be relevant in some cases. For example, in *Moon (Guardian Ad Litem Of) v. Campbell River Indian Band* (1996), 136 D.L.R. (4th) 383 (F.C.T.D.), aff'd (1999), 176 D.L.R. (4th) 254 (F.C.A.), the limitation period for a breach of trust was ten years but the limitation period for a breach of fiduciary obligation was not stated and it was argued that a six-year period would apply in the absence of an express limitation period. The Court decided that there was a breach of trust. See chapter 5, text accompanying note 231.

[170] *Supra* note 1 at 376. Note that the United States law generally applies traditional principles of trust law to the relationship between the government and Aboriginal peoples; see chapter 7, text accompanying notes 51 and 140 *et seq.*

[171] *Supra* note 1 at 386–87. It has been suggested by Professor Bartlett that Dickson J. adopted, *sub silentio*, the language of a *sui generis* relationship from a student note on the decision of the United States Supreme Court in *Mitchell II*, 463 U.S. 206 (1983): Richard H. Bartlett, "Indian Reserves and Aboriginal Lands" in *Canada: A Homeland* (Saskatoon: Univ. of Saskatchewan Native Law Centre, 1990) at 197 note 102. Professor Flannigan has observed that Justice Dickson "uses the phrase *'sui generis'* three times, first in relation to the Indian interest 'in the land' (at 339), then the 'relationship' (at 341) and then the 'fiduciary obligation' (at 343). Taken literally, he has characterized as *sui generis* both the Indian/Crown relation and the fiduciary obligation that governs the relation. The latter, however, does not necessarily follow from the former": Robert Flannigan, "The Boundaries of Fiduciary Accountability" (2004) 83 Can. Bar Rev. 35 at 63 note 81. As he comments, this adds a measure of uncertainty.

[172] *Supra* note 136 at 774.

[173] *Supra* note 18 at para. 96. See also *Haida Nation v. British Columbia (Minister of Forests), supra* note 111 at para. 18 in which McLachlin C.J.C., writing for the Court, said, "The content of the fiduciary duty may vary to take into account the Crown's other broader obligations."

[174] Before his appointment to the Supreme Court of Canada, Justice Binnie commented that "the description first coined in *Guerin*, has been repeated in subsequent cases as if repetition will make it a definition as opposed to an adamant refusal to essay a definition": W.I.C. Binnie, "The *Sparrow* Doctrine: Beginning of the End or End of the Beginning?" (1990) 15 Queen's L.J. 217 at 222. He referred to the description of Aboriginal rights as *"sui generis"* as "really a non-description" and "in the grand tradition of Supreme Court of Canada cases that have raised ambiguity about the content of Aboriginal rights to a high art form," *ibid.* at 221. However, giving the judgment of the Court in *Wewaykum, supra* note 18, he continued the practice of referring to the relationship in this way.

[175] Rotman, *supra* note 2 at 155–56.

[176] *Ibid.* at 155.

[177] [1975] 1 Q.B. 326 at 341(Eng. C.A.).

[178] *Supra* note 18 at para. 92.

[179] [1992] 2 S.C.R. 138 at 149.

[180] *R. v. Neil*, [2002] 3 S.C.R. 631.

[181] *Supra* chapter 6, text accompanying note 58 *et seq.*

[182] *Supra* note 111; see chapter 5, text accompanying note 129 *et seq.*

[183] *Ibid.* at para. 17; see chapter 1, text accompanying note 14.

[184] *Ibid.* at para. 18.

[185] *Ibid.* See *Wewaykum, supra* note 18, text accompanying notes 55 and 111 *et seq.*

[186] See chapter 4, text accompanying note 56, and *supra* text accompanying note 159.

[187] See *supra* text accompanying note 170.

[188] *Supra* note 16. See chapter 5, text accompanying note 127 *et seq.*

189 *Supra* note 45; see chapter 6, text accompanying note 21 *et seq.*

190 See chapter 10, text accompanying note 49 *et seq.*

191 *Supra* note 4 at 1107.

192 (1981), 34 O.R. (2d) 360 at 367.

193 *Supra* note 4 at 1108–9.

194 [1996] 2 S.C.R. 507 at para. 24.

195 [2001] 1 S.C.R. 911.

196 *Supra* note 18 at para. 80.

197 Leonard Rotman, "*Wewaykum:* A New Spin on the Crown's Fiduciary Obligations to Aboriginal Peoples" (2004) 37 U.B.C. L. Rev. 219 at 257–8.

198 *Supra* note 1 at 384.

199 (1994), 117 D.L.R. (4th) 161 at 173.

200 See chapter 6, text accompanying note 58 *et seq.* for the duties of a fiduciary.

201 249 N.Y. 458 at 464 (C.A.); see chapter 6, text accompanying note 69 for a fuller quotation.

Notes to Chapter 9

1 (2000), 186 D.L.R. (4th) 36 (Ont. C.A.).

2 (5 November 1996), Vancouver C914572, (B.C.S.C.), See generally M.V. Ellis, *Fiduciary Duties in Canada*, looseleaf (Toronto: Carswell, 2002) at 21–22.

3 [2001] 2 C.T.C. 96 (Ont. Sup. Ct.). It was held in *Proconic Electronics Ltd v. Wong* (1985), 67 B.C.L.R. 237 (B.C.S.C.) that particulars must be given for allegations of misconduct based on breach of fiduciary duty. The defendant is not obliged to answer a bald allegation of a breach of fiduciary duty.

4 *Beaver First Nation v. A.T.N. Farms Ltd.*, 2001 ABQB 748; see also *Lax Kw'Alaams Band of Indians v. Hudson's Bay Co.*, 2000 BCSC 378, additional reasons, 2000 BCSC 455.

5 (1998), 156 D.L.R. (4th) 56 at paras. 22, 99.

6 (1995), 24 C.C.L.T. (2d) 191 (B.C.S.C.), aff'd (1996), 30 C.C.L.T. (2d) 53 (B.C.C.A.); see also *M.M. v. P.M.*, 2000 BCSC 1597. In Ontario, s. 108(2) of the *Courts of Justice Act*, R.S.O. 1990, c. C43 provides that claims for equitable relief are to be tried without a jury.

7 2000 BCSC 379; see also *Delgrosso v. Paul* (1999), 45 O.R. (3d) 605 (Ont. Gen. Div.).

8 [2001] 2 S.C.R. 534.

9 (1999), 64 B.C.L.R. (3d) 80 (B.C.C.A.).

10 L.I. Rotman, "Balancing the Scales of Justice: Fiduciary Obligation and *Stewart v. C.B.C.*" (1999) 78 Can. Bar Rev. 445 at 470–71 [Rotman, "Balancing the Scales"], citing *Erlanger v. New Sombrero Phosphates Ltd.*, [1877] 3 App. Cas. 1218 (H.L.) and *Brickenden v. London Loan & Savings Co.*, [1933] 3 D.L.R. 161 (S.C.C.), aff'd [1934] 2 D.L.R. 465 (P.C.); see also L. I. Rotman, *Parallel Paths: Fiduciary Doctrine and the Crown–Native Relationship in Canada* (Toronto: Univ. of Toronto Press, 1996) at 183–84 [Rotman, *Parallel Paths*].

11 (1995), 99 F.T.R. 1.

12 *Ibid.* at para. 491.

13 [1992] 2 C.N.L.R. 54 at 103–4 (F.C.T.D.); chapter 5, text accompanying note 23 .

14 *Ibid.* at 76–77.

15 *Sub nom. Roberts v. Dick*, [2000] 3 C.N.L.R. 303 at para. 124.

16 *Ibid.* at para. 124.

17 [2002] 4 S.C.R. 245 [*Wewaykum*].

18 *Ibid.* at para. 121. He went on to note, however, that "[t]his is not to say that historical grievances should be ignored or that injustice necessarily loses its sting with the passage of the years": *ibid.* at para. 123. See generally Graeme Mew, *The Law of Limitations*, 2d ed. (Markham, Ont.: Butterworths, 2004).

19 *Ibid.* at para. 135.

20 [1992] 3 S.C.R. 6.

21 [1948] 3 D.L.R. 797 (Exch. Ct.); *supra* chapter 1, text accompanying note 65. It is also illustrated by the refusal of the federal government to allow the Allied Tribes of British Columbia to retain their own counsel in litigation to decide the question of Aboriginal title in the province during the first decades of the twentieth century: see *Order in Council*, P.C. 751 dated 20 June 1914 quoted in *Report*

and Evidence of the Joint Committee of the Senate and House of Commons Appointed to Inquire into the Claims of the Allied Tribes of British Columbia, Journal of the Senate of Canada 1926–27 at ix. There were no lawyers representing the Aboriginal peoples involved in critical cases affecting Aboriginal rights such as the *St. Catherine's Milling* case (1888), 14 A.C. 46 (P.C.).

[22] [1982] 2 F.C. 385 at 411. See chapter 3, text accompanying note 82 *et seq.* In the early 1900s, the Department of Indian Affairs refused to allow members of the Six Nations in Ontario to use their funds to pay for the costs of a legal education for one of their members: Forest E. La Violette, *The Struggle for Survival* (Toronto: Univ. of Toronto Press, 1961) at 165.

[23] Section 6 of *An Act to Amend the Indian Act*, S.C. 1926-7, c. 32, which was reproduced as s. 141 of the *Indian Act 1927*, R.S.C. 1927, c. 98. See chapter 2, text accompanying note 102 .

[24] *Supra* note 22 at 411, 418–19; see also chapter 3, text accompanying note 18.

[25] See Jack Woodward & Donna Jordan, "Limitation Periods for Breach of Fiduciary Duty in the Context of Aboriginal Claims" in *UFOs—Unidentified Fiduciary Obligations* (Winnipeg: Canadian Bar Association, 28 May 1994). It has been suggested that, in light of the difficulties faced by Aboriginal peoples in enforcing their rights in the courts and the inequity between their limited means and the vast resources available to the Crown, "to have the Crown escape liability for its actions because of the effects of its own legislation appears fundamentally unjust": Leonard I. Rotman, "*Wewaykum*: A New Spin on the Crown's Fiduciary Obligations to Aboriginal Peoples?" in *Canadian Aboriginal Law 2003* (Ottawa: Pacific Business & Law Institute, 2003) at 26–27.

[26] *Supra* note 20. The explicit exception for equitable claims no longer appears in the current Ontario *Limitations Act* (S.O. 2002, c. 24) but see ss. 2(2)(f) and 2(2) excluding from its operation "proceedings based on equitable claims brought by aboriginal peoples against the Crown" and stating that such proceedings are to be governed by the former law; see also Alberta *Limitations Act*, R.S.A. 2000, c. L-12, s. 13 which provides: "An action brought on or after March 1, 1999 by an aboriginal people against the Crown based on a breach of a fiduciary duty alleged to be owed by the Crown to those people is governed by the law on limitations of actions as if the *Limitations of Actions Act*, R.S.A. 1980 c. L-15, had not been repealed and this Act were not in force."

[27] R.S.B.C. 1996, c. 266; see Rhys Davies, "Remedies for Breach of Fiduciary Duty" in *Torts – 2001* (Vancouver: Continuing Legal Education Society of British Columbia, 2001).

[28] See *Wewaykum*, *supra* note 17 at para. 131.

[29] In *Moon (Guardian Ad Litem of) v. Campbell River Indian Band* (1996), 136 D.L.R. (4th) 383 (F.C.T.D.), aff'd (1999), 176 D.L.R. (4th) 254 (F.C.A.), the Court decided that a band council held funds for distribution to members under a trust. It found a breach of trust rather than a breach of fiduciary duty and so applied the ten-year limitation period rather than a six-year period as argued for the band council.

[30] *Supra* note 17 at paras. 132, 136; see *infra* notes 75–78.

[31] R.S.C. 1985, c. F-7.

[32] [1995] 4 S.C.R. 344 at para. 107.

[33] *Supra* note 17 at para. 114.

[34] *Wewaykum*, *supra* note 17 at para. 108. See generally Mew, *supra* note 18 at 37–44.

[35] R.S.O. 1990, c. L.15. See also British Columbia *Limitation Act*, *supra* note 27, ss. 2(a)(b) and the Alberta *Limitations Act*, *supra* note 26, s. 10.

[36] *Supra* note 20 at 70.

[37] (1806), 9 R.R. 119.

[38] *Supra* note 20 at 71–76.

[39] (London: Stevens & Sons, 1932).

[40] *Supra* note 20 at 74.

[41] Rotman, *Parallel Paths*, *supra* note 10 at 192, citing Graeme Mew, *The Law of Limitation* (Toronto: Butterworths, 1991) at 23.

[42] *Ibid.*

[43] On the relationship between trusts and fiduciary relationships, see chapter 8, text accompanying note 156 *et seq.*

[44] *Supra* note 20.

[45] (2000), 195 D.L.R. (4th) 135 at para. 298. See also *Wewaykum*, *supra* note 17 at para. 110. For the U.S. law, see *Sherrill (City of) v. Oneida Indian Nation of N.Y.* (29 March 2005), No. 03-855 (U.S.S.C.).

[46] *Supra* note 20 at 77–78, emphasis in original. The citation for *Lindsay Petroleum Co. v. Hurd* is (1874), L.R. 5 P.C. 221.

[47] *Supra* note 17 at para. 111.

[48] *Ibid.*

[49] *Ibid.* at para. 135. He noted that, on the facts, there was no repetition of an allegedly injurious act that would have given rise to a new cause of action that was not barred by the *Limitation Act*. See also *Fairford First Nation v. Canada*, [1999] 2 F.C. 48 at paras. 295–99 (F.C.T.D.).

[50] See *Blueberry River, supra* note 32, Gonthier J. at 365–66 and McLachlin J. at 405–6; *Semiahmoo Indian Band v. Canada* (1997), 148 D.L.R. (4th) 523 at 546.

[51] *Semiahmoo, ibid.* at 547; see chapter 5, text accompanying note 39 *et seq.* for the facts.

[52] *Supra* note 32; see chapter 5, text accompanying note 25 *et seq.* for the facts.

[53] *Ibid.* at 365; see also McLachlin J. at 405–6.

[54] *Guerin v. The Queen*, [1984] 2 S.C.R. 335 at 390, Dickson J.

[55] See chapter 3, text accompanying note 83; chapter 4, text accompanying note 63. For a discussion of the law of fraudulent concealment, see *M.(K.) v. M.(H.), supra* note 20 at 51–59, La Forest J.

[56] *Supra* note 54; see also decision of Collier J., *supra* note 22 at 423–25.

[57] *Supra* note 50.

[58] *Ibid.* at 552–54.

[59] *Supra* note 27.

[60] See the decision of Collier J. in *Guerin, supra* note 22 at 426–27.

[61] *Nielsen v. Kamloops*, [1984] 5 W.W.R. 1 (S.C.C.); *M.(K.) v. M.(H.), supra* note 20 at 28–34, La Forest J.

[62] See Mew, *supra* note 18 at 48–62.

[63] *Supra* note 32.

[64] *Supra* note 50.

[65] *Ibid.* at 555.

[66] *Supra* note 17 at para. 124.

[67] (1980) E.T.R. 219 (S.C.C.).

[68] *Ibid.* at 228.

[69] [1991] 3 S.C.R. 534.

[70] [1987] 2 N.Z.L.R. 443 (C.A.).

[71] *Supra* note 67.

[72] *Supra* note 69 at 590. See on the supposed fusion of law and equity that would result in the possible application of contributory fault to equitable claims such as breach of fiduciary duty: *infra* note 81.

[73] (2001), 180 A.L.R. 249 (H.C.A.).

[74] [1999] Lloyd's L.R. 359 (Ch.), Blackburne J. at paras. 62–63.

[75] *Supra* note 27. The current Ontario *Limitations Act*, see *supra* note 26, provides in s. 15 for an ultimate limitation period of fifteen years.

[76] *Wewaykum Indian Band v. Canada* (1995), 99 F.T.R. 1 (T.D.) at para. 199. McLachlin J. commented in her judgment in *Blueberry River, supra* note 32 at para. 107, that "[t]he 6- and 10-year limitations [under the British Columbia *Limitations Act*], *but not the general 30-year ultimate limitation,* may be postponed in certain circumstances." [emphasis added]

[77] *Supra* note 32 at paras. 106–11.

[78] *Supra* note 17 at para. 132.

[79] M.V. Ellis, *Fiduciary Duties in Canada*, looseleaf (Toronto: Carswell, 2002) at 20–21. See also: Ian E. Davidson, "The Equitable Remedy of Compensation" (1982) 3 Melbourne U.L. Rev. 349; W.M.C. Gummow, "Compensation for Breach of Fiduciary Duty" in T.G. Youdan, ed., *Equity, Fiduciaries and Trusts* (Toronto: Carswell, 1989); T.G. Youdan, "The Fiduciary Principle: The Applicability of Proprietary Remedies" in T.G. Youdan, ed., *Equity, Fiduciaries and Trusts,* (Toronto: Carswell, 1989); John D. McCamus, "Remedies for Breach of Fiduciary Duty" in *Special Lectures of the Law Society of Upper Canada 1990—Fiduciary Duties* (Scarborough, Ont.: De Boo, 1991); Michael Ng, *Fiduciary Duties: Oligations of Loyalty and Faithfulness,* looseleaf (Aurora, Ont.: Canada Law Book, 2003) at 13:1–13:21; Kent Roach, "Remedies for Violations of Aboriginal Rights" (1992) 21 Man. L.J. 498; Derek J. Davies, "Equitable Compensation: Causation, Foreseeability and Remoteness" in Donovan W.M. Waters, ed., *Equity, Fiduciaries and Trusts* (Toronto: Carswell, 1993); Rhys Davies, "Remedies for Breach of Fiduciary Duty" in *Torts—2001* (Vancouver: Continuing Legal Education Society of British Columbia, 2001). For

equitable remedies generally, see: I.C.F. Spry, *The Principles of Equitable Remedies,* 6th ed. (London: Sweet & Maxwell, 2001); J. Berryman, *The Law of Equitable Remedies* (Toronto: Irwin, 2000); R.J. Sharpe, *Injunctions and Specific Performance,* looseleaf (Aurora, Ont.: Canada Law Book, 2000).

[80] *Ibid.* at 20:26–20:27.

[81] For the history of equity and fiduciary law, see chapter 1, text accompanying note 38 *et seq.* Some cases have suggested, particularly for remedies, that there has been a "fusion" between law and equity so that there is no longer any distinction between the causes of action: *Canson Enterprises Ltd v. Boughton & Co.,* [1991] 3 S.C.R. 534 at 582, La Forest J. [*Canson*]; *Chippewas of Sarnia Band v. Canada* (2000), 195 D.L.R. (4th) 135 at para. 289 (Ont. C.A.), leave to appeal dismissed without reasons, [2001] 4 C.N.L.R. iv (note); reconsideration dismissed [2002] 3 C.N.L.R. iv (note). For reasons that I have set out elsewhere, it is submitted that this suggestion is contrary to the weight of authority and would throw the law into disarray in numerous areas: see James I. Reynolds, "Aboriginal Title: The Chippewas of Sarnia" (2002) 81 Can. Bar Rev. 97; Paul Perell & Jeff G. Cowan, "In Defence of *Chippewas of Sarnia Band v. Canada (Attorney General)*" (2002) 81 Can. Bar Rev. 727; James I. Reynolds, "A Reply to 'In Defence of *Chippewas of Sarnia Band v. Canada*'" (2003) 82 Can. Bar Rev. 122.

[82] [1997] 2 S.C.R. 217 at para. 34. For the flexibility of equitable remedies, see J. McGhee, ed., *Snell's Equity,* 30th ed. (London: Sweet & Maxwell, 2000) at 645–46; Spry, *supra* note 79 at 1–25.

[83] In *Pilmer v. Duke Group Ltd. supra* note 73 at para. 151, Kirby J. of the High Court of Australia noted that "[i]n affording remedies for a fiduciary's breach of its obligations, equity is seen, depending on one's point of view, at its flexible pragmatic best (or worst)," quoting from Underhill's *Law Relating to Trusts and Trustees,* 13th ed. (London: Butterworths, 1979) at 11.

[84] McCamus, *supra* note 79 at 58. See *Wewaykum, supra* note 17 at para. 94, in which Binnie J. referred to "an array of equitable remedies."

[85] *Wewaykum, supra* note 17 at para. 107.

[86] 39 B.C.L.R. (20) 177 at 182. Not all these remedies will be available in each case. In *Soowahlie Indian Band v. Canada (Attorney-General)* (2001), 209 D.L.R. (4th) 677, 2001 FCA 387, the Federal Court of Appeal rejected an application for an injunction to prevent the expropriation of reserve lands on the basis that damages would be an adequate remedy.

[87] *Supra* note 81 at 563.

[88] Ellis, *supra* note 79 at 20–22.

[89] (1993), 117 D.L.R. (4th) 161 at 199 (S.C.C.) [*Hodgkinson*].

[90] *Supra* note 54 at 360–61.

[91] [1966] 2 N.S.W.R. 211 at 214–16, Street J.

[92] *Supra* note 79 at 20:61.

[93] Wilson J. in *Guerin, supra* note 54 at 362; see also *Hodgkinson, supra* note 89 at 207–8.

[94] *Ibid.* at 362–63.

[95] *Infra* note 108.

[96] [1942] 1 All E.R. 378 at 386; see also judgments of Lord MacMillan at 391 and Lord Wright at 392.

[97] (1973), 40 D.L.R. (3d) 371 (S.C.C.) at 392. See also Ellis, *supra* note 79 at 20-4 and *Carl B. Potter Ltd. v. Mercantile Bank of Canada, supra* note 67.

[98] Ellis, *supra* note 79 at 20-5; *Island Realty Investments Ltd. v. Douglas* (1985), 19 E.T.R. 56 (B.C.S.C.); Rotman, "Balancing the Scales," *supra* note 10 at 471; L. Rotman, "Developments in Fiduciary and Trust Law: The 1998–99 Term" (2000) 11 Sup. Ct. L.Rev. 483 at 508.

[99] The case of *Canson, supra* note 81, supports the proposition that remoteness may sometimes be considered; see also *Waxman v. Waxman* (30 April 2004) C38611, C38616, C38824 at paras. 659–62 (Ont. C.A.). However, the majority opinion of the Supreme Court of Canada in *Hodgkinson, supra* note 89 at 201, stated "*Canson* held that a court exercising equitable jurisdiction is not prohibited from considering principles of remoteness, causation and intervening acts where necessary to reach a just and fair result. *Canson* does not however, signal a retreat from the principle for restitution; rather it recognizes the fact that a breach of fiduciary duty can take a variety of forms, and as such a variety of remedial considerations may be appropriate." *Canson* was a case of a third-party intervention causing the loss. The Court noted in *Hodgkinson* at 202 that "in *Canson* there was no particular nexus between the wrong complained of and the fiduciary relationship." On the relevance of causation, see Justice Tipping, "Causation at Law and in Equity: Do We Have Fusion?" (2000) 7 Canterbury L. Rev. 443; *Swindle v. Harrison,* [1997] 4 All E.R. 705 (Eng. C.A.); Rotman, "Balancing the Scales"

supra note 10 at 474–79.

[100] *Supra* text accompanying note 90 quoting from Street J. in *Re Dawson, supra* note 91. See also *Semiahmoo, supra* note 50 at 563; *Cadbury Schweppes Inc. v. F.B.I. Foods Ltd.*, [1999] 1 S.C.R. 142 at para. 50.

[101] *Supra* note 32.

[102] *Ibid.* at para. 103.

[103] *Supra* note 89.

[104] *Supra* note 32 at para. 103.

[105] *Supra* note 50 at 558; see also *Hodgkinson, supra* note 89 at 208–9. See chapter 1, text accompanying note 43 *et seq.* for the rationale for imposing fiduciary obligations.

[106] *Infra* note 82 at 220.

[107] *Norberg v. Wynrib* (1992), 92 D.L.R. (4th) 449 at 506; *M.(K.) v. M.(H.), supra* note 20 at 82; Ellis, *supra* note 79 at 20:32.1. See *Harris v. Digital Pulse Pty. Ltd.*, [2003] 56 N.S.W.L.R. 298 (N.S.W.C.A.) for a detailed review of the law in different jurisdictions including Canada. The Court held that, under the law of New South Wales, exemplary damages could not be awarded for breach of fiduciary duty.

[108] *Supra* note 50 at 558–59. See chapter 5, text accompanying note 39 for the facts of this case. For a general discussion of the law relating to constructive trusts, see L.I. Rotman, "Deconstructing the Constructive Trust" (1998) 37 Alta. L. Rev. 133. For constructive trusts as a remedy for breach of fiduciary duty, see Ng, *supra* note 79 at 13:30.10.

[109] *Ibid.* at 559–60.

[110] *Lac Minerals Ltd. v. International Corona Resources Ltd.* (1989), 61 D.L.R. (4th) 14 (S.C.C.).

[111] *Ibid.* at 49–52.

[112] *Supra* note 50 at 562.

[113] *Supra* note 82.

[114] *Supra* note 50 at 556.

[115] [1980] 2 S.C.R. 834.

[116] *Supra* note 50 at 557.

[117] *Ibid.*

[118] *Ibid.* at 558.

[119] *Supra* note 82.

[120] *Ibid.* at para. 1.

[121] *Ibid.* at para. 34. This statement was described as having "the disadvantage of being very general" in *Terra Energy Ltd. v. Kilborn Engineering Alberta Ltd.*, [1999] 6 W.W.R. 483 at para. 51 (Alta. C.A.). The Alberta Court of Appeal said that, in applying *Soulos*, courts must have regard not merely to do what is "fair" in a general sense but to other situations where courts have found a constructive trust.

[122] *Ibid.* at para. 45.

[123] *Supra* note 54.

[124] [1997] 3 S.C.R. 1010 at para. 169.

[125] *Supra* note 50 at 562.

[126] *Ibid.* at 563–64. See also *Ithaca Ice Works Pty. Ltd v. Queensland Ice Supplies Pty. & Amor*, 2002 QSC 222 at paras. 14–17 for a review of the relevant principles. In *Cadbury Schweppes Inc. v. F.B.I. Foods Ltd*, Binnie J., giving the judgment of the Supreme Court of Canada, said "It is well established that equitable rules may produce a more generous compensation than their counterpart in tort" citing, *inter alia, Guerin, supra* note 100 at para. 50.

[127] *Ibid.*

[128] *Guerin, supra* note 54 at 360; ; *Hodgkinson v. Simms, supra* note 89 at 208; *Frame v. Smith*, [1987] 2 S.C.R. 99 at paras. 79–83, Wilson J.

[129] *Halsbury's Laws of England*, vol. 48, 4th ed. (London: Butterworths, 1980) at 531. See *Regal (Hastings) Ltd. v. Gulliver, supra* note 96; Ng, *supra* note 79 at 13:20.20.

[130] *Supra* note 50.

[131] *Ibid.* at 565.

[132] R.S.B.C. 1996, c. 79.

[133] *B.(K.L.) v. British Columbia* (1998), 163 D.L.R. (4th) 550 (B.C.S.C.), rev'd on the question of liability for breach of fiduciary duty (2001), 197 D.L.R. (4th) 431 (B.C.C.A.), aff'd [2003] 2 S.C.R.

403; see Ng, *supra* note 79 at 13:9.

[134] *Supra* notes 93–95, 128.

[135] *Supra* note 133 at 563 (see *K.L.B. v. British Columbia*).

[136] (1995), 99 F.T.R. 1, aff'd without consideration of this point [2000] 3 C.N.L.R. 303 (F.C.A.); aff'd [2002] 4 S.C.R. 245. See, however, *Beattie v. Canada*, [2004] 3 C.N.L.R. 18, 2004 FC 674, in which Lafreniere P. suggested at para.103 that compound interest is not available against the Crown as equitable compensation.

[137] *Supra* note 13.

[138] *Supra* note 136 at para. 602; see *infra* text accompanying note 170 *et seq.*

[139] *Supra* note 54.

[140] *Supra* note 22.

[141] *Supra* note 50.

[142] *Supra* note 136.

[143] *Supra* note 13.

[144] *Supra* note 22. For a criticism of this award based on the facts of the case, see chapter 3, text accompanying note 95 *et seq.*

[145] *Ibid.* at 430.

[146] [1977] 2 S.C.R. 302 at 320, Dickson J.

[147] *Supra* note 22 at 437.

[148] *Ibid.* at 441.

[149] *Ibid.* at 441–42.

[150] *Supra* note 54 at 390–91.

[151] *Ibid.* at 356–64.

[152] *Supra* note 50.

[153] *Supra* text accompanying note 108 *et seq.*

[154] *Supra* note 50 at 566.

[155] *Supra* note 94.

[156] *Supra* note 50 at 564.

[157] *Ibid.* at 564–65.

[158] *Supra* note 136. See chapter 5, text accompanying note 52 *et seq.* for the facts of this case.

[159] *Ibid.*

[160] *Ibid.*

[161] *Supra* note 54.

[162] *Supra* note 81.

[163] *Supra* note 136 at paras. 596–97.

[164] *Ibid.* at paras. 607, 610, 613.

[165] *Ibid.* at para. 607.

[166] *Ibid.* at paras. 607–8.

[167] *Ibid.* at paras. 613, 619.

[168] *Ibid.* at para. 620.

[169] *Ibid.* at paras. 623–26.

[170] *Ibid.* at paras. 601–2, 644.

[171] R.S.C. 1985, c. C-50. See chapter 3, text accompanying note 98.

[172] *Supra* note 136 at paras. 648–49.

[173] *Supra* note 136 at para. 146, McDonald J.

[174] *Supra* note 136.

[175] *Supra* note 13. See chapter 5, text accompanying note 23 *et seq.* for the facts of this case.

[176] *Ibid.* at para. 269.

[177] *Outstanding Business. A Native Claims Policy* (Ottawa: Minister of Indian Affairs and Northern Development, 1982).

[178] William B. Henderson & Derek T. Ground, "Survey of Aboriginal Land Claims" (1994) 26 Ottawa L. Rev. 187 at 216.

[179] *Ibid.* at 225.

[180] See Alan Pratt, "Validating Claims under the *Specific Claims Resolution Act* (And Beyond!)" in Pacific Business and Law Institute, *Analysis of the Specific Claims Resolution Act* (Vancouver: Pacific Business and Law Institute, 2004). According to information provided by the Specific Claims Branch of the Department of Indian Affairs and Northern Development, only 233 of 1,154 specific claims advanced between 1 April 1970 and 30 June 2002 have been settled: Canada, Parliament, "Bill C-6: The Specific Claims Resolution Act," Legislative Summary LS-431E, 10 October 2002, revised 29 March 2003 by Mary C. Hurley at text accompanying note 27.

[181] Assembly of First Nations & Specific Claims, DIAND, *Report of the Joint First Nations–Canada Task Force on Specific Claims Policy Reform*, November 25, 1998, available on-line: Assembly of First Nations <http//:www.afn.ca/Programs/Treaties%20and%20Lands/IndependentClaims.htm.>

[182] S.C. 2003, c. 23. For a description and analysis of the Act, see Hurley, *supra* note 180.

[183] See documents on-line: Assembly of First Nations, *supra* note 181.

Notes to Chapter 10

[1] [1984] 2 S.C.R. 335.

[2] See the preface for the many references to the contribution made by *Guerin* to the law.

[3] See chapter 4, text accompanying note 46 *et seq.*

[4] [1990] 1 S.C.R. 1010. See chapter 5, text accompanying note 68 *et seq.*

[5] *Constitution Act, 1982*, being Schedule B to the *Canada Act 1982* (U.K.), c. 11. See chapter 1, text accompanying note 37.

[6] See chapter 6.

[7] Ronald St. John Macdonald (Chairman, Research Committee), *Research Project on Treaty and Aboriginal Rights of Canadian Indians and Eskimos* (Indian-Eskimo Association of Canada, 1970) at 201.

[8] See chapter 3, text accompanying note 133 *et seq.*

[9] Larissa Behrendt, "Lacking Good Faith: Australia, Fiduciary Duties and the Lonely Place of Indigenous Rights" in *In Whom We Trust* (Toronto: Irwin Law for Law Commission of Canada and Association of Iroquois and Allied Indians, 2002) at 264–65. The Australian law is considered in chapter 7, text accompanying note 64 *et seq.*

[10] See chapter 7, text accompanying note 66.

[11] *Supra* note 5. It is also important to note that large parts of Canada, including most of British Columbia, have been without treaties and that most treaties were negotiated under unequal conditions which led to limited benefits for the Aboriginal group.

[12] See *Johnson v. British Columbia (Securities Commission)* (1999), 67 B.C.L.R. (3d) 145 at para. 25 (B.C.S.C.), Allan J.

[13] Richard H. Bartlett, "Survey of Canadian Law—Indian and Native Law" (1983), 15 Ottawa L. Rev. 431 at 500. See chapter 5, text accompanying note 66 *et seq.*

[14] (1987) 66 Can. Bar Rev. 727.

[15] S. 35 did not apply because the action was commenced before it came into effect.

[16] *Supra* note 14 at 728.

[17] *Ibid.* at 730.

[18] [1973] S.C.R. 313. See chapter 1, text accompanying note 35 *et seq.*

[19] *Supra* note 14 at 731.

[20] *Ibid.*

[21] Brian Slattery, "Making Sense of Aboriginal and Treaty Rights" (2000) 79 Can. Bar Rev. 196 at 197; see chapter 1, text accompanying note 34 *et seq.*

[22] See chapter 4, notes 31, 72. The "monster" of political trust has not been completely vanquished: see chapter 1, notes 70, 145.

[23] *Supra* note 5.

[24] *Supra* note 4; see chapter 5, text accompanying note 68.

[25] [1996] 1 S.C.R. 771. See chapter 5, text accompanying note 95.

[26] [1997] 3 S.C.R. 1010. See chapter 5, text accompanying note 91.

[27] *Ibid.* at para. 162.

[28] *Ibid.* at para. 167–69. For a proposal for principles of compensation for infringement of Aboriginal or treaty rights based on fiduciary law, see Robert Mainville, *An Overview of Aboriginal and Treaty Rights and Compensation for Their Breach* (Saskatoon: Purich, 2001) at 104–29.

[29] *Infra* text accompanying note 33 *et seq.* See chapter 5, text accompanying note 125 *et seq.* for the duty to consult and accommodate Aboriginal rights.

[30] Chapter 4, text accompanying note 11 *et seq.*

[31] [1995] 4 S.C.R. 344; *supra* chapter 5, text accompanying note 25.

[32] *Supra* note 26 at para. 169. Michael Hudson, a lawyer for the Crown, estimated in 1997 that there were over three hundred actions against the Crown for breach of fiduciary obligation with approximately $2 billion at stake: Michael Hudson, "Crown Fiduciary Duties under the *Indian Act*" in Andrea Morrison & Irwin Cotler, *Justice for Natives—Searching for Common Ground* (Montreal: McGill & Queen's Universty, 1997) at 257–58.

[33] See *Haida Nation v. British Columbia (Minister of Forests)* (2002), 5 B.C.L.R. (4th) 33 at para. 62 (B.C.C.A.) [*Haida II*], Lambert J.A., aff'd with respect to the provincial government on the grounds that, in cases where there has not yet been a judicial determination of Aboriginal rights or title, the duty to consult and accommodate is based on the honour of the Crown rather than a fiduciary duty, (2004), 24 D.L.R. (4th) 33, 2004 SCC 73 [*Haida-SCC*] at para. 18 and rev'd with respect to the forestry company, *ibid* at paras. 52–56; see chapter 5, text accompanying note 125 *et seq.*

[34] *Ibid.*

[35] *Haida II, supra* note 33 at para. 104.

[36] *Haida-SCC, supra* note 33 at para. 47.

[37] *Haida II, supra* note 33 at para. 101. For some suggestions on economic accommodation, see James I. Reynolds, "Preparing First Nations for Business" in *Aboriginal Self-Government: What Does It Mean in Practice?* (Ottawa: Canadian Bar Association, 2002). Impact and Benefit Agreements and Memorada of Understanding have been signed by some corporations and Aboriginal groups covering such matters as training, employment, and business opportunities; see, for example, the *Diavik Diamond Project Socio-Economic Monitoring Agreement*, 2 October 1999, online: <http://www.diavik.ca/pdf/socioeconomic.pdf>.

[38] *Haida II, ibid.* at para. 119.

[39] For a differerent view, see W.I.C. Binnie, "The *Sparrow* Doctrine: Beginning of the End or End of the Beginning?" (1990) 15 Queen's L.J. 217 at 241, suggesting that *Guerin* was an important turning point in converting at a stroke thousands of political claims and controversies into legal disputes. By taking upon itself the responsibility of dealing with Aboriginal grievances as a matter of law, the Supreme Court of Canada let politicians off the hook. In his opinion, "[m]any politicians were pleased to see the transfer of these awkward and often embarrasing *dossiers* from the halls of government, where Native pressure groups had enjoyed considerable success, to the Supreme Court building": *ibid.*

[40] Chapter 8, text accompanying note 53.

[41] *In Whom We Trust, supra* note 9.

[42] Mark L. Stevenson & Albert Peeling, "Probing the Parameters of Canada's Crown–Aboriginal Fiduciary Relationship" in *ibid.* at 7. See also Patrick Macleam, "First Nations, Self-Government and the Borders of the Canadian Legal Imagination" (1991) 36 McGill L.J. 382 at 410–14.

[43] Gordon Christie, "Considering the Future of the Crown–Aboriginal Fiduciary Relationship" in *ibid.* at 289.

[44] See chapter 7, text accompanying note 121, discussing the New Zealand law, which bases the fiduciary relationship on the partnership between Maori and non-Maori.

[45] Chapter 8, text accompanying note 132 *et seq.*

[46] [2000] 3 C.N.L.R. 4 at para. 19. In *Bonaparte v. Canada (Attorney General)*, [2003] 3 C.N.L.R. 43 at para. 32 (Ont. C.A.), the Court observed, "as Binnie J.'s review of the law in *Wewaykum Indian Band* reveals, fiduciary law in Canada, particularly in respect of the Crown's relationship with Aboriginal peoples, is a very dynamic area of Canadian law. The nature and extent of the particular obligations that may arise out of this relationship are matters that remain largely unsettled in the jurisprudence." Professors Borrows and Rotman have commented, "The application of fiduciary law to Crown–Native relations is neither a finished work nor even a nearly completed one. . . . [F]iduciary law's connection to Crown–Native relations remains a project in its infancy": John J. Borrows & Leonard I. Rotman, *Aboriginal Legal Issues—Cases, Materials & Commentary*, 2d ed. (Markham, Ont.: Butterworths, 2003) at 244.

[47] (1998), 166 D.L.R. (4th) 475 at para. 84.

[48] Clea Parfitt & Melinda Munro, "Developments in the Law of Fiduciary Duty" (1999) 33 U.B.C. L. Rev. 199 at 200.

[49] *Supra* note 47. See chapter 7, text accompanying note 69 for criticism by the High Court of Australia of the Canadian law. Without referring to *Critchley*, Professor Flannigan makes a similar criticism: Robert Flannigan, "The Boundaries of Fiduciary Accountability" (2004) 83 Can. Bar Rev. 35 at 67, suggesting that it may be time that the fiduciary obligation of the Crown to Aboriginal peoples should be "formally disconnected from the general jurisprudence."

[50] *Ibid.* at para. 84.

[51] *Ibid.* at para. 85. It may be noted that, in order to reverse the development of the law on fiduciary obligations as suggested by Chief Justice McEachern, courts will also have to ignore the *Blueberry River* decision of the Supreme Court of Canada, *supra* note 31. In that case also, the Crown did not take advantage of the band for its own advantage but was held liable for a breach of fiduciary duty. Likewise, in *McInerney v. MacDonald*, [1992] 2 S.C.R. 138, chapter 6, text accompanying note 13, the doctor received no personal advantage in withholding the patient's records and, in *Canson Enterprises Ltd. v. Boughton & Co.,* [1991] 3 S.C.R. 534, chapter 6, text accompanying note 12 , the defendant solicitor did not derive any personal benefit from the secret profit made by the vendor. It would seem rather late in the day for law to be rewritten as suggested by McEachern C.J.

[52] Justice Beverley McLachlin, "Restitution in Canada" in W.R. Cornish, ed., *Restitution, Past, Present and Future* (Oxford: Hart, 1998) at 275–76; on the relationship between restitution and fiduciary obligations, see chapter 6, text accompanying note 100.

[53] See chapters 5 and 6.

[54] Michael Bryant, "Crown–Aboriginal Relationship in Canada: The Phantom of Fiduciary Law" (1993) 27 U.B.C. L. Rev. 19 at 20.

[55] See chapter 1, text accompanying note 39.

[56] Sir Frank Kitto, "Foreword to the First Edition" in R.P. Meagher, W.M.C. Gummow & J.R.F. 'Lehane, *Equity—Doctrines and Remedies*, 3d ed. (Sydney: Butterworths, 1992).

[57] See chapter 1, text accompanying note 39 *et seq.* for a brief account of the history of equity. In his foreword to the 30th edition of *Snell's Equity*, Lord Millett observed, "equity is on the march again. After long years of slumber during the post-war period—it is now fully awake. Indeed, it is rampant.": John McGhee, *Snell's Equity*, 30th ed. (London: Sweet & Maxwell, 2000). On equity as a force for greater justice, see *Dudley, Lord, and Ward v. Lady Dudley* (1705), 24 E.R. 118 at 244 (Ch.), Sir Nathan Wright L.K.: "Now equity is no part of the [common] law, but a moral virtue, which qualifies, moderates, and reforms the rigour, hardness, and edge of the law, and is an universal truth"; *Pettkus v. Becker* [1980] 2 S.C.R. 834 at 847–48, Dickson J.; James I. Reynolds, "Aboriginal Title: *The Chippewas of Sarnia*" (2002) 81 Can. Bar Rev. 97 at 119–20.

[58] Aboriginal rights are "a form of intersocietal law": *R. v. Van der Peet,* [1996] 2 S.C.R. 507 at 546, Lamer C.J.C., and can only be understood by reference to both the common law system and Aboriginal legal systems: *Delgamuuk, supra* note 26 at 1081, Lamer, C.J.C.; see generally John Borrows, *Recovering Canada: The Resurgence of Indigenous Law* (Toronto: Univ. of Toronto Press, 2002).

[59] See chapter 2 at note 102; chapter 9, text accompanying note 21 *et seq.*

Bibliography

Anyone seeking information on the Canadian law of fiduciary duties generally should refer to the following texts:

Ellis, M.V. *Fiduciary Duties in Canada,* looseleaf (Toronto: Carswell, 2002).

Ng, Michael. *Fiduciary Duties: Obligations of Loyalty and Faithfulness,* looseleaf (Aurora, Ont: Canada Law Book, 2003).

Anyone seeking information on general Canadian Aboriginal law should refer to the following texts:

Borrows, John J. & Leonard I. Rotman. *Aboriginal Legal Issues—Cases, Materials & Commentary,* 2d ed. (Markham, Ont.: Butterworths, 2003).

Isaac, Thomas. *Aboriginal Law: Commentary, Cases and Materials,* 3d. ed. (Saskatoon: Purich, 2004).

McNeil, Kent. *Emerging Justice? Essays on Indigenous Rights in Canada and Australia* (Saskatoon: Native Law Centre, 2001).

Woodward, Jack. *Native Law,* looseleaf (Toronto: Carswell, 1999).

For an overview of Aboriginal and treaty rights, see:

Mainville, Robert. *An Overview of Aboriginal and Treaty Rights and Compensation for their Breach* (Saskatoon: Purich, 2001).

Further references will be found in the notes to each chapter.

The following bibliography includes only those texts that deal primarily with the fiduciary obligations owed to Aboriginal peoples rather than fiduciary duties or Aboriginal rights generally:

Aitkin, Janice. "The Trust Doctrine in Federal Indian Law" (1997), 18 N. Ill. U.L. Rev. 115.

Aldredge, Jim. "*Haida Nation v. British Columbia and Weyerhaeuser.* Differing Perspectives—The First Nations Perspective" (2003) 61 The Advocate (B.C.) 177.

Amankwah, H.A. "Is the Limit of the Equitable Doctrine of Fiduciary Liability Determinable?" (1996) 3 James Cook U. L. Rev. 102.

Anaya, S. James, Richard Falk & Donat Pharand. "Canada's Fiduciary Obligation to Aboriginal Peoples in the Context of Accession to Sovereignty by Quebec," *Report of the Royal Commission on Aboriginal Peoples: International Dimensions,* vol. 2 (Ottawa: Supply and Services Canada, 1995).

Bartlett, R.H. "You Can't Trust the Crown" (1984–85) 49 Sask. L. Rev. 367.

———. "The Fiduciary Obligation of the Crown to the Indians" (1989) 53 Sask. L. Rev. 301.

———. *Indian Reserves and Aboriginal Lands in Canada: A Homeland* (Saskatoon: Univ. of Saskatchewan Native Law Centre, 1990), Part IV.

———. "Fiduciary Obligation, Traditional Lands, and Aboriginal Title in Australia" in Law Commission of Canada, *In Whom We Trust, op. cit.*

Barsh, Russel Lawrence. "Trust Responsibility and the Coordination of Aboriginal Issues in the United States: Potential Applications in Canada" prepared for the Aboriginal Justice Implementation

Commission (Manitoba), June 2000, online: Aboriginal Justice Implementation Commission: <http://www.ajic.mb.ca/federalaid.pdf>.

Batley, Paul. "The State's Fiduciary Duty to the Stolen Children" (1996) 2:2 Austl. J. of Human Rights 3.

Behrendt, Larissa. "Bargaining on More Than Goodwill: Recognising a Fiduciary Obligation in Native Title" in Lisa Strelein, ed., *Land, Rights, Laws: Issues of Native Title*, vol. 2:4 (Canberra: Native Title Research Unit, Australian Institute of Aboriginal and Torres Strait Island Series, 1999).

————. "Lacking Good Faith: Australia, Fiduciary Duties, and the Lonely Place of Indigenous Rights" in Law Commission of Canada, *In Whom We Trust, op. cit.*

Binnie, W.I.C. "The Sparrow Doctrine: Beginning of the End or End of the Beginning?" (1990) 15 Queen's L.J. 217.

Blowes, Robert. "Governments: Can You Trust Them with Your Traditional Title" (1993) 15 Sydney L. Rev. 254, reprinted in *Essays on the Mabo Decision* (Sydney: The Law Book Company, 1993).

Borrows, John J. & Leonard I. Rotman. *Aboriginal Legal Issues—Cases, Materials & Commentary*, 2d ed. (Markham, Ont.: Butterworths, 2003) at 244–335.

Brennan, Frank. "*Mabo* and the *Racial Discrimination Act*: The Limits of Native Title and Fiduciary Duty Under Australia's Sovereign Parliaments" (1993) 15 Sydney L. Rev. 206.

Bryant, Michael J. "Crown–Aboriginal Relationships in Canada: The Phantom of Fiduciary Law" (1993) 27 U.B.C. L. Rev. 19.

Canadian Bar Association, *UFO's—Unidentified Fiduciary Obligations* (Winnipeg, 28 May 1994).

Carter, Nancy Carol. "Race and Power Politics as Aspects of Federal Guardianship Over American Indians: Land Related Cases 1887–1924" (1976) 4 Am. Ind. L. Rev. 197.

Cassidy, Julie. "The Stolen Generation: Canadian and Australian Approaches to Fiduciary Duties" (2002) 34 Ottawa L. Rev. 175.

Cave, Rodine. "Simplifying the Indian Trust Responsibility" (2000) 32 Ariz. St. L.J. 1399.

Chambers, Reid Peyton. "Judicial Enforcement of the Federal Trust Responsibility to Indians" (1975) 27 Stamford L. Rev. 1213.

Chambers, Reid Peyton & Douglas B.L. Endreson. Testimony to Senate Committee on Indian Affairs Oversight Hearings on the Management of Indian Trust Funds (26 February 2002).

Christie, Gordon. "Considering the Future of the Crown–Aboriginal Fiduciary Relationship" in Law Commission of Canada, *In Whom We Trust, op. cit.*

Coyle, Michael. "Loyalty and Distinctiveness: A New Approach to the Crown's Fiduciary Duty Towards Aboriginal Peoples" (2003) 40 Alta. L. Rev. 841.

Cross, Raymond. "The Future of International Indigenous Trust and Fiduciary Law: A Comparative Analysis" in Law Commission of Canada, *In Whom We Trust, op. cit.*

"Crown's Fiduciary Obligations Towards Native Peoples," Editorial Comment (1985) 1 Admin. L.J. 49.

Dacks, Gurston. "Commentary" in Law Commission of Canada, *In Whom We Trust, op. cit.*

Di Marco, Lisa. "A Critique and Analysis of the Fiduciary Concept in *Mabo* v. *Queensland*" (1994) 19 Melbourne U.L. Rev. 868.

Donegan, Gerald. *Analysis of the Function and Application of the Doctrine of Fiduciary Obligation* (LL.M. Thesis, McGill University, 1996) [unpublished].

Donohue, Anne. "Aboriginal Land Rights in Canada: A Historical Perspective on the Fiduciary Relationship" (1990) 15 Am. Ind. L. Rev. 369.

Dorsett, Shaunnagh Grace. *The Crown's Fiduciary Duties to Indigenous Australians* (LL.M. Thesis, University of Calgary, 1996) [unpublished].

Dupuis R. & K. McNeil. "Canada's Fiduciary Obligation to Aboriginal Peoples in the Context of Accession to Sovereignty by Quebec," *Report of the Royal Commission on Aboriginal Peoples: Domestic Dimensions*, vol. 2 (Ottawa: Supply and Services Canada, 1995).

Edmond, Paul D. "Case Comment: *Guerin v. R.*" (1986) 20 E.T.R. 61.

Edwards, Bryce. "Towards a Bilateral Fiduciary Relationship: Recognizing Mutual Vulnerability in *R. v. Marshall*" (2001) 1 U. T. Fac. L. Rev. 107.

Elliott, David W. "Aboriginal Peoples in Canada and the United States and the Scope of the Special Fiduciary Relationship" 24 Man. L.J. 137 (1996).

————. "Much Ado About Dittos: *Wewaykum* and the Fiduciary Obligation of the Crown" (2003)

29 Queen's L.J. 1.

Ellwanger, Kimberly T. "Money Damages for Breach of the Federal–Indian Trust Relationship After *Mitchell II*" (1984) 59 Wash. L. Rev. 675.

Florio, Roger. "Water Rights: Enforcing the Federal–Indian Trust After *Nevada* v. *U.S.*" (1987) 13 Am. Ind. L. Rev. 79.

Freedman, Robert C. & F. Matthew Kirchner. "The Return of the Political Trust: Recent Developments in the Fiduciary Duty as Applied in the Crown–First Nation Context" in *Aboriginal Law in Canada 2001* (Vancouver: Native Trade and Investment Institute, 18–19 January 2001).

Getches, David H. "Federal Fiduciary Obligations to Indian Tribes in the United States" in Canadian Bar Association, *UFO's—Unidentified Fiduciary Obligations," op. cit.*

Green, L.C. "Trusteeship and Canada's Indians" (1976) 3 Dalhousie L.J. 104.

———. "North America's Indians and the Trusteeship Concept" (1975) 4 Anglo-Am. L. Rev. 137.

Griffiths, Owen B. "Case Comment on *Blueberry River:* Is the Crown Fiduciary Obligation in the Currents of Change?" (1996) 3 C.N.L.R. 25.

———. "Sui Semantics and Generis Gratuities: The Conundrum of Crown Fiduciary Obligations to Aboriginal Peoples" (1995) 6 Windsor Rev. Legal Soc. Issues 39.

Hall, Donna. "The Fiduciary Relationship Between Maori and the Government in New Zealand" in Law Commission of Canada, *In Whom We Trust, op. cit.*

Hannon, Gord. "A Number of Questions About Fiduciary Duties of the Provincial Crown to Aboriginal People" in Canadian Bar Association, *"UFO's—Unidentified Fiduciary Obligations," op. cit.*

Henderson, James Sákéj Youngblood. "Commentary" in Law Commsision of Canada, *In Whom We Trust, op. cit.*

Howard, John. "*Haida Nation* v. *British Columbia and Weyerhauser:* Differing Perspectives—The Industry Perspective" (2003) 61 The Advocate 190.

Hudson, Michael. "The Fiduciary Obligations of the Crown Towards Aboriginal Peoples" in Frank Cassidy, ed., *Aboriginal Title in British Columbia: Delgamuukw v. The Queen.* (Lantzville, B.C.: Institute for Research on Public Policy and Oolican Books, 1992).

———. "Crown Fiduciary Duties under the *Indian Act*" in Andrea Morrison & Irwin Cotler, eds., *Justice for Natives—Searching for Common Ground* (Montreal and Kingston: McGill & Queen's University, 1997).

Hughes, Camilla. "The Fiduciary Obligations of the Crown to Aborigines: Lessons from the United States and Canada" (1993) 16 U.N.S.W. L. Rev. 70.

Hughes, Richard W. "Can the Trustee Be Sued for Its Breach: The Sad Saga of *U.S.* v. *Mitchell* (1981) 26 S.D. L. Rev. 447.

Hunter, John J.L. "Fiduciary Obligations to First Nations: Recent Developments" in Continuing Legal Education Society of British Columbia ("C.L.E."), *Fiduciary Obligations—2003* (Vancouver: C.L.E., 2003).

Hurley, John D. "The Crown's Fiduciary Duty and Indian Title: *Guerin v. R.*" (1985) 30 McGill L.J. 559.

Hutchins P., D. Schulze & C. Hilling. "When Do Fiduciary Obligations to Aboriginal People Arise?" (1995) 59 Sask. L. Rev. 97.

Jamieson, Roberta. "Commentary" in Law Commission of Canada, *In Whom We Trust, op. cit.*

Janes, Robert J.M. "Enforcing the Fiduciary Duty: The Evolving Law of Crown Responsibility for Aboriginal People" in Pacific Business & Law Institute, *Canadian Aboriginal Law 2002* (Vancouver: Pacific Business & Law Institute, 2002).

Johnston, Darlene M. "A Theory of Crown Trust Towards Aboriginal Peoples" (1986) 30 Ottawa L. Rev. 307.

Kennedy, Priscilla. "Case Law in Canada Since *Guerin*" in Canadian Bar Association, *UFO's—Unidentified Fiduciary Obligations, op. cit.*

Knoll, David. "Improvident Surrenders and the Crown's Fiduciary Obligations: *Blueberry River Band v. Canada* " (1996) 54 The Advocate 715.

Kono, Kevin. "The Trust Doctrine and the *Clean Water Act:* The Environmental Protection Agency's Duty to Enforce Tribal Water Standards Against Upstream Polluters" (2001) 80 Or. L. Rev. 677.

Lafontaine, Alain. "Coexistence of the Fiduciary Obligation of the Crown and the Aboriginal Right to Self-Government" in Canadian Bar Association, *UFO's—Unidentified Fiduciary Obligations,* *op. cit.*

Laforme, Harry. "Commentary" in Law Commission of Canada, *In Whom We Trust, op. cit.*

Lajoie, Andree. "With Friends Like These . . . Two Perspectives on Fiduciary Relationships" in Law Commission of Canada, *In Whom We Trust, op. cit.*

Lambert, Gail M. "Indian Breach of Trust Suits: Partial Justice in the Court of the Conqueror" (1980) 33 Rutgers L. Rev. 502.

Law Commission of Canada & Association of Iroquois and Allied Indians. *In Whom We Trust: A Forum on Fiduciary Relationships* (Toronto: Irwin Law, 2002).

Lazor, Yan. "Commentary" in Law Commission of Canada, *In Whom We Trust, op. cit.*

Mainville, Robert. *An Overview of Aboriginal and Treaty Rights and Compensation for their Breach* (Saskatoon: Purich, 2001) at 53–60.

McHugh, Paul. *The Maori Magna Carta* (Auckland: Oxford University Press, 1991) at 239–64.

McMurty W.R. & A. Pratt. "Indians and the Fiduciary Concept" (1986) 3 C.N.L.R. 19.

McNeil, Daniel. "Trusts: Towards an Effective Indian Remedy for Breach of Trusts" (1980) 8 Am. Ind. L. Rev. 429.

McNeil, Kent. "The Lands and Trust Services Initiative: Its Potential Impact on the Federal Government's Fiduciary Obligations," Part I (August 1998), Part II (December 1999), a research paper prepared for the Assembly of First Nations.

———. "Fiduciary Obligations and Aboriginal Peoples" in Mark R. Gillen and Fayle Woodman, eds., *The Law of Trusts: A Contextual Approach* (Toronto: Emond Montgomery Publications, 2000) at 807–65.

———. "Fiduciary Obligations and Federal Responsibility for the Aboriginal Peoples" in Kent McNeil, *Emerging Justice? Essays on Indigenous Rights in Canda and Australia* (Saskatoon: Univ. of Saskatchewan Native Law Centre, 2001).

———. "Section 91(24) Powers, the Inherent Right of Self-Government and Canada's Fiduciary Obligations," research paper prepared for the Office of the B.C. Regional Vice-Chief of the Assembly of First Nations, reproduced in Pacific Business & Law Institute, *Canadian Aboriginal Law 2002* (Vancouver: Pacific Business & Law Institute, 2002).

———. "Culturally Modified Trees, Indian Reserves and the Crown's Fiduciary Obligations" (2003) 21 Sup. Ct. L. Rev. (2d) 105.

———. "Aboriginal Autonomy and the Crown's Fiduciary Obligations," paper prepared for the Canadian Bar Association's 2004 Canadian Legal Conference and Expo (Winnipeg, 15–17 August 2004).

Monture-Angus, Patricia. "The Experience of Fiduciary Relationships: Canada's First Nations and The Crown" in Law Commission of Canada, *In Whom We Trust, op. cit.*

Morellato, Maria. "The Crown's Fiduciary Obligation towards Aboriginal Peoples" in *Canadian Aboriginal Law 1999* (Vancouver: Pacific Business & Law Institute, 1999).

Morse, Brad. "The Landmark Musqueam Case" (1985) 4 Ont. Lawyers Weekly 16.

Nahwegahbow, David C., Michael W. Posluns, Don Allen & Douglas Sanders, *The First Nations and the Crown: A Study of Trust Relationships,* research report prepared for the Special Committee of the House of Commons on Indian Self-Government (April 1983) [unpublished].

Newton, Nell Jessup. "Enforcing the Federal–Indian Trust Relationship After *Mitchell*" (1982) 31 Cath. U. L. Rev. 635.

———. "Symposium: The Indian Trust Doctrine After the 2002–2003 Supreme Court Term— Introduction" (2003) 39 Tulsa L. Rev. 237.

Olney, Howard. "Who Owes What to Whom: The National Government's Fiduciary Obligation/Trust Responsibility Versus Aboriginal Self-Determination. An Australian Perspective" in Pacific Business and Law Institute, *International Indigenous Forum* (24–25 October 2002).

Owen, D.P. "Fiduciary Obligations and Aboriginal Peoples: Devolution in Action" (1994) 3 C.N.L.R. 1.

Pelz, Arne & Luningning Alcuitas-Imperial. "Fiduciary Obligation as a Source of Remedies Against Public Officials: The Aboriginal Context and Beyond" in A. MacInnes and B.M. Hamilton, eds., *Fiduciary Duties/Conflicts of Law,* 1993 Isaac Pitblado Lectures, Law Society of Manitoba.

Perkins, Matthew. "The Federal Indian Trust Doctrine and the Bald and Golden Eagle Protection

Act" (2000) 30 Envtl. L. 701.

Phipps, Eugenia A. "Feds 200, Indians 0: The Burden of Proof in the Federal/Indian Fiduciary Relationship" (2000) 53 Vand. L. Rev. 1637.

Pratt, A. "Aboriginal Self Government and the Crown's Fiduciary Duty" (1993) 2 N.J.C.L. 163.

Pryce, Charles. "Commentary" in Law Commission of Canada, *In Whom We Trust, op. cit.*

"The Re-emergence of the Trust Relationship After *U.S.* v. *Mitchell,* Note (1983) 18 Land & Water L. Rev. 491.

Reiter, Robert A. "The Crown's Fiduciary Obligations to Indians" in *The Fundamental Principles of Indian Law* (Edmonton: First Nations Resources Council, 1990).

"Rethinking the Trust Doctrine in Federal Indian Law" Note, (1984) 98 Harv. L. Rev. 422.

Reynolds, James I. "*Guerin* After Sixteen Years" in Pacific Business & Law Institute, *Canadian Aboriginal Law 2000* (Vancouver: Pacific Business & Law Institute, 2000).

———. Research Note to *Guerin* in Joseph Magnet, *Constitutional Law of Canada*, 8th ed. (Edmonton: Juriliber, 2001).

———. "Aboriginal Title and the Transmission of Fiduciary Obligations from the Crown to Business—Is the Leap of Logic Galactic or Synaptic?" in Continuing Legal Education Society of British Columbia (C.L.E.), *Fiduciary Obligations—2003* (Vancouver: C.L.E., 2003).

Reynolds, James I. & L. Harvey. "The Fiduciary Obligation of the United States and Canadian Governments Towards Indian Peoples" in Continuing Legal Education Society of British Columbia ("C.L.E.") *Indians and the Law II* (Vancouver: C.L.E., 1985).

Rotman, Leonard I. "Provincial Fiduciary Obligations to First Nations: The Nexus Between Governmental Power and Responsibility" (1994) 32 Osgoode Hall L.J. 735.

———. *Parallel Paths: Fiduciary Doctrine and the Crown Native Relationship in Canada* (Toronto: University of Toronto Press, 1996).

———. "Conceptualizing the Crown–Aboriginal Fiduciary Relationship" in Law Commission of Canada, *In Whom We Trust, op. cit.*

———. "Crown–Native Relations as Fiduciary" in The Canadian Bar Association Aboriginal Law CLE, *Aboriginal Ownership and Management of Resources in Canada: An Analysis of Litigation and Negotiation. Getting to Win–Win?* (Halifax, N.S.: The Canadian Bar Association, 25–26 April 2003).

———. "Developments in Aboriginal Law: The 2002–2003 Term" (2003) 22 S.C.L.R. (2d) 1.

———. "*Wewaykum*: A New Spin on the Crown's Fiduciary Obligations to Aboriginal Peoples" in Pacific Business & Law Institute (P.B.L.I.), *Canadian Aboriginal Law 2003* (Ottawa: P.B.L.I., 2003), revised version (2004) 37 U.B.C. L. Rev. 219.

Salembier, J. Paul. "Crown Fiduciary Duty, Indian Title: Legacy of *Apsassin v. The Queen*" (1996) 3 C.N.L.R. 1.

Sanders, Douglas. *The Friendly Care and Directing Hand of the Government: A Study of Government Trusteeship of Indians in Canada* (22 February 1977) [unpublished, archived at Musqueam Band Office].

Skibine, Alex Tallchief. "Integrating the Indian Trust Doctrine into the Constitution" (2003) 39 Tulsa L. Rev. 237.

Slattery, Brian. "First Nations and the Constitution: A Question of Trust" (1992) 71 Can. B. Rev. 261.

Stevenson, Mark & Albert Peeling, "Probing the Parameters of Canada's Crown–Aboriginal Fiduciary Relationship" in Law Commission of Canada, *In Whom We Trust, op. cit.*

Stevenson, S. Ronald. "Is the Fiduciary Role of Government Changing?" in *2001 Isaac Pitblado Lectures: Practicing Law in an Aboriginal Reality* (Winnipeg: Law Society of Manitoba, 2001).

Tan, David. "The Fiduciary as an Accordion Term: Can the Crown Play a Different Tune?" (1995) 69 Aust. L.J. 440.

Tsosie, Rebecca. "The Conflict Between the 'Public Trust' and the 'Indian Trust' Doctines: Federal Public Land Policy and Native Nations" (2003) 39 Tulsa L. Rev. 271.

Waters, D. "New Directions in the Employment of Equitable Doctrines: The Canadian Experience" in T.G. Youdan, ed., *Equity, Fiduciaries and Trusts* (Toronto: Carswell, 1989).

"Whom Can the Indians Trust After *Mitchell,*" Note (1981), 53 U. Colo. L. Rev. 179.

Wood, Mary Christine. "Indian Land and the Promise of Native Sovereignty: The Trust Doctrine

Revisited" (1994) Utah L. Rev. 1471.

―――. "Protecting the Attributes of Native Sovereignty: A New Trust Paradigm for Federal Actions Affecting Tribal Lands and Resources" (1995) Utah L. Rev. 109.

―――. "Fulfilling the Executive's Trust Responsibility Towards the Native Nations on Environmental Issues: A Partial Critique of the Clinton Administration's Promises and Performance" (1995) 25 Envtl. L. Rev. 733.

―――. "The Indian Trust Responsibility: Protecting Tribal Lands and Resources Through Claims of Injunctive Relief Against Federal Agencies" (2003) 39 Tulsa L. Rev. 355.

Woodward, Jack & Donna Jordan. "Limitation Periods for Breach of Fiduciary Duty in the Context of Aboriginal Claims" in Canadian Bar Association, *UFO's—Unidentified Fiduciary Obligations, op. cit.*

Index